W9-DIT-706

The Work of Words

Susanna Moodie has long been acknowledged as a key figure in pre-Confederation Canadian literature but most of her work has been overlooked or ignored by scholars and readers. *The Work of Words* not only provides the first comprehensive examination of the whole of Moodie's writing but also revolutionizes Moodie scholarship by overturning the myths that have cast her as pioneer heroine, one-woman garrison, or paranoid schizophrenic.

Thurston considers the whole of Moodie's literary career including her poems, short fiction, novels, and non-fiction, beginning with her youthful writing in England and culminating in an extensive analysis of her best-known work, *Roughing It in the Bush*. He establishes the biographical foundations of her writing using recently discovered correspondence and describes the historical issues and events that shaped her life and writing.

Using current historicist and feminist literary criticism, Thurston achieves new insights into Moodie's writing. Locating tensions of class, gender, and race within her work, he places Moodie both in the now-established tradition of nineteenth-century British women writers and in the less-familiar tradition of North American class conflict. For the student of Canadian literature, *The Work of Words* is an indispensable resource on the author and her works.

John Thurston is a writer, researcher, and editor living in Ottawa.

The Work of Words

The Writing of
Susanna Strickland Moodie

JOHN THURSTON

McGill-Queen's University Press
Montreal & Kingston • London • Buffalo

Legal deposit first quarter 1996
Bibliothèque nationale du Québec

Printed in the United States on acid-free paper

This book has been published with the help of a
grant from the Canadian Federation for the
Humanities, using funds provided by the Social
Sciences and Humanities Council of Canada.

McGill-Queen's University Press is grateful to the
Canada Council for support of its publishing
program.

Canadian Cataloguing in Publication Data

Thurston, John, 1955-
   The work of words : the writing of Susanna
   Strickland Moodie
   Includes bibliographical references and index.
   ISBN 0-7735-1287-X
   1. Moodie, Susanna, 1803-1855 —Criticism and
   interpretation. I. Title.
   PS8426.063Z88 1995   C813'.3   C95-900783-0
   PR9199.2.M65Z93 1995

To the memory of my dear mother, Phyllis Ruth Thurston, 1923-1995

Contents

Acknowledgments

This study has had a long and varied life, during which I have incurred many debts. Mary Jane Edwards, as general editor of the Centre for Editing Early Canadian Texts while I was a research assistant there, first gave me the opportunity to study in-depth the bibliographic details of *Roughing It in the Bush*. John Moss allowed me to make some of my thoughts on this text public when he accepted my proposal to deliver a paper at a conference he was organizing. Heather Murray's response to this paper and subsequent ones on Moodie led me to believe there was an audience for my work. As I began this study in earnest, Leslea Keevil and David Leahy were supportive in opposed but complementary ways. My doctoral supervisor, Leslie Monkman, more than anyone else enabled me to complete this work. My examiners, especially Margery Fee and Joy Parr, made many useful recommendations. Jack Healey was also an examiner, but my gratitude to him extends before and after this task to the encouragement and advice he has freely given for the last decade.

Donald Akenson, as editor at McGill-Queen's University Press, early on showed an interest in this work, and he and Roger Martin, also at the Press, have shepherded me on the journey from thesis to book. Misao Dean and Margaret Turner both read the thesis and urged me to attempt this journey. David Staines, as head of the Department of English at the University of Ottawa, was largely responsible for a productive atmosphere wherein to pursue this work, and Camille La Bossiére, Gerald Lynch, and Irene Makaryk made personal contributions to that atmosphere. The assessors of the manuscript for the

Canadian Federation for the Humanities and for the Press provided much helpful criticism. Susan Kent Davidson as my editor and Joan McGilvray as coordinating editor at the Press have contributed greatly to the transformation of the typescript into type. Through the extra effort of Jo-Anne McFarlan – in her "spare time"– this project was finally finished.

I deeply regret that my mother did not live to see this book in print. From her I have gained the tenacity necessary to see it through to the end. She, my father and my two sons have all given me reasons to do what I do. They and Debra Weinber, my partner, have given me a life beyond the study and so enabled me to return to it relatively sane and refreshed. To Debra in particular, thanks for letting me cook in my own way.

I gratefully acknowledge support from the Social Sciences and Humanities Research Council through doctoral and post-doctoral fellowships during much of the research and writing of this book.

Abbreviations

CEECT   Editorial material in the Centre for Editing Early Canadian Texts' edition of *Roughing It in the Bush*, supplied by researchers at the Centre and by editor Carl Ballstadt (Ottawa: Carleton University Press 1988).

EO   *Enthusiasm; and Other Poems* (London: Smith, Elder 1831).

FL   *Flora Lyndsay* (New York: De Witt and Davenport 1854).

GM   *Geoffrey Moncton* (New York: De Witt and Davenport 1855).

Intro   Introduction to the English edition of *Mark Hurdlestone*,
to *MH* rpr in *Life in the Clearings*, ed. Robert L. McDougall (Toronto: Macmillan 1959), 286-93.

LC   *Life in the Clearings* (Toronto: McClelland and Stewart 1989).

LG   *Literary Garland* (Montreal 1838-51).

Letters Editorial material in *Susanna Moodie: Letters of a Lifetime*, ed. Carl Ballstadt, Michael Peterman, and Elizabeth Hopkins (Toronto: University of Toronto Press 1985).

letter   Letters as numbered by the editors of *Letters of a Lifetime*.

MH   *Mark Hurdlestone* (New York: De Witt and Davenport 1854).

PHEC   Patrick Hamilton Ewing Collection of Moodie-Strickland-Vickers-Ewing Family Papers, Rare Book Room, National Library of Canada.

RI   *Roughing It in the Bush* (Toronto: McClelland and Stewart 1989).

TFC   Traill Family Collection, National Library of Canada.

"Trifles"   "Trifles from the Burthen of a Life," rpr in *Voyages: Short Narratives of Susanna Moodie*, ed. John Thurston (Ottawa: University of Ottawa Press 1991).

VM   *Victoria Magazine* (Belleville 1848-49).

Voyages   *Voyages: Short Narratives of Susanna Moodie*, ed. John Thurston (Ottawa: University of Ottawa Press 1991).

The Work of Words

Introduction

My Autograph

What – write my name? –
　　How vain the feeble trust,
To be remember'd
　　When the hand is dust.
Grieve rather – that the talents freely given
Were used for earth – not treasured up for Heaven.

Susanna Moodie

Alas, that one should have to work for money. But it cannot be helped, and I ought not to feel ashamed of turning the capacity God gave me to account, but ought rather to be grateful; still, it paralizes the mind having to tax it for daily supplies.

These two texts, written around the same time, say much about Susanna Moodie's work of words.[1] She always felt that her talent was innate, a God-given gift. She frequently felt guilty about not using it for strictly religious purposes; at other times it was something not to be wasted. Much of her writing was work for money to support successive domestic economies. Its worldly purposes exceeded the crassly material, however, encompassing recognition, compensation for social dislocation, fame, resistance to limitations, and, involving them all, the ongoing production of some sense of self.

That five out of six of the Strickland sisters became authors seems to establish their innate talent. They, however, recognized its connection to their poverty, Susanna for instance writing that, since "they dared to be poor," they had to "make the talents with which the great Father had liberally endowed them, work out their appointed end" (*RI*, 196). If she had not had "to work for money," she might not have worked at all, perhaps writing as a hobby for herself and friends, as many of her contemporaries did, without turning professional. Still, taxing her mind "for daily supplies" to exchange for supplies for her children or her larder may have curtailed her development and brought her career prematurely to a close.

Despite its humility, that Moodie wrote "My Autograph" (and signed it) shows her pride in the recognition she had. She has been remembered long since her hand was dust. This study of her life and work, another act of remembrance, is also an attempt to reorient and add to the terms by which she is remembered, developing them to account more fully for the ambivalences and complexities of the woman revealed in even these two brief passages.

The bibliographical analysis of *Roughing It in the Bush* that was my first serious engagement with Susanna Moodie revealed a text – described in detail in chapter 7 – that seemed seriously unstable in its most basic features. Recent criticism implicitly acknowledges this instability in its special pleading for an essential unity beyond those features. Earlier commentary is more concerned with using a selective version of Moodie's story to establish an outcome happy both for her and for the nation she is seen to be involved with in a representative way. The more I learned about her writing and her life, however, the less these two approaches seemed able to account for. This study will lay out those textual and biographical details that need to be accounted for and attempt to demonstrate that they are best addressed together, in a theoretically and historically informed context. Its version of Moodie's life and writing, especially in the case of *Roughing It*, around which so much commentary has accumulated, runs contrary to the versions found in that commentary.

The immediate colonial response to *Roughing It in the Bush* was largely hostile. On the eve of Confederation, however, Henry Morgan, a founder of the Canada First movement, began the canonization of Susanna Moodie, including her in *Sketches of Celebrated Canadians* and *Bibliotheca Canadensis*. Not wanting to be among Morgan's "list of Canadian worthies" because she was "by birth and education English," she resisted appropriation by nascent Canadian nationalism.[2] Morgan was the first to place *Roughing It* at the foundation of her reputation. She and it appear in every collection of Canadian national biography and survey of English Canadian literature since. Early cultural historians promoted the view that Moodie "was fully naturalised when she published 'Roughing it in the Bush'" and that she was "the chief poet and chronicler of pioneer days in Ontario."[3] By the early twentieth century this "pioneer of Canadian literature" was both a literary pathbreaker and a settler who wrote.[4]

To become a representative figure, Moodie had to be made a Canadian. Her nationalistic statements in the introduction to the first Canadian edition of *Roughing It*, although partly a deflection of criticism for its still-apparent distaste for colonial life, were accepted. She and her compatriots became "loyal, loving daughters of their adopted land"; they metamorphosed from "cultured English men and women ... into loyal citizens with a strong sense of nationality and unbounded faith in the future of Canada."[5] The repugnance for the colony evident in *Roughing It* was gradually lost sight of as the book came to be read as proof of this metamorphosis. By 1914 it was "a veritable Canadian classic" (Marquis, 545).

The surveys of the 1920s continued to present Moodie as a happy Canadian and *Roughing It* as "a national classic" (Baker 1920, 121). While believing in its realism, these critics also often emphasized that Moodie's story is "a romance in itself" (Pierce 1927, 156). Anthologists, excerpting from her work, created the Moodie they felt was most representative.[6] Critics and teachers of Canadian literature constituted both "the Canadian identity" and a Moodie congruent with it through a grid of acculturated proclivities founded on national optimism and faith in the romance of history.

A spate of biographical essays on Moodie and book-length group biographies including her appeared in the first twenty-five years after the Second World War.[7] They focus on *Roughing It*, passing quickly over her years both in Suffolk and in Belleville. They stress her hardships, her spirited confrontation of them, and her happy ending as a true Canadian heroine. In typological fashion, they read her life-text as inscription in small of the destiny of a nation; they credit her with helping us, in Robert McDougall's words, "to form a correct notion of our national identity" (1959, xi). This centralist, conservative privileging of continuity ensconced Moodie in its version of the English Canadian canon. As a construction of Moodie it is undermined, however, by the wealth of biographical information supplied since the early 1980s by Carl Ballstadt, Michael Peterman, and Elizabeth Hopkins.

Before that information was widely disseminated, however, another critical orthodoxy had crystalized. Others have noted the importance of the *Literary History of Canada* (1965) to the formation of the English

Canadian canon.[8] Moodie's presence in the first volume is unmatched by any other pre-Confederation writer. Ironically, the comments therein of Carl Klinck and Northrop Frye on Moodie spurred an interpretation of *Roughing It* that lacked historical perspective. Interpretive critics displaced the romantic, typological reading of Moodie with an ironic, archetypal reading of *Roughing It*. As the link between literature and nation shifted from "the Canadian identity" to "the Canadian imagination," the basis for valorizing this text shifted from its historical content to its literary form.[9]

Klinck first suggested that *Roughing It* was a novel in 1959, complaining that it had "been regarded as representative of colonial history rather than of colonial literature" (76). If it was really a work of creative fiction, then the wedge of irony could be driven between its author and "her Mrs. Moodie-character," with her now-embarrassing class and racial biases.[10] In his edition of 1962 Klinck created a short, fast novel from a long, tedious life-document, so lifting *Roughing It* over another barrier to its appreciation by students of Canadian literature. In his introduction to this edition he locates this "novel" at "a further stage in the growth of immigrant literature," when modern existential dilemmas first found expression in "stable literary forms" (1962, xii). His thesis that it is unified by the centrality of the author encouraged attention to it as artefact rather than document.

Frye's brief remarks on Moodie in his conclusion to the *Literary History* present her as archetypal isolated monad confronted by an undifferentiated environment of bush and barbarianism. Margaret Atwood completed the transference of Moodie to a transhistorical but geographically bound collective unconscious. Moodie haunted Atwood's dreams until she realized she was being spoken to of "obsessions still with us" (1970, 62). The "paranoid schizophrenia" of Atwood's Moodie beleaguered a monad that was as cut off from society and history as Frye's "one-woman garrison." Containing her concept of "violent duality" within an individual psychology, Atwood provided a paradoxical principle of unity in tension, attributable to the unifying heroine of Klinck's novel. In their imaginings Moodie became the mother of the Canadian imagination. The socially determined internal disunity and generic instability of *Roughing It* were willed away in the discovery that it is really a psychological novel after all.

With few exceptions, interpretive critics of this text in the 1970s and 1980s continued to devote their energies to finding in it a unified literary artefact detached from history. While practical, sensible Catharine Parr Traill did not attract analysts of Canada's psyche, the attention paid to *Roughing It* suggests its active reconstruction to support the topocentric and archetypal penchants of much of the criticism of those years.[11] That national unity and difficulties deriving from the foundation of the colony have been recurrent public issues further entangles *Roughing It*, Canadian literature, and the Canadian nation.

The interpretive tropes of alienation from the wilderness, the ironic novelist, and doubleness of vision, attached to Moodie in the surveys of D.G. Jones, John Moss, and Atwood, were developed in essays devoted solely to *Roughing It*. While Moss constituted her his most typical "Immigrant Exile," Hallvard Dahlie called his second chapter of *Varieties of Exile* "Roughing It in Exile." Gaile McGregor drew her Moodie from Atwood, whom she surpassed only in the extremity of her rhetoric on *Roughing It*. Clara Thomas early followed Klinck in finding Moodie's text unified by the character of the narrator, although she may have initiated the claim that Moodie "transcended" suffering by writing and "moved from the raw world she lived in towards the timeless reality of a contained world of the imagination" (1972, 16, 18).

R.D. MacDonald offered one of the first sustained attempts to rebuild *Roughing It* as a novel of the divided psyche. Through qualification and selectivity he creates unity in duality, "a single significant pattern" (24), at the expense of multiplicity. William Gairdner finds in Moodie the "psychological dangers" of confronting "the overwhelming emptiness of the Canadian wilds" (1972, 37, 36) by concentrating almost exclusively on the second half of *Roughing It*. David Stouck unifies the "opposition or tension" in the text through recourse to its "imaginative dimension" and isolates "three definable aspects of her experience that seem to be continuous in Canadian life" (1974, 464, 470). In his one interpretive essay on Moodie, Carl Ballstadt claims that she "articulate[s] the central issue and problem of the creative writer" in Canada, "to move upstream into the heart of the cedar swamp and to develop a language and form adequate to that experience" (1974, 109). T.D. MacLulich defines *Roughing It* as "a fantasy of living in a world without other people" (1976, 119). The mythopoeic imagination as constructed in Canada in the 1970s is happiest in an empty landscape.

Carol Shields takes issue with Atwood and MacDonald for distorting Moodie but reverts to Klinck's thesis that the "unifying force" of Moodie's Canadian books "is the overriding sense of her own personality" (1977, 6). Gerald Noonan, noting the reductiveness of criticism of *Roughing It*, promises "a strategy of fiction which amalgamates the disparate findings and the elements of the book into a cohesive if multifaceted flow" (1980, 280), but the strategy is again to read it through the focus of "the narrating persona" (283). Marion Fowler adds the finishing strokes to a portrait of the novelist as a middle-aged pioneer.

For her, *Roughing It* and *Flora Lyndsay* are in "the same style of English sentimental fiction" (1980, 80). She excuses Moodie's digressions from "the main narrative" (84), but what qualifies for Fowler's narrative is about 15 per cent of *Roughing It*.

These essays blot out history with myth. This text was remade as a novel about a heroine's confrontation with the archetypal wilderness. It became a major exhibit in the attempt to construct a canon based on the putative uniqueness of the Canadian relationship with the land. The other qualities necessary to a canonical figure, artistic accomplishment and acceptance of her country, accrued to Moodie along the way.

Challenges to this consensus are often weakened by assumptions shared with their targets. Robin Mathews places Moodie at the head of an evolving Canadian tradition, since she "treats questions and subjects that we shall not be free of in Canada for a long time, employing techniques and archetypes that describe both the Canadian fact and the ways in which Canadians deal with it" (1975, 43). David Jackel stresses "the fundamental incoherence of Moodie's book" but, since he valorizes unity as the essence of literature, rejects it completely (1979, 9). When she published her comparison of Moodie and Mrs Trollope, Janet Giltrow's linking of aesthetics and economics was unique in criticism on Moodie. Laura Groening dismantled Atwood's Moodie, but still affirmed Moodie's "acceptance of Canada as her new homeland" (1983, 179).

By 1986 Heather Murray could characterize "thematic criticism" as "until recently preponderant" (80). Much of the commentary on Moodie in the late 1980s and early 1990s builds on the rejection of previous orthodoxies while avoiding any attempt to synthesize a new one.[12] Interest in Moodie remains strong, but the canon she once anchored and that anchored her has increasingly come under attack. The connection of Canadian literature with a teleological interpretation of the Canadian nation, the primacy of the land as a theme in Canadian literature, the insulation of unified literary artefacts from social and political issues – these once common givens of English Canadian literary criticism are no longer secure.[13] W.H. New has observed that *Roughing It* is not just "a document of its time" but "a changing document of changing times" (1989, 72).

The present study seeks to participate in the current fluidity of Canadian criticism. Its project is not to displace Susanna Moodie from the canon but to replace one Moodie with another. The Moodie this study constructs is one more in accord with the drift of canonical values away from topocentrism and nationalism and towards concern with issues of class and gender. This Moodie appears when *Roughing It* is read with her other works in their full context. This Moodie is one whose life in England is as important as her life in Canada, whose relationship to society is more important than her relationship to the wilderness. This Moodie is more than pioneer heroine, one-woman garrison, or paranoid schizophrenic.

Why did Susanna Moodie write the way she did? Writing was for her implicated at every level – from structure to punctuation, characterization to theme, point of view to style and tone, physics to metaphysics – with her political, social, and economic environment, yet she tried to control that environment through it. This study attempts to establish both what her writing is and what its determinants were. It aims not for another overarching conception of what constitutes the Canadian writer, not even the English Canadian female writer, but for an understanding of how one woman inscribed herself in the literary texture of her time by consistently dealing with its social text. With no hasty saltations to all-encompassing generalities before the close examination of specific cases, this work attempts to produce local knowledge.

This study rests on three interrelated assumptions.[14] The first is that literary texts cannot be understood in isolation from the historical relations within which they were produced. Moodie's dates fall in the period of British history when industrial capitalism was consolidated as the dominant economic system, and manufacturing and mercantile interests coalesced in the hegemony of the middle class. The year she emigrated the first Reform Bill passed into legislation after years of agitation during which her middle-class family suffered economic disaster but avoided relegation to the working class. Susanna and her sisters Elizabeth, Agnes, Jane, and Catharine responded to their change in fortunes by writing for a living. An alternative response involved Susanna, Catharine, and brother Samuel in the massive emigration of the 1830s. Her writing responds to economic exclusion; it survives due to the dissemination of English by the same forces that drove her away from England. Her writing is inextricable from its time, at once made by history and making history.

A second assumption is that literary texts reveal the gaps and contradictions characteristic of their historical moment. Rather than interpret Moodie's texts, this study will analyse the determinants of those texts that best explain their various features. Two of their main features are discontinuity and heterogeneity. This perception runs contrary to the belief that *Roughing It* has a unity that justifies its study, albeit one that requires the effort of the interpreter to find. Moodie may have tried to negotiate for herself a unified identity through writing, but if personality is a function of language radically dispersed through the system of exchange that is language, then her attempts necessarily failed. The disunity of her self-textualizations implicates the circumstances of their production.

The third assumption is that literary activity is partly determined, and especially so in Moodie's case, by the representations of dominant class interests, and that writers can both resist and reiterate the social text of rival ideologies. Her writing reproduces social conflict as she tries to harmonize herself with contending forces. She acknowledges her subjectivity by responding to the various voices that hail her, but while she tries to correct disconcerting distortions of her identity when she answers, she is restricted to the terms those social voices allow her to speak. Submitting to definitions imposed by her class and gender position, she reproduces them in an attempt to reconcile their contradictions. The partial success of her attempts only highlights the limits within which they were made.

The structure of this study elaborates a basic chronology. The first six chapters are organized into two groups corresponding with the two main phases of Moodie's writing life, that in England and that in the colony. Chapters 1 and 4 provide a narrative of those features of her biography found pertinent to this study, from 1803 to 1832 and from 1832 to 1855 respectively. The correspondence and published texts are drawn on for information in these chapters but not analysed. Chapters 2, 3, 5, and 6 examine selected texts. These chapters are synchronic, each set of texts providing an opportunity for slicing across its historical moment and more thoroughly integrating history, life, and writing. Without being callous by denying the suffering, privation, and struggle that largely characterized Moodie's life, the aim of this study is to approach, not its lived texture, but its social determinants.

By establishing the relationship of those determinants to Moodie's writing, features of that writing that are often excused or glossed over can be more fully confronted. Chapter 7 shows that the disunity and instability of *Roughing It in the Bush* are partly accounted for by the conditions of its production in a context of shared authority in which the distribution of control ran largely against Moodie. The chapter argues that the text's strengths are its multivocality and heterogeneity, its integrity in reproducing dialects and dialogues, charivaris and other carnivalesque social rituals that are threatening to its author. In her attempt to construct her identity through writing, most clearly in *Roughing It*, Moodie's representations of mad Englishmen may unwittingly come closest to her self-image. Chapter 7 attempts to reamplify that text's dissonant voices, hitherto unheeded as its price of admission to the canon. *Roughing It's* play of dualities and contradictions can be reactivated, now that the English Canadian literary canon has itself come into play. I will deal with the salient features of Moodie's life and writing by grounding them in history and literary theory, so to construct, for this time, a workable relationship between us and the portion of our past she captured in her own peculiar way.

1 Between Establishment and Dissent: Susanna Strickland's Youth, 1803-1832

During the turmoil and instability that marked early nineteenth-century England, Susanna Strickland lived with her family in Suffolk county. While she grew to young womanhood, Napoleon bid for European supremacy and the British Empire was consolidated; the Prince of Wales had his regency, then rule, and Evangelicism gained control of middle-class morality; the Test and Corporation Acts were repealed and Catholic emancipation passed; the Industrial Revolution advanced and the landed gentry lost hegemony; the first European cholera plague struck and British emigration to North America peaked.[1] Susanna was born on 6 December 1803, ten weeks after Robert Emmet was hanged for his part in the Irish insurrection that year. She sailed for British North America on 1 July 1832, three weeks after the Reform Bill received royal assent. England was prepared for the more settled reign of Victoria. But Susanna, by then Mrs Moodie, was gone before she could relax with fellow citizens in peace and prosperity.[2]

To read for the social determinants of Susanna Strickland Moodie's literary production, it is necessary to establish the class within which she was raised. Her father, Thomas Strickland, from the salaried segment of the middle class, sought to improve his social position by joining the landed gentry rather than challenging it.[3] While neither he nor his daughters, ineligible because of gender, participated in politics, they were caught up in the social and economic tensions of their day in the more "private" areas of family, education, and religion. Involvement in the latter exposed Susanna to the precariousness of a position between establishment and dissent.[4]

Susanna's grandfather, a Lancashire yeoman, lost hereditary land at the return of a relative with prior claims. He shifted laterally from freehold farmer into the wage-earning end of the London middle class. After he got a job, he married and had eight children. Thomas, Susanna's father (b. 8 December 1758), became an employee of Hallet and Wells, shipowners, with whom he rose to the level of "master and sole manager" of their Greenland Dock.[5] His first wife, Susanna Butt, died childless, and in 1793 he married Elizabeth Homer (b. 1772), from "an old but decayed Dorsetshire family" (TFC, 8187-88). In 1803, after his wife had borne him five daughters, his health "required change and he left the Dockyard to live first near Norwich and subsequently at Stowe House near Bungay on the banks of the Waveney."[6] At this time he made business connections in Norwich and bought a house there. Susanna, the last daughter, was born soon after the family took up residence at Stowe House.

In December 1808 they moved into the recently purchased estate with tenant farms, just inland from Southwold, a town on the North Sea.[7] "Thomas Strickland, Esq. of Reydon Hall, Suffolk," retaining his town house, "quietly settled down as a country gentleman" to raise his family above the business milieu of London and Norwich.[8] All his children had been born, his two potential heirs last. The rural idyll did not proceed as hoped. At some time in the previous years he "had invested the chief part of his property" (Strickland 1887, 7) in a partnership with a near relation of his wife in Norwich and since then "allowed his name to remain as a ... guarantor" (FitzGibbon 1894, xii). Soon after the move to Suffolk and throughout the 1810s, he was forced to spend more time in Norwich than he had planned.[9] Among the girls, Eliza and Agnes were most often with him there. Eliza, his "amanuensis and confidante in all business," alternated with her mother between Norwich and Reydon Hall, caring for and educating the younger girls when Mrs Strickland was in Norwich.[10] During this period Catharine was sometimes also in town with her father, sisters, and brothers, "form[ing] friendships and acquir[ing] the tone of society" (Strickland 1887, 8); Sarah, Jane, and Susanna remained in Suffolk.

Few facts are available about the financial demise and ensuing death of Thomas Strickland on 18 May 1818. Catharine relates "the sudden tidings of the failure" of the firm "and the consequent loss of the principal part of his private income." Susanna writes of having "seen riches melt away from our once prosperous home." Jane notes "pecuniary losses which compelled" their mother "to practise a rigid and unsocial economy" after the father's death. His will, witnessed 10 April 1818, lists "Thomas Strickland and Company, Coach Manufactory of St. Giles Gates," Norwich, as the business that failed. Although the will left the family no liquid assets, Mrs Strickland was bequeathed "Reydon Hall, with freehold and copyhold estates from which she would receive rents and profits from the cultivation of land, a house in Norwich, and stock in the coach manufactory."[11] The house in Norwich was "given up the year of [their] father's death" (TFC, 9965) and part of Reydon Hall closed off.

Although Strickland strove to attain the security of belonging to the landed interest, his rents must not have been great enough to protect him and his family: earnings from industry were still needed. Norwich had been a prosperous woollen centre until its decline in the late eighteenth century due to the industrialization of cotton manufacturing. Economic distress led to serious labour disturbances. While initially a good location for Strickland to consolidate his earnings as dock manager by investing them in coach-making, Norwich felt the brunt of the receding post-1815 economy. The Stricklands toppled from their precarious perch among the gentry. Although they were particularly vulnerable and their fall was especially disastrous, they were but one of many families to suffer from the post-war depression. In E.J. Hobsbawm's words, "the nightmare shadow of bankruptcy or debt sometimes lay over their lives, and we can still recognize it in the novels of the period: the trust in an unreliable partner, the commercial crisis, the loss of middle-class comfort, the women-folk reduced to genteel penury, perhaps even emigration to the dustbin of the unwanted and the unsuccessful, the colonies."[12] This precisely describes the end of Thomas Strickland's career and the life he left his wife and daughters.

"The village of Reydon was an agricultural one, and afforded the young ladies of the Hall no companions," writes Jane (1887, 5-6), and so when they moved there the paternal and self-education of the girls began in earnest. Before his financial reverses began to occupy him, their father attended to the education of Eliza and Agnes. According to Agnes, he "approved of educating girls upon the same plan as boys" and believed "that few ladies ... know how to converse rationally, because they have been taught in a superficial manner."[13]

Susanna remarks that Agnes's "love of history" was satisfied by their "good old-fashioned Library" (letter 117). The English histories in it concentrated on the Civil War and Restoration.[14] Jane puts "Harrison's 'Survey of London'" in their reading, and Susanna mentions "a very ancient Geography and History of Europe."[15] Their library also contained philosophy. Catharine and Susanna tried "Lock on the Human Understanding" and "Descartes Philosophy," works over which the taint of English deism and French scepticism lingered. The two "made small progress in *that direction*" but found a "book of divine morality ... *too dry*" (TFC, 8413).

According to Jane, their father did not permit the older girls the "use of books of amusement, unless these were of a superior order, and were calculated to form their minds and morals; nor did he allow them to choose for themselves from the stores of his own library." The only poetry they were allowed at first was Pope's translations of Homer (1887, 2-3). Jane tells how the interdiction against poetry was lifted when they accidently encountered Shakespeare: "He gave them leave to read Shakespeare in future, considering that their infant innocence would prevent them from receiving injury from those loose passages which the coarse manners of the age in which they were written had not only tolerated, but probably admired" (3). Miss Strickland implicates her father in the market Dr Bowdler's *Family Shakespeare* (1818) met. Susanna describes how the "little ones" gathered to hear Agnes perform scenes "from Shakespeare; and often she would frame little Romances for us, founded upon passages from English history."[16] Agnes was given access to poetry as a curb to her own versifying, not to encourage her enjoyment of ornamental literature. Besides Shakespeare and Pope, she was allowed to read Milton, Gray, and Collins.[17] These poets evince a taste similar to that suggested by the prose writers: nonconformist and instructive, traditional and popular – at least for the generation prior to their father's.

All the books the girls mention date from the period prior to or shortly after their father's birth. They reflect the concerns of a displaced northern yeoman in London in the middle of the eighteenth century, rather than those of a rising City businessman at its end. With only their grandfather's books, the girls could have had little contact through their reading with the debates of their own time or even of their father's. They would have been unable to follow the development of response to the French Revolution, which led Wordsworth, Coleridge, and Southey, among others, from radicalism to conservativism. They would not have known the poetry of the younger Romantics – Byron would have been the name of scandal rather than of a popular poet. Their awareness of the aesthetics and politics of Romanticism would have been derived from hearsay. Jane tells how "romances and novels were almost unknown" to Agnes until her first trip away from home (1887, 6). In her account of the reading of the younger girls Catharine mentions "old magazines of the last century" (TFC, 8412) but no contemporary journals. Thus isolated from the popular book and periodical press and from philosophical and religious disputes, the Strickland sisters grew up with a cultural frame of reference some fifty or sixty years out of date. Only time away from Suffolk would have allowed them contact with contemporary issues, and Susanna did not get much time away until her early twenties.

Although his teaching resources were out of date, Strickland put them to progressive use. The education he gave his elder daughters does not conform to what was prescribed even for the majority of their male peers, let alone contemporary females. That he had them write abstracts of books he provided combines with evidence of the early beginnings of the girls' writing endeavours to complete a picture of a pedagogy strikingly like the Benthamite utilitarian program: "'Useful knowledge' became the watchword: ... writing and arithmetic ... plus the rote learning of geographical locations, historical dates, and elementary 'science.'"[18] The only item lacking in the Strickland curriculum is science. Sexism would have weighed against the older sisters' retention of scientific learning, had they, as Eliza seems to have, acquired it.[19] They learned from a mid-eighteenth-century library; that they learned anything at all is due to their father's connection with the early nineteenth century.

What has been described is the education of Eliza and Agnes. The evidence for Susanna's schooling sketches a less formal picture. The education of the elder girls establishes a domestic intellectual superstructure composed of early eighteenth-century north-county nonconformity, late eighteenth-century City mercantilism, and early nineteenth-century middle-class aspiration. While seemingly unaffected by reaction against the French Revolution and English reform agitation, it was thoroughly undermined by the destruction of its domestic economic base.

Religion among the Stricklands can be approached through another element in their intellectual atmosphere, Thomas's admiration for William III. Susanna writes of Agnes that "the Father and his child politician seldom agreed upon historical subjects. He was a Whig and a great admirer of William III, whom she detested being a devoted champion of the unfortunate House of Stuart."[20] William III, popular with the Protestant majority, was never accepted by much of the ruling class. This debate is between a newly-risen businessman's allegiance to the Whigs and constitutional monarchy, under which commerce and industry had been allowed to flourish, and the already-risen daughter's allegiance to the Tories and absolute monarchy, with its cachet of ancient lineage and High Church. Upon this crux, divergences in the religious and social affiliations of the Strickland women can be distinguished.

Agnes, twenty-two at her father's death, had for ten years been encouraged to consider herself a gentlewoman. So pronounced was her literary exhibition of High Church sympathies that she had continually to fend off accusations of secretly being a Roman Catholic.[21] From 1843 she kept a "Stuart Album." The Stuart sympathies displayed in her biographical work drew attacks like one in the Whig *Edinburgh Review* charging that she stood for "the pernicious doctrine of the divine right of Kings."[22] According to Jane, who associates their Stuart loyalties with the putative connection to the Catholic Stricklands of Sizergh Castle, Eliza held the same opinions as Agnes (1887, 5). She at least acceded to them by working with Agnes on *Lives of the Queens of England* (first series 1840-48). Jane takes great pains throughout her *Life of Agnes Strickland* (1887) to defend the views on monarchy and religion held by her two older sisters.

Susanna, fourteen when her father died, was perhaps unsure of what she was. Her, Sarah, and Catharine's religious and class affiliations contrast markedly with those of the other three. In the mid-1820s Sarah and Susanna became friends with the Childses of Bungay, a family of nonconformist printers who later gained a reputation for confronting state repression.[23] In 1831 the Childses testified before a parliamentary committee that they had been legally circumventing the King's Printer's Patent, restricting who could print Bibles, by annotating their editions. One of them was later imprisoned for refusal to pay church rates, which brought castigation of him by Peel in the House of Commons as "the Bungay martyr." He was among the "church rate martyrs" produced by the campaign organized by dissenters and Benthamites to agitate for disestablishment of the Church of England.[24]

Sarah and Susanna's relations with the Childses are well attested to. In the late 1820s Sarah's marriage to Robert Childs "had to be hushed up for Dissenters were socially low and Chapel folk were regarded askance by Church people."[25] Susanna did not reject Sarah, welcoming Sarah's aid throughout her first pregnancy (letter 34). Catharine and Susanna each portray Robert Childs in a story. At the beginning of 1829 he asked Susanna "to write a small volume of Psalms and Hymns," and they discussed how to get the necessary "sanction of the Bishop of London" (letter 12). The printer's imprint to Susanna's *Enthusiasm; and Other Poems* reads, "BUNGAY: PRINTED BY J.R. AND C. CHILDS" (John had a son, Charles).

In April 1830 Susanna "shocked her family by undergoing conversion" and being received into a community of dissenters (Pope-Hennessy 1940, 20, 25). Catharine writes of her sister's guidance into a noncomformist chapel "under the ministration of the Revd Mr. R—" (TFC, 9883). The editors of the *Letters* discuss her "brief but emotional conversion to Congregationalism" and cite the Wrentham Congregational Chapel's record book, which shows that she was brought into the assembly by Pastor Andrew Ritchie on 2 April 1830. They conclude that she "does not appear to have remained a 'Dissenter' for long," since her marriage was performed in an Anglican church a year after her conversion.[26] It would not, however, have been possible for her to get married in a Congregationalist chapel in 1831. An old puritan sect appealing to rural yeomen and urban businessmen, Congregationalists helped found a nonconformist lobby for repeal of the Test and Corporation Acts. Successful in gaining repeal, nonconformists did not achieve the right to marry in chapel until a civil register was established in 1836. In April 1831 the Presbyterian J.W.D. Moodie and the Congregationalist Susanna Strickland had no choice but to celebrate their marriage in the Church of England. Her commitment to Congregationalism would reappear in the colony.

In her *Life of Agnes Strickland* Jane is explicit about Agnes's Royalist and High Church affinities so to exonerate her of Jacobitism and Romanism and to affirm her allegiance to the Hanoverians and the established church. She does not, however, mention Sarah's marriage to Robert Childs or Susanna's involvement with the same family and conversion to Congregationalism. Sarah's marriage ended with the suicide of her husband in 1837. Five years later she married the Reverend Richard Gwillym of the established church. At this event Jane joyously welcomes her back into the narrative. According to Agnes's other biographer, "the Stricklands were not at all proud of the Childs connection ... Sarah's second marriage to a clergyman of the Establishment was, it is made clear, a source of pride and satisfaction to the entire family" (Pope-Hennessy 1940, 45-6).

Jane relegates the marriages of Catharine and Susanna to Scots Presbyterian soldiers to a footnote and never mentions their emigration. She briefly refers to the two youngest girls once more in connection with Agnes's socializing in Edinburgh, and alludes to Susanna a final time to support her contention that the "poetical talents" possessed by Agnes and Eliza ran in the family (1887, 388). Jane does not acknowledge the youngest brother, Thomas – perhaps because he became a sailor – but makes much of Samuel, the colonial patrician, in the story of his return to England to replace a second wife who had died. Both Agnes and Jane praise his talent as an author, although nothing is said about the publications of Susanna and Catharine, not even *Roughing It*, which preceded Samuel's book by a year and had been dedicated "to Agnes Strickland, Author of 'Lives of the Queens of England'" (v). Jane narrates at length the deaths of her mother, Samuel, Agnes, and Eliza. Susanna's death, two years before her book was published, is not mentioned.

There is something to be made of the gaps and silences of Jane Strickland's biography of Agnes, something beyond a story of family rivalries and allegiances or the oblivion into which the emigrant sank.

Eliza and Agnes set and fulfilled their goals for London literary careers. Jane, at Reydon Hall caring for their mother, followed them from afar and made attempts to emulate them. None of these three married or strayed from commitment to the High Church. Sarah, Susanna, and Catharine, by contrast, flirted with nonconformist sects and members of them, marrying outside the Church of England. Further, Catharine and Susanna, by resigning themselves to lives of hardship far from the imperial metropolis, acknowledged the family's loss of caste.[27]

Catharine's memoirs speak of their isolation from "the resident farmers and their families" due to their status (TFC, 8343). While their father was alive, there were "formal visits ... and dinner parties at stated times," but as he became too ill for company, these ceased: "We lived very much alone" (8312, 8341). After his death, their "former liberal income ... reduced to doubtful means of keeping up our status in society," even "the better sort" of "agriculturalists" treated them with "cold distant civility but no warmth": "Society there was none, we stood alone in our parish ... Only among our poor neighbors there was kindly affection and great respect" (8486-7). Agnes had begun to publish in literary magazines, however, and soon after their father's death she went to London to capitalize on her literary connections. The society that she and Eliza cultivated seems to have been based on their literary endeavours, and all outside Suffolk.[28] At home the "chief want" felt by the "elder sisters was congenial society" (TFC, 8337).

The Strickland girls may be grouped according to religion, marital status, and class affiliation: "The tendency of the aristocracy was automatically to ignore people in the position of the Stricklands, just as the tendency of the Stricklands, as Church folk, was automatically to ignore Chapel folk" (Pope-Hennessy 1940, 21). This easy conflation of class and religion makes Eliza and Agnes the representives of the Stricklands and forgets that Sarah and Susanna during this very period were "Chapel folk" themselves.

"Our religious training had been strictly as the children of High Church Protestant parents," Catharine writes: "We were taught reverence for the church and our clergy, obedience to the state and its rulers and deference to parents and our elders." She notes their strict Sunday observances but also stresses the formal and disciplinary elements of their training and concludes: "This was a firm but a fruitless faith."[29] The other sisters do not supply direct evidence of Thomas Strickland's religious orientation. The connection with the Childses may date from the days at Stowe House, and Susanna was allowed to associate with Quakers as a girl, raising the possibility that Strickland had nonconformist associations before his temporary elevation to the gentry.[30] That their religious instruction was confined to Sundays is negative evidence that their father may have been latitudinarian in his beliefs. The affinity that his educational program had with late eighteenth-century rationalism justifies the speculation that he may, at some time in his economic rise, have been drawn towards "the Socinian wilderness of Unitarianism."[31]

The growth of nonconformism during this period made it the "midwife" of "the new class system," instrumental in the "emancipation of the middle ranks and lower orders" from "the dependency system" (Perkin 1969, 196). Mobility within the religious hierarchy occurred "as one moved up – or down – the social hierarchy" (202). The stages of religious affiliation paralleling class affiliation took a "member of the lower orders who raised himself" out of the Broad Church and into "one of the Independent congregations." Continued elevation would lead to a Presbyterian or Quaker chapel: "Finally, if he became so successful as to be able to buy an estate and retire from business he or his family would return to the Anglican fold" (204). Susanna's religious development, the reverse of her father's, follows an "or down" scenario.

Una Pope-Hennessy positions the girls among the class and gender pressures of their time. Following the matter of the marriage and emigration of Catharine and Susanna, she writes: "Actually the Miss Stricklands' chances of making good marriages were not very favourable as socially they fell between two stools, being neither of the county nor yet connected with a business. It is evident that though their circumstances were genteel, their upbringing gentle, and their residence a Hall, they were not at this time accepted by the county families who avoided all suspicion of contact with trade or the middle-class" (1940, 20-1). Catharine shows how the stakes were raised by the family events of 1818: "In those days poverty was regarded almost as a crime" (FitzGibbon 1894, xvi) – especially if one were not born to it and a woman. That three of the sisters did not marry says more about class allegiances and gender politics than about their personal proclivities.

The line dividing the "two stools" of church and chapel, gentry and middle class, between which the Stricklands fell can be erased. Manufacturers and merchants had to choose whether to join the ruling class as individuals or to work in solidarity with the rest of the amorphous middle class, even the working class, to change the existing system and, as happened, instal themselves as a new hegemony. Thomas Strickland chose the first option but failed to retain his place in the gentry. His wife and daughters, unable to participate in business or politics, were locked in the precarious heritage he bequeathed them. Their only recourse was to attempt to resolve the contradictions of their position by writing.

Until 1832 Anglicans were politically and socially unified and non-Anglicans marginalized. Carl Ballstadt, Michael Peterman, and Elizabeth Hopkins mention that "Suffolk was a notorious Nonconformist region during the early 1800s" (*Letters*, 16). Susanna characterizes the locals as "mostly Methodists" (letter 4). A Southwold member of Parliament, a knight, "would not tolerate a Dissenter as tenant but this may be explained perhaps as much on political as religious grounds" (Pope-Hennessy 1940, 45). In Norwich dissenters led political radicals. Dissenters were condemned as unpatriotic, and the rural chapel was an insult to the local elite, both religious and political.[32]

Through religion, Eliza, Agnes, and Jane clung to the upward trajectory their father had established before his business failure. Agnes, with her Roman Catholic sympathies, sought to confirm her solidarity with a class to which she did not belong. Her writing testifies to a nostalgia for the *ancien regime*, even the pre-Reformation. She resolved her dilemma by affirming a mythical ancestry, writing endless tomes on bygone queens and circulating at the highest levels of society.

Sarah, Catharine, and Susanna followed the downward trajectory initiated by that business failure. That Susanna would attend chapel shows the extent to which her religious and class allegiances had diverged from those of the older sisters. According to Catharine, "her secession from the Established Church was very distasteful to our mother and sisters, and for a while, was the cause of disunion and a withdrawal of the old harmony and confidence which had hitherto existed in the family" (TFC, 9884). So much younger when her father died, Susanna vacillated among various alternatives: a literary career in London, dissent, marriage to a romantic Scots soldier, and, finally, "the dustbin of the colonies." She gave in to her reduced status and grappled with its meaning. Her writing records her attempts to resolve the conflicts within herself and in so doing dramatizes the class conflicts of the society within which she was raised. No matter how far into historical territory she travels, she does not lose sight of the disquieting class and religious features of the landscape around her. Susanna Strickland's writing is an ideological map that refuses to yield the location of the safe home the post-war depression erased from it. It carries the tracks of her unfinished journey between establishment and dissent.

2 Writing as Resolution: Literary Production 1822-1830

Susanna Strickland, caught between established church and nonconformist chapel, was in her writing caught between convention and exploration. Pressure on her to cleave to the church and deny the reality of her social position was compounded by pressure on her to exploit the conventions of the literary marketplace and overcome that position. Her decision to join Congregationalism was an acceptance and affirmation of her class, parallel to her decision to write from her own experience, with the incumbent problems. Writing formalized her solutions of the tensions between desire and reality. The recurrence of these tensions, however, dramatizes how writing is always re-solution for her, until moral resolution leads to questioning the efficacy of writing itself.

The Strickland women developed literary careers with their social allegiances during the 1820s. Catharine and Susanna began writing fiction in early 1816.[1] Agnes's poem on Princess Charlotte's death (1817) was the first publication of the sisters. A collection of Catharine's children's stories (1818) was their first book publication. Susanna relates how a friend of her father, shown a manuscript of hers "as a literary curiosity," thought it worth publishing, and so her first book, *Spartacus* (1822), appeared.[2] This book initiated a concern with independence consistent in her subsequent stories, as well as her displacement of that concern on to male heroes. Peterman describes the story as dealing with "the difficult course between devotion to the ideal of freedom and an unwillingness to rebel violently against the prevailing Roman order" (1983, 69). The young woman's desire for dignity is correlated with a male slave's; resolution is sought through inscribing nineteenth-century morality upon a historic substratum.

Catharine was "grateful" to use money earned by her first book "to eke out the now reduced income of the home" (FitzGibbon 1894, xv). Following Catharine, all the sisters but Sarah published children's books.[3] Susanna, noting that the girls were "remarkable for their literary attainments," tells how their "very misfortunes became the source from whence they derived both energy and strength": "they dared to ... make the talents with which the great Father had liberally endowed them, work out their appointed end" (*RI*, 196).

Accompanied by her sisters, Susanna may not have realized just how daring it was for them to enter what was still, despite growing numbers of women writers, the predominantly male world of publishing. Like many first publications among their counterparts, the majority of the Stricklands' early works were children's books, considered a minor genre specifically the preserve of women, and many of these were published anonymously, presumably to avoid the castigation due to this sort of public display.[4] In another strategy of indirection through which Catharine, Susanna, and Agnes fulfilled their desire to write without betraying the modesty of their sex, they wrote for their own and their family's amusement. Catharine and Susanna hatched the scheme of writing stories "first to amuse ourselves," and then to read them at night to Sarah.

The encounter with another domestic coterie of writers and readers must have been one of the main reasons Catharine, upon reading Gaskell's *The Life of Charlotte Brontë* later in life, exclaimed that "the early days" of the Brontës "remind[s] me of *our own early years.*"[5] Significantly, Catharine and Susanna's first books were mediated to publishers by male friends of their father, without the girls taking part. Their payment for these books – probably for most of their publications before emigration – was entirely in the hands of their de facto agents and publishers.[6]

According to Jane, "poverty was the means of bringing forth talents that might have remained buried had circumstances been less adverse." Economic pressure forced them to ignore the limits of gender. They took advantage of the commodification of literature in the nascent stage of the literary profession. Believing that writing was what talented romantic geniuses did, they began publishing with the tacit awareness that it was a marketable skill. The sisters probably considered teaching, one career alternative, but there were few opportunities.[7]

By 1828 Susanna had published a series of children's books.[8] Her decision to name the eponymous hero of what proved to be her most popular story Hugh Latimer seems intentionally to address Agnes's

High Church and Stuart sympathies. The historical Hugh Latimer gained prominence through his support for the annulment of the marriage of Henry VIII and Catherine of Aragon, and was promptly martyred by the daughter of this union, Mary Tudor, when she returned the English church to Rome. Agnes later wrote a novel that featured Henry and Catherine happily married, and in her biographical work defended their daughter, a.k.a. Bloody Mary. But the name of the friend and helper of the fictional Hugh, Montrose Graham, alludes to John Graham, earl of Montrose, a Stuart supporter, and the story may enact a rapprochement between the two sides in the Strickland family's domestic politics. Susanna's hero shares no more than a propensity for martyrdom with his namesake, but his name and that of his friend would resonate among the sisters, heated as they were by the history and presence of England's religious broils.

The fictional character does share more with his author: a grandfather who lost the family farm; a father who died broke; a mother struggling to support the family. The epigraph to *Hugh Latimer* comes from Hugh's speech to a repentant persecutor: "Worth consists neither in rank nor riches, though it adds a lustre to both." This moral became a standard feature of middle-class doxa in books like Samuel Smiles' *Self-Help*. In the first third of the century, however, it was part of the middle-class attempt to manipulate ambiguities associated with the idea of the gentleman so to challenge the gentry's exclusive ownership of the idea.[9] The impecunious gentlewoman resolves her personal turmoil by writing a story that demonstrates that gentility is based on morality, not social position. Through didacticism, displacement, and plotting, she freights this story with autobiographical import and, through fictional conventions, solves her dilemma. She deals with her experience while hiding its reality from herself and her readers.[10]

The story replaces social and economic explanations for loss of caste with pure contingency. Hugh's grandfather loses his farm not because of another heir's prior claim but through fire. Hugh Sr loses his family not because of a divergence in social and religious commitment but through smallpox. Hugh Jr loses his patrimony not because of his father's business failure but through his supreme sacrifice saving his commander in the Peninsular War. Unaccountable, "natural" contingency displaces material causality.

His mother supports Hugh and his wise old uncle by keeping a shop. The disdain of his aristocratic schoolfellows for a shopkeeper's son is not, however, shown to be supported by an underlying social fabric.[11] While they are well-versed in "distinctions of rank" (8), identifying themselves as "*gentlemen*" (9) and Hugh as a "beggar's brat" (8), they are not really gentlemen. They are cruel and cowardly, among "those who wantonly commit crime, because they think that their rank shields them" (10). The boarders are poor students compared to poor Hugh, a day-student on a foundation: he is made an example to "the young gentlemen" (29). The true gentlemen, Montrose Grahame and his uncle, Colonel Grahame, see beyond his lack of rank and riches to the lustre of Hugh's worth: humility, duty, compassion, and intelligence transcend unredeemed materiality, as "the good and sensible part of mankind" recognizes (9). The artificial hierarchy of rank is negated by the "natural" one of worth, so allowing the moral displacement of Hugh's dilemma. Those who embrace rank are bad, while the virtuous transcend social limitations. As in Samuel Smiles, when the gentlemanly ideal is interpreted in moral rather than social terms, the "'True Gentleman' [is] essentially classless" (Gilmour 1981, 99). Still, the bad characters do all belong to the upper ranks.

Providence, a name for contingency that implicates God's hand in its operation, determines social position, and the acceptance of Providence dissolves social limits.[12] Hugh's dependent uncle tells him, "a good and gracious God will add *his* to *my* feeble blessing, if you do your duty, and walk uprightly in that station of life to which it has pleased his Almighty Providence to call you" (23). Colonel Grahame, the good aristocrat, has "learned to consider those whom Providence has wisely ordained to move in a lower sphere of life, in a more just and benevolent point of view" (57). The uncle's admonishment never to set "too much value on riches, which have once, and can again, take to themselves wings and flee away" (74–5) affirms that God, not economics, determines economic station. This popular moral suasion was expressed by Wilberforce, who would placate the poor by teaching them that "their more lowly path has been allotted to them by the hand of God; that it is their part faithfully to discharge its duties and contentedly to bear its inconveniences; ... that the objects, about which worldly men conflict so eagerly, are not worth the contest" (1797, 309). This endorsement of the status quo underlies the story.

God's blessing extends beyond the bestowal of grace to show itself materially. Curbing his pride, Hugh triumphs at school. He gains the friendship of the most admired boy in the class and welcome in his genteel home. As head boy in his final year, Hugh represents the school by reciting a Latin speech to a visiting lord, known to him as his father's former commander. His Lordship, reminded by the boy's face of the soldier who died for him, uncovers Hugh's identity and bestows a commission on him and fifty pounds per annum on his mother. Colonel Grahame, who had intended to do the same, settles for equipping Hugh to go "forth into the world as befits a gentleman" (160). In the denouement Hugh is knighted. Virtue is more than its own reward.

The wish-fulfilling plot, putting Providence at the service of the rising middle class, accounts for the story's popularity, as does its brief opening on class conflict and immediate blurring of the view. Here too are the ambiguities of the middle-class appropriation of the gentlemanly ideal: Hugh is a born gentleman, but he can be accepted as one only after he has achieved the tangible signs of rank.

Writing a children's romance illustrating these ethics, Susanna resolves her own economic and sexual dilemma even as she hides from herself the realities of that dilemma. Hugh's problems are caused by "natural" disasters, not by economic determinants. Even to achieve this resolution she has to use a male hero; this enactment of desire was not available to females. Her writing helps her to adjust to subjection and create an image of community, providing her others – her readers – to share in that subjection.

The Little Prisoner, another of Susanna's children's books, demonstrates the taming of Ferdinand Charlton's passionate temper with Christian patience. A gentleman's son, like Hugh's schoolmates he persecutes his inferiors, in this case his father's servants. Ferdinand is called a madman and wild beast and treated as a criminal. To subdue his spirit his father has him imprisoned in the governor's castle. During his rehabilitative confinement he is subjected to Christian homiletics, like a sermon illustrating the anti-Rousseauian belief that "Man, left to himself ... can do nothing but commit evil; he remains in a savage, unenlightened state of existence, yielding, on all occasions, to ... bad passions" (55). Hannah More, influential writer of moral tracts and friend of Wilberforce, thought it a "fundamental error to consider children as innocent beings": they have "a corrupt nature and evil dispositions."[13] The contradiction that this wisdom must be enforced by punishment is effaced when Ferdinand is convinced that he makes his own prison: "At present, your mind, like your person, is in prison," he is told: "If you ... regulate your words and actions by the precepts laid down for us in God's blessed book, he will bestow on you that liberty, of which no earthly power can deprive you" (57). In Susanna's situation, no reformation would gain her release from her less tangible prison, but this faith provided spiritual liberation from economic bondage.

Susanna's children's stories demonstrate the necessity of subduing ungovernable passions. A useful life requires resignation to duty. She attempts to prove, by recourse to patriarchal middle-class morality, the error of resisting her place as a woman in a family of reduced means. Pride is humbled; the solution sought in Christian humility is demonstrated through the syllogisms of children's didactic fiction. Pride and passion must be repressed, their return in story after story showing that repression is never quite complete. These stories are Susanna's attempt to acquiesce to her lowly path, to make peace with a situation that protest could not change. But the writing of these stories is evidence that she did resist the social structure that bound her and had difficulty subduing her pride and anger.[14]

Susanna invested in the power of writing to lift her out of the social station that humility would teach her to accept. At a turning-point in the relations of literary production, she straddled this contradiction. She could still idealize writing as what the genteel amateur indulged in to fulfil the creative yearnings of his or her soul. It occupied an abundant leisure due not to independent means or the largesse of a patron but to the isolation incumbent on her family's circumstances. Meanwhile, she turned this gentle pastime to utilitarian purpose: it helped eke out the family income. Writing was both supplemental and essential, both leisure pursuit and substitute for other work.[15]

When the Strickland women began making excursions to London, they had two cousins of their father with whom to stay. Thomas Cheesman, an artist, and Rebecca Leverton, a wealthy widow, both lived in the neighbourhood of the British Museum. The sisters, except Jane and Sarah, paid many calls from Suffolk to this fashionable part of London, staying with Cheesman and his niece in the first part of the 1820s and with Mrs Leverton later in the decade.[16] Eliza became a professional woman of letters earliest, editing a fashionable London periodical in the 1830s.[17] Eliza, the recluse, and Agnes, the socialite, spent much of their time in London from the early 1820s on.

The literary networking of the elder sisters began in the mid-1820s. Under Mrs Leverton's "chaperonage" Agnes "entered into society," meeting many of the magazine editors, and women writers like Lady Morgan, Letitia Elizabeth Landon, Anna Jameson, and Anna and Jane Porter, becoming good friends with the latter.[18] The burgeoning periodical and book press, especially that controlled by Henry Colburn, extracted products for mass consumption from this fashionable literary society. The circle of Agnes's acquaintances was unlike what is known of Susanna's, and supplies evidence of the social articulation of the distinct ideological positions the sisters occupied.

Of Agnes's London friends, only Thomas Pringle figures in Susanna's life. The Stricklands may have met him through Thomas Harral, described by the editors of the *Letters* as "a fervent Tory and royalist" who "published polemical essays in opposition to parliamentary reform and in strong support of George IV at the time of what he called 'the follies of Queen Caroline'" (6). His daughter, Anna Laura, Susanna calls "one of the friends of [her] girlhood." Harral edited periodicals in Suffolk and was "for several years Editor of *La Belle Assemblée*" (letter 59). Apart from, in Susanna's words, "struggling with unusual pecuniary difficulties" in 1828 (letter 10), his ideological profile is closer to Agnes's than to hers. That Susanna was a close friend of his daughter and Catharine had a long engagement to his son indicates that up to a point the younger girls shared the aspirations of their older sisters. Susanna later describes Harral as "a great sceptic on religious matters" (letter 68), but her discussion in 1827 of his request for a story shows that she was then closer to his religious beliefs than she was to those of her Methodist neighbours (letter 4).

La Belle Assemblée's alternate title, *Court and Fashionable Magazine*, suits its self-description as "Containing Interesting and Original Literature, and Records of the Beau-Monde," and also suits what is known of Harral's proclivities. The opening engraving of one "of the Beauties of the Court of George the Fourth," the series "forming a Picture Gallery of the Female Nobility of Great Britain," is followed by short memoirs of the illustrated ladies. A sketch or fiction instalment appears, then a page of "Original Poetry." A few coloured pages of fashionable women, accompanied by an "Explanation of Illustrated Fashions" and the notes of the Paris or Italian correspondent on continental styles, constitute the fashion section. Brief notices on the arts and sciences occupy the penultimate part, and the magazine closes with a personal page on royalty or the titled. Harral himself irregularly contributed sketches of writers like Coleridge and Bulwer-Lytton.

Susanna began writing for adults with poems and sketches in *La Belle Assemblée* in the spring of 1827. "I have written a little sketch for *La Belle* which I despatch today. I rather think of becoming a regular contributor to the Mag, but must do so, on the usual terms," she tells a friend (letter 2). "The Witch of East Cliff," in the July issue, is headed "Sketches from the Country. No. I." Connections with male friends featured in most of her publishing relations. Her first juvenile book saw print thanks to a family friend, and her first sketch appeared in a periodical edited by a friend's father. Over the next three years Harral published more than forty pieces by her.

Susanna admired the work of Mary Russell Mitford, a writer of popular rural sketches. In mid-1829 Pringle passed on letters between the two, and a correspondence ensued.[19] These two women shared much in their orientation to the dominant male ideology. The elder woman wrote to support her father's gambling. Her sketches showed Susanna how a woman writer could tap nostalgia for a rural past to earn a living. Susanna's poem to Mitford is mainly about a "Nature" the love of which she imagines sharing with her. Despite her modesty, there is an ambition to emulate: "Never to me will Nature teach the art / To sketch the living portrait on the heart" (letters 15). In later letters she admires

Mitford's sketches but does not indicate any systematic study of their particular craft.

Susanna published five "Sketches from the Country" in *La Belle Assemblée*. The second, "The Two Fishermen," is told to the frame narrator by an old man. Two brothers of contrasting temperaments marry two sisters. Following an argument, one of the men disappears; the other turns up with blood on his hands. The vanished brother's wife dies in childbirth, and the surviving brother is hanged for murder. The surviving sister cares for her nephew until his father returns six years later; then she dies. He had been kidnapped by smugglers and goes on to outlive them all, passing his story on to Susanna. This story is, as its later subtitle proclaims, "A Tale of the Coast," not a sketch. The improbable plot demonstrates the moral elaborated upon it. The problem that brings "the little prisoner" to grief shatters the tranquillity of these families. One brother, "handsome, gay, passionate, and thoughtless," possesses an "unfortunate temper" and is jealous of the other's happiness (110). When the latter disappears, it is the flawed brother's reputation that convicts him of fratricide. Passion is not only disruptive; it can be lethal. Social hierarchy is transcended through the happily married brother, who, content with his wife's love, "envied not the luxuries of the great" (110). As in her children's stories, controlling passion leads to a contentment and social adjustment that can ignore social disabilities.

The first four sketches, published within a space of six months, are melodramatic stories that various old-county characters are set up to narrate. They may be based on Suffolk legends, but their contrived plots suggest considerable invention. Plot, framing narrative and archaic setting make them generically closer to tales than sketches. The fifth, published after an interval of almost a year from the fourth, is the only one to conform to the loose conventions of the sketch. In "Old Hannah; or, The Charm" Susanna deals with her experiences with a maid at Reydon Hall. This sketch, without the developed plots and frame narratives that constrain the others, is formally closer to the type of sketch with which Mitford worked. Susanna's admiration for Mitford was an influence on her negotiations with the press, not a literary influence. After Mitford created a market for stories of rural life, Susanna could use county characters and settings, but she shaped them with the fictional conventions she had used in her children's stories.

One of Susanna's putatively historical tales for *La Belle Assemblée* strays from the didacticism of her prose up to this point. "The Pope's Promise," an apocryphal anecdote from the life of Pope Sixtus V, has no truly good or bad characters, and everyone gets his reward. A poor shoemaker makes shoes for a friar who comes up short for the payment. The shoemaker scorns the friar's promise of recompense when he becomes pope, but more than twenty years later he is summoned to Rome. He obeys, in fear of the Inquisition, and it is the friar-become-pope who has issued the summons. After a bit of verbal jousting he grants a purse of gold to the shoemaker's wife and a bishopric to his son. No consistent moral can be derived from the story. Neither pope nor shoemaker deserves elevation. The story might have shown power bound by honour as weakness by poverty, except the pope's payment is due more to vanity than honour. Like other characters, the shoemaker is afflicted with a bad temper, but he is not punished, for in venting his anger he expresses orthodox Protestant prejudice. The exclusive object of his ire is "a rich community of Franciscan monks."[20]

Legitimate targets though Catholics were, the shoemaker's words seem charged with his author's displaced anger at the laxity of some of the Anglican clergy: "Oh, these monks are ... too spiritual to attend to any temporal wants but their own ... They live on the general contributions of the public, and take good care to want for nothing that can be obtained by way of extortion. ... O, 'tis a dainty life! whose very motto is 'laziness.' They are the hooded locusts that devour the substance of the land" (6). The righteous chagrin of the stalwart middle class against pluralists and placemen can be felt in every word. An evil character in one of Susanna's later stories points to the local rector's hold on "five rich livings" as sufficient incentive to seek his own fortune in the Church of England, and relishes the life of luxury he will lead as a "Right Worshipful Rector" (MH 109). Counter-Reformation Italy, worse than Broad Church England, can supply no one to correct the shoemaker's temper and lead him to patience; experience must be his teacher: "Poverty, and the increasing cares of a large family, tamed the vivacity of the Scarpetáro's spirits" (9–10). Projecting her imagination into a remote time and place, Susanna critiques the effects of an established church and social hierarchy. Distance from her story frees her from didacticism and allows her to reveal more about contradictions in her own moral experience than she usually does.

The bulk of Susanna's contributions to La Belle Assemblée was poetic. Her verse is clichéd in expression and sentiment, like the work of other forgotten poets who had a readership in their time. While they do not repay close textual analysis, these poems do bear upon what drove her to write and how her writing articulated with the literary market. Once more, dispossession impelled her to seek refuge in contemporary morality. Her first substantial poem in La Belle Assemblée was "The Earthquake."[21] It depicts the destruction of a vaguely archaic city, representative of human society, and ends with a gloomy wilderness where once the city in "pomp and splendour rose" (l. 50). Susanna had never experienced any natural disaster worse than a North Sea storm strayed inland. What drew her to imagine an apocalyptic event beyond anything she knew?

A piece of a possible answer is in her variation on the *ubi sunt* motif, "On the Ruins of Walberswick Church in Suffolk."[22] The poet asks, "What hast thou seen in olden times?" and the church answers for the rest of the poem. These ruins know where the hordes of yesteryear have gone: "Here thousands find a resting place ... Forgotten save by God" (ll. 41, 48). Hierarchies are levelled by the fate all share. In death can "The soil-bound slave forget his woe, / The king resign his crown" (ll. 31–2). Death erases the transient distinctions of the living: "The prince – the peer – the peasant sleeps / Alike beneath the sod" (ll. 45–6). That all die should console those living with inequality, especially the peasant. Despite the specificity of its title, the poem knows neither time nor place because "human hearts are still / In every age to nature true" (ll. 58–59). "The Nameless Grave" similarly spurns the concrete to express the eternal truth that "Thou art living to-day and forgotten tomorrow!" (l. 12).

"The Old Ash Tree," like "The Earthquake" and "On the Ruins" written in 1827 and published in *La Belle Assemblée*, helps in tracing the lineaments of Susanna's imagination to the source of her apocalyptic visions:

Thou beautiful Ash! thou art lowly laid,
    And my eyes shall hail no more
From afar thy cool and refreshing shade,
    When the toilsome journey's o'er.
The winged and the wandering tribes of air
    A home 'mid thy foliage found,
But the graceful boughs, all broken and bare,
    The wild winds are scattering round.

The storm-demon sent up his loudest shout
    When he levelled his bolt at thee,
When thy massy trunk and thy branches stout
    Were riven by the blast, old tree!
It has bowed to the dust thy stately form,
    Which for many an age defied
The rush and the roar of the midnight storm,
    When it swept through thy branches wide.

I have gazed on thee with a fond delight
    In childhood's happier day,
And watched the moonbeams of a summer night
    Through thy quivering branches play.
I have gathered the ivy wreaths that bound
    Thy old fantastic roots,
And wove the wild flowers that blossomed round
    With spring's first tender shoots.

And when youth with its glowing visions came,
    Thou wert still my favourite seat;
And the ardent dreams of future fame
    Were formed at thy hoary feet.
Farewell – farewell – the wintry wind
    Has waged unsparing war on thee,
And only pictured on my mind
    Remains thy form, time-honoured tree!

The metaphoric structure suggesting the ravages of maturity has an extended purpose: unhappiness is aligned with natural process. That the poet bids farewell to compensatory dreams of fame makes this process less natural than the poem's formal structure suggests.

"Autumn" presents the same equation of natural and human processes and encompasses the consolation of "On the Ruins." With the dying of the year the poet hears "a spirit sigh" (l. 16), which tells her "all must die, / As the leaf dies on the ground" (ll. 19–20). Not just bodies but

The brightest hopes we cherish,
    Which own a mortal trust,
But bloom awhile to perish
    And moulder in the dust. (21–4)

Only the soul transcends process to "live again with God" (l. 4) in a heaven of eternal spring. In "Stanzas" the calm before the storm is the same as the "speechless expectation" before "sorrow lays our fondest wishes low," and the linked human and natural phenomena are subsumed in the "brighter hope" of faith, which allows the soul to "[soar] over earthly ill."[23]

All are subject to death. The Christian finds consolation through faith in a life after death. From these commonplace themes it does not follow that the vicissitudes of the living are as inevitable, as subject to "natural" laws, as birth and death or that Christian faith necessarily entails resignation to these vicissitudes. What, besides literary fashion, led a healthy young woman to ruminate on these themes in poem after poem? An answer lies in family circumstances, which led her in youth to fantasies of future glory and, as naïveté gave way to experience, forced her to abandon those fantasies.[24] She confesses to wasting "precious hours and talents ... in forming those vain theories, those fanciful dreams of happiness that have faded in my grasp" (letter 19). Her dreams of happiness met disappointment; she sought relief in the moral that human life conforms to natural process and that nature reveals the higher happiness of Christian faith. Providence decrees unhappiness so that the soul can transcend nature and join with God. The repressed desire for worldly happiness, as pride and passion in the stories, returns throughout her poetry.

In this light, and recalling how in *Hugh Latimer* she displaces the economic catastrophes of her own life into a narrative of fated events, "The Earthquake" may now be read as an allegory for pending social and political cataclysm in pre-Reform Bill England. The French Revolution had swallowed "stately towers and temples" in "Its fiery depths" (ll. 45, 47) as inexorably as the earthquake. Perhaps an English revolution was coming. Perhaps in some corner of her mind Susanna Strickland wished it would. One other poem from *La Belle Assemblée* helps to extend this argument. "The Dream" is of the poet's dead lover. A love poem would not suit *Enthusiasm*, where it later appears, but this poem is about the peace that a corpse is imagined enjoying, not the loss of the living on which a profane love poem might concentrate:

> Whilst on thy lips the placid smile that played,
>   Proved thy soul's exit to a happier sphere,
> In silent eloquence reproaching those
> Who watched in agony thy last repose. (ll. 5–8)

Love is sublimated in the hope of immortality. The poem harmonizes with religious tracts of the period, celebrating a holy death as the only goal the suffering might long for without guilt. Susanna's poetry articulates with a religious conditioning that defers the sexual and material desires of the poor into a wish for death as the only freedom from living.

Susanna also contributed to *La Belle Assemblée* two poems addressed to Harral's daughter, Anna Laurel. The editors of the *Letters* speculate that her "original link to Harral was through his daughter" and that "perhaps Harral's willingness to publish his daughter's poetry ... led Susanna to submit her own work."[25] She submitted her last work to *La Belle Assemblée* in late 1829 or early 1830. During the period that she was writing for Harral she began submitting work to the gift-books and annuals. She made her first gift-book contribution to *The Pledge of Friendship* in the fall of 1827, a few months after "The Earthquake" had been published. By 1829 she was contributing to at least five different annuals.

The annuals, an early triumph of capitalist publishing, depended on a new control by publishers of the production of commodities attractive to an emergent middle-class market. The first annual appeared in November 1822 as a Christmas gift-book, and they peaked ten years later with sixty-three titles.[26] Their vogue was due to innovations in design and the ability to mass-produce illustrations cheaply following the advent of steel-plate engraving in 1819. Increasing competition and expenditures made them unprofitable, and they began to disappear.

The annuals stressed style over content, constantly experimenting with ornate bindings. Sometimes engravings were gathered first and writers then commissioned to illustrate the illustrations. Fashionable writers were sought over more serious authors. Writers for the annuals made texts as others made textiles, as a way to sell their labour. The marks of these relations of production are upon Susanna Strickland's work for them.

The annuals had a reputation for piety. There is no contradiction in Susanna's contributing to them after she had experienced doubt about authorship. She could easily see her work in them as fulfilling a moral, not literary purpose. She joined the annuals with "Stanzas on War," an appropriate subject for a poem written in the same period as "The Earthquake" and *Hugh Latimer*, where the Napoleonic War is a natural phenomenon like smallpox. The war apostrophized in the prosopoetic first stanza is an abstract force, a "Dark spirit!" found in "every age" and immune to explanation, like plague or natural catastrophe.[27] This poem accepts armed conflict and its attraction for the men who die in it. After the first two stanzas, dealing with war in general, the remaining ten relate a pathetic incident set in the English Civil War. The soul of a young warrior is freed by death in combat for "flight" to "its native shore" as "A spirit robed in light" (ll. 50–2). War and history are excuses for this moral tale.

The Iris: A Literary and Religious Offering was edited by the Reverend Thomas Dale. "The Overthrow of Zebah and Zalmunna," in the volume for 1830, is Susanna's first published biblical paraphrase.[28] It narrates Gideon's defeat of the Midianites and underwrites the religious rationale for war. Gideon is an agent of "the vengeance of the Lord" against Baal (l. 9). The God motivating this conflict is as abstract as the "Dark spirit" of "Stanzas on War." In the next *Iris* Susanna provides another biblical poem, this one recalling "The Earthquake" except that, in "The Deluge," apocalypse is demanded by the corruption to which humanity has sunk.[29] The absence of Noah's name and God's covenant combines with the anachronism of a walled city and the dress of its inhabitants to detemporalize the poem, making its setting, as with "The Earthquake," someplace between contemporary England and the antediluvian Middle East. As in "On the Ruins," social distinctions are noted only to be dissolved "in the living mass" (l. 27). All are to be destroyed because of the corruption all share. The apocalypticism previously related to the threat of civil strife now carries an evangelical moral force.

Several poems in the annuals again suggest the personal anguish behind Susanna's apocalyptic visions. "The Captive" and "The Release of the Caged Lark" are variations on the theme of captivity.[30] "The Captive" is a citizen of a conquered nation, whose family has been slain and who has herself been removed to the king's palace. She reacts to her confinement by crying – "Oh, 'tis a luxury unrestrained to weep: / She feels a joy in that wild waste of woe" (ll. 36–7) – and dreaming of her happy childhood. The reappearance of this theme in "The Release of the Caged Lark" increases the suspicion that her figures of imprisonment are self-projections. In this poem a "lovely tyrant" enjoys the music of her bird (l. 16), unmindful of the source of the bird's song:

> Whilst here, all the day,
>   I pour my sad lay;
>   And whilst I complain,
>   So tender's the strain,
> That my mistress looks up to rejoice in my pain. (ll. 11–15)

The bird protests:

> Oh, call it not music! when sorrow is pouring
> Her sighs to the breeze, in low accents deploring
> The loss of that liberty – life's dearest blessing –
> Which renders me cold to your playful caressing. (ll. 31–4)

At last her mistress feels compassion and releases the bird. Susanna's poetry, like the lark's song, has its source in the distress of constraint, only her bars are economic and sexual. The advice to "the little prisoner" to seek liberty through Christian faith looks increasingly like advice she was trying to believe in herself.

One group of Susanna's gift-book verse, her nature poems, is perhaps her most conventional contribution.[31] While the Romantic poets use nature for varied philosophical musings, her nature inevitably leads to God. "O Come to the Meadows" beckons a friend to see the flowers, but they realize that the flowers, "Like us, but bloom to fade" (l. 44). As in "Autumn," this is not all that passes: "The hope that owns a mortal trust, / As quickly fades and dies" (ll. 51–2). They turn to a "brighter wreath" (l. 53), "the flowers of virtue" that "only bloom in heaven!" (ll. 55–6). "The Spirit of Spring" is lightly evoked in the poem of that name until the last lines, when it all leads beyond nature: "In thee we claim a brighter dower, / The day-spring of our God!" (ll. 39–40). The same movement occurs in "There's Joy when the Rosy Morning," one of Susanna's few paeans to the positive things in life, after the "fleeting ray" (l. 58) of earthly joy becomes as nothing:

> But there's a better joy than earth,
>   With all her charms can give,
> Which marks the Christian's second birth,
>   When man but dies to live! (ll. 61–64)

A hymn to joy that ends in the hope of death is characteristic of Susanna and her internalization of the morality of her day. "Awake!" and "The Wood Lane" are similar. The poet exhorts her readers to awake to the beauty of bird-song before demanding they "Awake! – to Him who formed the light" (l. 13). "The Wood Lane" elaborately enumerates flora and fauna, then finally asserts they should lead us "To Look, through Nature, up to Nature's God!" (l. 40). The quotation from Pope's *Essay on Man* points to the confluence of deism and dissent.

By early 1829 Susanna had begun to contribute to the *Ecclesiastic*, a new periodical, and late in that year she appeared in several explicitly Christian annuals.[32] "O Come to the Meadows," "The Spirit of Spring," "Zebah and Zalmunna," and at least two other poems from late 1829 were signed "Z.Z." This pseudonym may have been suggested by its typographical similarity with her own initials, as was another, "Sophia Sandys." Ballstadt, Peterman, and Hopkins, noting "her uneasy feelings about her literary worth, the goal of literary fame, and the disagreeable aspects of familial rivalry," say that she soon dropped this "affectation" (14). These pseudonyms appear during her moral crisis and may signal conflict amongst spiritual, literary, and feminine selves. The initials of the two leaders of the Midianites are Z.Z. Perhaps literary fame was as much a false god as Baal.

In many of her poems and stories, history is the substratum upon which Susanna elaborates personal moral concerns. Sending "The Son of Arminius" to an editor in 1829, she comments: "I wish I could say that it was strictly historical. This you will perceive it is not ... Tacitus has given us the promise in his history of these singular adventures ... The record is lost. ... I have presumed to fill up the blank thinking that the story might interest the ardent minds of youth, as I well remember when a child, being most deeply interested in those tales that were founded on ancient history."[33] She connects history, story, and childhood. In her historical tales she fills gaps in the record with romance. She later defends a conception of history as romance. "The Son of Arminius" opens with the triumphant return of the Roman legions from Germany. The captive wife of the German Arminius enters in paragraph 6 as the syntagm returning the story to the tone characteristic of Susanna's other stories. Like "The Captive," the wife suffers much, going to the extreme of dying from her "wounded spirit and broken heart."[34]

The son of Arminius, named Thumelicus and raised as a Roman by his uncle, becomes devoted to the country he believes his own and shares in the revelries of his peers. He is recalled from debauchery one evening by a fateful voice asking, "Is it the son of Arminius that degrades his name and country by becoming the leader of a band of licentious bacchanalians?" He has never heard his father's name but does not hesitate to bear the judgment and apply "to study, and to learning the use of arms" (79). His moral rejuvenation is hastened when his uncle reveals their shared origin and exhorts Thumelicus to return to Arminius. He does so, is accepted into his father's army without disclosing their kinship, is killed in battle, and only then is revealed as the long-lost son. Susanna refrains from giving a pagan the Christian faith that frees her other captives, but the story of Thumelicus is also a lesson in nineteenth-century morality. His uncle tells him to greet Arminius by declaring, "Father! I have been a slave at Rome; – I come to Germany to fight beneath your banners – to die in the cause of liberty!"[35] Yet again, the path to freedom lies through subjection to duty in the name of the father. Thumelicus must cast off the chains of luxury and pleasure, a satisfying moral for one who could not experience the weight of those chains.

The opposition of pleasure and honour is less first-century pagan than nineteenth-century middle-class. While the uncle dies from guilt at being a traitor to Rome, Arminius is held up as the ideal patriot. Susanna's acceptance of the nineteenth-century German view of Arminius as a national hero is necessary for the racial theory underlying the story. Thumelicus, knowing only of Rome and his allegiance to it, retains the traits Tacitus ascribes to the Germanic tribes. Once he learns he is German, he naturally switches his allegiance and easily fits in with the tribe to which he returns. No amount of romanizing can overcome his German blood. Biological determinism and the inexorable name of the Father produce a fatalistic vision. This fatalism is redeemed in other stories by inscription as a beneficent Providence. The individual must accept fate since he or she has no choice but to live that fate out. The desire for dignity, confronted by degradation, finds a transcendent dignity in resignation to duty. To align one's will with the will of God is to be a good Christian; to do otherwise changes nothing but one's moral condition.

From Spartacus to Thumelicus, captivity is determined by God's inscrutable design. So is poverty. The remaining five stories in the annuals all deal with cash shortage.[36] Three have central characters who have fallen from financial well-being to penury. The autobiographical parallels are unavoidable. "My Aunt Dorothy's Legacy," the slightest, concerns the disposition of the legacy.[37] "The Disappointed Politician" dwells on marriage for love or money among the governing classes of Sweden. Love wins. By the time she was writing it Susanna had met and married the fortuneless J.W.D. Moodie.

"Black Jenny: A Tale Founded on Facts," like *The Little Prisoner*, begins with two sons of gentry, one of whom has transgressed his father's rules and been punished, while the other suffers with him. At the sight of their mutual devotion the father relents and rewards them with a trip to London to buy archery equipment from a "fashionable shop." As the boys indulge in pastries after their coach ride, "a respectable-looking man, in very mean apparel, entered the shop, leading by the hand a pale emaciated little boy, of six years old" (8). He is begging scraps. A blacksmith who came to London to try his fortune, in the course of his work he rescued an orphaned foal. This is Black Jenny, whom the family nursed to maturity in their fourth-floor garret. Since then the blacksmith has broken his arm and his master has died, landing him in poverty. Though they must sacrifice their bows, the boys adopt Jenny, the blacksmith, his sick wife, and their five children. Their father removes the whole menagerie from their garret in St Giles and transports them to the pastoral fields of Richmond.

Here is another fall from economic grace precipitated by fate – the broken arm, the master's death – rather than economics. Equally fated, indeed providential, is the plot's alignment of compassionate gentry and humble pauper. Extreme poverty is again met by the benevolence and philanthropy of wealth. Stories like *Hugh Latimer* and "Black Jenny" that exhibit the beneficence of responsible paternalism implicitly endorse the status quo. If there was a true gentleman like Colonel Grahame or the father in "Black Jenny" for every indigent, then economic inequality would be solved. The problem is posed, but ethics obviates economics. God's presence is built into every turn of this story: Providence arranges the salvation of the fallen in combination with an opportunity for the elevated to feel satisfied with their own goodness. Providence, in Susanna's stories, always works with the status quo. The writing of fiction becomes an act of faith that her life could not match.[38]

In two of her stories for the annuals, published in late 1831, Susanna grapples with her own immediate dilemmas. "The Vanquished Lion" and "The Picture Lost at Sea" are the closest she comes at this time to fictional autobiography. The first was written to accompany an illustration that is only glossed on the last two pages, where a mother saves her infant from a lion. Once more the elaborations on this slight plot repay examination. The story opens with a distressed mother who, delivering the message of many of Susanna's children's poems, tells her ten year old he can "little know the trials which await" him. But in this story as in no other the author goes on to produce what she knew of the economic and social determinants of her own trials. The mother explains to her son:

A few weeks ago, your father was a rich man. This fine house, and these beautiful gardens ... were his own property; and every body looked up to him with respect, and treated him with attention. A great change has taken place. Your father has lost all his fortune. He is now ... a poor man. This house is no longer his. It has been sold ... to pay his creditors ... The friends who came hither so often, when we could afford to entertain them, have deserted us in our distress.[39]

Susanna does not go into the causes of the financial failure but condenses her own experience and her mother's: this father, instead of dying, decides to emigrate to the Cape colony. Susanna herself had married in April 1831, was pregnant by summer, and first mentions emigration in her correspondence on 31 August (letter 32), before she would have had to submit this story. In it she connects loss of fortune and the imperative to emigrate.

The attempts of her fictional character to deal with the prospect of emigration are proleptic of Susanna's own attempts, reiterated up to twenty years later in *Roughing It*. The mother tells her son that "God will give me strength, for your sakes, my dear children, to support this great trial," that "I may learn to love" the colony "for your sake," that "God ... has appointed the future," and that "to submit with cheerfulness to the dispensations of Providence is to overcome the world" (32–3). Providence is the last resort for a woman who finds that control of her life is in the hands of others. Through it she avoids facing economic determinism. The burden of the mother's grief is never resolved. She next appears in the foreground of the story before the lion clutching her child, when she utters a "prayer to the Father of Mercies to protect her from evil." God listens, as "One who had compassion upon her grief" (41), and she attributes her success to him: "the Almighty Power ... had assisted her in the hour of danger, vanquished the lion, and delivered her child from death" (42). Psychological distress opens the story but is displaced into physical distress by its close. By this detour Susanna proves that God answers prayers. She must not have tested him by praying against emigration.

She also sublimates her own experience into romance in "The Picture Lost at Sea." In a plot hinging on coincidence, a beneficent Providence shows its interest in the faithful. In the frame-narrative Ludovico, an Italian painter naturalized in England, is forced by penury to sell a painting he has inherited. This necessity leads him to tell the story of the painting to his son. Ludovico's father, "the son of a rich jeweller" (153), aspired to be a painter, but, since he "never gained that celebrity as an artist which his talents deserved" (154), survival was a struggle. He gained the patronage of a prince who, unfortunately, soon died. The painter decided to emigrate to London. In a shipwreck they lost everything, including a painting given them by the prince, which brought on the painter's death. Ludovico and his sister, the painter's children, having learned his art, sell their wares in the street. Their land-lady has connections with a marquis and arranges for Ludovico to petition him. In the interview Ludovico sees the lost painting, which had washed up on the marquis's coastal estate. He proves that it be-longs to his family, and the marquis, good aristocrat and true gentleman that he is, returns the painting plus its value in sterling. The frame-narrative is resolved by the appearance of a customer, now able to pay for the painting he had commissioned because a dead uncle had left him "a fine fortune" (167).

The mother equates plot and "that gracious Providence ... who so marvellously provides for the children of the distressed" (166). The plot proves that "Providence never forsakes those who are true to them-selves" (168). The one action Susanna attributes to free will in this story, and one of the few in any of her stories, is the painter's decision to leave his father's home and live on his art. This exercise of choice is a "rash and criminal step" leading to "poverty and ruin" (154). Respon-sible for the indigence of his family, he dies bereft of any reward, whereas his children and his wife arrive at a happy ending. To place faith in individual ability rather than Providence invites disaster. That Susanna may have been writing a fictional demonstration of the validity of this lesson to herself is suggested by details of the painter's life which con-form to her own. His father scorns his work; Eliza scorned her writing. The painter is "puffed ... up with vanity" to make his art public (153); she called her "desire for fame" a vanity (letter 19). The painter and his son, Ludovico, fail to achieve fame and must sell their work to survive; perhaps she was conceding that her work's worth was best measured by the money it brought her family.[40] She was a literary worker in a system of production for extracting surplus value from her labour. For the painter, art "lost much of its attraction when he was forced to pur-sue it to earn his daily bread" (154).

Susanna's writing during these years dramatizes the conflict of de-sire and reality, value and necessity. In her prose, when desire for dignity confronts humiliation, a higher dignity is attained by trusting Provi-dence and accepting duty. This solution is formalized through the conventions of didactic fiction, so that plot becomes the display of Provi-dence's workings. In her verse, when desire for happiness confronts disappointment, a higher happiness is attained by recognizing in fate the workings of a natural process ordained by God. This solution is formalized through the conventions of sentimental poetry, so that meta-phor becomes the display of God's order. These demonstrations are performed over and over as repressed desires return. By the end of the decade, however, the compensations and consolations of literature had begun to wear thin. Susanna's religious and moral crisis of 1829–30 may have partly been due to frustration with the failure of words to secure the safe haven she sought. The moral resolve that writing was to have demonstrated turned back and questioned writing as resolution.

3 Literary Affiliation and Religious Crisis: Literary Production 1830-1832

As Susanna learned the futility of attempting to accommodate herself to her social position through writing, the struggle between ambition and resignation to Providence was exacerbated. The moral ideology she reproduced became more insistent and independent of its literary means of production. The evidence of her moral and religious crisis in the late 1820s includes changing friendships and changing publishing relations. She rejected assimilation by the fashionable middle class and bound herself to the middle-class oppositional faction of Evangelicism. This transformation made her crisis more acute because it required severing filiative links and forging an affiliative network.[1]

After publishing steadily with *La Belle Assemblée* for two and a half years, Susanna's last contribution to it appeared in early 1830.[2] Her first poems in the *Lady's Magazine* appeared late that year. Between the two, during this year of religious crisis and reorientation, she had nine pieces in the *Athenaeum*. In the early 1830s she, Eliza and Agnes published regularly in the *Lady's Magazine*, which Eliza may have been editing. *La Belle Assemblée* and the *Lady's Magazine* provided similar coverage of the interests of that portion of the middle class aspiring to gentry status, especially of their infatuation with activities at court. While the death of George IV in June 1830 was welcomed by the nation at large, the fashion magazines mourned profusely. In the July *Belle Assemblée* Harral abandoned the usual format to print a black-bordered engraving and memoir of the late king. By writing for the *Athenaeum*, a literary review begun in 1828 as an antidote to the church and Crown bias of the court and fashionable magazines, Susanna broke her association with the establishment.

Susanna's work for the *Athenaeum*, bridging her work for the other two periodicals, marks a transition in her publishing relations. She used all her signatures in it: her two pseudonyms, her maiden name, and her married name. She signs "Love and Ambition," in January 1830 her first poem in the *Athenaeum*, Z.Z. In the following weeks she offers "Thou Wilt Think of Me Love" and "To Water Lilies" over the name Sophia Sandys. In these poems she continues to sublimate desire and dwell on the impossibility of happiness. In two poems on linked historical subjects in the spring and summer she continues her characteristic treatment of the past.[3] "The Besieged City," signed Susanna Strickland, is in blank verse aspiring to Miltonic grandeur. At the heart of the poem are vignettes of a starving girl and her lover, a woman cooling "the burning brow / Of her young lord" (ll. 61–2), and a mother and dying children. The city's rescue is greeted by the cry "It is the aid of God!" (ll. 91, 93). In "Francis I. In Captivity" Francis rails against those who "talk of freedom! – who have never known / But half the value of the good they prize" because they have never had "their hopes o'erthrown" and "All liberty, save that of thought, denied" (ll. 7–8, 9, 11). He has recourse to moral consolation: "All – all is lost! – but honour still is mine"; "crooked policy / May bind a slave – it cannot chain the free!" (ll. 67, 71–2).

Susanna's first review for the *Athenaeum* suggests correlatives for these two poems and advances the conception of history that enables all her poems and tales set in the past. In late 1830 she reviewed Leitch Ritchie's *The Romance of History – France*.[4] She describes this work as consisting of "tales, each founded on some historical incident," beginning with Charlemagne and ending with Louis XIV. She finds congenial Ritchie's view of history and the display of ancient "habits, superstitions, and opinions" in his tales. She disparages "all the cant about 'enlightened views,' and a 'taste that despises the marvellous,'" and claims that, at Christmas at least, "we look back upon old times, and old observances, – aye! even upon old superstitions, with a kindly feeling"; in "that season so dear to our simple-minded forefathers, we read the old black-letter romaunt, or wild lay of faerie, with a pleasure that recalls to our minds the all-believing days of our childhood" (769). She fuses the childhood of European civilization and personal childhood. Her one complaint, revealing her own proclivities, is that Ritchie brings his book "so near to modern times as the age of Louis XIV., for it is in the earlier periods of history, in describing the fierce and lion-like bravery of semi-barbarians, or the intense yearnings after freedom of the serf, who 'knew his rights,' but who unhappily could not 'maintain,' nay, even assert them, and in painting scenes of knightly prowess and courtliness, that he excels." In her creative work she too is drawn to "romantic incidents, and startling surprises, and sudden, and, what in a more settled state of society would be unnatural, changes." Anyone who "has lingered among the brilliant and spirit-stirring scenes of the romantic period, cannot but find a great deficiency of interest in the incidents of more modern times" (771).

Susanna defends the medievalism so important to nineteenth-century culture from Scott and Keats to the Pre-Raphaelites. She laments that "worthy matter-of-fact people," objecting to Ritchie's work, will "iterate, for the thousandth time, those commonplaces about taking unwarrantable liberties with historical events, or infusing a love of romance into youthful minds ... and ... charge these volumes with teaching people to mistake fiction for fact." Her self-defence becomes transparent as she tells how she has been "both surprised and irritated at these futile charges being again and again brought forward by people who really ought to have known better." She makes three claims: first, "all youthful minds worth anything ... breathe in the sunny atmosphere of romance"; next, for those "who cannot afford leisure, or obtain facilities ... for an enlarged knowledge of the state of society during the middle ages, the historical novel is absolutely necessary"; finally, historical fiction delivers "the real, the peculiar character of those times" by focusing on "the minutiae of dress, and scenery, and manners ... [and] the peculiar opinions or superstitions of the period" (771).

Besides Ritchie, Susanna's support for these claims is the Scott of "Ivanhoe and Kenilworth." History equals medieval history equals romance. She was drawn to romance, not history. Sixteen months before this review she admitted that "from the age of twelve years" she had "roamed through the beautiful but delusive regions of Romance, entirely to gratify my restless imagination, to cull all that was bright and lovely, and to strew with flowers the desert path of life" (letter 19). The review makes clear her distaste for "modern times" and her belief that in historical settings romance seems "natural." Her "historical" stories project her own dilemmas onto male heroes, resolving them through romance plots. She gives form to a belief in Providence that helps her to cope with the realities of her life in tales set far enough away in time to be unconstrained by those realities.

Thomas Pringle held an editorial post with the *Athenaeum* in 1830. In the same letter in which she numbers the Ritchies among her new friends, Susanna says her reviews were for Pringle (letter 5). That he favoured both her and Ritchie may explain why her review was featured on the first page of the number in which it appears. Her review of William Kennedy's *An Only Son* is shorter and in the middle of the first *Athenaeum* of 1831. Its most notable statement is that commending Kennedy for selecting "his hero, – not from the peerage, as is customary with the ragged regiment of discarded footmen and abigails, – but out of the middle, the really intelligent and intelligible rank of English society" (7). She exercises her class consciousness at the expense of the serving class rather than the gentry. Her other review for the *Athenaeum* is of Charles Swain's *Beauties of the Mind, a Poetical Sketch; with Lays, Historical and Romantic*, a collection of his gift-book contributions. She extracts two poems and writes a paragraph more critical than she had been of Ritchie and Kennedy. She admits, "I like reviewing very much indeed but I fear Mr. Swain will not like what I say of his."[5]

Susanna's "God Preserve the King!" appeared in the *Athenaeum* in the fall of 1830. Six weeks later she claims that the "*Sunday Times* and the *Dramatic Gazette* speak of it in such terms and of its writer that it would almost make me write songs for the time to come."[6] She had long been writing songs; there is no question of her loyalty; and the loyal song was an accepted genre in the periodicals to which she contributed: yet this was her first loyal song. George IV did not inspire her. She was among the London crowd singing "God Save the King" at the proclamation of William IV.[7] Her song was elicited by the hope that William would be a more righteous ruler. It is driven by "loyal zeal" and belief in "these favoured isles" (ll. 4, 6). She has faith that he will "long their rights maintain" under "Freedom's banner" (ll. 9, 12). She wants "united voices" to sing for his preservation (l. 16). She could not pledge allegiance to an immoral king, but at the prospect for moral rejuvenation provided by his death she joined the chorus of the loyal and devout welcoming William. She published "England's Glory: A Loyal Song" in January 1831, "Britannia's Wreath" in August, and "London: A National Song" in February 1832. She later described a publication with Agnes: "*The Patriotic Songs* ... was a joint volume of music and songs, dedicated by permission to King William IV, who had just ascended the throne. We each furnished three songs ... The King ... wrote us a very complimentary letter ... which made the two country girls very glad."[8] In *La Belle Assemblée* and the *Lady's Magazine* notices of the collection appeared in 1831, likely by Harral and Eliza Strickland. This flow of patriotic songs shows how much happier Susanna was as a subject of the new king than she had been of his brother.

Pringle left the *Athenaeum* at the end of 1830, and Susanna left with him. She had one further poem in the journal in the fall of 1831. She was not at a loss for publishers, however. As well as being able to proclaim her loyalty to William IV, she was more at ease because of her new religious identity. Both factors, and Eliza's association with the *Lady's Magazine*, allowed her to re-enter the fashionable periodicals through it. In October 1830 "The Captive Squirrel's Petition" was published in the *Lady's Magazine*. She had returned, her preoccupation with captivity intact.

Susanna's other pieces in the *Lady's Magazine* deploy genres and themes already discussed. "The Royal Election: A Historical Sketch from Polish History" and "On the Fall of Warsaw" are, respectively, prose and verse concerned with freedom in historical settings. The nostalgia of "Home" would suit characters in "The Captive" or "The Vanquished Lion." She also published several nature poems. "The Spirit of Motion" concludes that this spirit must ever be "Known alone to him who gave / Thee sovereignty o'er wind and wave" (ll. 31-2). "The Forest Rill" develops the metaphor of life as a stream, resolving the mystery of source and mouth, birth and death, in the transcendental signifiers, God and eternity. This poem, again characteristically, carries a personal note:

> The Christian will not mourn her lot,
> ...
> Though in the crowded page of time
> The record of her name may die,
> 'Tis traced in annals more sublime,
> The volume of eternity! (ll. 50, 53–6)

Susanna was still trying to reconcile herself to living and dying in obscurity. The death of compensatory dreams of fame was still harder to accept than physical death.[9]

Besides "The Royal Election," Susanna, likely due to Eliza's disposal of her papers, had two other stories in the *Lady's Magazine*. "The Miser" after several versions became *Mark Hurdlestone*. "The Doctor Distressed. A Sketch from Life," like "Black Jenny: A Tale Founded on Facts" and her "Historical Sketches," is fiction that may derive from fact.[10] That her subtitles stress the veracity of her stories suggests her awareness that, especially in those with contemporary settings, their contrived plots might make them seem "unnatural." But since plot is evidence of Providence, she cannot allow herself to doubt that these stories accurately represent reality, as ordained by God, even when, in "The Doctor Distressed" and many others, Providence arranges financial matters.

"The Doctor Distressed" is a comic anecdote with a satirical edge. Mrs Mary Orams, housekeeper to the Reverend Dr Beaumont, has served him for twenty years "in the hope of inducing him to pay her disinterested services by making him her wife," an idea he thinks "too ridiculous" (46). He plans to leave his money to his widowed sister and her children. Mrs Orams "hated them, for they were his natural heirs; were pretty and genteel, and young" (47). The discharge of his nephew, another heir, from the army prompts her threat to marry a local steward and leave the reverend. He capitulates. The satirical twist comes in the last paragraph. Within a year Mrs Dr Beaumont, from the "fat and indolence" induced by her new station, "expired one morning of obesity." The doctor soon follows, and his relatives "not only came in for all their uncle's property, but for his wife's savings" (48). Apart from the reverend's legacy, his nephew's finances are a problem. He explains to Mrs Orams that "the half pay of lieutenant in the army is but a trifle, a mere trifle. I must allow him *something* yearly to keep up his place in society" (43). When Mrs Orams suggests the nephew "look out for a rich wife," Dr Beaumont declares "The boy would never be so absurd. In his circumstances 'twould be madness" (44). Neither did J.W.D. Moodie, a second lieutenant on half-pay, find himself a rich wife, perhaps realizing the absurdity of his circumstances. The barbs aimed at the established church and the serving class also have an autobiographical keenness. The reverend, an "indolent divine" and a gourmand, is "not wholly dead to natural affections" (46). Mrs Orams' pretensions are hurt by the heirs. Her steward suitor's qualification is "plenty of money" (45). At the reverend's proposal, "Avarice, revenge, and pride were alike gratified" (48). Susanna brought her ideological conundrums into the *Lady's Magazine*.

Susanna left a clear record of religious and moral crisis, connecting it to her shifting relations with the literary profession, in letters from this period to James and Emma Bird, whom she met in the fall of 1826.[11] They may have met through Harral, who, as editor of the *Suffolk Chronicle* and *La Belle Assemblée*, published his friend Bird's poetry. Bird's *White Hats* (1819), a mock-heroic poem attacking radical reformers, shows that for a time the two men shared the same politics.[12] Susanna's remarks on Bird's 1831 satire about rotten boroughs make apparent his change in politics: "Tell the Bard that I laughed heartily over the disfranchise of Dunwich. ... Tell him to write on Eye. The member having lost his Eye will make no bad joke" (letter 33). She and Bird now supported the middle-class appropriation of the radical Reform program.

The Stricklands bought paper and books in Bird's shop; he sold their books and distributed prospectuses for subscriptions to *Enthusiasm*. Susanna's letters to him often refer to the publications of them both. Her self-mockery in a letter from late 1827 reveals her ambivalence about literary society and her status as a poet. On borrowing a donkey in order to visit the Birds, she writes, "poor Poets must put up with all shifts, such trifles do not ruffle them." She realizes she "must descend" from her "poetic dignity," and wonders what "the fashionables ... in Bedford Square" would say could they see her. Priding herself on her independence, she "almost" wishes they could, then quotes Burns's "For A' That and A' That" as her text: "Had I been a man that should have been my song" (letter 3). She sees the folly of aspiring to join Agnes's London circle, but rejects the option by affirming independence, not egalitarianism. Her next letter to Bird, also in late 1827, exposes a latitudinarian levity about religion. Instead of saying her "prayers like a good girl at church," she is being "very ungodly" in "writing a saucy epistle." Her witticism about writing "a tale on the Devil" and shocking the Methodists exhibits the same worldliness (letter 4). Her sophistication has a determinant in Bird's religious orientation. The Birds "were formally members of the Church of England, but his religious sympathies were broad and he was, according to John Glyde in his 'Suffolk Worthies' ... 'a disciple of the Unitarian school'" (Letters, 37 n 1).

By November 1829, however, when she recalls Bird's "Unitarian Tracts" and "letter on the subject," she needs "a serious and less hurried hour to answer them" (letter 20). By this point she was taking religion very seriously, and the implications for her friendships were forcing themselves upon her. The morality formalized in writing was returning as antithetical to more than just the lived contradictions it was intended to resolve.

To understand Susanna's struggle for religious and social self-definition, Bird's Unitarianism must be situated. From the late eighteenth century the label "Unitarian" was applied to heterodox dissent. Unitarians were associated with radical reform, denying the divine sanction of the state along with the Trinity, the divinity of Christ, the Atonement, and the Bible's authority. Anglican-aristocratic hegemony and Unitarian-republican challenge clashed in the eighteenth century, but by 1791 the Unitarians and their commitment to reform were broken.[13] They remained outside of toleration and subject to the Blasphemy Act until 1813. Heterodox dissent arose again in the 1820s with the renewal of radical agitation. This time Unitarians were allied not just to orthodox dissent but to utilitarianism.[14] Unitarians pressed for repeal of the Test and Corporation Acts and, unlike orthodox dissenters, supported Catholic emancipation. The object of repeal and emancipation "was not toleration, which Dissenters enjoyed already, but the destruction of Anglican ascendency" (Clark 1985, 350).

Susanna's friendship with the Birds compounded her link, as with the Childses, to the forces of disestablishment. Bird's proselytizing of her in 1830 signals the fervour of a conversion that would have complicated his friendship with Harral (Letters, 6). Harral's associations with fashionable London and sycophancy towards the court make it likely that he was Broad Church. Susanna notes his religious scepticism (letter 68). Bird may have shared the discretion of other Unitarians wishing to avoid persecution and been canny enough to keep religion out of his relations with Harral, unwilling to risk alienating a promoter of his poetry.

In the spring of 1831, a year after Susanna's last contribution to Harral's *Belle Assemblée*, Catharine's engagement to his son was broken off. Susanna tells how "Mrs. Harral has been annoying [Catharine] in the most unwomanly way, and to shew her spite put the announcement of Katy and Frank's marriage into the *Globe*."[15] Susanna's Congregationalism, her and Sarah's intimacy with the Childses, and the Harrals' disdain for members of their class fraction who let their pretensions slip explain the severing of their relations with the younger girls. But Harral became disenchanted with Susanna before her conversion in April 1830.

No correspondence between Susanna and Harral has been found. She mentions him in eight of nineteen letters between her first reference to *La Belle Assemblée* and her conversion. After her conversion she drops the respectful "Mr" and names him simply "Harral" (letters 29, 32). With *Enthusiasm* published, she abandons any dependency she may have felt: "What a contemptible review was Harral's of my book. A good sound manly hiss would have done more for me than such invidious praise ... It is on a piece with the shabby manner in which he has treated me and is a liberal mode of paying old debts" (letter 32). From her association with Harral she retained confidence in her literary abilities, the habit of periodical publication, and several friendships flexible enough to survive fluctuations in her class affiliations. Their relations ended during the period of her ripening independence and deepening moral certainty. Her divergence from him was the reflex of her newly-confirmed allegiances, an expression of relative freedom and security from the censures of those with whom she disagreed.

In the fall of 1828 Susanna, as part of her personal creed, had expressed abhorrence at "selfishness" and at "extravagant people [who] are the most mean and selfish people," in contrast to "the independent spirit" she venerated in Cowper (letter 8). She claimed independence from "extravagant people" as she posed Burns's "honest independent Man" against "fashionables." She later proclaimed her discovery of what "real interest" is, connecting it to her feeling that friends are "of more value than the mere gratification of the selfish affections" (letter 17). During the stress of her conversion to Congregationalism in April 1830 her "only cheering conviction was that I was obeying the dictates of conscience and that I was right" (letter 22). The virtue of independence and the vice of selfishness were her defensive and offensive weapons against those who would diminish her.

By early 1829 Susanna had "nearly discarded the Muses." Her only creative work was on "a couple of sacred pieces" for "a small volume of Psalms and Hymns" requested by Robert Childs. She may have learned recourse from social contradiction into sacred verse from Cowper, whom she had recently first read, but she remained ambivalent about writing, now because of piety: "I feel a great diffidence in my own powers; the subject itself requires so much serious consideration that I tremble lest I should throw a discredit on it." She was preoccupied with religious and moral difficulties. She transcribes one of the hymns written for Childs, asking for Bird's opinion on the project. The hymn is in praise of the coming of "The Bridegroom," his conquest of death and sin and ascension as "the King of Heaven." It concludes, "To Him! be praise and glory given / To Father! Son and Holy Ghost!"[16] She must not have been aware of Bird's Unitarianism.

In the spring of 1829 Susanna replaced previous cordiality to Harral with anxiety: "My communications to Mr. Harral were of that nature which made me dread his displeasure and his silence had wound up my feeling to a pitch somewhat beyond anxiety and I fear even now to open his letter when it shall arrive" (letter 14). A month later, she feared she would lose the "friendship and confidence" of the Birds, as well. Her closeness with the Birds and her frankness in discussing religion with them enabled her to broach questions of belief. She begins the letter, "I should think myself unworthy of life if I could regard any sect of Christians with indifference because they did not agree with me on *doctrinal points*" (letter 17). Among High, Broad, and Low Anglicans and the orthodox dissenting sects there was little dispute on doctrine. They are all orthodox Protestants, diverging only in ecclesiastical organization and social status. Her reference to doctrine was not meant to justify hers but rather to release the Birds from any fear of her rejection because of their heterodoxy. Only the Unitarians disagreed "on *doctrinal points*" with the other early nineteenth-century sects.

In this letter Susanna refers to "mental struggles"; in her next she reminds Bird that she "expected to lose some of [her] friends in consequence of the step [she] had taken." She did not join the Congregationalists for another year, but here refers to being "termed a mad woman and a fanatic" and to "the despised faith [she] had forfeited the good opinion of the world to claim" (letter 18). What step had she taken? What was this faith? Why did she fear the rejection of both Harral and Bird? While remaining in the established church, she had joined an Evangelical group. Catharine later described how her sister was "suddenly awakened" from spiritual indifference by "the energetic preaching of an enthusiastic Clergyman of the English Church rousing her sensitive nature to a consideration of the importance of her spiritual state – A great conflict was going on in her mind at this time." Contrasting this clergyman's zeal with the "deadness and supineness" in the neighbouring churches, Catharine notes that "the sermon that had aroused" Susanna was "the first truly gospel sermon [they] had heard preached in Reydon church for years."[17] Susanna had been led across the rationalism/enthusiasm axis cutting through Broad Church Anglicanism and Nonconformism. Evangelicals sought to correct the vices of the gentry.[18] Susanna found in the Evangelical Cowper "a Reformer of the Vices of mankind to stand unrivalled" (letter 8). Her "dread" of Harral's displeasure implies that she had attempted to reform his vices or those of his *Belle Assemblée*.

On 31 July 1829 she wrote of her anguished religious doubts about the pursuit of fame to Miss Mitford. She pleads that her publications are not "worthy of notice, and ... were written more with the view of serving several dear friends ... than with any idea of establishing" a reputation. She distances herself from Agnes's circle as a "plain, matter-of-fact country girl" who, unlike her "very talented and accomplished" sister, is "totally unfitted to mingle with the world." She rises to an emotional pitch as she admits her culpability: "A desire for fame appears to me almost inseparable from an author, especially if that author is a poet. I was painfully convinced that this was one of my besetting sins." When Mitford ranked Susanna her peer, "all my ambitious feelings rose up in arms against me, till, ashamed of my vanity and presumption, I stood abashed in my own eyes, and felt truly ashamed of being so deeply enamoured with a title I did not deserve, and I felt that that insatiable thirst for fame was not only a weak but a criminal passion." She confesses that she has "employed those abilities with which heaven had endowed me, doubtless for a wise and useful purpose, entirely for my own amusement, without any wish to benefit or improve my fellow creatures." She has "resolved to give up my pursuit of fame, withdraw entirely from the scene of action, and, under another name, devote my talents to the service of my God."[19] Z.Z. and Sophia Sandys would henceforth write for Jehovah, not Baal.

Susanna's involvement with Evangelicism began in the spring of 1829 and ended a year later when she joined the Congregationalists. The emotionalism of her letter to Mitford suggests this involvement brought further agitation, not peace. In the fall of 1829 she "frightened all the girls by fainting" (letter 20). She was unsettled, seeking a system of belief that would relieve her of acute contradictions among various fragmentary allegiances and reconcile her need to write with the world for which she wrote. Evangelicism aggravated these dilemmas by demanding that she extricate herself from worldly bonds. She burned some verse tragedies, persuaded, she later said, "by foolish fanaticks, with whom I got entangled ... it being they said unworthy of a christian to write for the stage" (letter 61).

In "The Hymn of the Convalescent," published in the fall of 1830, Susanna was thankful for the return of health the previous spring: "sickness bowed my feeble frame / Through winter's cheerless hours."[20] When she writes,

> The joyful heart one moment bounds,
> Then feels a sudden chill,
> Whispering in vague uncertain sounds
> Presentiments of ill (ll. 45–48),

it is clear that her fluctuating health was not due to physical disease. When sick she was unable to pray or raise her "thoughts on high" (l. 54). Her cure came with the settlement of religious crisis, when "light from heaven, like April's ray, / Broke through the stormy sky!" (ll. 55–6).

If Susanna's Trinitarian hymn did not elicit Bird's tracts, perhaps her emotional instability did. He may have thought her needy of Unitarian rationalism. She dispassionately relates to him her traumatic admission to chapel. Despite the tears and trembling she describes, there is a palpable calm about this letter. She takes care to avoid having Bird think her "a mere visionary enthusiast." With her new-found conviction and equanimity apparent, she now confronts his heterodoxy: "You disputed with me dear friend the truth of the atonement and defied me to produce the text mentioned. I now give you it, just to show you that our glorious hope in remission of sins through the blood of the blessed Redeemer has its foundation in holy writ." She has "received the noble hope of life eternal through the blood of [her] redeemer."[21] A religious and social crisis had driven her into the arms of Anglican Evangelicals. She did not abandon these allegiances to recline into the Broad Church latitudinarian lap or embrace the High Church. Grasping for her own social and religious body, she found nonconformity.

Susanna's renewed Christian faith had extensive social implications. She tells Bird of feeling tied to the Congregationalists "by the indissoluble bonds of Christian union," of being given "the right hand of fellowship in the name of the whole congregation" and of rejoicing that she "was the member of a free church and blessed with such a friend and spiritual adviser" as her new pastor. She says, simply, "I am happy now." She banishes "worldly thoughts" that "this step would ultimately make me an alien to all my friends." According to Catharine, Susanna received "rest and comfort" from her new pastor, but for the family, "staunch adherents of the English Church, ... to enter that of a nonconformist was regarded ... as bordering on heresy."[22]

Susanna risked alienating her mother, three sisters, the Harrals, and the Birds. Her filial link to the gentry had been in decay since her father's death; she now severed the sororial ligament. Forced by moral imperatives, she rejected the London literary world, home to Agnes and Eliza. Her conversion may have relieved her anxieties, so apparent in her poetry, about the instability and frustrations of worldly life. She needed a community in accord with her uncertain social position. That she returned to the world and married within the year is no evidence of inconstancy: no available affiliation could tie together all the strands of her life.

Enthusiasm absorbed Susanna's social, literary, and religious conflicts. In it she collected poems written mainly from her mid-twenties, with some written specifically for the book, initiating the creative frugality characteristic of all her book publications.[23] The *Athenaeum* announced it in early April 1830, so its conception preceded Congregationalism. By the next fall her new pastor was managing arrangements between the publishers and the Childs press. She sent prospectuses to Unitarians, Quakers, and Independents but also to Miss Mitford, and "several friends" in London (letters 23–5). She was concerned about its reception in the fashionable periodicals. Connecting the book to her economic predicament, she tells Bird she "must depend upon [her] wits to buy [her] wedding clothes" (letter 23), and she later attributes its "deep tone of melancholy" to "the sorrows of a very unhappy home" (letter 54). When she concludes that the "curse of authorship like the garment of Hercules cleaves to [her] and nothing but death will release" her (letter 25), the mantel of doomed Romantic creator is enfolded in religious and social drapery. By dedicating the book, "Jan. 1st. 1831," to James Montgomery, Moravian, radical newspaper editor and abolitionist poet, she reaffirmed her connection with reform and dissent. It was published in the spring of 1831. She later claimed that "the edition of 500 copies, sold, paying its own expenses, and leaving ... a profit of some 25 or 30 pounds," but she brought one hundred unbound copies to the colony.[24] *Enthusiasm* was "the major publishing event of her English years" (*Letters*, 14).

"Enthusiasm" is the most ambitious poem Susanna Moodie ever wrote. Questions of worldly ambition aside, this devotional poem must rise to the grandeur of its subject. It is 458 lines of blank verse in eighteen verse paragraphs. An accrescence of shorter poems on a common theme, it does have elements of the epic formula. Its latinate syntax and grandiloquent diction attempt the epic's elevated decorum; the biblical phrases and allusions reflect contemporary sermons; the invocation of the muse echoes Milton:

Oh, thou bright spirit, of whose power I sing,
Electric, deathless energy of mind,
Harp of the soul, by genius swept,
Inspire my strains, and aid me to portray
The base and joyless vanities which man
Madly prefers to everlasting bliss![25]

Here also is the epic theme. The poem will distinguish the varieties of enthusiasm and defend the only kind disparaged by the world, religious enthusiasm.

Susanna conception of enthusiasm is expansive and she ratifies the religious variety by associating it with secular engagements at the beginning of her second verse paragraph:

Parent of genius, bright Enthusiasm!
Bold nurse of high resolve and generous thought,
'Tis to thy soul-awakening power we owe
The preacher's eloquence, the painter's skill,
The poet's lay, the patriot's noble zeal,
The warrior's courage, and the sage's love.[26]

Lacking enthusiasm, we are mere animals, but we condone it only for worldly purposes: "Zeal in a sacred cause alone is deemed / An aberration of our mental powers" (ll. 49–50). In light of her religious turmoil and "mad woman" phase, the autobiographical explanation of the poem as a defence of her evangelical moment is unavoidable. Through crisis she attained closer contact with Christian faith, but its precipitation into Congregationalism marked the end of emotional zeal and the beginning of intellectual commitment. It is unlikely that she wrote "Enthusiasm," crafted and reasoned as it is, while she was an enthusiast. The poem justifies her past experience by giving it form in a poetic receptacle.

Enthusiasm is derogated because "The sons of pleasure cannot bear" those who, "conscious of their guilt," seek "Through faith in Christ's atonement, to regain / The glorious liberty of sons of God!" (ll. 51, 53–6). In contrasting profane and spiritual freedom, Susanna elevates the powerless. The "redeemed" find their "chief joy" in celebrating Christ's love, "That called them out of darkness into light" and "gave Hope wings to soar again to heaven!" (ll. 57, 59, 62). This last line points again to the clipped wings of early hope.

The rest of the poem puts on display the vanities of the unredeemed. She makes examples of the painter, the sage, the scientist, the warrior, and, especially, the poet. In "Fancy and the Poet" Fancy tells how "Happiness, when from earth she fled," gave Fancy a wreath for "the sons of sorrow" (ll. 7, 11). Fancy formed from the wreath "many a song divine" to give poets so they can "tell of a world brighter than their own!" (ll. 14, 42). She presents herself as "one of Fancy's spoiled and wayward children" (letter 19). The poet in "Enthusiasm" has received some of the "glorious forms" that "atone / For all the faults and follies of his kind" (ll. 84, 86–7). Despite his reclusiveness, he is not independent: "his lovely dreams" and "earthly hopes" (ll. 115–16) will end in "penury and dire disease, / Neglect, a broken heart, an early grave!" (ll. 117–18). If this poet were to follow the example of "Enthusiasm" itself and tune his "harp to truths divine" (l. 119), he would, as she has vowed she will, avoid this end.

Susanna laments the inadequacy of words before "Visions of glory" vouchsafed her "mental eye," including "the New Jerusalem" (ll. 369, 368, 374). When the "rapid stream of time" makes her wonder how "naked spirit" could traverse it to heaven, her answer in Christ returns her to the main theme:

> His universal sovereignty demands
> That deep devotion of the heart which men
> Miscall enthusiasm![27]

The equation of fanatical "Zeal" (l. 411) with sincere Christian faith does not fit either definition of enthusiasm in the early nineteenth century. The first meaning, possession by a god, by the eighteenth century connoted misdirected, extravagant religious emotion. Susanna was labelled by friends and family an enthusiast in this sense. Current with this definition was the modern meaning of enthusiasm as intense involvement with something.[28] This meaning does not preclude religious involvement but would not need defending, as possession by a god would. In her transformation from Evangelicist to Congregationalist, she transformed her religious enthusiasm from the eighteenth-century sense to the current sense, from extravagant religious emotion to intense faith in Christianity. She rationalizes her earlier fanaticism with the depth of faith she salvaged from it by causally relating them. She uses the polysemy of enthusiasm to condemn previous critics and affirm present grace. Her closing lines trace her treck from inspiration to faith:

> Never, while reason holds her steady rein,
> To curb imagination's fiery steeds,
> May I to joyless apathy resign
> The high and holy thoughts inspired by thee! (ll. 455–8)

Reason now reins in her fiery imagination, controlling her once visionary religious opinions and providing the sanction for her deep but regulated faith.

Susanna versifies her reservations about fame in the second poem in *Enthusiasm*.[29] In "Fame" she complains about its ephemerality and tendency to turn its pursuers from the one source of everlasting glory: "In heaven alone the promised blessing lies" (l. 63). Criticizing those chasing renown, she faces her failure to achieve it: "How many pages have been blotted o'er / With heartfelt tears, that now are read no more" (ll. 73–4). She again raises the disadvantaged over their superiors:

> For splendid talents often lead astray
> The unguarded heart, and hide the narrow way,
> While the unlearned and those of low estate,
> With faith's clear eye behold the living gate. (ll. 119–22)

Once she assumes a Christian elite, she dismisses the tolerance of her letters and stories:

> The child of pleasure may despise his aim,
> And heap reproach upon the Christian's name,
> May laugh his faith, as foolishness, to scorn: –
> These by the man of God are meekly borne. (ll. 157–60)

She finds no middle ground between ascetic and "infidel" (l. 161). The hedonist pretends to enjoy himself, but amid the "festive throng" hears "A death-bell" and "seeks in pleasure's cup to drown / The dread that weighs his ardent spirit down" (ll. 169, 171, 177–8). At his end, too late conceding inevitable damnation, he can only, "despairing, die!" (l. 184). Earthly renown and heavenly glory are mutually exclusive in this poem. "Fame," by reducing experience, contains its complications.

Seven biblical poems that similarly reduce Old Testament complexity to evangelical morality follow "Fame." These include the previously published "The Deluge" and "The Overthrow of Zebah and Zalmunna," and "The Avenger of Blood," which equates murder and manslaughter, nullifying the Mosaic law distinguishing the two.[30] Three biblical paraphrases stress God's power while, by rendering roughly a third of their source chapters, they avoid details that would require a more complex understanding of that power. Starting from the same trope, two poems imagine the destruction of a corrupt people. "The Deluge" begins when "Visions of the years gone by / Flash upon my mental eye" (ll. 1–2); "The Destruction of Babylon" begins when "An awful vision floats before my sight" (l. 1). These poems are begot by the seed of apocalyptic vision coupling with the social confusion around her.

Susanna extends the religious range of the collection in two memorial poems. The first is "To the Memory of Mrs. Ewing," the wife of a Scots minister and missionary. At death, her "faith unshaken *showed that all*

was right!" (l. 12). In a poem to "R.R. Jun.," "Late of Ipswich, and one of
the Society of Friends," she sustains throughout the note sounding in
the last lines:

> Who that has mourned the tyranny of sin,
> The strong temptations which assail the breast,
> The fiery passions warring still within,
> But does not envy thee thy heavenly rest.[31]

A mother's reaction to the death of another son evokes "The Christian
Mother's Lament," and the same consolation:

> ... the smile on thy pale lip that lies,
> Now tells of a joy that no language can speak.
> The fountain is sealed, the young spirit at rest,
> Ah, why should I mourn thee – my loved one – my blest? (ll. 14–17)

She also uses this theme, somewhat incongruously, in "Lines on a New-
born Infant." He is "A stranger as yet to the storms and the strife," and
his "cry is the herald of anguish and woe," but the last line seems morbid
in a poem celebrating a birth: "May the sunbeams of hope gild thy path
to the tomb."[32]

"Uncertainty" posits doubt about the future as worse than past
disappointments. Joy, in memory, survives beyond its frustration, but
uncertainty is a "tormenting fiend, / Beneath Hope's pinions screened,"
which "Makest her promise vain" (ll. 15–16, 18). Faith provides the one
hope of "The land of joy and peace, / Where doubts and sorrows cease"
(ll. 55–6). Religion is the only consolation for living in a "present – scarce
our own" (l. 42). Doubly dispossessed by class and gender, one of
Susanna's doubts may have concerned marriage. The poem following
"Uncertainty" is about the end of a romantic involvement. "The
Warning" opens at the turning away of the lover's eyes, when "O'er
the bright sun of hope float the dark clouds of sadness, / And youth's
lovely visions recede with the ray" (ll. 3–4). The poetic persona rejects
worldly attachments for "the day star of gladness above" (l. 22). At
sixteen Susanna went "to London for a change of air" and had her "first
mortifying knowledge of the world" through an unhappy love affair.[33]
In September 1828 she was engaged to someone called Asker but
was "vexed with him on many accounts," including his apparent
indifference, and finally struck "the death blow to the hopes of years"
by dismissing "the author of [her] Sufferings" (letters 8, 10). Before
Moodie, all her love poems, including the few in *Enthusiasm*, deal with
its severing through male faithlessness or natural disaster. In her poetry
love always ends in a parting to be rectified, if at all, in heaven.[34]

"The Ruin" presents a stranger version of broken plight. Set on the same Suffolk coast where the ruins of the church sit, the ruin of the title is, however, "a female figure" whose appearance "Bespoke a mind in ruins," marked by "Despair" (ll. 58, 60, 61). This character speaks a long "mournful requiem of her perished hopes" (l. 73). The poet explains:

Hers was a common tale – she early owned
The ardent love that youthful spirits feel,
And gave her soul in blind idolatry
To one dear object. (ll. 129–32)

The loss of that object drove her mad. Speaking with the voice of experience, the poet tells the "poor maniac" (l. 124) what should have been her course:

Thy hopes, thy wishes centred all in earth –
Earth has repaid thee with a broken heart!
Love to thy God had known no rash excess,
For in his service there is joy and peace. (ll. 141–44)

The hysteria of lost love should have been channelled in the hysteria of religious enthusiasm. In this poem Susanna explores an alternative outcome to her experience from fall 1828 to the next spring. The "Love" eulogized in the poem of that name is of course *agape*, "Immortal principle" and "attribute of Deity" (ll. 3, 14), not *eros*.

Susanna's projections of disappointed love, captivity, madness, and poverty accumulate. *Enthusiasm* also contains a figure, seen already in "The Vanquished Lion" and "The Emigrant's Bride," who will absorb the others. "The Lament of the Disappointed" is sung by "a poor exile, whom Sorrow had banished / From Joy's golden halls" (ll. 17–18). Exile here is metaphoric and sorrow due to economic ineligibility for the social pleasures open to others. "The dark chain ... Of sorrow and sin" (ll. 26–7) is another displacement of the chains of penury, the freedom offered by God, once more the only attainable freedom. A poem to "The Sugar Bird" concentrates on the reaction to it of "exiled eyes" (l. 15). The poem tells of immigrants unhappy with the bird's alien clime. The poet, unsure whether "memory to their dreams may bring / Past scenes, to cheer their sleeping eye" (ll. 17–18), is certain that from the bird "The captive turns in sullen woe / To climes more dear and scenes less fair" (ll. 23–4). On such slight pretext she hangs her preoccupations. That exile so draws her imagination tells of her foreboding that emigration is the corollary of economic imprisonment.

"Night's Phantasies" in *Enthusiasm* is the strangest poem Susanna ever wrote. In this "Fragment" she "dream[s] sweet dreams of a summer night" (l. 1) with the resonance of the unconscious missing from her other dream poems. Her sense of its incompleteness may be due to her inability to tether this poem to a moral post. Lacking moral purpose, the poem reverberates in a way little of her writing does. "Night's Phantasies" begins unexceptionally with the dichotomy between the depressingly diurnal and prospective eternal bliss. The poet, lulled by the sea, drifts off in sleep. Then,

> ... a magic spell on my spirit was cast,
> And forms that had perished in ages past,
> Were by Fancy revealed to my wondering view,
> As the veil of Oblivion she backward drew. (ll. 19–22)

Though now attuned to "songs divine" (l. 35), the vision she receives is not the expected heavenly one. Instead, a figure "radiantly bright" floats over the waves (l. 45). She describes this figure conventionally enough but then develops an allusion that, though standard, is unparalleled in her work. The apparition reminds her of "that sea-born goddess ... of old, / ... / The queen of beauty and joy's fair bride" (ll. 65, 66). Other than the odd naiad or nymph, Susanna has excluded classical deities from her work. This figure, while no Venus, is of pre-Christian provenance. She is "The desolate spirit of things that were," holding "Oblivion's iron key" (ll. 80–1). She sings of her underwater realm, wherein "Lie the shattered domes of the ancient world" (l. 85). She has seen "a thousand ages" roll over edifices "the giant kings possessed of old," and she cages "The spirits of earth and air" (ll. 86, 88, 93).

The spirit makes the poet an offer: "if thou canst banish all mortal dread, / Thou shalt view that world of the mighty dead" (ll. 98–9). The song ends; the poet is left listening to "the night winds" (l. 103) – and that is all. Susanna, suffering a failure of imagination at the threshold of a pagan world, has still let the poem stand, without the resolving leap to the transcendent. Its atmosphere is the ambiguous, hazy one of dream and fantasy. This poem is evidence that poetry was not inevitably didactic and religious for her. In "Night's Phantasies" she attempts to stretch her imagination beyond the platitudes to which her poetry is otherwise devoted.

Enthusiasm is a nexus between Susanna's relations of production and her friendships. It is her attempt to weave the unruly strands of the dominant patriarchal ideology into a seamless fabric. The unhappiness and dis-ease evidenced by the poet, without the distance that artistic accomplishment and imaginative strength might have interposed, are explained by the life of the woman. The tactics she uses to cope with her state, while they arise from profound Christian faith, are expedient and purposeful arrangements of the only forces available to her in her struggle to survive.

Susanna developed anti-slavery sentiments, perhaps in conjunction with her evangelicism, during her contact with Thomas Pringle. He, an Edinburgh graduate, editor, and writer, emigrated to South Africa only to return within six years due to trouble with the governor. In London he associated with anti-slavery activists and the Clapham Sect, which recruited him as secretary to the Anti-Slavery Society in March 1827. Susanna knew him from the spring of 1828.[35] While in fear that her enthusiasm would offend Harral and Bird, she refers to "Papa Pringle," and this usage continues after her conversion to Congregationalism (letters 20, 22). He is her "dear adopted father" who "has ever shown himself a kind and disinterested friend" (letter 24). In the summer of 1830 she tried, with his urging, to recruit Bird for the anti-slavery movement. By this point she was calling it "our cause ... because it ought to be the cause of every free man who enjoys the privilege of freedom" (letter 23). While living with the Pringles for several months in 1830–31 and writing for the *Athenaeum* and the Anti-Slavery Society, she once more decided "to try [her] fortune in the world of letters" (letter 29).

In constituting Pringle her adopted father, Susanna recast an affiliation in filiative terms. His affiliation was with the Clapham Sect, a critical faction within the developing middle-class hegemony. In morals and on the slave question they stood with the Evangelicals. Working for Pringle, she enlisted in the service of intellectuals engaged in shaping the dominant ideology in their image. While her writing did not change, her attitude towards it did. Her service to God provided an affiliative network that relieved the contradiction between her material circumstances and the ideology her writing once promoted. She did not fall from moral rejuvenation into the fashionable world; she would instead use literature to reform morals and free slaves: Hannah More is now her model, not Agnes Strickland.

In late 1830 Susanna wrote "An Appeal to the Free" for the *Athenaeum*, concluding that the free "are slaves! – for the freeborn in mind / Are the children of mercy, the friends of mankind."[36] Her sympathy for slaves had been overdetermined by her experience of the chains of class and gender and her adoption of evangelical morality. That winter she recorded "Mr. Pringle's black Mary's life from her own dictation ... adhering to her own simple story and language without deviating to the paths of flourish or romance" (letter 29). In recording Mary's life, Susanna explicitly eschewed techniques she had used in treating other stories taken from life. When in "Trifles from the Burthen of a Life" Rachel M— is told that "the History of Mary P—" is "an imaginary tale got up for party purposes," Rachel vouches for it personally: "I know that narrative to be strictly true, for I took it down myself from the woman's own lips" (228).

Pringle's preface to *The History of Mary Prince ... Related by Herself* is dated 25 January 1831.[37] That the penniless white woman is a guest while trying to establish herself but the black woman works as a servant while fighting for her freedom is linked to another contradiction in the same letter of early 1831 in which Susanna refers to Mary. After mentioning that "the thoughts of Revolution here have died away," she describes "Hunt's procession into Islington." The July 1830 Revolution in France fading from memory, the leader of a potential English revolution is the butt of her anxious humour:

I think my dear friend Bird you would have laughed yourself into pleurisy. It was indeed
    March my boys in your radical rags
    Handle your sticks and flourish your flags.
Mr. Hunt ... rode foremost ... Then came the incomparable blacking mass filled with trumpeters who had expended all their breath ... and dirty blacking boys who with red Cockades upon their hats shouted "Hunt for ever" and "Radical Reform" till our ears would gladly have shut themselves against their teeth jarring jargon.

Here are the disaffected poor, not the good, humble poor who people Susanna's stories. She calls them a "motley band of rag tag notoriety" and is pleased with her witticism "that M.P. after Henry Hunt's name signified 'mischievous person.'"[38]

Susanna transcribes Orator Hunt and Mary Prince within the same system. In her and the Anti-Slavery Society's eyes this system's few problems could be ameliorated through a consensus of right-thinking men and an increase in godliness. Others, however, stressed the hypocrisy of abolitionists colluding, by their silence, with the oppression of the working class.[39] The slaves of colonial capitalists were objects of sentiment and moral dogma, especially when they were exotic spectacles in London.[40] The slaves of domestic capitalists were taught to resign themselves to Providence and look to the hereafter.

Mrs Pringle asks Susanna, after she has recorded Mary's story, to sign a letter to the "Birmingham Ladies' Society for Relief of Negro Slaves" testifying to Mary's scars. This supplemental inscription will add to her "own testimony that of Miss Strickland (the lady who wrote down in this house the narratives of Mary Prince and Ashton Warner)."[41] In his preface, Pringle discusses the pamphlet's production:

The narrative was taken down from Mary's own lips by a lady ... residing in my family as a visitor. It was written out fully ... and afterwards pruned into its present shape; retaining, as far as was practicable, Mary's exact expressions and peculiar phraseology. ... It is essentially her own, without any material alteration farther than was requisite to exclude redundances and gross grammatical errors, so as to render it clearly intelligible. (1831a, 45)

Pringle supplies footnotes, a supplement and pruning.

Mary Prince contains themes associated with Susanna but at a level of generality that cannot mark authorship and points only to a shared moral fabric. Mary's narrative was shaped and censored into that of a conventional, morally upright example of nineteenth-century womanhood. "Of course my name does not appear" (letter 29), Susanna writes, noting the possibility while cancelling it. She resisted transforming the text with "flourish or romance." It cannot be ascribed to an individual. Pringle states that "any profits ... will be exclusively appropriated to the benefit of Mary Prince" (1831a, 46), granting her royalties she could not legally claim. The shaping of *Mary Prince* into an intelligible, linear, grammatically correct narrative has taken this text away from Mary. It is a corporate text – Mary, Susanna, Pringle – that finally only the Anti-Slavery Society could be said to author.

Before Mrs Moodie emigrated from her precarious position in England, marriage, too, conflicted with literary aspiration. In October 1830 she had placed herself among "the blue stocking fraternity" (letter 25). Ten days later she was engaged. By the new year she thought the engagement "too hasty"; "circumstances," she informs Bird, caused her to end it: "I will neither marry a soldier nor leave my country for ever and feel happy that I am once more my own mistress." Then, immediately, she describes her stay with the Pringles and the London literati with whom she has become "intimately acquainted." She has been promised help in getting "on in the literary world" and lionized at a popular painter's reception, but is "almost tired with compliments and sick of flattering encomiums on [her] genius" (letter 29). Here are "circumstances" that preclude marrying a mere soldier on half-pay set on emigrating. *Mary Prince* may also have brought her to the uncomfortable conjunction of eros and enslavement. Much of her writing issued out of struggle, but its recognition by the righteous lifted her, for a time, above it.

On 4 April she married her soldier. "What do you now think of the vagaries of woman kind?" Catharine asks Bird, adding: "The dear girl kept up her spirits pretty well though at times a shade of care came over her brow" (quoted in *Letters*, 62 n 2). When five days later Mrs Moodie tells Bird this "piece of now old news," she exhibits no excitement but does reveal renewed doubt about authorship. Of "that ugliest of all pebbles, a critical stone," she writes: "That illnatured weapon of offensive, and defensive notoriety, has broken more hearts than you or I ever cracked nuts, for the life of me, I wish they were all pounded up in a mortar." Her collection of poetry not yet released, she says her "Enthusiasm ... begins to cool, and if the printers and editors, who have dawdled so long over it, do not quicken their movements, it will soon be extinguished altogether" (letter 31). After her lionizing, fame brought its fickle side home to her.

Writing and marriage had become incompatible: "My blue stockings, since I became a wife, have turned so pale that I think they will soon be quite white." Yet she was still torn between two possible futures. A paragraph that begins wistful of the "charm in literary society which none other can give" ends by declaring "that the noble art of housewifery is more to be desired than all the accomplishments, which are to be retailed by the literary and fashionable damsels who frequent these envied circles" (letter 31). With emigration planned, she asserts that her children will be farmers and she "will whip every literary propensity out of them. I have quarreled with rhymes," she continues, "ever since I found out how much happier we can be without them. Domestic comfort is worth all the literary fame that ever pu[lled] a youthful Bard onto the pinnacle of pub[lic] notice" (letter 33). She confirms the rightness of leaving literary life. The possibility that she felt excluded from this life is occluded in an explanation that makes the choice her own.

Susanna Strickland began writing in a filial alignment with her father's aspirations. She could not, as Agnes and Eliza, cleave to this line, and her writing is fraught with conflict between the dominant ideology and her economic situation. Her appropriation of ideology through morality led to questioning the worldly aspects of that ideology and partly determined her religious crisis. This crisis precipitated her into affiliation with Evangelicism, nonconformity, and the Anti-Slavery Society. Her marriage grew out of these affiliations. Having broken with her older sisters made it easier for her to abandon England and literary life altogether. Emigration had been prepared for many years before she conceded to it.

4 Emigration/Immigration: The Moodies and Upper Canada 1832-1855

Immigrants to Upper Canada/Canada West from the British Isles in the second third of the nineteenth century reasserted Old over New World demographic dominance and helped to quadruple its population to almost a million. Land policies created scarcity of land, urban centres on the Lake Ontario front, and Indian reserves. After intense strife, the old representative system and Tory oligarchy gave way to responsible government and capitalist plutocracy. Paternal labour relations became impersonal industrial relations; the open labour market became restricted, predicated on unemployment. With an infrastructure in place by mid-century, the railway boom began the colony's industrial revolution. Once more Susanna Moodie lived through instability that issued in the hegemony of the business and industrial class. The Moodies left England in 1832 as part of a massive population redistribution intended to solve problems spread across the British Empire. In 1855 the last novel of Mrs Moodie's major period of production was published, and the Taché-Macdonald government used newly-won powers to pass the Grand Trunk Railway Relief Act, giving Grand Trunk a monopoly on public financing. Her position did not change so much as did the politics of the society in which she found herself, until a middle class with which she could identify coalesced. But, as in England, she wrote before this outcome was assured.

Emigration was crucial to the culture of post-Waterloo England.[1] J.W.D. Moodie's first emigration, to the Cape, was connected to the Highland Clearances. In 1816 he had "no prospect of employment"; his father, the ninth laird of their Orkney estate, was near death; his oldest brother had tried "in vain to save the family property ... from the grasp of the creditors," then gone to South Africa. John followed in 1819, and another brother in 1820. The Moodies were successful settlers.[2] John "had plenty of land, and of all the common necessaries of life," but made a trip to England "with the resolution of placing [his] domestic matters on a more comfortable footing" – that is, to find a wife. He left South Africa in 1829 "with the intention of returning to that colony, where [he] had a fine property, to which [he] was attached in no ordinary degree."[3] He also hoped to arrange publication of his book on the colony. His friend Pringle had been publishing on South Africa since leaving in 1826. Susanna's Flora Lyndsay is "bored to death about the Cape, by our good friends the P—'s."[4]

Susanna had known emigrants before Pringle. James Black, the friend of her father who arranged for the publication of *Spartacus*, left for Upper Canada in the early 1820s, and her brother followed with his aid in 1825. In 1826 Catharine published anonymously *The Young Emigrants; or, Pictures of Canada*, commenting in the preface that it contained information "communicated to the writer by the members of a very amiable family, who emigrated to America in 1821."[5] In a letter from the winter of 1829–30 Susanna names Catharine the author of this story, and remarks on Samuel:

He ... promises to do something for himself in the country to which he has emigrated, and to which I often feel strongly induced to follow him, having many dear friends in that land "of the mountain and the flood." He gives me such superb descriptions of Canadian scenery that I often long to accept his invitation to join him ... But I fear my heart would fail me when the moment of separation came, and my native land would appear more beautiful than any other spot in the world, when I was called upon to leave it. (letter 21)

The sisters played with ideas of one day joining the demographic shift of the early nineteenth century even before they met half-pay officers bent on the colonies.

Moodie's courtship required convincing Susanna to leave family, friends, and country for a life in the colonies with him. They met soon after her conversion to Congregationalism in April 1830, and by July they were engaged.[6] In August it is "very likely" that within "a few months" she will "bid adieu to [her] native land ... forever," but in the fall Moodie discusses the options of a frugal life in Suffolk or the Orkneys.[7] So in love that she "should be happy with Dunbar anywhere if beneath the burning suns of Africa or building a nest among the eagles of the storm encircled Orkneys," she finds the latter more appealing.[8] Within three months she decides against marriage and emigration; in three months more she is married, but does not plan to emigrate.[9] By

August 1831 the couple "entertain serious thoughts of going next spring to join [her] brother in Canada" (letter 32).

Susanna suppressed thoughts of emigration until after the wedding. "Trifles from the Burthen of a Life" opens with "a question rather suddenly put to his young wife, by Lieutenant M——": "Rachel, have you forgotten the talk we had about emigration, the morning before our marriage?" And indeed, "it had long been forgotten by his wife" (160). When left to recall the conversation, she remembers that "in the blessed prospect of becoming his wife, it had not then appeared to her so terrible." During the first months of wedded bliss "all thoughts upon the dreaded subject of emigration had been banished" (162–3). In the story the heroine's pregnancy causes her husband to resurrect the subject; in *Roughing It* Mrs Moodie attributes to their first child's birth acceptance of emigration.[10] She knew she was pregnant by the end of July 1831. In both fiction and autobiography the husband argues his heirs' case against his wife. From his early twenties Moodie had been committed to a role as settler and civilizer in Britain's colonies. Owning land at the Cape, he only lacked a wife to populate his estate. Susanna Strickland, friend to the recently returned Pringles, with a brother who had emigrated and little means to support herself, could provide him heirs. After the marriage she discovered that she had accepted emigration along with him: "If you intended to remain in England you should not have married a poor man," says M——; "When you married for inclination, you knew that emigration must be the result of such an act of imprudence in over-populated England," says Moodie.[11] That his wife later reiterates his arguments demonstrates her attempt to cleave to the patriarchal lead.

Besides worrying her about a child, Moodie wore down his wife's resistance by giving up his plan to return to South Africa. He believed her "invincible dislike to that colony" arose because "the wild animals were her terror," and she notes her heroine's "terror of the wild beasts – those dreadful snakes and lions!"[12] When Moodie tries to convince her that they can lead a normal life in Africa, she quotes his book "triumphantly in confirmation of her vague notions of danger" (*RI*, 220). He articulates an alternative motive in his account of the capitulation: "At last, between my wife's fear of the wild animals of Africa, and a certain love of novelty, which formed a part of my own character, I made up my mind, as they write on stray letters in the post-office, to 'try Canada'" (221). Moodie later claims full responsibility for directing the family, presenting this second motive as sufficient in itself: "This was my *first* mistake – viz., in going to Canada instead of returning to South Africa; but, I suppose, the love of adventure ... was too strong for me" (1866, ix). In *Flora Lyndsay* it is John Lyndsay's "choice of Canada, hoping that it might be more to [her] taste," that finally overcomes "all Flora's obstinate scruples." Because he displays "such affectionate earnestness for her happiness more than his own – for it was no small sacrifice to Lyndsay to give up going back to the Cape – " (8), she gives in.

Moodie had no ties to England. Breaking his wife's attachments was his final step in getting her to accept emigration. Lieutenant M— achieves this submission with disarming ease:

"the only obstacle in the way is your reluctance to leave your friends. Am I less dear to you, Rachel, than friends and country?"
   "Oh! no, no. You are more to me than all the world. I will try and reconcile myself to the change." (162)

Mrs Moodie's devotes her work to reconciling herself "to the change." The narrative trope requires a romantic hero and heroine facing the prospect of the wilderness alone, so the family and friends sharing Rachel's exile are not mentioned.

Between becoming aware of her pregnancy and deciding to emigrate, the Moodies were visited by Samuel's father-in-law, in England on business.[13] Their plans were sealed by Strickland's acquisition of land for them near his own as early as August 1831. Catharine became part of the plan with her marriage in May 1832 to Moodie's fellow officer and Orkneyman, Thomas Traill, whom Moodie had been entertaining at the Southwold cottage; Traill took land between Moodie and Strickland. Tom Wales, a Suffolk friend, joined the group and departed ahead of them all. James Bird sent his twelve-year-old son, and, on Moodie's insistence that his wife take a nurse, her mother sent her pregnant but unmarried servant.[14] The Moodies would join a substantial group of friends and family once they made it to Douro Township. Her baby born, its future among an English landed class in Upper Canada seemingly secure, Susanna's one letter on the prospect is hopeful and buoyant (letter 34).

These gentlefolk thought they were peopling a wilderness. The narrator of *Flora Lyndsay* notes the perception in Suffolk that "the caprice of a husband" was forcing Flora into "a rude, uncultivated wilderness" (18). In the 1830s "the idea of anything decent [in clothing] being required in a barbarous desert, such as the woods of Canada, was repudiated as nonsense." Rachel "fancied that her lot would be cast in one of these remote settlements, where no sounds of human life were to meet her ears"; to her Upper Canada "was a vast region of cheerless forests, inhabited by unreclaimed savages, and rude settlers doomed to perpetual toil" ("Trifles," 182). The narrator views in retrospect Rachel's ignorance "of the manners and customs of the colony" and comments on "the false notions formed by most persons at home, of Canada," who think it "a barbarous country, so thinly peopled, that settlers seldom resided within a day's journey of each other."[15] This idea of Canada as a wilderness, fertile for the dissemination of British civilization by half-pay officers, younger sons, and frustrated gentry, accounts for much of the shock of Mrs Moodie's first years in the colony.[16]

His first child having been born in February 1832, Moodie spent most of the spring in London making arrangements for their emigration.[17] In "Trifles" the M—s are delayed in reaching Edinburgh and miss the boat, losing their deposit of half the fare. Both the M—s and the Moodies spend June in Edinburgh looking for passage, finally booking on the "brig *Anne*, one hundred and ninety-two tons burden," the season's last ship for Canada, which sailed 1 July. Becalmed off the Grand Banks for three weeks, they arrived at Grosse Isle 30 August.[18] The Moodies were the only cabin passengers, while there were seventy-two in steerage. They ate with the captain and had beds; steerage came with one stove and an open lower deck on which to set up house. This ratio among passengers on the *Anne* reflects the ratio of working- to middle-class emigrants in general.

Due to delays the Moodies did not arrive at Cobourg until 9 September 1832. Their intention had been to "settle near Peterborough within a mile of [Susanna's] brother," where he had secured one hundred and forty-six acres of uncleared land for them.[19] By the time they reached Cobourg they were no longer determined to proceed to Douro; they stayed in a hotel for three weeks while Moodie sought to buy cleared land locally.[20] He gives no reason for the change: "Though my wife had some near relatives settled in the backwoods, ... I had made up my mind to buy a cleared farm near Lake Ontario."[21] Mrs Moodie does not refer to a change of plan but mentions their anxiety to take over the Cobourg land as soon as possible in order "to plough for fall wheat" (81). William Cattermole, whose lectures on emigration Moodie had heard, advised the emigrant to "embark early in the season, that he may have the summer before him ... before winter sets in."[22] The husband in *Flora Lyndsay* is angered by his wife's reluctance to travel in a ship leaving two weeks earlier than the *Anne*. The Moodies did not arrive in time to prepare for the winter, and during their first year had to live entirely on Moodie's capital.

When the Moodies arrived, the Lake Ontario front was under cultivation, and the frontier had moved inland. Loyalists had settled as far west as the Bay of Quinte; administrative and military centres had attracted the few early British immigrants; American settlers had converted the front into farmland. Americans founded Cobourg in

1798.[23] By 1830 Upper Canada was "a relatively well-established and prosperous province" with "a relatively cohesive and integrated society" (Errington 1987, 89, 91). The elite wanted a colony unified by loyalty and the principles so entailed. Growing political divisiveness, as the interests of settlers began to diverge from those of the Tory oligarchy, was readily attributed to republicanism and American influence.[24] The British immigrants who were to overwhelm this influence were confronted in the settled districts "by a pattern of life already existing ... a developed community of opinion" (Rashley 1958, 8). Only away from the front, on the interior frontier where the military grants now were, did a void await their Old World culture. Although Moodie's land was spread over Fenelon, Verulam, and Douro townships, the very place for English gentlemen, he bought a cleared farm on the Yankee front.[25]

To those attached to British institutions, American settlers were equated with "the spirit of independence" and "ideas of equality and insubordination": "many were generally judged to be 'bad citizens'" (Errington 1987, 47). By the 1830s British immigrants saw both Canadians and Yankees as Americans.[26] Attempting to use mass immigration as a restraint on demands for reform, the government, according to one newspaper, exerted its influence to teach immigrants to call the old settlers "Yankees, Republicans, &c., by way of reproach ... Hence the supercilious deportment of Europeans towards Canadians when they first come amongst them."[27] The Moodies were amenable to this indoctrination. Their reaction to the American – Yankee and Canadian – community surrounding them at Cobourg implicates them in the ideological struggle that convulsed Upper Canada in the 1830s.

Had the Moodies stayed on the Cobourg farm they could have participated in growing wheat exports to England. With twenty years' hindsight Moodie saw how he might have prospered: "had I only followed my own unassisted judgement ... and quietly settled down on the cleared farm I had purchased, in a well-settled neighbourhood, ... I should now in all probability have been in easy if not in affluent circumstances" (*RI*, 218). With "about £300 when [he] arrived in Canada," he was able to buy cleared land eight miles from Cobourg with "an extensive orchard ... two log houses ... a large frame-barn," and an "uncleared part ... on the flat, rocky summit of a high hill." The family moved there on 22 September 1832.[28] Moodie believed that his money was "advantageously invested in a cleared farm," and had he been content with it "and purchased two adjoining cleared farms, ... [he] should have done well."[29]

In the first edition of *Roughing It* the bush segment begins in volume two. J.W.D. Moodie's concluding chapters to volume one detail the transactions that resulted in taking up the land Strickland had secured for him. When "an intimation from the War-office appeared in all the newspapers, calling on half-pay officers either to sell their commissions or to hold themselves in readiness to join some regiment," Moodie chose the former option (254). The speculator who had familiarized him with colonial land sales was on hand to exchange his commission for steamboat company stock. Moodie believed he was cheated of a hundred pounds in this transaction. Due to disagreements between stockholders, the boat profited no one. When it was sold, Moodie received one hundred and fifty pounds, "about a fourth part of [his] original stock."[30] Besides the loss of his half-pay there were other factors in his decision to leave the Cobourg area for his Douro holding. He fell "into the common error of [his] countrymen, of purchasing wild land, on speculation, with a very inadequate capital." His capital came from the sale of the Cobourg farm back to his usual land speculator and a legacy Mrs Moodie received in 1834.[31]

Moodie's naïve capitalist ventures and Mrs Moodie's reactions to the Cobourg settlement are linked. He avers that "some of [their] neighbours were far from being agreeable" and "allude[s] more particularly to some rude and demoralised American farmers from the United States ... who composed a considerable part of the population, [and] regarded British settlers with an intense feeling of dislike" (250-1). Some of these settlers were second-generation Loyalists whose families had been there since 1797. More annoyingly, "new settlers of the lower classes were then in the habit of imitating their rudeness and familiarity, which they mistook for independence." About the mixing of "higher class" and "labouring class" he concludes that "the fermentation arising from the strange mixture of discordant elements" makes "the state of society ... anything but agreeable or satisfactory" (251). To the Moodies, "its state at C—, in 1832 ... was so distasteful, that ... [they] began to listen to the persuasions of [their] friends, who were settled in the township of D—" (251-2).

Instead of a wilderness awaiting the onslaught of displaced English gentlemen, the Moodies found an established society that refused to accommodate their desires for hierarchy and deference. So, rather than become a merely prosperous farmer amidst other prosperous farmers in the levelled society at the front, he took a chance at a place amidst a nascent estate-owning elite. In the winter of 1833 Moodie made

some flying visits to the backwoods, and found the state of society ... more congenial to our European tastes and habits; for several gentlemen of liberal education were settled in the neighbourhood ... All these gentlemen had recently arrived ... and all the labouring class were also fresh from the old country, and consequently very little change had taken place in the manners or feelings of either class. There we felt we could enjoy the society of those who could sympathise with our tastes and prejudices. (252)

He sold his cleared farm in November 1833 and moved his family to Douro in February 1834.

An anonymous article titled "The Emigration of 1832" appeared in the *Canadian Literary Magazine* in 1833, directly following a review of *Enthusiasm*. This article stresses that, while before 1830 immigration "was almost exclusively confined to the laboring, and poorest classes of the British population," in 1832 "the Emigration ... has included ... a large proportion of men of wealth, intelligence and enterprise ... Men of Literature and science; and respectable professional persons of every description; including a large number of half-pay, and retired Officers" (110). The "gentlemen of the Army and Navy" are taking grants in the Newcastle District (115), while the "greater proportion of the labouring Emigrants" are going further north and west (118). Traill, Moodie, and Strickland are on the article's list of "Officers and other gentlemen of property" settling in the Newcastle District; Stewart appears as a legislative councillor and Reid as a magistrate.[32] Strickland had found Douro Township open for investment of capital he had accumulated with the Canada Company, and was Moodie's land agent. In the distribution of military land grants, influence with the Executive Council, directly or through a local elite, meant choice of location. One immigrant gives "the power of forming a neighbourhood of select friends" as an advantage of settling bush land.[33]

Isolated from York, local officials held real power in the settlements. Strickland's association with the Douro elite was instrumental in gathering the Traills and the Moodies to his area. The local power bases were dependent on the favour of the central elite, which "hinged upon personal relationships, and had little to do ordinarily with forms of merit other than the political."[34] Due to the exercise of influence "Douro Township ... experienced something like a complete transplant of the social structure of the old country."[35] The society the Moodies encountered in the Cobourg area was well-rooted in North American conditions; they rejected it for the social structure in Douro, a hothouse transplant that, for lack of fertile economic soil, eventually withered.

Roughing It reveals how poorly the English social structure took to its new soil. Of all Moodie's extended prose, the second volume of *Roughing It* has the least to say about society. In contrast to volume one, social tensions seldom disturb her backwoods life. Presenting an isolated heroine whose main antagonist is nature, she neglects social reflections. The Stricklands, the Traills, Moodie's friend Emilia Shairp, and her husband are characters incidental to the main drama pitting the author against the wilderness. One of her few references to society in the second volume of *Roughing It* occurs in a paragraph where she regrets that her husband is working elsewhere and laments the abandonment of the bush by her sister, brother-in-law, and friend. There is no diminishing the extent of the misery, hard work, suffering, endurance, misfortune, and fortitude she depicts in volume two. But the social void is more important to the Moodies' retreat to the front and is emblematic of the failure of their transplanted English social structure to survive in Upper Canada. That failure can be partly attributed to the political and economic disturbances of the colony in the 1830s.

Thomas Need supplies one reason for the enhanced land values in Douro Township that Strickland, Traill, and Moodie sought to exploit: "the settlement of three or four persons of education and capital in a Township always attracts notice, and increases the value of property" (1838, 74). Another attraction resided in proposed improvements to inland water transportation. First proposed in 1827, this plan for the navigation system was by the fall of 1833 driving the price of land up. According to Mrs Moodie, "the prospect of opening the Trent and Otonabee for the navigation of steam-boats and other small craft, was ... a favourite speculation, and its practicability, and the great advantages to be derived from it, were so widely believed as to raise the value of the wild lands along these remote waters to an enormous price."[36] In 1833 the government announced plans to begin work on the system and the next summer Lieutenant-Governor Colborne came to view the contemplated improvements. In 1836 and 1837 money was appropriated. The economic boom ended in 1836, and after the rebellion there was no money for large-scale public works. Reformers opposed massive developments because they believed that they enriched the elite without aiding the settlers whose money paid for them. Means for the back-township farmers of the Newcastle District to get their produce to market were not provided: "because of the political and financial dislocation ... little had been accomplished at the time of Union" to open up the Trent system.[37]

The failure to open up inland navigation led not only to economic but to social problems. Traill, in late 1834 projecting the "incalculable advantage" to be derived from "this noble work," believed it would lead to "settling many of the back townships bordering upon these lakes" (1836, 209). In 1837, among circumstances "depress[ing] the energies of the settlers of this township," was the lack of "navigable streams for the conveyance of commodities to market" (TFC, 9688-89). Without waterways to Lake Ontario, the settlers could not get their wheat cheaply to market and the influx of immigrants they had expected to populate their fledgling British community did not arrive.

Shipping difficulties compounded the Moodies' problems with poor crops, finding help, livestock loss, injury, and fire. By mid-1835 their "ready money was exhausted" (*RI* 352). Mrs Moodie summed up the situation in 1836–37: "We had involved ourselves considerably in debt, in order to pay our servants and obtain the common necessaries of life; and ... for clearing ten more acres upon the farm. Our utter inability to meet these demands weighed heavily upon my husband's mind" (353). "Anxious to free himself from the thraldom of debts which pressed him sore," Moodie tried to sell two hundred acres; the deal fell through when the buyer returned to England (408). With money from various sources, by mid 1838 "their large debt [was] more than half liquidated" (423). But even with his militia pay, they found it "impossible to pay several hundreds of pounds of debt; and the steam-boat stock still continued a dead letter. To remain much longer in the woods was impossible."[38]

Susanna's attitude, that "of all evils, to borrow money is perhaps the worst" (88), shows that English scruples about dependency clouded the Moodies' assessment of the situation. Throughout the many years it took to bring an Upper Canadian farm into full production, "the farmer's need for capital must have tended to exceed his income" (McCalla 1978, 188). Since a farmer invested his own and his family's labour, to accumulate debt to supply necessities was "a reasonable investment strategy" (189). Those who survived the uncertainty of the 1830s prospered in the 1840s. The opening up of the southern half of the Trent system after 1841 increased the profitability of farming north of Rice Lake. As with the Cobourg farm, if Moodie had retained his Douro holding, he could have become a substantial landowner and successful farmer.

The Moodies' most direct involvement in political events was during the rebellion of 1837. Mrs Moodie's later claim that, prior to "the revolution which was about to work a great change ... for Canada," they "knew nothing, heard nothing of the political state of the country" is somewhat disingenuous.[39] She read the Cobourg *Reformer* in their first month in the colony; she knew of republican sentiments in the settlements; there were grievance meetings in Peterborough from 1833, and there was a reform candidate for the riding in 1836. Strickland, with his ties to Councillor Stewart and Magistrate Reid, knew of the growth of political opposition during these years.[40] Politics was talked about only by the gentlemen, but Mrs Moodie was aware of colonial factionalism. The alacrity with which her husband responded to the loyal call-to-arms suggests his knowledge was more detailed.

Mrs Moodie first heard of the rebellion from her servant, in "strange and monstrous statements" derived from the visit of "some gentleman" who had "left a large paper, all about the Queen and the Yankees" and "a war between Canada and the States." The "elucidation" of these "marvellous tales" was "a copy of the Queen's proclamation, calling upon all loyal gentlemen to join in putting down the unnatural rebellion."[41] Ten years after the event Moodie implied that the servant was inaccurate, but these statements are what would be expected from a "gentleman" carrying rumours of revolt. The metonymic chain with which the Tory faction bound together reformism-republicanism-Americanism-U.S. imperialism was well-forged by this time, and an uprising provided the final link – treason. Regardless of the issues and participants involved, rebellion was reduced to a conflict of the Queen v. the Yankees, Canada v. the United States, loyalty v. the unnatural.

Her husband "instantly obeyed ... the imperative call of duty," while Mrs Moodie, her "British spirit ... fairly roused" against "the enemies of [her] beloved country[,] ... did what little [she] could to serve the good cause with [her] pen" (411, 413). She includes two propaganda poems in *Roughing It* to "amuse" her readers; they speak of treason and loyalty, despotism and freedom, republicanism and monarchy, atheism and religion. While still maintaining that "the political struggles that convulsed the country were scarcely echoed in the depths of those old primeval forests," she ends her chapter on "The Outbreak" with a long poem written at the time in praise of the patriots and damnation of the traitors (425–6).

Moodie never saw what little action there was in the rebellion. His wife attracted more attention with her poems. While their commitment to "the good cause" was sincere, that cause served them in turn. Mrs Moodie's first loyal poem appeared 20 December 1837 and was, as she says, "widely circulated."[42] Moodie was back by mid-December, but on 20 January left to become a captain in the militia drawn up to defend the colony against rebel incursions from the United States; this was "a signal act of mercy" since it meant "full pay" (416). "Just at this period" John Lovell invited Mrs Moodie to write for the *Literary Garland*, having become acquainted with her work through her loyal poems.[43] In July 1838, with Thomas Traill's approval, she wrote to the new lieutenant-governor, Sir George Arthur, asking him to keep Moodie in the militia, but with its reduction that month, he was out of work.[44]

Arthur had "instructions to emulate Head's policies"; to restore order "he was to place full confidence in the loyal elements that had saved the province."[45] He proved more reactionary than the Colonial Office desired, but when he was made assistant to Governor General Thomson (later Lord Sydenham) in late 1839, he had to help break up the oligarchy by winning moderate Tories to the union proposal. During his reorganization of colonial defence in late 1838 he may have been, as

Moodie believed, responsible for her husband's appointment as militia paymaster, a job that lasted less than eight months.[46] His next government job was definitely Arthur's doing. In October 1839 Moodie was appointed to "the much coveted, newly created office of sheriff of Hastings County."[47] Mrs Moodie writes that her husband, "though perfectly unacquainted with the difficulties and responsibilities of such an important office, ... looked upon it as a gift sent from heaven" (*RI*, 475–6). He viewed it as "evidence that [his] services met with the approval of the Government" (1866, x), even though he knew of the intercessions of his wife and his commanding officer with the lieutenant-governor. She thanked God and Sir George Arthur.

Mrs Moodie's letter to Arthur has not survived. She was inspired to "write to the Governor; tell him candidly all you have suffered during your sojourn in this country; and trust to God for the rest," and called the resulting letter "a simple statement of facts" (424). Three facts distinguished this petition from others like it: the loyal songs she wrote after the rebellion; her husband's response to the rebellion, rank in the militia, and service as paymaster; and the connection of them both with the Douro elite. Prior to becoming Thomson's assistant, Arthur made "a burst of eleventh-hour appointments" (*Letters*, 72). These installed loyal forces at the local level, in grudging acceptance that at the provincial level the influence of the "Constitutional party" – even its control over patronage – was waning. When Moodie appealed to Arthur over difficulties in assuming his post, he was reassured: "as to your loyalty and attachments to British Institutions, it was unnecessary for you to say one word – I took it for granted that you must possess both, or you would not have been the husband of Mrs. Moodie" (quoted in Morris 1968, 177–8). Moodie himself was not remiss in claiming the loyal label, so potent in the aftermath of the rebellion.

At the end of the 1830s the Belleville area had a reputation as a radical stronghold. A political union had been formed in the town under Mackenzie's influence in 1837, and there were many arrests that December. In December 1838 Moodie found the land of the Bay area enticing, "but there are few British settlers, and the mass of people are disaffected"; he had doubts "whether the society is particularly desirable." By early 1839, however, he was "pretty *thick*" with one Loyalist descendent and decided that "the old loyal settlers ... are a fine honest respectable set of fellows far superior in character to the Cobourg folks who are demoralized."[48] His wife and children joined him in Belleville in January 1840. The rebellion was the catalyst releasing them from the settler's life. Since Moodie's first paymaster appointment in late 1838 they had been seeking a way off their bush farm.[49] They gained a livelihood and status through their connection to the old order. Mrs

Moodie was the main writer for the *Literary Garland*; J.W.D. Moodie was a local government official, second only to the district judge. But the political conflict had yet to work itself out. The fragmentation of the conservative faction that Durham and the union proposal caused was yet to settle into a stable realignment. The Moodies in Belleville were forced gradually to shift their position until they ended up with an orientation apparently the opposite of the one they had previously occupied.

Established Bellevillians, not the disaffected, were the first and most persistent source of difficulties for Moodie.[50] The town had been founded by Loyalists in 1790 and settled by them. In the 1820s and 1830s only poorer immigrants, mainly Irish, had stayed in the area.[51] The main demographic difference between Cobourg and Belleville was the lack of post-1798 American immigrants in the latter. "Loyalty" meant two different things to the gentlefolk of Douro and the Loyalists of Belleville. Loyalty for the recent English immigrants entailed principles: hierarchy, deference, and privilege. The Loyalist concept was pragmatic: loyalty confirmed association with the ruling class.[52] Before the influx of middle-class British immigrants, appearance on the United Empire list increased eligibility for government patronage. As Moodie put it, "the name of U.E. (United Empire) Loyalist or Tory came to be considered an indispensable qualification for every office in the colony" (*RI*, 499). The newly-arrived British gentlemen expected patronage to be spread amongst them. Needing support for union from moderates of all stripes, Sydenham set long-settled, extreme Loyalists at odds with more recent and moderate immigrants over patronage. Mrs Moodie says the heirs of "the first settlers ... form the aristocracy of Canada": "From this class her legislators and local officers are generally chosen; and they are exceedingly jealous of foreigners interfering, in any way, with what they consider *their rights* as *Canadians born*."[53] Moodie walked into this situation with his government appointment as sheriff of Loyalist Belleville.

Arthur, not in Upper Canada long enough to become sensitive to local elites, may not have known how important to retaining their support patronage appointments were. The Moodies had connections in Douro but none in Belleville or, more importantly, Toronto.[54] The wrath of local Tories at his appointment was symptomatic of the breakdown of old alliances after 1840. While the shrievalty went far towards alleviating physical privation, it once more embroiled the Moodies in conflict. His first antagonists were Thomas Parker, a local Tory who had expected the sheriff's job, and Benjamin Dougall, who became district court judge at the same time Moodie received his appointment.

William Ponton was an early ally whom Moodie recommended to the lieutenant-governor for registrar because Ponton's "character and habits" would be a "powerful influence ... in raising the standards of morals amidst a vicious community."[55] Mrs Moodie was equally unimpressed with the town's physical appearance in 1840, describing it as "an insignificant, dirty-looking place" (*LC*, 29).

The shrievalty was worth approximately two hundred and fifty pounds a year, enough to keep the Moodies in middle-class comfort had there not been difficulties collecting it. Since government services were self-supporting, Moodie's income came from fees charged for the performance of his duties: the officials and lawyers who opposed him delayed or withheld payment.[56] He was on a sheriffs' committee that petitioned the governor in 1842 for reform of the system, particularly requesting payment for the peacekeeping duties that occupied most of their time, but for which they had no one to charge. Despite this unpaid work, Moodie claimed his duties seldom took "more than two or three hours daily," and by October 1841 he was requesting additional appointments.[57] His enemies repeatedly filed nuisance suits against him, which, although dropped as readily as begun, involved him in legal expenses. He later summed up his situation between the time of his appointment and his resignation in January 1863: "I have had to contend with a succession of suits at law got up by parties *on speculation*, or with the object of creating a vacancy in my office, which they thought might be filled by one more deserving than myself. Though I generally escaped the snares laid for me, *I was poor*, and the tear and wear, and anxiety, were undermining my naturally robust constitution."[58] In print Mrs Moodie tangentially comments on her husband's problems with fees and litigation when she decries the "great deficiency among our professional men and wealthy traders of that nice sense of honour that marks the conduct and dealings of the same class at home" (*LC*, 41); she is more forthright in condemning "*legal thieves*" in her correspondence.[59]

Moodie's battles with Belleville Tories were intensified by politics in the election of 1841. Sydenham had to secure a pro-union majority while keeping promoters of responsible government at bay. He won Robert Baldwin's support when Baldwin accepted the office of solicitor-general in 1840. The Belleville incumbent, Edmund Murney, had been elected on Head's cry of loyalty. In the first union election Sydenham, as his predecessor, interfered to run Baldwin against Murney on the appeal to loyalty. Murney was supported by the strong local Orange Lodge. Parker and a nephew of Judge Dougall were Orangemen. One of the sheriff's peacekeeping duties was to be returning officer. The riots on the six days of voting were worse in Belleville than elsewhere. Baldwin, to whom the rebel label would not stick since he was running for Sydenham, won by thirty-six votes. Moodie was attacked in a petition to the Assembly for "wilful and unwarrantable partiality" and being "grossly biassed in favour of the said Robert Baldwin."[60] Given the tone of elections during the period, the Tory complaints against the Baldwin election committee's use of gangs of "armed shanty-men, bullies and ruffians" were likely just, if hypocritical. The Assembly dismissed the petition. Moodie's friendship with Baldwin and reputation as a reformer date from this time. In this "difficult constituency with a large Tory vote," he had consolidated and augmented the ranks of those opposing him.[61]

Baldwin had won the acknowledgment of British colonial officials through the Durham Report but had yet to complete his work for responsible government. His Belleville adviser was a Toronto lawyer who went on to become president of the Grand Trunk Railway and an official in Macdonald's government. Responsible government, necessary for the ascendance of the middle class in the Canadas, was made possible by severing all associations with independence. Baldwin resigned from the Executive in June 1841 because of disagreement with Sydenham over responsible government. When the problem of Assembly recalcitrance resurfaced for Sydenham's successor in the fall of 1842, Bagot recreated the Baldwin-Lafontaine ministry. Baldwin turned again to Hastings County to seek re-election.

The election of October 1842 was more violent and chaotic than the previous one. Moodie called up the militia, asked for and received two army companies, and closed the polls early several times. His request for extension of the poll was denied. Murney won by a slight margin, but his election was disallowed because Moodie would not certify that the writ had been properly carried out.[62] Moodie was made a scapegoat, but it was his good fortune that he was henceforth not called as returning officer. Now he was unequivocally branded a reformer, but he also lost friends in the local reform faction. After Baldwin's election in Rimouski their relationship was maintained through correspondence. Mrs Moodie's discussion of the politics of the time shows the effects on her while "the demon of party reigned pre-eminent": "Even women entered deeply into this party hostility; and those who, from their education and mental advantages, might have been friends and agreeable companions, kept aloof, rarely taking notice of each other, when accidentally thrown together" (LC, 56).

Besides being involved in local factionalism, the Moodies were perceived as aliens. In July 1840 they named their sixth child George Arthur; three years later they named their last Robert Baldwin. Not only do these nominations evince their response to the shifting political tides around them: they inscribe upon their children a certain pride, also seen in Moodie's laconic admission to Baldwin in 1843 that he was "aware of the *objection to strangers* in this country."[63] Their class biases, shocked into rigidity at Cobourg and positively reinforced in Douro, remained strong ten years after their arrival in Upper Canada. Besides Baldwin, the friends they made in the 1840s had backgrounds similar to their own. Among them was Dr William Hope, who had come to Belleville in 1838 from medical training in Kingston, Dr James Lister, who had immigrated to the colony in 1841, and William FitzGibbon, who came from Toronto early in 1843 as Bagot's replacement for Murney as clerk of the peace.[64] All these men were gentlemen, professionals, and outsiders.

While Moodie may have stumbled unawares into a virulent local conflict just as it was being exacerbated by shifts in power at the provincial level, he soon engaged fully in that conflict. Due to trouble securing his sheriff's bond, he had accepted two prominent local men unknown to him as sureties. One of them made his motives clear when he expected the new sheriff's support in a lawsuit. Moodie instead acceded to the request of the opponent of his surety, with "common humanity" his motive.[65] The surety, accusing Moodie of dereliction, withdrew his sponsorship. The new bond brought Moodie into the toils of Judge Dougall, who had to approve it. The matter was finally settled in May 1842 after the direct confrontation of Dougall and Moodie. Moodie took his revenge in 1843 when Dougall, then lawyer for the plaintiff in a suit against Moodie, was consulted by the coroner on the composition of the jury. Moodie brought charges against them both before the Executive Council, and a judicial inquiry led to Judge Dougall's dismissal. Moodie's principled identification of the integrity of the law with his own conduct as his best justification, his only defence, and his ultimately effective offence reveals how considerations of power are at once supported and concealed by legalistic and bureaucratic principles.

The Moodies did, if only briefly, build contacts with some local citizens, one of whom would rise to some prominence in the new relations of power that settled into place by mid-century. These contacts derived from Mrs Moodie's Congregationalism. Of the two Belleville churches they would otherwise have felt at home in, the Presbyterian and the Anglican, the former was led by a minister too Calvinistic for their liking and the latter was dominated by their Tory enemies. So in August 1844 they helped to found the Congregationalist Church of Belleville. They are among the twelve signatories to the constituent preamble that opens the minute-book of the church.[66] In the minutes themselves, that five new members are noted to have come from

American Presbyterian churches points to the New World reunion of these two denominations that had begun together in the seventeeth century, and further explains why J.W.D. Moodie was willing to join his wife in founding a church for her sect. Beside the Moodies' names on the founders' list, "Expelled" has been written. The minutes for March and April 1845 record the events leading up to this expulsion. The Moodies seem to have become lax in their performance of church duties – a serious offence among Congregationalists, who expect the active participation of all members. The Moodies sought religious consolation after the drowning of their six-year-old son in June 1844. The church they helped to form does not seem to have met their needs. Neither did it fulfil its promise of establishing a continuum in Mrs Moodie's religious experience or of providing broader social connections.

The Moodies continued to be involved in the mix of power and principle at the local level of the provincial struggle. Metcalfe tried to hold back gains that reform had made under Bagot and, responding once more to the loyalty cry, the electorate in 1844 gave him an Assembly he could manage. One sign of Tory resurgence was in Hastings, where, with Baldwin gone and Moodie no longer returning officer, Murney won handily. By now politicians on all sides accepted responsible government. Without Elgin's intervention in the election of 1848, the loyalty label could not be claimed by either faction, and a unified reform party won an overwhelming majority. With the Great Hunger in Ireland and the threat of another uprising, with Chartist agitation in England and revolutions on the Continent, the Colonial Office was happy to see a peaceful rotation of office taking place in the Canadas.[67]

Moodie had been seeking additional or different appointments from the time he arrived in Belleville. Yet he tells Baldwin in early 1845 that he has "for some time back … carefully abstained from taking any part whatever in politics and did not even vote in the last election." He may have abstained from voting because the contenders for Hastings in 1844 were Murney and Dougall. When he claims that he has been injured by "the selfish indifference … and the base treachery" of local reformers who also covet his office, and says that he cannot "feel … called on to ruin [himself] to please them," he falls just short of an admission of partisanship in his administration of the previous elections.[68] He now confined his political participation to appeals for patronage. In September 1848, six months after Baldwin returned to the Executive Council with control of patronage granted, he offered a new job to Moodie, who rejected it, hoping that "something better may turn up."[69]

While her husband sought to improve his official situation, Mrs Moodie was adjusting to her reputation as Belleville's most famous author. At Cobourg she had felt that authors were "held in supreme detestation" as worse than useless, and so she had "tried to conceal [her] blue stockings" and "avoid all literary subjects" (*RI*, 201, 202). But throughout the 1840s she was writing for the *Literary Garland*, and she says her work was received in a "flattering manner ... by the Canadian public" (Intro to *MH*, 290). In *Life in the Clearings* she portrays the "highly amusing" conception "that some country people form of an author." A schoolboy has the idea from his mother that "Mrs. M— invented lies, and got money for them" (64), and "the wife of a rich farmer" is surprised on finding "the woman that writes" but "a humly body after all" (65). Two other women experience the same disappointed expectations: "We have seen Mrs. M—, and we were so surprised to find her just like other people."[70] Her generalization that "the sin of authorship meets with little toleration in a new country" is based on her view of her own experience. She supports this opinion with a sketch of one of "several persons of this class" who has found "few minds that could sympathize with" him (66). When a lecture she attends turns out to be on "Great women, from Eve down to Mrs. M—" she leaves, not wanting to be made "a laughing-stock" (99). In 1854 she still conceals her blue stockings: "I always *drop* the *profession*, and never allude to *authorship*" (letter 55). By the late 1850s there were those who identified her on the streets of Belleville with respect rather than derision. She took little solace in her reputation, unless, as with her husband, it was the solace of believing that her inability to assimilate herself to Belleville society was a sign of innate superiority. The Moodies were respected in Belleville, but never accepted.

During the Moodies' first two decades in the colony the extremes at both ends of the political spectrum withered. The association of responsible government with independence and republicanism was broken. By 1845 it was considered fully in accord with the maintenance of the British connection and the operation of a constitutional monarchy. The Moodies rode out the rough ideological seas while retaining their conservative mooring. Each provides the same analysis of political changes in the 1830s and 1840s. J.W.D. Moodie tells how extreme "toryism and high churchism" impeded development until deadlock between the Assembly and the Executive resulted: "Such a state of things could not last long; and the discontent of a large portion of the people, terminating, through the indiscretion of an infatuated local government, in actual rebellion, soon produced the remedy" (*RI*, 500, 501). The remedy was responsible government, "and the people being thus given the power of governing by their majorities in Parliament, improvements of all kinds are steadily advancing" (501). "The Tory party," Mrs Moodie explains, "arrogated the whole loyalty of the colony to themselves," and the rebellion occurred "not without severe provocation." The rebels' "disaffection was more towards the colonial government, and the abuses it fostered, than any particular dislike to British supremacy or institutions" (*LC*, 56). Under the reform administration "the colony has greatly progressed" (59).

Mrs Moodie could have allied herself with any of the colonial ideologies struggling for hegemony: agrarian radicalism, ultra-Tory conservativism, or moderate reformism. Her eventual orientation towards the last was determined by her experience of these factions. The agrarian radicalism at Cobourg left her with a repugnance for what she perceived as Yankee republicanism. In Douro Township, where she might have begun to understand the forces impelling settlers towards radical solutions, she was instead attached to a local elite with an interest in preserving the status quo. The move to Belleville occurred as extreme conservativism was losing ground and brought her into contact with Baldwin just as he was about to achieve his greatest success. While her stance towards Upper Canadian radicals softened after they were broken, she retained her conservativism even when she adopted some reform principles.

The Moodies participated in quelling the rebellion because they were attached to England. They feared the United States and democracy, and Baldwin helped them to see that responsible government did not imply a love of either; by 1840 there were no radicals left in Upper Canada who would dare to suggest that it did. The association of Loyalists such as Dougall and Murney with an embattled status quo, vociferously and with ever less credibility proclaiming its loyalty, made the Moodies more amenable to Baldwin's arguments. By the mid-1840s moderates from all sides accepted that responsible government could provide a way of constructively channelling factionalism without interrupting the workings of government. One of the appeals of responsible government, as both the Moodies attest, was that it worked.

By the end of the 1840s the indigenous business and professional class in Upper Canada had a secure basis for its development of hegemonic status. Those who held the ideology of established church, aristocracy, and tradition had never become secure in their grip on the state apparatus. But the ideology of industry, commerce, and wealth did become fully established in the Canadas. Capital is more easily exported than are titles. The British constitution remained intact in both colony and mother country throughout the transfer of hegemony.[71] At mid-century the constitutional balance was maintained not by the weight of a few lords against the populace but by the weight of a few wealthy men. That the Moodies identified with the new hegemonic class is indicated by the dispensations of some of their children: in 1850 Agnes married another son of Colonel James FitzGibbon, Thomas, a lawyer practising in Toronto; in 1853 Donald was sent to McGill University to study medicine; in 1855 Catherine married John Vickers, a successful Toronto businessman. Between 1832 and 1855 Mrs Moodie transformed from an emigrant whose main identification was with values left behind to an immigrant who reluctantly accepted the values she found dominant around her.

5 The Ideal and The Real: Literary Production 1832-1852

A backward glance, to the idealized homeland she had been forced to leave, conditioned Susanna Moodie's writing in Upper Canada. As with a character in one of her novels, "the *ideal* vanished, and the hard, uncompromising *real* took its place" (*GM*, 17). England haunts her writing as the lost ideal, the desired object, only because she had left it. The colony, as the real, suffers in comparison. She wrote to reclaim the ideal and preserve it from the real.

Moodie began her colonial literary career while still in England, and by addressing the tastes of emigrés. In the fall of 1831 three of her poems appeared anonymously in the Cobourg *Star*, likely through the agency of her brother Samuel.[1] In Cobourg a year later the Moodies met "the *Star*'s Tory editor, R.D. Chatterton," establishing her as the author of the poems, and in the fall of 1832 five poems from *Enthusiasm* were in the *Star*.[2] She gave Chatterton previously published work, initiating a practice that would become habitual, but early in 1833 she wrote to the editor of the New York *Albion*, Dr John Bartlett, "ambitious of the honour of contributing to its pages" and enclosing "the first flight of [her] muse on Canadian shores." If Bartlett would accept "the assistance of a pen, deemed not unworthy of public notice in [her] native land," she would continue to submit, "from time to time, a few small original poems." She did not yet deem the "chilly atmosphere" of Upper Canada worth the expenditure of creative energy, as was Bartlett's "more liberal channel of communication with the public" (letter 35). One of these poems tells how "The strains we hear in foreign lands, / No echo from the heart can claim," and yearns for "The music of our native shore."[3]

Colonial music left her cold. Bartlett published two poems, with her letter, and five more in the *Albion* up to January 1835; he also included her work in his *Emigrant and Old Countryman*.[4] She later regretted rejecting "his kind offer to come to New York, and become one of his regular contributors" (letter 78). So soon after her arrival, she looked beyond the colony for media oriented towards England.

The anglophile *Albion*'s popularity cost Moodie her first colonial venue, but did provide compensation.[5] Chatterton's remarks, prefacing his reprint of the *Albion* letter and poems in the *Star*, shows how slighted he felt. He never published her again. The one recognizably and positively Canadian poem she had so far written, "The Sleigh-Bells," was also reprinted from the *Albion* in two York papers and the *Canadian Magazine*. The reception of this poem encouraged Moodie to participate in attempts to raise what recent British middle-class immigrants perceived as the earth-bound horizons of Upper Canadians. In March 1833 she submitted new work to the *Canadian Literary Magazine*. She later notes the "patronage of the Lieutenant-Governor, Sir John Colborne," over it.[6] The editor, John Kent, was hired upon his arrival in 1833, when he was also hired for Upper Canada College, established by Colborne in 1829. In his first editorial Kent appeals to "every individual who feels a desire that Canada should possess a literature of its own."[7] Two poems and a story by Moodie appear in the first number of this magazine concocted to reproduce British culture in the colony. The bemusement of Upper Canadians at a publication that printed poems asking, "Oh Can You Leave Your Native Land?" undoubtedly contributed to its failure after three issues. Among recent immigrants, only a minority had, as the addressee of this poem, hands "unused to toil"; to even fewer would her "loved isle" ever appear "An Eden" (ll. 13, 19).

Moodie again found ears responsive to the call of British civilization in an American periodical that sought to tap nostalgia for British cultural ideals. Sumner Lincoln Fairfield gathered her work from various sources, including the *Canadian Literary Magazine*, and introduced it in the *North American Quarterly Magazine* in December 1834. He or "some unknown friend" sent this issue and two others to the Moodies in Douro. This gift prompted her to send him a copy of *Enthusiasm*, which he had "noticed in such flattering terms." She also took the "opportunity of enclosing a few original poems." Apart from this offer, she declined Fairfield's invitation to become a regular contributor because "the expense of transmitting articles to such a great distance is beyond [her] means, and [her] time is too valuable to waste in the pursuit of fame" (letter 36). She later recalled this relationship:

I had been requested by an American author, of great merit, to contribute to the *North American Review*, published for several years in Philadelphia; and he promised to remunerate me in proportion to the success of the work. I had contrived to write several articles after the children were asleep, though the expense even of the stationery and the postage of the manuscripts was severely felt by one so destitute of means; but the hope of being of the least service to those dear to me cheered me to the task. I never realised anything from that source; but I believe it was not the fault of the editor. (*RI*, 417)

From 1835 to late in 1837 Fairfield was her sole North American publisher, printing nine of her poems.

Among the *North American Quarterly Magazine* poems, two expressive of her experience in Douro are probably the "articles" to which she refers. In "Oh Canada! Thy Gloomy Woods!" and "Home Thoughts of an Emigrant" she voices her initial response to the backwoods.[8] Her pre-emigration poems identify with nature and find in it a path to God, but Canadian nature repels her. Like other immigrants trying to snag an alien reality in a familiar net, she can barely see the New World:

> Oh Canada! thy gloomy woods
> Will never cheer the heart;
>
> In the depths of dark forests my soul droops her wings;
> In tall boughs above me no merry bird sings;
> The sigh of the wild winds – the rush of the floods –
> Is the only sad music that wakens the woods.[9]

Despondent, she recalls natural settings left behind:

> But ever as a thought most bless'd
>   Her distant shores will rise,
> In all their spring-tide beauty dress'd,
>   To cheer my mental eyes.
> ("Oh Canada! Thy Gloomy Woods!" ll. 17–20)
>
> In dreams, lovely England! my spirit still hails
> Thy soft waving woodlands, thy green, daisied vales.
> ("Home Thoughts of an Emigrant," ll. 23–4)

With patriarchal, middle-class values of independence and duty she tries to suppress her pain:

> But independent souls will brave
>   All hardships to be free;
> No more I weep to cross the wave,
>   My native land to see. ("Oh Canada! Thy Gloomy Woods!" ll. 13–16)

The stern voice of duty compell'd me to roam,
From country and friends – the enjoyments of home;
But faith in the future my anguish restrain'd
And my soul in that dark hour of parting sustain'd.
("Home Thoughts of an Emigrant," ll. 13-16)

In these poems she first attempts to assimilate creatively the reality of the backwoods. She wrote and sent them to Philadelphia at an expense of time and money she could ill afford, hoping that she would be paid for them. The poetry of cultural deprivation arises in the midst of material deprivation. These poems are the only evidence that she wrote anything between the end of her first year in Douro and the Rebellion of 1837.

While the alien landscape stifled Moodie, Upper Canadian politics opened an opportunity for writing in a familiar vein. She put her earlier experience with patriotic songs to use in the defence of her ideal in the unsettled Canadas of 1837. Similarly, the mockery she directed at "Orator" Hunt in that earlier time reappears transformed in the vilification she pours on Mackenzie. The distance she had travelled adds a new urgency to themes with which she once only played.

The colonial press fully covered Mackenzie's activities in October, and by early November the Tory papers were calling on government supporters to arm themselves against a possible revolt.[10] Mackenzie's "popular Constitution" was widely circulated in mid-November. Moodie entered the press battle with "Canadians Will You Join the Band," which, despite her claimed innocence of colonial politics, she wrote two weeks before the rebellion occurred. Warning Canadians not to join "the factious band," she rouses them to "crush the traitors" (ll. 1, 40). The poem is a pre-rebellion warning to Mackenzie and his followers, advising "the baffled traitor" and "the rash, misguided band" to "sue for mercy, ere too late" (ll. 29, 26, 27). Charles Fothergill published this "Loyal Song" in the first issue of his *Palladium of British America* on 20 December, and her next poem on the rebellion, "On Reading the Proclamation Delivered by William Lyon Mackenzie," in mid-January.[11] The latter is her response to Mackenzie's "Proclamation ... of the Provisional Government of the State of Upper Canada," delivered on 14 December, the first day of his occupation of Navy Island.

Both poem and proclamation are rife with contradictions, enamoured with mirages. Referring to Mackenzie as "a self-elected demagogue" (l. 8), Moodie disregards his seven elections to the Assembly. She contrasts him with a heroic Washington; in his proclamation he had justified his actions by citing "the enduring principles of the Revolution of 1776" (1837, 155). She charges the "sons of anarchy" with violent abuse of the rights and property of "peaceful citizens" (ll. 31, 33), but government forces had burnt two homes to the rebels' one, and Mackenzie enjoined his followers to set "the praiseworthy example of protecting the houses, the homes, and the families" of their enemies (155–6). What most provokes her is his characterization of Upper Canada's rulers as "military despots, strangers from Europe" (152) and his demand for an independent republic. To her these are "Men who have sworn / Faithful allegiance to their lawful prince" and "bless the parent land from whence they sprung, / And deem their highest privilege is still / To live beneath her mild maternal sway" (ll. 33–4, 36–8). His "hired red coats of Europe" (155) are her "fathers! husbands! brothers!" (l. 76). They agree only in their association of freedom with England: she refers to "free-born Britons" (l. 64), he to "the blessings of British freedom" (156). He attacked the British connection that she needed, for her own peace, to retain. The rebellion threatened her identity. Writing on it she fought for that identity and appealed to the audience with whom she shared it.

Moodie supplied the newly formed market for patriotic verse with British productions suited to the climate of civil war and potential invasion from the United States. "The Banner of England," "War," and "The Avenger of Blood," all published by 1831, reappeared in the *Palladium* in early 1838.[12] She then gave Fothergill a new poem. "The Burning of the Caroline" was "partly written at the period when the important event it celebrates occurred," but she was "hindered from preparing it for publication at the time." Although in submitting the poem almost a year after its occasion she did not want "to keep alive the public excitement, so widely displayed on the perpetration of that gallant action," it remains a poem of good versus evil.[13] Its hero has "taught the dastard foe / That British honour never yields / To democratic influence, low" (ll. 82–4). Another poem in the *Palladium,* her last on the rebellion, "The Oath of the Canadian Volunteers," similarly proclaims loyalty to England as the highest good:

The stars for us shall never burn,
　The stripes may frighten slaves,
The Briton's eye will proudly turn
　Where Britain's standard waves. (ll. 28–31)

Transforming civil strife into conflict between the United States and England, democracy and monarchy, the real and the ideal, she forecasts the extirpation of republicans like those who annoyed her at Cobourg. Her husband employed by the winning side, she put aside her loneliness in the oppressive Upper Canadian woods by celebrating a triumphal British culture that would find one of its nuclei in Douro.

The reform newspapers that printed Moodie's first Canadian poems were closed to her after her propaganda poems began to appear.[14] She now became a regular in Tory papers like the Kingston *Chronicle and Gazette*, the Bytown *Gazette*, and the St Catharines *Journal*, each of which reprinted at least one loyal poem from the *Palladium* among several others. The *Chronicle*, in 1838, was the first to publish "There Is Not a Spot in this Wide Peopled Earth," another nostalgic encomium on "the land of our birth" (l. 2). "The Waters," later titled "A Canadian Song," appeared in the Bytown paper in 1839. This poem, Canadian only in its invitation to "launch the light canoe" (l. 1), was nevertheless her first attempt to rediscover God in New World nature. This rediscovery was related to the discomfiture of the godless in which she was participating.

The apparent victory of her British ideal partly accounts for her change in attitude to publishing in the Canadas. As the prospect that J.W.D. Moodie might become a permanent employee of the military arose, the couple began to consider the development of a remunerative literary career for her. In December 1838 Moodie, in Belleville, wishes he had a copy of *Enthusiasm* for his commanding officer who has asked about her.[15] Replying in a letter that she might be able to get a copy to him, she discusses Agnes's recommendation that she send her Canadian songs to a British musician, "as it *might*," Susanna reports, "*perhaps bring* [her] *poetry a little into notice*"; she would, however, "rather now be popular in the country of [her] adoption than at home." Her husband asks her for copies of her British collection to satisfy inquiries at Kingston, but he is also thinking of a colonial career for her: when next in Kingston he will try to "get an offer for a *new volume of poems with* [her] *Canadian poems added*."[16] In March she raises an idea they would act upon eight years later: "What if you and I were to edit a newspaper in some large town on conservative principles and endeavor to make it a valuable vehicle for conveying intelligence respecting the colony to the old country as well as this ... The successful Editors of papers ... find it a sure step to preferment ... Without much effort I think our paper would soon be the first in the Provinces."[17] She conceived the *Victoria Magazine* in the bush. Amongst a number of others, it was the one literary scheme to extricate the Moodies from their cultural and economic plight. The plan arose from her desire for communication with "the old country" and for "preferment" in the new, for maintenance of her hold on the ideal and enhancement of her conditions in the real.

Had they pursued the idea when it first arose, a "conservative newspaper" edited by the Moodies might have shared the success of the *Literary Garland*. The reform cause blighted by the rebellion, Tory fortunes were at their height in the late 1830s, but the Moodies made their way out of the bush without taking the risk of establishing their own publication. By the fall of 1839 publishing opportunities and preferment were opening up through events earlier set in motion. A week after its *Palladium* appearance "Canadians Will You Join the Band" was reprinted in the *Transcript*, a Montreal newspaper begun by John Lovell in 1836. "The Banner of England" and "The Burning of the Caroline" also went straight from the Toronto to the Montreal paper. Soon after reprinting the latter poem, Lovell asked Susanna for contributions to his new magazine.

Moodie recognized the *Garland* as successor to the *Canadian Literary Magazine* and the *Canadian Magazine*, which she called "unfortunate attempts at a national periodical." While they began when reform was ascendant, it "was established at the most exciting period of Canadian history, on the eve of her memorable rebellion, which proved so fatal to its instigators" (Intro to *MH*, 290). The *Garland* was in fact established as the disaffected were emigrating en masse to the United States and middle-class immigrants and Loyalists were securing control through the militia and the press. It satisfied the tastes of the fraction of the population raised on genteel periodicals in England who enjoyed, at the *Garland*'s inception, the backing of the state. Carl Klinck, noting the "vogue of gentility" within which it thrived, describes its appeal: "The temptation to be English in the aristocratic or upper-gentlefolk manner was ... especially strong in the British colonies, where class distinctions lived a precarious life among only the favoured few. ... The life portrayed was obviously foreign to most Canadian readers, who shared in these things neither before nor after emigration" (1965, 159–60). Alfred Bailey writes that "the middle-class piety and sentiment of contemporary England ... were exemplified" by the *Garland* (1965, 79). Its success as the pre-eminent pre-Confederation periodical is linked to the program of the Colonial Office and colonial elite to anglicize the colony and re-establish a British hierarchy. While most Canadians did not read the *Garland*, it served those who would rule them.[18]

Moodie commented on an early issue of the *Garland* sent to her by Lovell: "tis a wretched performance – but the typography and paper is good – I must say I do not much like being the lioness of it." Lovell asked her to name her own terms. By mid-1839 their dealings had begun:

I sent ... two small MSS down to Mr Lovel, ... for which I asked 5£. He has returned me a very kind gentlemanly answer – accepting the MSS and promising to transmit the money the first week of June. He likewise hopes that any papers I can spare I will send him putting upon each a price and if they can possibly afford to purchase them they will – Though they are not able to offer much, yet this will open up a little fund for me which may enable me to pay Jenny's wages and get a few necessaries for the children –[19]

The two items she refers to are "The Otonabee" and "The Oath of the Canadian Volunteers," her only Canadian works in the *Garland* in 1839. While she published three more poems and three stories in this first volume, they had all been written before emigration.[20]

While Moodie produced new work for the *Garland* in 1840, six of eleven pieces in the second volume had already been published. Every year from 1840 to 1851, except 1849 and 1850, she submitted at least one new serialized prose work, apart from the "Canadian Sketches," always fiction. Of over one hundred pieces in the *Garland*, nearly half are reprints. Of the remainder, forty-one are European in subject. Nineteen have colonial content. Nineteen poems from *Enthusiasm* reappear in the *Garland*, three of them twice. She completed versions of the stories "The Royal Quixote," "The Miner," "Jane Redgrave," and "The Miser and His Son" in England.[21] Remarking that "the Old English tone was supplied by Mrs. Moodie," Klinck concludes that "cultural tenacity was the clue to everything in the *Garland*" (1965, 160–1). Ballstadt mentions its "emulation of Old World models" (1975, xx).

These observations apply literally in Moodie's case: not only did she rely on British models when submitting work, but half the time she relied on poems and stories pre-approved by a British audience. Her mining of pre-emigration ore was multiply determined. Her British publications were unavailable in the colony. Since nothing came of her husband's plan for a Canadian edition of her poems, she may have felt obliged to satisfy interest in her early poetry through other means. Apart from the interest expressed in Belleville and Kingston, the steady transfer of her poems from newspaper to newspaper also indicated that she had a market. These reprints were unauthorized and unremunerated. By controlling the reissue of her work through the *Garland,* she could earn money.

Beyond maintaining her reputation and making a living, there was a psychological and social rationale for this recycling: reprinting publications of the young woman in England, she sealed an identity between that woman and the married, middle-aged immigrant she somehow turned out to be. Presenting the Canadas with "The Banner of England" and "London: A National Song," she told herself and Canadians that they lived under the same regime as the one under which she had written them. "War," "The Earthquake," and "The Destruction of Babylon," oblique responses to civil disorder in England in the late 1820s, became equally relevant ten years later in the New World. "An Appeal to the Free," published in 1830 to support the anti-slavery cause, might succour American abolitionists in 1850. She wanted to believe that "Autumn" described the same season in 1828, 1832, 1840, and 1846, "The Spirit of Spring" the same season in 1829, 1840, and

1848. By superimposing "The Wood Lane" and "The Forest Rill" on Canadian nature, she might conquer its recalcitrance. She reaffirmed her early experience by resurrecting "The Lament of the Disappointed" and "The Hymn of the Convalescent." The metaphor of "The Old Ash Tree," uniting the destruction of a tree and of youthful hopes, meant as much in 1841 and 1849 as in 1828. The twenty-five- and the forty-six-year-old were the same. Through this obsessive republication of early poems she sutured the wound of emigration. To make the real bow to the ideal, she bargained for a stable identity at the linguistic bourse. This psychic and creative economy refigured the stringencies of her domestic economy.

Reduplication continued into the *Victoria Magazine*. While she brought out some previously published prose, most of her reissued work was verse. Up to 1838 the majority of her new titles had been poems; as she wrote for the *Garland*, this ratio changed. From 1839 she published more new pages of prose each year than of verse. By 1846 she was writing only one or two new poems a year. She accounted for this shift in her production: "Time to me was money – it belonged by right to my family, and was too valuable a commodity to give away. I therefore named five pounds per sheet, as the price required for articles from my pen, which had to be written after the labours of the day were over, and the children were asleep in their beds. The magazine was of large size, with double columns, and in very small type. It required a great deal of writing to fill a sheet" (Intro to *MH*, 286). A piece-worker, she more easily earned her pay writing prose than verse. Instead of seeking anew each night the inspiration to launch a lyric, she returned to a story in progress, letting a plot already under way carry her on. This concentration on prose stood her in good stead in the 1850s, when she completed the return circuit of this system of exchange, republishing her colonial prose in England. While she never had a second collection of poetry, Bentley made books out of half her prose from the *Garland* and the *Victoria Magazine*. *Roughing It* and *Life in the Clearings* have lengthy sections written specifically for them, but of the forty-seven poems by her in these two books, no more than five were not already written, some as early as 1827.[22]

When Moodie began to write serialized fiction for the *Garland*, she returned, with a difference, to her preoccupations of the late 1820s. She wanted to subtitle her first novel in it "the Memoirs of a poor relation" (letter 50), and her second was "The First Debt." Morality, inseparable from money, remained her other thematic dominant. To an extent she retained her youthful division of the world into good and evil, but she created more complex characters with mixed morals. As in her children's stories, her good male characters fail due to passionate natures, but she now deploys secondary male characters who have plunged into dissipation before learning the error of their ways. Also new to her mature fiction is the attribution of real crime to the antagonists: robbery, fraud, murder, and adultery all occur with some frequency, although never directly depicted. Unable to see in the colony the type of society upon which the European novel relied, she retained British settings. In Carole Gerson's words, "Moodie's now-forgotten fiction imaginatively enacts a return to England no longer possible in her own life."[23]

Some of Moodie's serial works, like "Jane Redgrave," published as a two-part story in *La Belle Assembleé* and expanded to twelve instalments for the *Garland*, and "Trifles from the Burthen of a Life," published in four parts in the *Garland* and fleshed out to become the novel *Flora Lyndsay*, are short stories lengthened with character sketches, sub-plots, stories within stories, and other digressions. In "Geoffrey Moncton," because its hero conveys in the first person the mystery that plagues him, several other lengthy first-person narratives are needed to unravel the plot. Moodie usually titled her novels after their main characters. "Geoffrey Moncton," published in the United States under this title, appears in Bentley's edition as *The Moncktons*.[24] George Moncton, present from page thirty-eight on, carries as much interest and meaning as the titular hero. The mysteries surrounding the two entwine. For George to satisfy Geoffrey's curiosity regarding his past, his voice takes over for a quarter of the novel. Three other Monctons are central: Sir Alexander, Geoffrey's rich second uncle, morally upright after a profligate youth; Geoffrey's first uncle, Robert, an unscrupulous and wealthy lawyer; and Robert's son, Theophilus, more evil than he. Bentley had reason for renaming the novel.

The initial disequilibrium of good dependent on evil in *Geoffrey Moncton* is righted through plot; for the real social contradiction that the unprincipled may thrive, an imaginary resolution is found.[25] This novel, as *Hugh Latimer*, demonstrates that the gentlemanly ideal is moral, not social, but the final proof remains the social recognition of the moral gentleman. Both eponymous characters begin in passion and dependency and end in virtue and wealth. In their essential qualities and the fates assigned them there is little to distinguish a Hugh Latimer from a Geoffrey or George Moncton. Naming her novels after their main characters, Moodie foregrounds one of her heroes' few marks of individuality. Her characters are not so much "characters" in the usual representational sense as they are manifestations of a system of meaning existing independent of them. While in her juvenile fiction she does not fill all the various positions that can be extrapolated from her values, in her mature novels she elaborates characters from all the inherent possibilities.

Passion must be controlled but is none the less a positive quality in her later texts, since through it her characters achieve independence and affirm their faith. Passion is an analogue to enthusiasm and, as spiritual wealth, a prime value. The opposite of spiritual wealth in her novels is material wealth, when undeserved. The opposition of spirituality/materiality is basic, while its negation is lack of spirit/lack of money. At the beginning of the novel Geoffrey Moncton combines spirituality and poverty, while Robert Moncton combines materiality and lack of spirit or profanity. Theophilus, waiting to become his father's heir, is the synthesis of the negations, lack of spirit and lack of money. Sir Alex ideally synthesizes spirituality and materiality but is apparently without an heir. Robert's conspiracies seem headed for success; Theophilus will then absorb the wealth of Sir Alex. This outcome would cancel the ideal of materiality fused with spirituality and confirm the demonic synthesis of materiality and profanity. The novel strives to solve the contradiction of evil triumphant. The final stasis it arrives at is this solution. Robert's plot is foiled and he is murdered: the demonic synthesis is left an empty, untenable position. Theophilus is disinherited and driven into the depths of poverty: the true fruits of evil are degradation. Geoffrey and George, their passions tempered by suffering into spirituality, gain all the wealth in the novel – plus the pure women. They are dual heirs to Sir Alex, confirming the rightness of spirituality's getting its earthly rewards, the righteousness of morality's achieving social recognition.

In *Mark Hurdlestone*, the other *Garland* serial that became a British novel, Moodie distributes her characters more schematically than in *Geoffrey Moncton*. Its first title, "The Miser and His Son," is more accurate than the title of the book. The miser, Mark, is merely the source of lack, while his son, Anthony, is the hero. Once more the *agon* turns on the struggle for an inheritance. Anthony's real antagonist is his evil cousin Godfrey. Carol Shields, noting that "Mrs. Moodie employs a traditional means of revelation, that of comparing paired personalities," cites *Mark Hurdlestone* (1977, 24). Shields compares characters in strength and weakness, badness and goodness, but only their economic status explains plot developments. This novel's disequilibrium results from Mark Hurdlestone's greed and spiritual penury. He will not care for the passionate Anthony, who becomes dependent on his wealthy but untamed uncle Algernon Hurdlestone. Algernon's son, Godfrey, has the greed of his uncle and the dependency of his cousin. This distribution of characters is analogous to that at the beginning of *Geoffrey Moncton*. Algernon occupies Sir Alex's place; Mark occupies Robert's; Godfrey occupies Theophilus's; and Anthony occupies Geoffrey's. Algernon dissipates his son's inheritance; hence Godfrey must covet that which

Anthony expects on the death of his father. Godfrey murders the miser and frames his cousin. The imminent ascendance of evil is thwarted by feminine confessions, and Godfrey is hanged. At the end of the novel three of four positions are vacant as Anthony, spiritual heir to his uncle and material heir to his father, attains the ideal synthesis of spirituality and materiality. He too gets the desirable female for whom a rivalry had existed between him and his cousin.

Moodie's presentation of evil as unbridled materiality and good as spirituality belongs to the middle-class appropriation of the idea of the gentleman. Economic inequality in these novels allows evil to prosper; wealth must be redistributed, not across a social hierarchy but across a moral one. Her production of an ideal synthesis of materiality and spirituality is just that – ideal. In her desire to rise above circumstances, she retains Providence as the agency for restoring good to its proper station. Various characters in *Geoffrey Moncton* and *Mark Hurdlestone* rely on Providence at crucial points. The plots of these novels depend so much on coincidence that no other agency could account for them. The good characters all believe that an individual's fate is in the hands of God. His cousin's plot coming to fruition, Anthony Hurdlestone is told, "God is just. You are innocent; trust in him. Trust firmly, nothing wavering, and he will save you" (350). Godfrey exposed, Anthony's faith is confirmed: "The God in whom you trusted has been strong to save" (357). The wronged characters do not hesitate to apply the inverse of this trust to their transgressors. A victimized woman in *Geoffrey Moncton* believes that "there is one in heaven who will be my Avenger – who never lets the thoroughly bad escape unpunished" (250). The narrator of *Mark Hurdlestone* seconds her: "But the vengeance of Heaven never sleeps, and though the stratagems of wicked men may for a time prove successful, the end generally proves the truth of the apostle's awful denunciation: '*The wages of sin is death*'" (180). Geoffrey Moncton has ready to hand the moral bearing on his cousin: "the fate of Theophilus Moncton" illustrates "the awful text – 'There is no peace,' saith my God, 'for the wicked' and again – 'The wicked have no hope in their death'" (360). In her maturity as in her youth, Moodie contrives plots to prove that, despite appearances, Providence can be relied upon.

George Moncton momentarily steps outside the providential universe: "The station in which we are born, constitutes fate in this world; it is the only thing pertaining to man over which his will has no control. We can destroy our own lives, but our birth is entirely in the hands of Providence" (141). These are curiously ironic words. George at this point still thinks he is the son of a poor woman and is under an alias to escape his murderous grandmother. If he lived out either of these identities he would have to work for a living. When his true parentage is uncovered, he becomes Sir George and his life changes. The fate decreed by birth, determining the whole of life, cannot be escaped; the reach of will is circumscribed. George's example for the exertion of will is suicide. The novel closes even the small loophole for free will in George's idea of fate. Geoffrey's narration later supplies the correct view: "Our will is free to plan. Our opportunities of action are in the hands of God ... How, then, can any man affirm that his destiny is in his own hands, when circumstances form a chain around him, as strong as fate" (316). When Godfrey, forced to accept this determinism in *Mark Hurdlestone*, concludes that "none of us shape our own destinies" (269), he gives up a key belief of the evil characters in these novels. The good may trust in it; the evil may fear it; but no one can escape Providence. It ensures that social contradictions will be overcome.

Moodie opposes materiality and spirituality throughout her fiction. Paired brothers feature in *The Little Prisoner*, "The Two Fishermen," "The Son of Arminius," and her stories of the 1840s. In "Matrimonial Speculations" two lawyers articling for the same firm and angling for the same woman form a pair like that of Geoffrey and Theophilus, Anthony and Godfrey. Here again the gross materialist loses all while the man of spirit gets the girl and the fortune. In "Noah Cotton" Mr Carlos is the unrefined man of wealth, his illegitimate son Noah the dependent. Unaware of their relationship, Noah accidentally murders his father for money. After discovering the truth, his conscience so plagues him that Noah exposes himself, but before his execution he repents and finds the peace of Christ. The character system of "Richard Redpath" is more complete, less melodramatic. Robert Redpath is the low-spirited twin of the gay Richard. Robert thinks only of restoring the fortune lost in a shipwreck, Richard only of wooing a beautiful girl. Other corners are occupied by the evil Benjamin Levi and the rich Joshua Baynes. Levi ends up dead; Baynes continues in his unregenerate ways; Richard wins a beautiful heiress; and Robert weds the woman merchant for whom he works. Moodie sought to solve the problem of genteel penury in her fiction by showing that economic station is ordained by Providence, but her solution to the contradiction that the good and deserving may be poor is in every sense imaginary.

Moodie in the 1840s remained preoccupied with plotting solutions to economic dilemmas related to her own, but at the same time worked towards more direct literary self-representation. Because those solutions depend on a displacement of her dilemma on to male characters, women in the texts so far discussed are largely incidental. She does, however, invest some female characters – like Juliet Whitmore, the girl Anthony Hurdlestone wins – with significance exceeding their plot functions.

Juliet lives with her widowed father, under the tutelage of her stern spinster aunt. These relations are introduced through a dispute involving the discovery that Juliet "has the folly to write verses." The aunt's concern is that she herself "shall be called a blue-stocking" because she is Juliet's teacher (*MH*, 128). Juliet, upset "at finding her secret discovered" (130), was initially inspired when she surreptitiously removed Shakespeare's plays from the library. Poetry comes to her "without seeking" as "a great mystery," the possession of which makes her "very happy" (130). Juliet "laid no claim to the title of a *Blue* – she had not the most remote idea of being considered a literary lady"; "Her sins of authorship were undicted by ambition or the mere love of fame; but were the joyous outpourings of an artless mind" (153). Moodie here idealizes her own relations with reading, writing, and her older sister. Starting from this self-projection on to the romantic figure of a poetic young maiden, she writes beyond convention by having Juliet claim to possess "Enthusiasm!":

Enthusiasm is the eternal struggling of our immortal against our mortal nature, which expands the wings of the soul towards its native heaven. Enthusiasm! Can anything great or good be achieved without it? Can a man become a poet, painter, orator, patriot, warrior, or lover, without enthusiasm? Can he become a Christian without it? In man's struggle to obtain fame, enthusiasm is a virtue. In a holy cause it is termed madness. Oh, thou Author of the human soul, evermore grant me the inspiration of this immortal spirit! (154–5)

"An enthusiastic country girl," Juliet is "a novice in the world" (135). Her functional counterpart in *Geoffrey Moncton* is described by a sophisticate as "too sentimental and countrified" (123). When Juliet's father proposes a trip to London as the "best antidote to love," her aunt agrees, adding that Juliet wants "polishing – she is horribly countryfied" (317). A digression occupying a quarter of "Matrimonial Speculations" deals with the introduction to town life of a character who has no other role than to provide this story. This "slight sketch" of Rachel Beauchamp's first trip to London is a "moral lecture" on the folly of desiring metropolitan experience. Rachel's background aligns her, too, with Susanna. Her father "was the poor, proud representative of a noble, but ruined family." He retained "one small estate" to provide for his second wife and the children she bore him, but "he brought up [Rachel and her] six brothers and sisters with the most extravagant ideas of [their] consequence." When the father died, the "mother was left to struggle on with a large family, and very limited means." In 1820 Rachel travels from near Yarmouth via Ipswich to London, as had Susanna.[26] She concludes her story by recalling "the warm, kind hearts" she later became acquainted with in London (399).

Whereas in stories like *Hugh Latimer* and "The Vanquished Lion" Susanna displaces detached details from her background onto characters whose overall experience does not correspond with hers, in the early 1840s she approaches an open self-representation. In "Richard Redpath" she makes a different, related use of her experience. Published in 1843, this story is set in Jamaica. Susanna would later tell Bentley that "the incidents ... were related to [her] as *facts* by a West Indian Planter, whom [she] met on board a Steam Boat in 1831."[27] The main device of the story, the disguise of the title character as a black so that his brother can sell him into slavery and relieve their financial situation, requires an active slave trade, hence the colonial setting. This ruse probably encompasses "the principal events" related to her by the planter. The essentials of character and plot that encase these events do not differ from the stories set in England that she was writing at the same time.

Two elements in "Richard Redpath," neither required by the "voluntary slave" device or the plot, lead back to Moodie. The first is slavery itself. Blacks appear throughout as caricatured minor characters. Richard's sale at a slave market provides the opportunity for a digression against slavery stridently incongruous with this treatment of blacks. Two paragraphs of high rhetoric open chapter 3, rising to this peroration: "Most noble of all noble modern reformations! – the bloodless triumph of reason and humanity over the selfish avarice and cruelty of the tyrant man" (441). The third paragraph depicts the sale of a mother and children. This scene recalls the one in *Mary Prince* that Thomas Pringle had mirrored in his long editorial note on the sale of a family in a South African slave market. The tableau of a family torn apart by slavery is highly charged when domesticity is a transcendent value. Moodie's connection with the anti-slavery movement is coloured with sentimentality.[28]

The character of Benjamin Levi, a Jewish newspaper editor, is the other excessive element in "Richard Redpath." He has little function apart from providing what at first seems intended as comic relief. Shields, noting how "confusing, incomplete, and mysterious" this character is, speculates that Moodie may have "originally conceived a more ambitious role for Levi" but had "difficulty assimilating him into her fictional world" (1977, 18–19). Sending "Richard Redpath" to Bentley, Moodie provides the key to Levi's character: "The *Jew Editor*, is a true picture drawn from life, which so closely resembles the original, that it will be recognized by all who ever knew him, or fell under his lash. A man *detested* in his day and generation" (letter 54). Benjamin Levi's career parallels that of George Benjamin, who moved to Belleville in 1834 to start a conservative newspaper. Mackenzie Bowell, Benjamin's successor, acknowledged the accuracy of the portrait by referring to "the old office which was immortalized by the novelist in her Richard Redpath."[29] Benjamin, native of Sussex, was founding first master of the Orange Lodge of Belleville in 1834 and chief aid of Edmund Murney in the elections of 1841 and 1842. While few issues of Benjamin's newspaper have survived, J.W.D. Moodie's role as returning officer in those elections must have been censured in its pages. In "Richard Redpath" Moodie for the first time uses writing to retaliate directly against an individual who has offended her: "At least in fiction, Susanna could deliver Benjamin of his comeuppance."[30] Levi is the butt of gratuitous anti-semitism. The ignominious death from fright she finishes him with is her only departure from her original. By the early 1840s she had found that prose as well as verse could be used as a weapon.

Levi's journalism receives inordinate attention in "Richard Redpath." His newspaper is "a violent party paper, ... a perfect sink of iniquity, a receptacle for all that was low in morals and base in practice"; it is a medium for "the most malicious slanders ... falsehoods and artful insinuations." While Benjamin and his newspaper opposed the reform cause, Levi and his oppose the anti-slavery cause. Levi denounces abolitionists as "traitors to Great Britain, and enemies to their country" (483), the same charges that Tories in the early 1840s aimed at reformers. By switching the issue, Moodie establishes a basis for condemning her target with which most Canadians would concur, so avoiding the more contentious Tory/reform struggle. Her attack on the conservative Belleville paper cannot be construed as evidence of reform sympathies, since in "Tom Wilson's Emigration," written in the same period, she singles out the Cobourg *Reformer* for "the vulgar abuse that defiled every page" (*RI*, 83).

The politicization of the colonial press began with reform agitation in the mid 1820s. The administration thought "the many reform newspapers in Upper Canada ... were consciously fanning 'the rage of contending factions.'" Tories felt "that the distinction between liberty of the press and licentiousness was all too often lost."[31] The destruction of Mackenzie's press in 1826 is a concrete image of a hegemonic faction using the alibi of journalistic scurrility to control the press. Moodie habitually links "the glorious privilege" of the freedom of the colonial press with its "disgraceful abuse":

in a colony ... men may call one another liars, and thieves, and traitors in print, without the least fear of punishment.

Men, in Canada, may call one another rogues and miscreants ... through the medium of the newspapers ... without any dread of the horsewhip.

There is no restraint upon the freedom of the press in Canada. Men ... often run mad in the exuberance of their liberty, if you may judge of their sanity by the intemperate language used in these local journals.[32]

If the press had become as moral as she wanted, attacks on her husband would have ceased. But the opposition, reform or Tory, would also have lost one of its main outlets.

Since her portrait of Benjamin as Levi "is a true picture," disguised, moreover, as fiction, Moodie could believe it free of the slanderousness she criticizes. She rewrites the facts of Benjamin's career within the values of her fiction. From this period on her protestations concerning the truth of what she writes become particularly defensive. At the same time as she begins to write directly autobiographical fiction, she begins to write aggressively ideological fiction. Definition of self accompanies definition of other. "Canadian Sketches" and "Scenes in Canada" appear in 1847. Peterman connects these sketches to "a burst of autobiographical writing she seems to have begun in the mid-1840s" (1983, 83). His explanation is sound: "This interesting shift from novels to autobiography may have owed something to Moodie's age, her distance from the great adventure and sorrow of her life – emigration, and the fact that she saw before her an inescapable 'Canadian' destiny" (98 n 58). This shift also signals her acceptance that the ideal cannot solve the real. In these sketches she grapples openly with her life and contemporaries while employing techniques developed in her fiction.

The prose sketches on Canada had verse precursors. Apart from nature poems and political poems, Moodie wrote a number of Canadian poems that are dramatic. These include "The Sleigh-Bells," "The Canadian Herd-Boy," and "The Canadian Woodsman," published in 1833–34, and "The Fisherman's Light," "The Canadian Hunter's Song," and "The Dying Hunter to His Dog," all in the *Garland* in 1843. Focusing on specific characters, she avoids the vagueness of her nature poems set in Canada; presenting the characters as typical, she escapes the occasional quality of her political poems. All but "The Canadian Herd-Boy" are included in *Roughing It*, and that poem becomes part of *Life in the Clearings*. In the nineteenth century these were her most frequently reprinted poems, and among them are her only poems to survive into twentieth-century anthologies. In the three earlier poems she depicts scenes of cheerfulness in the wild. "The Canadian Woodsman" explicitly states the lesson, beginning with an injunction: "Son of the isles! rave not to me/Of the old world's pride and luxury" (ll. 1–2). The speaker, striving to be "contented in my rugged cot" (l. 25), presents one side of an argument between opposed responses to Canada. "The Fisherman's Light" and "The Canadian Hunter's Song" dramatize the acquisition of provisions. Only "The Dying Hunter to His Dog" conveys the melancholy of so many of her poems. But the hunter is resigned to his death and reminisces on the excitements of the hunt, which his dog survives to experience again. In "The Sleigh-Bells" and "The Canadian Hunter's Song" the poetic persona awaits the return of the absent male. In "The Canadian Herd-Boy" and "The Fisherman's Light" the poet observes the activities of others. "The Canadian Woodsman" and "The Dying Hunter" use male personae. In none of these poems does the poet occupy the centre of activity. Moodie is absent from the drama of her Canadian dramatic poems.

This passive stance continues into "Old Woodruff and His Three Wives," the first "Canadian Sketch." After opening with a description of the title character, the narrator reins herself in: "But to begin at the beginning, for I have a little outrun my story."[33] The beginning she returns to is the eve of her departure from the bush. She has been summoned by her husband to Belleville. The remaining first half of the sketch concerns the preparations made for her by her brother and his superintendence of their trip. She counterpoints this documentary frame with Woodruff's story. Half-way through the sketch the group arrives at Woodruff's and, after referring to her introductory portrait, the narrator records the dialogue between him and her brother. This exchange leads into Woodruff's narrative of matrimonial vicissitudes, a contrived monologue despite its colloquialisms, especially in contrast with the dialogue preceding it. Woodruff's story touches motifs found throughout Moodie's work: his first marriage was to a cousin for his uncle's money; this wife died in childbirth; his second was to a beautiful madwoman who killed herself; because of his second marriage, his uncle threatened to disinherit him; in revenge for his third marriage, his uncle "married his housekeeper, by whom he had soon a large young family" (180); a partner ran off with all of Woodruff's money, leaving him their joint debts. It was only at this juncture, in 1832, that he immigrated to Canada.

Woodruff is one of the few individuals named in *Roughing It* who has not been identified.[34] Moodie designates his story, simply, "A Canadian Sketch," suggesting that it precedes her conception of a series of these pieces. Her main deletion from "Old Woodruff and His Three Wives" when it is transformed into her last chapter in *Roughing It* is of Woodruff's story, which she passes over: "then he told us the history of his several ventures in matrimony, with which I shall not trouble my readers."[35] Considering Susanna Strickland's loose use of the term "sketch" to cover both fiction and non-fiction, the recurrence in this text of motifs from her fiction, the British setting, and her use of Woodruff to illustrate one of her common themes – "'What an unfeeling wretch!' thought I" (182) – "Old Woodruff and His Three Wives" likely vacillates between fiction and documentary. She retains the framework of this story in *Roughing It*, but drops Woodruff's narrative, as his original, if he had one, has disappeared from the historical record. Like the narrator of "The Two Fishermen," his level of reality is that of a person she knew who inspired her to create a story for him and have him relate it orally. A fictional core resides within the layers of the narrative.

With "The Walk to Dummer" Moodie pluralizes the subtitle and begins numeration. "Canadian Sketches. No. II" is more typical of the series than is "Old Woodruff." In this sketch she is an active participant, not just the passive poetic persona of the dramatic poems or the contriver of the occasion for the story of Old Woodruff. She unites techniques for self-dramatization adumbrated separately in "Matrimonial Speculations" and "Richard Redpath." Through narrative interjections and the story of a mission of mercy, she creates a linguistic presence for herself as she places others. The identities of the characters in this sketch, Jenny Buchanan, Emilia Shairp, Thomas Traill, and Captain and Mrs Lloyd, are well established.[36] Moodie's character appears in relief through the portraits of Jenny and Mrs Lloyd.

Although Captain Lloyd's career resembles Lieutenant Moodie's, she establishes the differences that will prevent her domestic life from ever plummeting to the alcoholic depths Mrs Lloyd's has.[37] In this sketch she develops the basic structure for the remaining four "Canadian Sketches." She introduces a character or set of characters and proceeds to dramatize her interactions with them. In "Our Borrowing" and "Uncle Joe and His Family" she is the main focal point in her battles with groups of vulgar neighbours. In "Tom Wilson's Emigration" and "Brian, the Still Hunter" the title characters bear the weight of their sketches, as these failed English gentlemen become proxies for the narrator. The sketches outline a character system with affinities to that in *Mark Hurdlestone* and *Geoffrey Moncton*. This character system is completed in the expansion of the sketches into *Roughing It*, where the narrator's main dilemma is her search for a stable position within the system of values she generates to account for her world.

In mid-1847, as Moodie was submitting the final "Canadian Sketch" to Lovell, she and her husband were at last acting on the idea she raised in 1839 of editing their own periodical. The opening editorial of the *Victoria Magazine*, "To the Public," hedges on its relationship to the *Literary Garland*, since the latter was her only paying venue at the time. The Moodies do not wish to rival "any other magazine in Canada," and Mrs Moodie will continue "her long connection with the 'Garland'" (*VM*, 1). The cheapness of their "periodical for the people" will allow it to circulate among poorer settlers, especially "among that most numerous and not least respected class of [their] fellow Colonists, – the rural population of the Province." The prospectus praises farming as a pastoral occupation "calculated to form a great, virtuous and intelligent reflective character" (2). By their last "Editor's Table" the Moodies have also acquired "the hope of inducing a taste for polite literature among the working classes" (287). They identified a market niche, but never reached it.[38]

The actual target audience of the *Victoria Magazine* was more restricted than that broadly appealed to by its editors in their initial address "To the Public." The Moodies edited the magazine for readers like themselves, those seeking an imaginative return to England, not naturalized Canadian farmers or recent working-class immigrants. Their readership can be assessed from the list of subscribers they provide in the last number. It is sprinkled with ministers and doctors, members of parliament and military officers, spinsters and widows. The Toronto subscribers are especially interesting. Along with Robert Baldwin is his solicitor general, William Hume Blake, but also John Beverley Robinson and Bishop Strachan. The *Victoria Magazine* did not cut across class lines but did straddle the narrow party lines of the late 1840s.

Moodie's "Scenes in Canada" are two of the few Canadian pieces in the *Victoria Magazine*. The "Scenes" follow a procedure different from the "Canadian Sketches." The dramatic incidents they contain are submerged within the narrator's reactions to the St Lawrence scenery. Just once more, when describing Niagara Falls, would she depict the sublime in Canadian nature as in these texts:

a thrill of wonder and delight pervaded my mind; the spectacle floated dimly on my sight, for my eyes were blinded with tears; – blinded with the excess of beauty. ("A Visit to Grosse Isle," 15)

How the mind naturally expands with the sublimity of the magnificent objects presented to your view, and soars upward in gratitude and adoration to the Author of all being, to thank Him, for having made this lower world so wonderous fair. ("Quebec," 65)

Each of these prose landscapes includes a mob scene. In the first Irish immigrants cavort on Grosse Isle; in the second the ship's steerage passengers panic after a collision in the night. In one way, then, the "Scenes" resemble the "Sketches." The narrator achieves self-identity by contrasting herself with those around her: she is the one to experience rapture before sublime scenery, while the lower orders swarm uncontrollably. Scenery and mob only supply occasions for her display of sensibility. The Irish travelling in steerage made up a larger portion of immigrants than any other group, especially during the "Great Hunger" of 1847. The first issue of the *Victoria Magazine*, the Grosse Isle scene in its middle, would not have gained it readers among this segment of the population.

The sketch is an amorphous genre. Before Moodie the term had been applied to a great variety of things, so it is unnecessary to posit a specific influence behind those of her texts to which the label can legitimately be applied. She did not apprentice herself to any writer. Her sketches are significant because in them she more directly represents her immediate dilemmas than in her fiction. In much of her fiction prior to the "Canadian Sketches" she seeks techniques for literary self-representation, either through displaced portraits of her youth or through disguised portraits of her contemporaries. Turning to the sketch, she drops the more conscious elements of the disguise. As Gerson points out, she "took no risks by attempting to transplant to Canadian soil the complex plots and stereotyped characters required by the sentimental novel" (1989, 43). Sufficient generations had not passed to provide a sense of society, stratified society, upon which that type of novel could be based. Through the sketch's lack of conventional strictures, she freed herself from the ideal so she could confront realities around her.

Moodie's use of the sketch was transitional. She published eight texts on Canada in 1847, then returned the next year to fiction, now unequivocally autobiographical. The serialization of "Rachel Wilde, or Trifles from the Burthen of a Life" began in January in the *Victoria Magazine*. This story expands on the background of Rachel Beauchamp in "Matrimonial Speculations." It covers Rachel's life from age six to twelve, from 1809 to 1815. Her father "lost a large fortune" and "purchased a small estate in the country," where he planned to superintend the education of his children. From "a well-furnished library" they read history, Shakespeare, the *Iliad*, Milton, and "musty magazines of the last century."[39] Rachel and Dorothea, representing Catharine, begin writing verse at a young age. The other children include Lilla for Eliza, Ann for Agnes, Selina for Sarah, and two unnamed younger brothers. Disaster overtakes Mr Wilde: "Her father had given his name as security to a gentleman, nearly related to his wife, who betrayed his trust, and dragged his generous benefactor down in his own ruin" (145). His health broken, he spends his time in a nearby city trying to recover his loss. Rachel and Dorothea continue their studies under their elder sister and begin writing stories on paper found in a "great Indian chest" (146). The last episode concerns Lilla's discovery and mockery of Rachel's "sacred Manuscript" (149). "Rachel Wilde," diffuse and plotless throughout, is brought to an arbitrary close with reference to the heroine's future literary fame and her decision to give it up for love, marriage, and the emigration thus entailed.[40]

Moodie reconstructs her girlhood as that of a young artist. Three incidents illustrate the chastening of Rachel's creative spirit: she is rebuked for her childhood drama; she is punished for drawing on wet paint; she is scorned for her first story. As an outcast artist Rachel worships the fallen angels, Napoleon, and Milton's Satan. She is "a solitary child ... with a mysterious consciousness of the great mystery of life" (138). Violent storms inspire her to "wild unmeasured, unwritten, spontaneous bursts of song." Like Anthony's Juliet, to Rachel "lofty visions ... came unbidden" (139): the outcast as visionary. At the commencement of her and Dorothea's writing, the narrator projects their future as authors: "The love and approbation of the few, and the envy and hatred of the many. To resign the joys of the present, and to live alone for the future. To be the scorn of vulgar and common minds; the dread of the weak and sensitive, to stand alone and without sympathy, misunderstood and maligned by most of their species" (147). While Rachel and Susanna gave up writing for love, the latter returned to it, and this description of the British romantic writer's relationship to society also applies to her place in Belleville. This story, in her periodical, might even broaden the horizons of the locals so that they could appreciate her.

Margot Northey, connecting the conception of the writer in "Rachel Wilde" to Moodie's sense of exile in Canada, argues "that the feelings of isolation, misinterpretation, and exile she expresses in *Roughing It in the Bush* are not simply a reaction to her particular physical circumstances but also a long-standing, inward-looking response to her vision of herself as artist" (1984, 125). Northey attributes this vision to something inherent in Moodie's psyche, that of "an exceptional spirit, driven by her own imagination, emotion, and spiritual sensibility" (120). The story provides evidence of more material determinants. While her life at home is idyllic, Rachel's first trip away involves her in social conflict. Taken by the friend she is travelling with to visit a rich uncle, she rejects him unseen because he is in trade: "Rachel was the daughter of a poor gentleman, had been brought up with very aristocratic notions, and the sight of the shop, called all her pride into active operation" (110). Rachel's hauteur dissolves in a subsequent episode when she enjoys a day spent with the shepherd of her friend's father. This rich gentleman thinks her "an ungrateful little baggage to prefer the shepherd's cottage to his own handsome house" (135). Her rejection of the tradesman and attraction to the shepherd confuses social class and literary pastoralism. Rachel, from the gentleman's reaction to her enjoyment of his labourer's company, learns "the first worst lesson of humanity": "the hard names that human pride had invented to separate into two distinct species, the rich and the poor" (136). As a guest of the rich gentleman she is treated as a charity case and deserted by all but the animals on the estate. Rachel's isolation is due less to her "spiritual sensibility" than to her being the daughter of a gentleman who had lost caste.

Moodie translates her past as outcast in Rachel's drama, and in the story's other main theme displaces her economic problem. The story begins with a meditation on destiny: "We are all more or less, the creatures of circumstance ... Others have formed links in our destiny ... Our very thoughts are not are own" (98). Landscape shapes character, as do "the pursuits, mode of thinking, nay, even the prejudices of those with whom we pass our early years" (99). She begins this representation of her youth by expounding the determinism consistent in her work from "The Son of Arminius" to "The Miser and His Son." The narrator's next philosophical interlude responds to the betrayal of Rachel by "a domestic slave": "Such neglected beings are more objects of deep compassion, than of thoughtless blame: – while contemplating their unmitigated wretchedness, we strive in vain to solve the great riddle of life" (123). She decides that some are born rich, some poor. When Rachel later asks the shepherd girl why this is, she responds: "'tis God's will, and it must be right; but it seems hard to us who are poor" (131). The narrator surpasses this explanation: "Pride must have broken the ancient bond of unity, which, at some remote period of the world's history, existed between its children" (123).

Rachel herself is guilty of pride. In contrast with Dorothea, who "had a perfect controll over her passions," she cannot see "that her own perverseness drew down upon herself, much of the misery, which shed a doleful gloom upon her mind and character." She fails "to make successful war against the imperfections of her own faulty temper, and ... head-strong passions" (137). Pride is blamed for an isolation partly economic. Following this analysis, Rachel buds as a visionary and begins to listen to "the tempting fiend" of fame (139). She reacts to isolation by becoming an artist. The perfunctory ending of the story attempts to complete the equation. Through her art, Rachel rejoins society: "The world ... gave the meed of praise so long denied." Moodie then invokes love as a supplementary explanation for an isolation unremedied by the recognition of Rachel's talent: "The desire to be loved by one noble heart was dearer to her than ambition, than the applause of the world; and she resigned the tempting wreath it offered her, to follow the adverse fortunes of the beloved – to toil in poverty and sorrow by his side – a stranger and an exile in a foreign land" (150).

Rachel voluntarily affirms her exile for the recompense of love. In fictionalizing her early life Moodie shies from its material determinants. She replaces them with other explanations – pride, vision, love. This juxtaposing of the development of an artist with an exposition of economic determinism, however, reveals much of what she could not write. The determinism of her other fiction is present in "Rachel Wilde"; what is missing is a plot that could redeem determinism by presenting it as Providence. In this respect the text is one of her more realistic. Northey is puzzled that, while the story begins with a discussion of "environmental determinism" (119), "we learn less about how circumstances shape Rachel's character than about how Rachel's temperament and innate sensibilities lead her to act and react as she does" (123). This gap between intention and execution exposes Moodie's blind spot, how reaction to the outside catalyses construction of the inside. When free to invent her plots she demonstrates the existence of a benevolent God. When living the plot out, no such easy solution was available.

Rachel Beauchamp's narrative parallels Susanna Strickland's life to age sixteen. "Rachel Wilde" covers in more detail the same life from six to twelve. The story of Rachel M— is a representation of Susanna Moodie's last months in England, ending when she embarks for a new world. This text became *Flora Lyndsay*, but in the *Literary Garland* in 1851 is another "Trifles from the Burthen of a Life." The same Rachel, now married, is its heroine. Even in its *Garland* form, before being expanded with character sketches, the narrative of the trans-Atlantic voyage, and "Noah Cotton," Rachel M—'s text bears formal similarities with Rachel Wilde's. It too is diffuse and plotless. When Moodie informs Bentley about the manuscript, she acknowledges its incompleteness: "I will send you ... a bundle of droll sketches of our adventures out to Canada and preparations for our emigration and all we met and saw on our voyage. This should have been the commencement of *Roughing It*, for it was written for it, and I took a freak of cutting it out of the MS. and beginning the work at Grosse Isle."[41]

At its end she strains to justify the story as a demonstration of benevolent determinism: "For those who doubt the agency of an overruling providence in the ordinary affairs of life, these trifling reminiscences have been chiefly penned" (239). The passengers on the ship the M—s missed died of cholera; the passengers on the second ship John M— wanted to take "died of small pox." The narrator neglects to ask why Providence deserted those other emigrants but does grasp the meaning of the M—'s safe passage: "How kind was the providence that watched over our poor emigrants" (240). Even with the extension of "Trifles" in *Flora Lyndsay*, safe arrival in Canada is not a happy enough ending to provide retroactively a providential plot. The endings of both story and novel are as arbitrary as that of "Rachel Wilde." While the unity of her fabricated texts redeems determinism by attributing it to

God's design, the honesty of her autobiographical stories would be compromised if they proved something of which she could never be sure – hence her inability to achieve satisfactory closure in these fictions. In her autobiographical fiction, free from the contrivances of plot, she demonstrates the very unprovidential nature of her life.

When Moodie displaces her economic dilemma on to male characters, she is able to resolve that dilemma happily. In "The Vanquished Lion" and "The Broken Mirror" she uses a female character to explore the South African option she did not take. In "The Sailor's Return" she explores another option she did not take by having a female character decline to emigrate with her fiancé. All three of these stories end happily, proving that "Providence is always true to those who are true to themselves." Her first story in the *Victoria Magazine* is her one fictional exploration of the option she did take. "The Well in the Wilderness" is her only fiction set in North America. The benevolent Providence that arranges the happy destinies of her South African immigrants is absent from this story. Wild animals never appear in her Old World fiction. By repeatedly expressing fear for them in her autobiographical work, she makes them emblems of her terror of the unsettled parts of the world. In 1831 Providence was a presence powerful enough to save the mother in "The Vanquished Lion" from the beast in the jungle. Fifteen years from England Moodie writes her most gruesome scene as she describes the mother in "The Well in the Wilderness" being devoured by a cougar "in the centre of a jungle" in the interior of North America.[42] The one time she tried to bring her fiction to her New World home she produced a shocking image of loss of faith in God's ability to engineer happy plots for immigrating heroines. She explores options not taken; she discovers the difficulty of inscribing a benevolent determinism upon her own life; she unravels European romance and replaces it with American tragedy – writing was her way of questioning decisions about her life that she felt she had had no choice but to make.

In her one essay of literary criticism, "A Word for the Novel Writers," published in the *Garland* immediately after "Trifles from the Burthen of a Life," Moodie confounds realism and romance as she had history and romance in her review of Ritchie's book. She defends novels from the charge of immorality by arguing that they instruct by amusing. A good novelist does not, in the interest of didacticism, make "his hero or heroine ... too good for reality," for this would sacrifice the reader's sympathy: "high moral excellence is represented as struggling with the faults and follies common to humanity" (348–9). Fiction acquaints the otherwise smugly insulated middle and upper classes with the degradation that exists around them. But the revelation of depravity must leave no doubt about the outcome: "In the writings of our great modern novelists, virtue is never debased, nor vice exalted." In her view "novels, or romances ... founded upon real incidents," fictions "true to nature," never show vice exalted, for this would be unrealistic. By this theory of fiction the romance resolutions of her stories are strictly realistic. She links the "unnatural" and the "immoral" (348). An immoral novel is an unnatural novel. Ideality in her texts, then, represents reality. Her own life, when she turned to writing about it, could not sustain this conception of reality.

By the end of the 1840s the realities of her publishing relations were impinging on Moodie's literary production. The last "Editor's Table" in the *Victoria Magazine* reveals that the journal is in trouble. After summing up the magazine's first year and projecting its second, the column breaks off: "Since writing the above, it has been deemed advisable not to commence the second volume ... until the first of January, 1849; when some new arrangement will in all probability be made." Either the Moodies will "become both Editor's and Proprietor's" (sic), or they may drop the magazine altogether (288). Problems had developed between them and its publisher, Joseph Wilson. He had been publishing *Wilson's Experiment* for some time and the previous month had begun *Wilson's Canada Casket*, a "Literary Periodical in the shape of a cheap newspaper" of fiction and poetry.[43] He was competing with the magazine the Moodies edited for him. Mrs Moodie would later write that "the failure of its proprietor, who was engaged in several literary speculations, put a stop to its further progress" (Intro to *MH*, 291). Later still she claimed that their subscribers wanted the Moodies to continue the magazine, but "the proprietor was such a dishonest fellow, that [they] declined it altogether" (letter 78). It may be that Wilson was not satisfied with the return he was getting from the *Victoria Magazine* and launched alternative ventures. To his unpaid editors his literary speculations would appear unprincipled. Plans for a second volume of the *Victoria Magazine* were dropped.

The *Victoria Magazine* would have been unprofitable for the same reasons that made the *Literary Garland*'s demise imminent. Klinck writes that the *Garland* was "ready for death because of something insecure in its British connection" (1965, 161). With an indigenous business and professional class led by Baldwin and Lafontaine, MacNab and Cartier, taking the United Province into the exercise of responsible government without damaging its colonial status, artificial encouragement of British culture became unnecessary. The wave of immigrants from the 1830s were assimilating to North American ways. Moodie resisted assimilation by reprinting British poems and writing British romances, but those interested in reading them were declining in number. Not all literary critics in the *Garland* confused realism and romance. Perhaps an oblique comment on "Jane Redgrave" since it falls between instalments of this fiction, W.P.C.'s essay "Our Literature Present and Prospective" complains that "of late, our manner of reading has, I fear, included too much of the ideal and romantic, and too little of the real and practical" (1848, 246). His or her call for more attention to colonial history shows a distaste for the attempt to transplant British culture in the colony.

During the *Victoria Magazine*'s existence, "Brian, the Still Hunter" was the only wholly new work by Moodie published in the *Literary Garland*. Internal temporal indicators in *Roughing It* imply that she produced it in 1849 and 1850, and in each of these years she gave Lovell just one new poem. She may already have been negotiating British book publication of periodical work. Five new prose texts in the *Garland*'s last volume become part of either *Life in the Clearings* or *Flora Lyndsay*. Her claim that one of these, "Trifles from the Burthen of a Life," was written for *Roughing It* suggests that by March 1851, when its serialization began, she had a commitment from Bentley to consider a work on Canada. While the *Garland*'s last issue was being published in Montreal in December 1851, *Roughing It* was being printed in London. The British ideal might yet save Moodie from her colonial reality.

6 Truths and Opinions: Literary Production 1852-1855

Susanna Moodie produced six books between 1852 and 1855, all derived from periodical publications of the previous decade. They consolidated the creative work of her forties. Her imaginative struggle for a stable identity is at its most intense in *Roughing It in the Bush*, the focus of the next chapter, where she balances precariously between dissolution and dogmatism. Her clearest expression of the personal truths upon which she was able, that book behind her, to pin her conception of self and society is *Life in the Clearings*. She did not distinguish between these personal opinions or truths and verifiable facts, and she defends the one as if it were the other by claiming that she only writes the truth.

Challenges to Moodie's work may have begun as early as her "true picture" of George Benjamin in "Richard Redpath." Benjamin's long and distinguished public career in elected and appointed positions is evidence that many people did not share her opinion of him. Even her husband, ten years after the contentious elections that brought him to the pillory of the Tory press, does not substantiate her venomous portrait; he refers to "G. Benjamin, Esq. ... to whose business talents and public spirit the country is largely indebted for its progress in internal improvements."[1]

Moodie's first essay of social commentary, "Education the True Wealth of the World," begins with an epigraph invoking "Truth, wisdom, virtue, the eternal three."[2] She opens her first autobiographical fiction, "Rachel Wilde," with an epigraph linking fiction and truth:

Fiction, however wild and fanciful,
Is but the copy memory draws from truth;

'Tis not in human genius *to create*;
The mind is but a mirror, which reflects
Realities that are. (98)

These lines recall the theory of fiction of "A Word for the Novel Writers,"
and indeed she uses them as the epigraph for that essay as well.[3] Since
her fiction embodied truth, so must her sketches. How disconcerted
she must have been, then, by "A Hint to Whom It May Concern," a
condemnation of her *Garland* sketch "Michael Macbride" in *The True
Witness and Catholic Chronicle*. The anonymous author questions "her
reputation for ... truthfulness" and attacks this English Protestant
characterization of Irish Catholics.

The events in "Michael Macbride" probably happened much as
Moodie relates them. But why did she select these events to write about?
She had wanted "Michael Macbride" to be a chapter in *Roughing It,*
and it has similarities with "Phoebe H–, and Our Second Moving." Both
sketches depict the deathbed scenes of unfortunate youths as Moodie
defies their mothers to read to them from the Bible, after which they
die in peace. Phoebe's mother is a Yankee atheist, Michael's an Irish
Catholic. These sketches contrast the ignorance of women who will not
trust in the efficacy of the Word of God with Moodie's own piety. In
her alignment of race and religion, her opposition of self and other, she
ties these sketches to her own specific position. She supplies a chapter
to replace "Michael Macbride," which she "had supressed, on account
of the Catholics, who considered that story as written against them,
although in every particular, *it was strictly true*" (letter 44). She cleaves
to her writing as true and not, in her very selection of events for "story,"
directed from her own ideological position.

The epigraph to *Roughing It* anticipates criticism and mounts a pre-
emptive defence:

I sketch from Nature, and the picture's true;
Whate'er the subject, whether grave or gay,
Painful experience in a distant land
Made it mine own.

Roughing It is only half set in the bush, so when Moodie calls it "a faithful
picture of a life in the backwoods" (489), another kind of selection is
operating. In *Life in the Clearings* she refers to "ten years ... residence in
the woods of Douro" (17) and claims that "when the greatest portion of
'Roughing it in the Bush' was written, [she] was totally ignorant of life
in Canada, as it existed in the towns and villages" (12). The Moodies
spent only six years in the bush. She did not recommence writing prose
until Lovell requested material for the *Garland* late in 1838. She herself

says that *Mark Hurdlestone* was "the *first*, of a series, that employed [her] pen during the long winter evenings of 1838-9 ... in the bush."[4] The prose pieces at the core of *Roughing It* do not appear until seven years into her residence in Belleville. The book was not compiled until the end of the 1840s; she could have factored in the broader awareness of life in the colony gained from ten years in Belleville. But *Roughing It* had to be the naive and limited view of a heroine isolated in the elemental wilderness.

Writing to Bentley of the abuse of her book in the Canadian press, Moodie claims that she has "said nothing of them beyond the truth, nor told half of what could, and ought to be said, of their unfaithful dealings, and utter disregard of all honorable feelings. ... It is *God's truth*" (letter 45). Sixteen years later she still calls the text a "true picture of [their] life and experience while residing among the grand old woods" (letter 89). Canadian reviewers found a great disparity between their view of the colony and hers. The truths she deals in could only be partial. Despite the multiplicity of quotidian truth, she claims a prerogative upon it as her sole defence against those who disagree with her.

The reception of *Roughing It* is inscribed upon *Life in the Clearings*. Between his first two issues of Moodie's first Canadian book, Bentley asked for a "picture of the state of society in the large towns and cities of Canada," one that would "present them ... as they were years ago and as they are now." This "picture" would be a "pendant" to the other Canadian text (quoted in *Letters*, 110). He wanted a text to compensate for the partiality of *Roughing It*, perhaps one short enough to include as a supplement to a reissue. Moodie initially responds that she "will think over the new Canadian work" (letter 45), but her next letter is more enthusiastic:

> It will give me great pleasure, to try and meet your wishes with regard to another book on Canada, and I send you a few pages which I wrote the other day, as a sort of introduction to such a book ... My idea was, to describe as much of the country, as I could in my trip to Niagara ... introducing as many incidents and anecdotes illustrative of the *present state* of *Canada*, as I could collect or remember, to form a sort of apendix to *Roughing It in the Bush*. (letter 46)

Having sent a manuscript to Bentley, she requests that it "be termed, as a companion to the other, 'The Clearings versus the Bush or Life in Canada,' – a Sequel to *Roughing It* etc" (letter 47). When reviews of the "Sequel" indicate that it is "a failure," she is surprised: "This seems strange, as it really is equal to *Roughing It* in every respect, that I can see. Had they made a *whole*, instead of separate works, we should have found it equally successful" (letter 49). But for her "freak of cutting it out," *Flora Lyndsay* would have been the beginning of *Roughing It*.

These three texts, *Flora Lyndsay*, *Roughing It*, and *Life in the Clearings*, constitute Moodie's Canadian trilogy, and contain all of the prose she devoted to the colony and much of the poetry. None of them, however, is an integrated whole, unified by a conscious intention. They are instalments in a serial writing project, a project directed at bringing her truth into alignment with the truth of the society around her, a project as unfinished and contingent as the life it shadows, the history it attempts to capture, and the truth it stakes its integrity upon.

Roughing It frames *Life in the Clearings*. The epigraph from the former reappears on the title-page of the latter. In the first sentence of the introduction Moodie refers to *Roughing It*, where she "endeavoured to draw a picture of Canadian life ... in the Backwoods" (9). She ends this introduction claiming to have "been repeatedly asked, since the publication of 'Roughing it in the Bush,' to give an account of the present state of society in the colony" (13). In the epigraph to the conclusion she sounds a familiar note, now more militantly:

Why dost thou fear to speak the honest truth?
Speak boldly, fearlessly, what thou think'st right,
And time shall justify thy words and thee!

S.M. (324)

Her marginal – epigraphic and epistolary – assertions of the veracity of text and author finally, in this conclusion, occupy the centre as she mounts a public defence of all she has made: "I have written what I consider to be the truth" (329). She turns on her attackers: "In 'Roughing it in the Bush,' I gave an honest personal statement of *facts*. I related nothing but what had really happened" (330). She names and challenges her critics: "I should feel much obliged to the writer in the *London Observer* to enlighten me on this head, or those editors of Canadian papers who, without reading for themselves, servilely copied a *falsehood*" (331). These last pages of *Life in the Clearings*, personal vindication at its most vehement, are inscribed with italics and emotion as she poses her truth against the truths of others.

Alert now to the possibility of others doubting her word, Moodie personally endorses *Flora Lyndsay* when she sends it to Bentley: "The characters and incidents are drawn from life. The book is no fiction" (letter 48). Within the text she says that one character is "no creature of romance," another "actually lived and walked the earth" (16, 32). She footnotes a ghost story told by a servant: "I have told the story exactly as it was told to me ... I have no doubt of the truth of the tale" (79). She tersely verifies two incidents with footnotes saying simply, "A fact" (202, 326). Meanwhile, she tells Bentley that other stories she sends are based on "facts" or are "true" (letters 46, 56). It is not necessary to agree with the mother who told her son "that Mrs. M— invented lies" (*LC*, 64) to see that her truths could not transcend the partiality of her personal ideology. Since that ideology was attached to a rising class that had yet to achieve hegemony, members of subservient class fragments were yet able to voice challenges from outside the soon-to-be dominant walls.

By the time she produced *Life in the Clearings* in late 1852, Moodie, at the peak of her reputation, was aligning herself with the status quo as it had congealed in the Canadas by mid-century. Seeing North America free of the rigid British class system, she supported a less institutional-ized form of hierarchy.[5] In "Trifles from the Burthen of a Life," divid-ing "the aristocracy of England" into "that of family, of wealth, and of talent" and arguing that "the one that ranks the last, however, should be the first," she asserts that in "America, the man of money would have it all his own way" (183). Despite "the mixed society" described in *Life in the Clearings*, "the lady and gentleman in Canada are as dis-tinctly marked as elsewhere. There is no mistaking the superiority that mental cultivation bestows" (59–60). She cannot acknowledge social equality, but preaches equality before God.[6] Convinced of the eternal necessity of there being rulers and ruled, she argues that "equality of station is a dream ... The rich and the educated will never look upon the poor and ignorant as their equals" (332–3). She justifies hierarchy as a principle of stability, and gives education and talent a place near the pinnacle that wealth was beginning to dominate.

During the production of *Life in the Clearings* Moodie was secure in her sense of belonging to a talented and educated elite. Lovell and Gibson of the *Literary Garland* printed all she sent them. She blamed the failure of the *Victoria Magazine* on its publisher. Her revived British career seemed destined for success, as she felt obliged to tell Bentley when she sent him *Mark Hurdlestone*: "*Roughing It in the Bush*, if I may judge from the reviews that have reached the Colony, has met with a favorable reception in England" (letter 44). She apprises him of the existence of eight more volume-length fictions ready for his press. She is flattered at having had *Roughing It* pirated by Putnam and spoken of "*most highly*" in the American press (letter 45). *Life in the Clearings*, compiled before she saw the bad reviews of *Mark Hurdlestone*, is the work of a writer who anticipates success throughout the English-reading world – except where she lives.

Moodie put together *Life in the Clearings* before 1853. The introduction, dated a day prior to the letter presenting Bentley with a "few pages" to see if they met his requirements, is likely the "sort of introduction" to which this letter refers (letter 46). Parts of the conclusion had been published in 1848. More than a third of the prose and most of the poetry had been previously published.[7] *Life in the Clearings* shares a haphazard and miscellaneous composition with *Roughing It*, but there are significant differences between the two texts. Signs of Moodie's belief in the previous book's success are in its sequel. She replaces the tense uncertainty of her Upper Canadian story of struggle in the Cobourg clearing and Douro bush with the banal complacency of an account of society in Canada West. There are no dramatic scenes of a heroine battling vulgar neighbours or a hostile nature. The one exception, "Michael Macbride," was intended for the other book. She presents character sketches like "Jeanie Burns" and "Grace Marks" as second-hand accounts. She makes no attempt to create a space for herself in the narrative, writes no dramas of self and other like those from the later 1840s. *Life in the Clearings* "is written more with a view to convey general impressions, than to delineate separate features" (252). By the time she puts it together she knows where she stands, and from that place she expounds her ideas of Canada to a British audience, with a sideways glance at her fellow colonials, hoping they too might benefit from her truths.

The colonials who could learn from Moodie are not those who, like Robert Baldwin, J.B. Robinson, or Egerton Ryerson, share her faith in the professional elite, but rather those who would prolong civil strife and interfere with the middle class's success in clinching hegemony.[8] While her social commentary does not extend the middle-class orthodoxy as it was developing, in *Life in the Clearings* she surely captures a nascent consensus. She comments on the family and social relations, literature and the arts, churches, political parties, the press, schools, the legal system, and labour. In the conclusion, momentarily forgetting that her book is being published in London, she summarizes one of her intentions: "These remarks are made with no ill-will, but with a sincere hope that they may prove beneficial to the community at large, and be the means of removing some of the evils which are to be found in our otherwise pleasant and rapidly-improving society" (329). By the end of the book it is clear that most of the evils to be removed arise from the persistence of other class factions in challenging the middle-class claim to hegemony.

In *Life in the Clearings* Moodie is often contradictory, as when discussing domestic relations. "The harmony that reigns among members of a Canadian family is truly delightful," and due to "the perfect equality on which children stand in a family, the superior claim of eldership ... never being enforced," she states at one point (60). "Age in Canada is seldom honoured," she later complains, and describes situations, "especially [among] the middle class," where "the mother ... almost invariably holds a subordinate position in her wealthier son or daughter's family" (325, 324). In the first discussion she favourably contrasts Canadian customs with those "upheld at home" (60); in the second she misses how "these things [are] ordered" in her "own country" (325). While she is happy to have "seldom found a real Canadian ashamed of owning a poor relation," she derogates them for fostering the "evil" of "the careless, disrespectful manner often used ... by children to their parents" (60, 329). The gap is between an equality among kin regardless of status and an equality that disregards the wisdom of the aged. The contradiction arises from her desire to elevate experience and education to a status equal to wealth.

Treating social relations, Moodie discusses drunkenness as it is linked to the family. "Alas! this frightful vice of drinking prevails throughout the colony," she writes. A domestic offender, the drunkard is "an active instrument in the ruin of himself and family" (68). She does not think temperance societies or legislation will eradicate drinking, and argues for fighting it where it has its worst effect: "we must prepare our children from their earliest infancy to resist the growing evil"; "Teach the child to pray against drunkenness, as he would against murder, lying, and theft" (71). The family is a site for social indoctrination. She ties drunkenness to caste: "nor is it exhibited by the lower classes in so shameless a manner as by the gentlemen settlers, from whom a better example might be expected." She attributes the prevalence of this "dreadful vice" among gentlemen to the "demoralizing" influence of the bush (12). She connects drink to a dominant theme in her writing on class in Canada, one reiterated when she defends *Roughing It* in *Life in the Clearings*. Her first book on Canada "was written as a warning to well-educated persons not to settle in localities for which they were unfitted by their *previous habits and education*" (330). Members of "the higher class" should "leave to the hardy labourer the place assigned to him by Providence" as "pioneer in the great wilderness."[9] Gentlemen should come to the colonies either to become speculators or to take cleared farms. They will thus contribute to civilizing society rather than participate in barbarizing it at the edges.

Moodie stratifies the very topography of the colony. She draws from her personal response to the bush as expressed in *Roughing It* a more generalized account for *Life in the Clearings*. After a paragraph on "the uniformity dreary in the extreme" of Canadian forests, she enters her caution: "those who look for an Arcadia of fruits and flowers in the Backwoods of Canada cannot fail of disappointment." When she describes "the blank look of desolation that pervades all new settlements," she entwines society and geography: because "property is constantly changing owners," settlers do not, as the English gentry whose land "remains for ages in the same family," bother to improve their estates.[10] Here is the aesthetic argument for primogeniture. The free circulation of land leads to a failure to beautify holdings.

The same values inform her descriptions of longer-settled areas. The land from Queenston to Niagara, one of the earliest-occupied regions and location of Carleton's first capital, "might justly be termed the garden of Canada, and partakes more of the soft and rich character of English scenery." The estates in this area, passing from generation to generation, have been nurtured to take on "an appearance of wealth and comfort, which cannot exist for many years to come in more remote districts" (295). Her description of another ex-capital carries similar overtones: "The streets are wide and well paved, and there are a great many trees in and about Kingston, which give to it the appearance of a European town" (190). The pinnacle of this topology linking length of settlement, the Old World, and class is reserved for the present capital and its immediate successor: "In large cities, like Montreal and Toronto, the higher classes are as refined and intellectual as ladies and gentlemen at home, and spend their lives much in the same manner. Their houses abound in all the elegancies and luxuries of life, and to step into their drawing-rooms you would imagine yourself still in England."[11] Although the colony is subject to levelling influences, one need only follow the lay of the land to rise from the demoralized, drunken gentleman and rude labourer in the wilderness to the urban gentry's drawing-room, where one would not know that one had left class-bound England. The comfort and refinement of "the higher classes" brings order to a society that must encompass the desolate bush of "the hardy labourer."

Moodie's remarks on literature and the arts in the colony convey her sense of the gulf between urban and rural. She ties her essay "A Word for the Novel Writers" to the setting of the chapter it becomes by mentioning "the handsome, well-supplied book stores" she was surprised to find in Toronto. That these bookstores flourish "speaks well for the mental improvement of Canada" since "some years ago."[12] The incongruity of this statement with the text's other discussion of colonial authorship is accounted for by the cultural contrast between city and settlement. Unable to find any in the Belleville area who could understand her role as author, she eulogizes "the unfortunate Dr. Huskins, late of Frankfort on the river Trent." One of the "unhappy fraternity" of writers, "he found very few who could appreciate or understand his mental superiority" and drank himself to death before he could "remove to a more favourable spot" (66, 67). She makes similar remarks on the other arts in Canada, writing, for instance, that "the opportunities of visiting the theatre ... only can be enjoyed by those who reside in the *cities* of Canada" (91). At an exhibition of Paul Kane's paintings at the agricultural show in Toronto, rather than describing the paintings, she is preoccupied with a man, "in the grey homespun of the country," whose manners on shoving her aside are worse than a bear's (286). In one respect, however, even towns like Belleville are becoming more refined: "You will find a piano in every wealthy Canadian's house, and even in the dwellings of most of the respectable mechanics."[13] There is hope that the clearings will take some of the roughness off the bush.

Describing manners in colonial society, Moodie again discloses her ambivalence. She mentions the repugnance the new immigrant is apt to experience at "the mixed society," then excuses that society: "A certain mixture of the common and the real, of the absurd and the ridiculous, gives a zest to the cold, tame decencies to be found in more exclusive and refined circles" (59). According to her, "the pretence and affected airs of importance, occasionally met with" are imported by immigrants who did not have just claim to them "at home" (60). At public balls she also encounters a "very mixed company," but each stratum keeps apart from the others, not even dancing at the same time (89). The one "affectionate, time-honoured, hospitable custom" of which she "cordially approve[s]" is that of the New Year's Day round of visiting. She admits there "may be some reasonable truth" to the complaint that "it gives a number of vulgar, under-bred men, the opportunity of introducing themselves to the notice and company" of genteel daughters, yet would not have it discontinued for this alone.[14] She is displeased excessively when she subsequently describes children's parties as "very pernicious." They "bring to maturity the seeds of *evil*," she claims, referring to the "flippancy" and "vanity" that young girls learn at them.[15] Neither does she have any liking for the week of receptions that newly wed brides endure, calling it a "trying piece of ceremonial" and "stiff complimentary nonsense" (326).

Moodie reserves her greatest chagrin for an "absurd custom[]" not restricted to the colony, "that of *wearing mourning for the dead!*" to which she devotes a chapter (161). Ostentatious and vain, like children's parties and wedding receptions, this custom she also considers superstitious and hypocritical. Her final argument is that it ignores the one form of social equality she has held from her earliest poems, that of "death, the great equalizer" (80): "the soul of man is of no rank, but of equal value in our eyes, whether belonging to rich or poor" (171). The custom of prolonged mourning also transgresses against her cherished belief that death is "a benignant angel, wiping away all tears, healing all pain, burying in oblivion all sorrow and care, calming every turbulent passion, and restoring man, reconciled to his Maker, to a state of purity and peace" (163). From the period of her evangelicism, when she was unwilling to dispute differences "on *doctrinal points*" with her Unitarian friend Bird, she had conceded that heaven's peace is attainable by all Christians, and she maintains this latitudinarian stance with the grieving Catholic mother of Michael Macbride: "It is not a question of creeds that is here to be determined, as to which is the best – yours or mine," she tells her; "I trust that all the faithful followers of Christ, however named, hold the same faith, and will be saved by the same means" (219). She none the less insists that the Bible, read by her to Michael, is a more effective means of introducing him to the presence of his maker than is extreme unction administered by a priest.

Moodie's Christian faith exists apart from her awareness of the church as a social institution in the colony. In the chapter "Camp Meetings" she relates a number of anecdotes told to her of the time before there were churches in Belleville, "and the travelling Methodist ministers used to pitch their tents on these plains, and preach night and day" (140). Samuel Strickland, in 1853 recounting how he did not see one Church of England minister in the Guelph area twenty years earlier, plaintively asks, "Why are we always the last to send labourers into the vineyard? No sooner does a small village ... spring up in the woods, than you find a Presbyterian, Methodist, or Baptist Church ... No wonder ... our church is losing ground." Others observed the same process.[16] While Anglican clergy were delivering sermons on public occasions to an educated Tory elite in the larger settlements, the Methodists and Baptists were carrying their missions to the Indians and pioneers. The Methodist Episcopal preachers whose "fanaticism and religious enthusiasm" she describes were from the United States (140). Their Yankee background partly explains the condescension that Moodie, who might have been sympathetic to their enthusiasm, displays towards the camp preachers. By the 1850s she had seen how lack of loyalty and orderliness could threaten Christian society and may have come to see Methodist enthusiasm as a dangerous extreme challenging the broad Protestant centre, which could only be held by the older churches, established or not.[17] The loyalty of Methodists in Upper Canada was suspect until mid-century.

When she writes of the Belleville churches, Moodie deals at length with the English Methodists: "The Wesleyans who have been of infinite use in spreading the Gospel on the North American continent, possess a numerous and highly respectable congregation" in Belleville. The conservative Wesleyans had not sent preachers to Upper Canada until 1816, twenty-five years behind the American Episcopal Methodists. The "Episcopal Methodist church" is passed off with one sentence, compared to the paragraph on the Wesleyan.[18] She discusses the two Scots churches, the Residuary and Free, and mentions the 1843 Disruption in the Church of Scotland, but her sympathies are with the more evangelical Free Church.[19] "The English church" and "its Catholic brother" have a prominent place in her description of Belleville. The former is "a great eyesore" and a "tasteless building" with an "ugly tower": "Doubtless its founders thought they had done wonders when they erected this humble looking place of worship," she concludes, "but now ... it should ... give place to a larger and handsomer edifice" (23–4). The identification of the Church of England with ultra-Toryism, and many of the Moodies' enemies, may have provoked the residual animus that colours her description.[20] Her portrait of the Catholic church, on the other hand, is conditioned by a willingness to compensate for what they had taken as her unjust treatment of them: "its elegant structure and graceful spire add[] to the beauty of the scene" (24).

A desire to avoid any imputation of insult actuates the treatment of Irish Catholics throughout *Life in the Clearings*, apart from "Michael Macbride."[21] Moodie has "found the Catholic Irish as faithful and trustworthy as the Protestants" (26). She contrasts the chastity of Irish women with the lack of it in "the female peasantry in the eastern counties of England" (27). She compliments the Irish and their priests on their wit and humour. Through her story of their Belleville fire and the kindness it elicited from Father Brennan she shows that "Catholics do not always act with hostility towards their Protestant brethren."[22] She ascribes the transplant of religious violence to the Orange rather than the Green, and wishes no longer to see "the orange banner flaunting our streets on the twelfth of July" (26). Superstition is the only fault, other than undue reverence for priests, she finds with Catholics. Her guard slips when she describes the religious "credulity" of the Irish Catholics, "as boundless as their ignorance," but she quickly declares her respect for "their child-like trust" (25).

Harking back to her period beyond the pale of the established church, Moodie appreciates the toleration of "all religions" in the colony (26). "Thanks to the liberal institutions of the country," distinctions between church and chapel "are unknown in Canada. Every community of Christian worshippers is rightly termed *a church*. *The Church* is only arrogated by one" (35). Before his wife joins him in Belleville, J.W.D. Moodie and his "countrymen go to the English Church" when the Presbyterian minister, who supports this practice, is absent: "The Episcopalians, however, are not liberal enough to follow this laudable example."[23] When *Life in the Clearings* was rejected in England, Mrs Moodie acknowledged to Bentley that "there are ... many things in it, which would give great offence to *bigots* of all denominations, but as the substance of it is strictly true, it may chance to make its way when more liberal sentiments are popular in England" (letter 52). British attitudes hardened in the wake of the Oxford Movement and the disestablishment of the Anglican church. What applied in England, where middle-class dominance was premised on the secularization of the state, applied even more in the Canadas, where Catholics were a greater force. The lingering Anglican aspirations to be "*the Church*" of the Canadas were disruptive. Moodie castigates Strachan for fawning over Durham: "What a contemptible figure Dr Strachan cuts with his half Radical letter."[24] While the Moodies favoured the separation of church and state in the colony, religion would still support social stability by enforcing public morality. Mrs Moodie follows her plea for the cessation of Protestant and Catholic hostilities by suggesting that they "meet each other half way, as brothers of one common manhood, inspired by the same Christian hope and bound to the same heavenly country" (26). Religion could promote stability and peace in their earthly country.[25]

The Moodies saw that civil conflict endangered the development of middle-class consensus. J.W.D. Moodie, paymaster of the militia, wrote his wife to this effect: "I sometimes wish I could clear out from this unhappy distracted country where I can see nothing but ultra selfish Toryism or Revolutionary Radicalism." With his appointment as sheriff he thought that, "but for this miserable petty party and national feeling [they] might be very comfortable" in Belleville.[26] Like their contemporaries, the Moodies saw changes in the old representative system leading to the dominance of moderate reformers. They believed one-party dominance necessary to stability, but the system was actually developing towards an institutionalized framework within which rotation of parties in office itself guaranteed stability. J.W.D. Moodie refers to the resolution of "the violence of party feeling which lately prevailed in Canada" when "the party generally most powerful in the Legislative Assembly ... obtained the position to which [it was] entitled." After an early reference in *Life in the Clearings* to the time "when party feeling ran high," Mrs Moodie later asserts that "the demon of party" has been quelled, since "the union of the provinces has kept the reform party in the ascendant."[27] Her one mention of the press in this text reiterates her belief that it should abstain from political partisanship: "The two rival parties ... occasionally abuse and vilify each other through the medium of the common safety valve – the public papers" (58–9).

Moodie addresses "the '*Clergy Reserves question*'" – a pre-rebellion issue hanging over the mid-1850s that encompassed politics, religion, economics, and education. She begins with a conclusion: "All parties were wrong" (57). The extended metaphor she uses to characterize "this vexed political question" epitomizes anarchic, selfish strife. The churches make up a pack of dogs fighting over a bone. In her allegory, "some benevolent individual, with a view to their mutual benefit, had flung a shank of beef, with enough upon the upper end to have satisfied the hunger of all, could such an impossible thing as an equal division, among such noisy claimants, have been made" (57–8). She tells how "a strong English bull-dog" managed "for some time ... to keep all the other dogs at bay." A "stout mastiff," the Methodists, first to show its resentment, was soon joined by "a wiry, active Scotch terrier." Meanwhile, "an old cunning greyhound, to whom no share had been offered ... stood proudly aloof," and "a multitude of nondescript curs" waited for "the few tit bits, which they hoped might fall to their share." She leaves her "ludicrous sort of caricature" with "the figure of Justice," ignored while "lifting her sword to make an equal division" (57–8). In 1840 legislation divided half the proceeds from the sale of reserves between the Churches of England and Scotland, leaving the other half to all the other denominations. That the moderate majority wanted this money used to develop education and the churches to support themselves led to further agitation in the 1850s; this accounts for the discussion of the reserves in *Life in the Clearings*: "If the Church of England were supported throughout the colony, on the voluntary principle ... the outcry about the ever-vexed question of the Clergy Reserves, would be merged in her increased influence and prosperity."[28] The "elegant structure" of the stone Catholic church and the "graceful structure" of the limestone Free Church are "capital illustration[s] of the working of the voluntary principle" (24, 34). If the Anglican church would cede its claim on public revenues, then religious contention would no longer disturb the peace of an ecumenical middle class.

The first Upper Canadian commission of inquiry into educational reform reported on lunatic asylums and prisons as well as schools. For bureaucrats and politicians, schools were among those other institutions intended for the control of unruly segments of the populace.[29] Moodie sees no need for further reform in her surveys of colonial provisions in these areas. She manipulates the framework of the voyage around Lake Ontario upon which *Life in the Clearings* is structured to enable her to comment on the Kingston penitentiary, then admits that it was three years prior to her present trip that she visited it.[30] In Toronto the only place she writes about is the asylum. Her accounts of the penitentiary and asylum stress how humane is the Canadian treatment of those who have transgressed the laws of society and of sanity. She is "surprised at the neatness, cleanliness, order, and regularity" of the jail. She is not surprised that some prisoners "preferred being there, well clothed and well fed, to gaining a precarious living elsewhere." She does not find the rule forbidding conversation among inmates harsh nor the narrow cells cramped, nor "a sort of machine" in which "mutinous convicts are confined ... the least painful" (190, 191). Her assessment of conditions at the penitentiary is at odds with the first investigation of them, released in 1849, which described cases like that of an eleven-year-old boy whipped fifty-seven times in less than a year for offences like smiling and staring.[31] She is similarly impressed by the "lofty, well lighted, well aired, and exquisitely clean" lunatic asylum. The mad have "no appearance of wretchedness or misery" but look "healthy and cheerful, nay, almost happy" (265). To complete her circuit, she crosses the street to look at Trinity College, a new institution for the coming generation of colonial leaders.

Moodie does not attempt to connect her chapter on education to the voyage around Lake Ontario that loosely holds together most of the book. As she is satisfied with provisions for the criminal and the insane, so do the educational arrangements recently made for dealing with the children of the poor gain her approval. Along with her attitude to clergy reserves went the moderate middle-class opinion on education, and since this opinion had yet to be fully institutionalized, she promotes it. She attributes to reform ascendance the creation of "free schools," and, in a few introductory words added to "Education the True Wealth of the World" to transform it into "Free Schools – Thoughts on Education" in *Life in the Clearings*, she applauds "the present liberal provision made for the education of the rising generation."[32] Praising the Common School Act of 1850, which laid the basis for a centralized system supported by a property tax, she recognizes the resistance to it: "These schools are supported by a district tax which falls upon the property of persons well able to pay it; but avarice and bigotry are already at work, to endeavour to deprive the young of this new-found blessing. Persons grumble at having to pay this additional tax. They say, 'If poor people want their children taught, let them pay for it: their instruction has no right to be forced from our earnings'" (78). She need not have worried. In the 1850 act free schools were optional, but most towns and cities supported them; in 1871 Ryerson obtained passage of a bill making them compulsory.

Moodie's argument for public education is that used by its promoters, among whom Ryerson stands out: "The education of these neglected children, by making them better citizens, will in the long run prove a great protection both to life and property" (78). Educational reform in the United States and Europe had been, since the 1830s, based on a conception of state-run education as tool for social control. In the Canadas after the rebellions, fear of American influence, Irish disorderliness, and working-class disaffection finally forced the middle class to accept some of the cost of educating disadvantaged children. Educational reformers convinced those with money that spending it to teach these children bought a more orderly population for themselves.[33] When Moodie argues that, since "ignorance is the fruitful parent of crime, we should unite with heart and voice to banish it from the earth," she pits ignorance against order to plead for education as a prophylactic against vice.[34] Property owners eventually saw that their contribution of a small portion of their wealth to a public education system actually helped to secure their possession of that wealth and property.

The conviction that clergy reserve revenues should be devoted to education was confronted by another objection to free schools – focused by Strachan's efforts to secure an educational system under the dominance of the Church of England – which Moodie also recognized:

Then the priests of different persuasions lift up their voices because no particular creed is allowed to be taught in the seminaries, and exclaim – "The children will be infidels. These schools are godless and immoral in the extreme." Yes; children will be taught to love each other without any such paltry distinctions of party and creed. The rich and the poor will meet together to learn the sweet courtesies of a common humanity, and prejudice and avarice and bigotry cannot bear that. (78)

While this defence is consistent with her commitment to religious tolerance, the same chord was struck in the public domain by Ryerson's intentions for the school system: "Christianity – the Christianity of the Bible – regardless of the peculiarities of Sects, or Parties is to be the basis of our System of Public Instruction, as it is of our Civil Constitution."[35] That the famine Irish would swell Canadian free schools was only a further argument for publicly funding them.

Moodie's support for free schools was anything but egalitarian. Teaching children "that there was no disgrace in labour, in honest, honourable poverty, but a deep and lasting disgrace in ignorance and immorality" would "produce the most beneficial results" (85). Public education was to provide, in Ryerson's words, "that instruction and discipline which qualify and dispose the subjects of it for their appropriate duties and employments of life."[36] This purpose would reinforce social hierarchy, as Moodie knew when she confronted the objection that educating "the poorer classes ... would render them familiar and presumptuous, and they would no longer pay to their superiors in station that deference which must exist for the well-being of society": "The man who knows his duty is more likely to perform it well than the ignorant man, whose services are compulsory, and whose actions are uninfluenced by the moral responsibility which a right knowledge must give" (81). The teaching of discipline and quiescence to the children of labourers must be central to the curriculum. Soon after J.W.D. Moodie arrived in Belleville he joined the local school board, an extension of his duties as sheriff. The educational system that the school promoters sought to institute and that Mrs Moodie lauded had as a goal the maintenance of order within a society based on inequality.

The paramount contradiction in Moodie's writing on Canada is in her attitude to the working class. Her own lifelong poverty and resistance to loss of caste was one source for this contradiction, but it took shape the way it did because of labour relations specific to the colony. Her personal background accounts for the uncertainty of her search for what her class allegiances were and should be, but the fluidity of Canadian class relations exacerbated this insecurity. From her earliest stories she was never insensitive to the plight of the working class and the miseries of the poor. When writing those stories she was insulated by the marks of her own status – Reydon Hall, reliable servants, literary friendships, and secure publishing relations – and they promoted individual independence, not social equality. In the colony she was deprived of all outward indications of gentility, and her writing is fissured by an extreme ambivalence to workers: her sympathy for them deepens, but for the first time a revulsion for her "social inferiors" arises. Here is the source of her increased regard for the poor:

It is almost impossible for anyone who has never earned his own bread by manual labour to feel an affectionate interest in the every-day workers of the world, or regard them really as brethren. Having experienced in my own person somewhat of their trials and sufferings, I never feel the least degraded by honourable poverty, or ashamed of owning that I have worked for daily bread, and would do so cheerfully again did occasion require.[37]

She implies that her own labour was confined to the years in Douro. She still does not view writing for money as work, and so it involves no loss of status. She speaks with the assurance that she was a gentlewoman in England and, when she reached Belleville, a gentlewoman again.

Moodie's congratulations to colonial labourers for making it to a colony where they have such improved economic prospects are the obverse of her cautions to genteel emigrants: "To the honest sons of labour Canada is, indeed, an El Dorado – a land flowing with milk and honey; for they soon obtain that independence which the poor gentleman struggles in vain to realise by his own labour in the woods."[38] She sees "a delightful contrast to the squalid want and poverty ... at home" in the "almost total absence of pauperism" in Canada.[39] At this point in *Life in the Clearings* she provides an entirely positive characterization of the change immigration makes in the deportment of members of the working class: "The consciousness of their newly-acquired freedom has raised them in the scale of society, in their own estimation, and in that of their fellows. They feel that they are no longer despised; the ample wages they receive has enabled them to cast off the slough of hopeless poverty" (36). She sounds a more ambivalent note later, during her discussion of "the mere pretenders in society" (61). Writing of "the affectation of wishing people to think that you had been better off in the mother country than in Canada," she asserts that "the very poorest are the most remarked for this ridiculous boasting" (62–3). This statement recalls her reaction in *Roughing It* to her fellow passengers: "I was not a little amused at the extravagant expectations entertained by some of our steerage passengers. The sight of the Canadian shores had changed them into persons of great consequence ... They talked loudly of the rank and wealth of their connexions at home" (40). Although workers can improve their economic status in the colony, it still behoves them to remain mindful of their place in the social hierarchy.

The place of the working class in the Canadas is, in Moodie's view, in the backwoods, in road and railway construction, or in service.[40] The members of the impoverished class with whom she has her greatest difficulty are servants. Perhaps chastened by the Toronto reviewer who had characterized her as "too poor to lie on a sofa and too proud to work for her bread," she does not in *Life in the Clearings* continue the harangue against servants found in her first book, although she reproduces that harangue in *Flora Lindsay*.[41] Merely to illustrate the affectations of "the very poorest," she includes mocking sketches of her "servant girl" and one of their "working men." In her sketch on the maid she again, as in *Roughing It*, reveals that her problems with servants are their disrespect and their unwillingness to do "hard work" (63). She accurately analyses why "the serving class" in the Canadas are so intractable: there are not enough of them, and their wages are too high. The need for reliable servants was part of a broader social demand for labourers, and as this demand contributed to policies that, with other developments, made it harder for them to get land, a fund of unemployed labourers formed.

Accounts of labour relations in the first half of the century, all from the perspective of middle-class settlers, continually stress the problem of finding and keeping good domestic help. They were buttressed by the state apparatus through the Master and Servant Act of 1847. By the 1850s working-class immigration had begun, in Strickland's words, "cheapening labour."[42] Middle-class women, however, were slower to benefit from this "cheapening," which had more of an effect on male labourers than on female domestics. Prior to 1850, *ad hoc* paternalistic labour relations predominated, but as workers became more numerous, they also became more organized, and employers, backed by the state, followed suit. A colonial working class existed by mid-century. Modern industrial labour relations, established first in urban centres, only gradually began to affect master and servant relations. For properly deferential and hard-working servants to become available, it was necessary that the conditions that allowed poor immigrants to gain independence and economic well-being – gains Moodie praises – be eliminated. For her to get the kind of "helps" she wanted, a pauper class had to be created.[43]

The blindness of middle-class settlers like Moodie and Traill to this contradiction in their view of colonial society also appears in their attitudes to crime. Traill writes a section extolling "security of person and property in Canada" for her guidebook. She concludes that "the inhabitants are essentially honest, because they are enabled, by the exertion of their own hands, to obtain in abundance the necessaries of life ... it is the miseries arising from poverty that induce crime. – Men do not violate the law of honesty, unless driven to do so by necessity" (1855, 45). Robbery occurs "occasionally" in "large towns ... for it is there that poverty is to be found" (45). Moodie approaches this observation when she notes that robbery is not a problem for the citizens of Belleville, but "in Hamilton and Toronto ... daring acts of housebreaking are of frequent occurrence" (195). She does not pursue an explanation, however, and while recognizing that poverty creates the conditions for drunkenness and its attendant crimes to thrive, she seems to believe in innate evil. The convicts in the penitentiary, for instance, display in their "very bad countenances" a proclivity for wrong-doing: "I never felt so much convinced of the truth of phrenology as while looking at their heads. The extraordinary ... *mal*-formation, of some of them, led me to think that their possessors were hardly accountable for their actions" (193). She finds the secret of Grace Marks, who incited murder for economic reasons, revealed by her descent into madness: "Let us hope that all her previous guilt may be attributed to the incipient workings of this frightful malady" (209). She seems unable to conceive of want as a motive for crime. Neither can she complete the equation implied by her praise of educational reform. Schools were needed to check the growth of crime due to the spread of economic privation. The first provincial penitentiary in the Canadas opened in 1836. In the 1840s, as available land decreased, crime increased. The conditions that forced servants to be deferential would force others to be criminal.

Traill congratulates herself and her neighbours, among whom the Moodies were numbered, with "having shaken off the trammels of

Grundyism," the conventional social pretensions she associates with England. But she then describes their society as "mostly military or naval; so that we meet on equal grounds, and are, of course, well acquainted with the rules of good breeding and polite life" (1836, 218). The English middle class disliked being patronized by those above them but equally resented the levelling urge from those below. Moodie appreciates the lack of "conventional prejudices that shackle the movements of the higher classes in Britain" (*LC*, 13) but is less happy with "the rude, coarse familiarity of the uneducated people" (*RI*, 197). In *Flora Lyndsay* the colony is described as "a country destitute of an hereditary aristocracy ... where the poorest emigrant ... may rise to wealth and political importance." It is "a semi-democratic country, where people get over their prejudices regarding superiority of blood and breeding, and must ... associate with persons on an equal footing, whom, in the old country, they would consider vastly inferior."[44] Traill is happy that among their neighbours "the lower or working class of settlers are well disposed, and quite free from ... annoying Yankee manners" (1836, 219). In Canada the English middle class escaped Mrs Grundy only to be buttonholed by Sam Slick.

Part of Moodie liked the lack of social stratification in the colony, but another part needed desperately to find a way to reinstate it. An economically distressed gentlewoman, she graded society by the non-material standard of manners and education. She portrays this view of hierarchy in *Hugh Latimer, Geoffrey Moncton*, and *Mark Hurdlestone*, where gentility is a moral, not a social ideal. It accounts for her obsession with criticizing sartorial ostentation in the colony: "The aristocracy of wealth is bad enough; but the aristocracy of dress is perfectly contemptible," she writes. The talent of a Raphael "in rags" would be dismissed in the New World: "Great and manifold ... are the evils arising from this inordinate love for dress" (*RI*, 203–4). She is more pointed in *Life in the Clearings*: "Uneducated, ignorant people often rise by their industry to great wealth in the colony; to such the preference shown to the educated man always seems a puzzle. Their ideas of gentility consist in being the owners of fine clothes, fine houses, splendid furniture, expensive equipages, and plenty of money ... They cannot comprehend the mysterious ascendancy of mind over mere animal enjoyments" (62). For Traill, too, "it is education and manners that must distinguish the gentleman in this country, seeing that the labouring man ... may soon become his equal in point of worldy possessions" (1836, 73). Their brother, with wishful insistence, reiterates a similar point, claiming that, while the "industrial classes" get rich, a "balance" is maintained where the "man of education and refinement" holds "offices in the Colony and responsible situations which his richer but less learned neighbour can never fill with ease or propriety."[45]

These genteel immigrants saw the rising colonial entrepreneurial class passing them by. With colonial wealth such a fluid quality, they wanted a further mark of superiority, one more difficult to obtain, to become the guarantor of caste. While the worker had to be taught the dignity of labour, the wealthy had to be shown the value of refined manners and mental superiority. *Life in the Clearings* attempts to convince the middle class that materialism must be leavened by a spirituality that only people like its author were qualified to supply.

Moodie grew increasingly aware that her role as ideologist for the colonial middle class was not gaining wide acceptance. In her letters she recognizes that the Canadians who might countenance her were not listening and those who were did not accept her opinions of them and their society. The fragmentation and diffuseness of her autobiographical texts show her unable to plot her own life to prove that Providence had destined her to be a literary spokeswoman for the colony. In *Roughing It* "Providence" is the answer when she asks what brought her to the bush: "Not for your own welfare, perhaps, but for the welfare of your children, the unerring hand of the Great Father has led you here ... It may be your lot to suffer, but others will reap a benefit from your trials" (267). No one reaped any benefit from those trials in the wilderness. The Moodies failed to secure an estate for their heirs. When in *Life in the Clearings* she avers that roughing it in the bush is "assigned to [the labourer] by Providence," she suggests that the Moodies themselves deviated from God's design. The passage that contains this assertion stresses the "thousand more advantageous ways in which a man of property may invest his capital" instead of "burying himself and his family in the woods" (10), and reads as a confession that the Moodies strayed from Providence into those woods. The one time in *Life in the Clearings* that she applies the salient term to her life is when she looks back from a steamboat's deck to the receding Belleville shores: "There stood my peaceful, happy home; the haven of rest to which Providence had conducted me after the storms and trials of many years" (19). But that "small stone cottage" is not the landed estate the Moodies came to Upper Canada to claim as a patrimony for their lineage. They later lost it and had to rent an even smaller house. By the 1850s, having achieved only modest success, she could no longer read her own life as a providential romance.

Through evangelicism and dissent Moodie abjured the external authority of the formulated theology of the established church. From that point on she had to find the guarantee of the piety of her life in her individual experience and personal conviction.[46] From *Hugh Latimer* to *Mark Hurdlestone* she created male heroes with backgrounds like hers and encased them in plots that prove their morality by providing them social recognition. In their goodness these characters resign themselves to the Providence that finally vindicates them, while the evil characters heretically believe they control their own destinies. When Moodie began to record her own life in the late 1840s, she could not discover a plot to prove that her resignation to Providence had been rewarded. "Rachel Wilde," "Trifles from the Burthen of a Life," *Roughing It, Life in the Clearings, Flora Lyndsay,* all plotless, fail to confirm the piety of their heroines through happy resolutions. Each time Moodie tried to discern an order behind her experience, she encountered disorderliness. Unable to fault God's design, she had to suspect that the problem lay in her failure to act in accordance with that design. What if emigration had been, rather than resignation to duty, mere wilfulness, the result of having been persuaded by her husband that they could control their own destiny?

Moodie concludes *Life in the Clearings* with a seemingly straightforward assertion that all is right with her world: "I no longer regard myself as an alien on her shores, but her daughter by adoption, – the happy mother of Canadian children, – rejoicing in the warmth and hospitality of a Canadian Home!" (333). The ambiguity of "daughter by adoption" is prised open by the book's verse conclusion, "For London, A National Song," a twenty-year-old paean to the mother country that had orphaned her. Had she adopted Canada, or had Canada adopted her? The colonial reception of *Roughing It* showed that the latter had not happened. If she intended the former, then she none the less remained lukewarm about her adoptive parent. The metaphor is also used in the introduction to *Life in the Clearings* when, writing about "the country of my adoption," she goes only so far as to say that "Canada has become almost as dear to me as my native land" (12). Both these declarations of adaptation arise from the defences of *Roughing It* they follow. While her regret at having been exiled from her first family, literally and metaphorically, lessened with time, it none the less persisted as a consistent factor in her relationship with the colony. While she accepted that she would live her life in the Canadas, her primary identification remained with England. She was one of those "inhabitants" Anna Jameson identified for whom the colony was "an adopted, not a real mother. Their love, their pride, are not for poor Canada, but for high and happy England" (1838, 66).

To ward off "persons who delight in misrepresenting the opinions of others" from accusing her of "republican principles," Moodie attacks the belief "that *perfect equality* can exist" on earth. As an alternative, she "advocates ... *equality of mind*," which amounts to a state in which "both master and servant will enjoy a reciprocal communion of mind, without lessening the respect due from the one to the other." All that is required for this state to be achieved is for "he who serves" to accept that he was born to serve. She has already mounted a similar criticism of the "fallacious chimera" of republicanism.[47] She is trying to maintain a balance that she fears she may have upset. Whereas Mackenzie's son-in-law had called *Roughing It* the work of an "ape of the aristocracy," she deals here with the dread that in *Life in the Clearings* she has overcompensated and that one of Bishop Strachan's protégés might call her an "ape" of the radicals. She once more rejects factionalism and seeks the middle way. Unfortunately for her sense of the colonial reception of her work, the other inhabitants of that middle ground did not come forth in public praise of her position.

Moodie was worn down by the residual partisan sniping that her books drew. She is obviously stung by the first Canadian reaction to *Roughing It*: "the little I have said of Canadian society has made me so unpopular with the natives, that I believe it would be better to leave them alone for the future, if I would hope to live in peace" (letter 45). After submitting *Flora Lyndsay*, she made a resolution she never broke: "After all, It shall be my last work on Canada. I am sick of the subject, and it awakens ill feelings in others" (letter 49). She broadened this resolution six months later: "I never mean to write for Canadian paper or magazine again, after their unjust abuse of me" (letter 57). Apparently in response to Bentley's request for fiction set in the colony, she inscribed her most expansive defence of *Roughing It* outside of *Life in the Clearings*, in a letter that lays bare the depth of her alienation, anger, and sense of rejection:

It is difficult to write a work of fiction, placing the scene in Canada, without rousing up the whole country against me. Whatever locality I chose, the people would insist, that my characters were *really* natives of the place. That I had a malicious motive in shewing them up, and every local idiom I made use of, to render such characters true to nature, would be considered a national insult. You don't know the touchy nature of the people. Vindictive, treacherous and dishonest, they always impute to your words and actions the worst motives, and no abuse is too coarse to express in their public journals, their hatred and defiance. Have I not already run the gauntlet with them? Will they ever forgive me for writing *Roughing It*? They know that it was the truth, but have I not been a mark for every vulgar editor of a village journal, throughout the length and breadth of the land to hurl a stone at, and point out as the enemy to Canada. Had I gained a fortune by that book, it would have been dearly earned by the constant annoyance I have experienced since its publication. If I write about this country again, it shall never be published till my head is under the sod. (letter 64)

Moodie stumbled into a political and social minefield and never understood that what hit her were versions of the truth that, because they spoke from different social and economic positions, could never correspond with hers. She remained defensive about *Roughing It* for over twenty years after its publication. Her last surviving reference to it, written at seventy-one, was to her "unlucky book."[48] As Providence deserted her when she entered the Canadian bush, so even was luck lost to her when she entered the colonial ideological wilderness.

7 *Roughing It in the Bush*: A Case Study in Colonial Contradictions

That Moodie dredges up recollections of her first years in Upper Canada when she first writes about it speaks of the emotional burden those years laid upon her. A desire to wrest meaning from her earliest experiences of the colony drives *Roughing It in the Bush*. It is as much an expression of her needs in the 1850s as a representation of her life in the 1830s. The pain charging her memories of Cobourg clearing and Douro bush comes partly from her nagging sense of that period as a void in the progress of her life. That suffering and trial had bought nothing and, if left unredeemed, might bankrupt the whole Canada venture. Carol Shields' description of Moodie's writing as "an attempt to find confirmation of ... an existence which was hidden in an alien wilderness and all but buried alive" applies best to *Roughing It* (1977, 32). Elizabeth Thompson suggests that "Moodie's inability to resolve" the tensions between gentlewoman and pioneer may, compared to Traill, "be the more accurate rendering" (1991, 32). Moodie became engaged in *Roughing It* as a negotiation with her images of Yankees and the bush for significance. En route to some kind of dogma concerning the colony, however, she skirts dissolution. The text needs to be explored to see how and why it leaves a deficit when she undertook it as a recovery of spiritual and emotional capital.

Moodie's one canonical text combines evident personal commitment with extreme diffuseness of voice, intention, and execution. In *Roughing It* the authority she reaches for escapes her grasp. She concentrates in this book the difficulty and anguish of her entire life, reaching back before emigration and eventually extending on into old age as she prepares it for publication in Canada in 1871. Whereas *Life in the Clearings* appropriates the colony for the mother country, *Roughing It* is Moodie's incomplete attempt to appropriate the colony for herself. It is the hinge upon which she articulates her colonial and her British reputations as an author. It is the only text in the realistic mode of *Flora Lyndsay* and *Life in the Clearings* upon which she attempts to inscribe the romance plot of her novels, but the text lacks the finality of resolution that the novels attain. The inscription is smudged.

If *Roughing It* is Moodie's most rewarding text, seeing it as an apprenticeship novel or a Gothic romance can no longer account for its interest. Rather than being provided an interpretation that attempts to accommodate its disparate elements and perceive its deep, internal organization, rather than being closed in on itself and found a work worthy of detached contemplation, an artifact of intricate, if elusive design, *Roughing It* needs to be opened up to its history and its discontinuities traced to the dispersed social and psychological energies it tries to contain. When *Roughing It*'s contradictoriness has been noticed, recuperation within a larger unity, either of an isolated monad labelled "Susanna Moodie" or of a collective unconscious labelled "the Canadian imagination," has soon followed. The text cries out to be unified; this abjured, its disunity remains to be explored.[1]

Moodie's is one hand among many involved in the production of this text. In the British market for books on the colonies, J.W.D. Moodie was the acknowledged author, not his wife. In 1832, just before they emigrated, he wrote to her that the firm that had published *Enthusiasm* was "still much inclined" to accept from him a work "on Canada."[2] When offering Bentley *Ten Years in South Africa*, Moodie provided a prospectus of this other book. It would be "a fair and impartial account ... a plain unaffected narrative of the progress and proceedings of a settler in this colony." By the end of this description the proposed book begins to sound like *Roughing It*: "My personal narrative would of course occupy a considerable portion of the work, and would be the more popular as containing not mere opinions but my actual experience in the country." Bentley declined, success being doubtful because "so much has lately been written on that country," but if Moodie proceeded he would "be happy to see the M.S." Moodie may even have begun writing his book on the colony.[3]

As they became established in Upper Canada, however, the Moodies divided their labour. After negotiations with Harpers in the early 1840s for the book publication of *Mark Hurdlestone* and *Geoffrey Moncton* lapsed, Mrs Moodie considered already existing connections: "If I had time, I would try Moodie's publisher, Bentley of London. My sister

Agnes's name would be a great help to me now in selling a book of my own" (letter 40). Moodie was involved with his sheriff's job; she had become the recognized author. None the less, and likely because he had already written on colonization, when they compiled the manuscript of *Roughing It* they included his four chapters and eleven poems. The poem that opens "The Whirlwind" was contributed by Samuel Strickland, as was almost half this chapter. Mrs Moodie arranged the manuscript, and at some point the negotiations with Bentley devolved upon her.[4] J.W.D. Moodie, pointing out that his wife's narrative would be "unintelligible" without the information he supplies, subordinates his text to hers: "one of my chief objects in writing this chapter being to afford a connecting link between my wife's sketches."[5] Although the text is collaborative, its emotional centre of gravity is in her contributions; his is "the informative, objective, and generally optimistic voice."[6] She revises sketches previously published in the *Literary Garland* and the *Victoria Magazine* and accompanies them with new material. Taking into account all three contributors' work, fully two-thirds of the manuscript sent to Bentley had appeared in periodicals prior to book publication.[7]

Moodie considered her potential audience when transforming these fragments into a book. She suppressed "Michael Macbride" to avoid further provoking Catholics, but her greater concern – or her editor's – was her English audience. Peterman analyses the revisions "for the tastes and assumptions of the particular audience she was addressing" and finds "the language ... more high-toned and poetic in the English edition" (1983, 84). Ballstadt suggests that some changes were "calculated to make it acceptable and appealing to her prospective British reading public," and others "rendered the narrative more exotic" (1988, xxvi). Both Ballstadt and Peterman note changes that seem intended to protect "the Victorian sensibilities" of "her English and feminine audience."[8] Among these changes are two of the few excisions from the sketches, those of Woodruff's story and of the full details of Brian's suicide attempt. To an extent she allowed her audience's demands, as she perceived them, to dictate the style and substance of the family work.

The next participants in the production of *Roughing It* were employees at the Bentley publishing house and John Bruce, the Moodie's London agent. Bruce "saw the work through the press, reading the proofs and making alterations and corrections" (*Letters*, 104). The first three "editions" of *Roughing It* contain hundreds of variants in accidentals and substantives, all of which are documented in the edition by the Centre for Editing Early Canadian Texts (637-44). There are a number of major substantive variants between the first two titular "editions": a page of dialogue in the periodical version of the first chapter, missing from the first issue, is reinserted for the second; the poems at the end of the penultimate chapter and the beginning of the last are shuffled, resulting in a change of title for the last chapter; some of the poetry is rewritten, with lines inserted or deleted; J.W.D. Moodie's "Canadian Sketches" surfaces for the first time in the second issue. The correspondence between Mrs Moodie and Bentley contains no evidence that any of these changes was made on the express wishes of her or her husband. Bentley in his "Advertisement" thinks it "right to state" that "she has not been able to superintend this work whilst passing through the press" (ix).

Bruce and the Bentley proof-readers and editors shaped the manuscript. On 27 December 1851 Bentley asks Bruce to revise it with "the view of omitting some of the poetry" (Parker 1979, 150). Two days later Bruce refers to "softnesses" he is eliminating at Bentley's request. Since the book was published on 29 January 1852, Bruce's activities ran concurrent with its setting. Bentley and Bruce also decided what was to be included in the final text. The Moodies sent two chapters to Bentley separate from the bulk of the manuscript. One was to replace "Michael Macbride," and one was to be a concluding factual and statistical chapter, which Bentley had requested. Only the latter, J.W.D. Moodie's "Canadian Sketches," becomes part of Bentley's edition, and its inclusion is due to several factors: it could be added on to the already set book more easily than his wife's chapter could be inserted in its middle; it broadens the market appeal to attract serious immigrants and speculators; it allows the description of the second "edition" as "with additions."

"Michael Macbride" and the sketch of Jeanie Burns and the lost children sent with "Canadian Sketches" do appear in *Life in the Clearings*, where the latter is divided into two chapters. That the responsibility for which chapters were included in *Roughing It* resides with Bentley and Bruce can be inferred from a note concerning these three chapters: "This ['Lost Children'], and the two preceding chapters ['Michael Macbride" and "Jeanie Burns"], were written for 'Roughing it in the Bush,' and were sent to England to make a part of that work, but came too late for insertion, which will account to the reader for their appearance here" (*LC*, 248). What seems to be Moodie's confusion over when "Michael Macbride" was sent and what her intentions for it were can be read, if the note is attributed to Bentley, as his attempt to conceal his hand in the creation of both texts. "Michael Macbride" accompanied the manuscript of *Roughing It*, and the other chapter was with "Canadian Sketches." Yet Bentley told Moodie that "Jeanie Burns" "arrived too late for insertion" (letter 44). There is no evidence that she authorized the inclusion of "Michael Macbride" in any of her books, and the attitude to Catholics it dramatizes is inconsistent with her apparent deference to them throughout *Life in the Clearings*. To a significant extent, Bentley was choosing what would go into Moodie's books and what would not.

Ballstadt claims that "Canadian Sketches" was added "to the standing type of the first impression" and that Bentley waited until after "the favourable reception of the book ... to issue a second impression, which he called a 'Second Edition, With Additions,' on 29 Nov. 1852" (1988, xxxiv). Bentley's "Second Edition" would have been of sheets printed, after extensive in-press revisions, in late 1851–early 1852. He could not have kept the type of a six-hundred-page book standing for six months between impressions and there is no record of plates being made. The Bentley archives do record the printing of 2,250 copies of *Roughing It* in early 1852.[9] He produced a third issue of this edition in 1854, calling it a "Third Edition, With Additions. In One Volume" and charging half what he had for the first and second issues. He was still looking for ways to dispose of the 2,250 copies printed two years before. The critical success of *Roughing It* did not translate into sales.

Bentley was responsible for a further detail – the title. The freedom he would exercise in titling "Rachel MacGregor's Emigration" *Flora Lyndsay*, and *Geoffrey Moncton, The Moncktons*, was conceded to him when he packaged Moodie's first prose book. He and Bruce refer to the manuscript as "Mrs. Moodie's Canadian Life" and "a work at present entitled 'Canadian Life'" in their correspondence (Ballstadt 1988, xxvii–xxix). She had no contact with Bentley before "Canadian Life" appeared with the title by which it has since been known. A few years earlier Bentley had published a book on Australia called *Roughing It in the Outback*. While his advertisement emphasizes hardship, Bentley's title also suggests that the Moodies were only doing what colonists were expected to do, preparing the land roughly for its subsequent full occupation. If his thoughts tended in either of these directions, then he was ignorant of the state of settlement in the colony in the 1830s, and the text failed to rectify his ignorance. However Bentley meant it, this book has always been read as an account of rough conditions.[10]

This varied evidence of editorial intervention suggests that the Moodie manuscript handled by Bruce needed work. Bentley's belief in its marketability must have been solid for him to expend so much time on it. He and Bruce must have felt a sense of responsibility to the Moodies as well as to their own interests. They supplied the patina to an inchoate work. The text's subsequent publishing history shows that they were not entirely successful. Each successive editor has assumed a freedom to remake the text according to his perception of it and of its market. The poetry was the first sacrifice to editorial prerogative, that taken by Charles Frederick Briggs in New York in the summer of 1852 and that retained by Bentley when he produced the yellow-back edition in 1857. Other chapters or verses were reduced or omitted by each new editor. Bentley and Bruce participated in a process of textual production initiated by the Moodies. Every editor since them has felt compelled to join.[11]

The Moodies did not claim the privilege of authorial autonomy. Neither did they have any stable intentions concerning the writing project that was in 1852 labelled by their publisher *Roughing It in the Bush*. They produced this text by engaging in a collaborative relationship with a publishing institution. They shared authority with Bentley and Bruce. To attribute autonomous authority to the Moodies is contrary to what is known of their publishing relations. Whatever unity this book of fragments has is due as much to intentions attributed to it by its editors as to any intentions the diverse sources of it may have had.

Roughing It is not the product of an autonomous author, nor can it be reduced to a hypothetical authorial intention. Moodie abdicated authorial responsibility. For the 1871 edition, the only one she oversaw, she mimicked the abscissions performed by other editors and muted the anti-Canadian tone that had drawn hostile reactions. With this book, authors, editors, texts, environments of writing, technics of production, market factors, paths of dissemination are in a relationship sufficiently unstable, shifting, and open-ended as to vitiate any configuration at the centre of which could be placed an autonomous author and her final intentions. The manuscript's unfinished quality, attested to by the labours of Bruce and Bentley, merely reflects this. There is no definitive text of *Roughing It*. Its outward emblems of flux are the wandering commas, spurs of exclamation, appearing and disappearing majuscules, variant spellings, substitutions, pages lost, found, rearranged, dialogue that is silenced, chapters that fail to make the Atlantic crossing or arrive shuffled, disoriented.

These emblems of *Roughing It*'s textual instability signal its internal instability. The Moodies could not find a genre within which to inscribe this book. Bruce and Bentley may have thought it was either an informative immigrant tract, an exotic travel narrative, a wilderness romance, or all three. Critics have been looking for a genre to confine this text ever since. Klinck defines it as an apprenticeship novel (1962, xiv). Ballstadt has tried to show that it is a series of sketches in the manner of Miss Mitford, but has since argued that it follows a narrative model established by Frances Trollope (1972; 1988, xxiii–xxiv). Marion Fowler tries to prove that it is in the tradition of the sentimental Gothic novel of Ann Radcliffe. Gerson says it is in "the indigenous genre of the fictionalized survival guide" (1989, 135). As Peterman summarizes it, "containing elements of poetry, fiction, travel writing, autobiography, and social analysis, it eludes definition" (1983, 81). That, in Susan Glickman's words, *Roughing It*" is a miscegenous work, resisting generic classification" (1991, 22), suggests that it is no single thing. Moodie had intentions, although no single one, and she sought to provide some larger structure for the individual chapters. But the various intentions clash, and the text displays an unfulfilled dream of unity. Its strengths derive from the mix of literary sociolects with local dialects, from the mix of the serious with the comic, from the multivocality and heterogeneity that Moodie, perhaps involuntarily, figured into it.[12]

When Bentley contracted to publish the book and what precisely he thought he was getting are not known. Ballstadt says that by "early 1851 the manuscript was sent to John Bruce"; that he, "perhaps at the Moodies' suggestion, offered the shortened manuscript to Richard Bentley"; and that "by December 1851 Bentley had seen the manuscript and had it assessed by readers" (1988, xxviii). With its provisional title, "Canadian Life," and J.W.D. Moodie's previous proposal in mind, Bentley may initially have believed it to be a documentary. The documentary qualities are supplied by J.W.D. Moodie, but there is too little information on the colony and too much on Mrs Moodie to qualify it for this genre. Neither is it an immigrant's handbook, like Traill's *Female Emigrant's Guide* or Strickland's *Twenty-Seven Years in Canada West*. Although "The Outbreak" and "Canadian Sketches" are historical, this is no history. The chronological development and internal correspondences and parallels make it more than just a collection of sketches. While autobiographical, it is not an autobiography, lacking as it does a narrator who stands outside of the narrative or has an understanding of the significance to her development of the period covered.

Moodie's stated intention cannot account for the diversity of the book. "I have given you a faithful picture of a life in the backwoods of Canada, and I leave you to draw from it your own conclusions," she writes, and then draws hers: "To the poor, industrious working man it presents many advantages; to the poor gentleman, *none!*" Among the sections of the book that fall outside this frame for her "picture" are the first volume and "Canadian Sketches." In her last paragraph she reiterates her intention, now as redemption: "If these sketches should prove the means of deterring one family from ... shipwrecking all their hopes ... in the backwoods of Canada, I shall ... feel that I have not toiled and suffered in vain."[13] Summing up "a long digression" added to "The Walk to Dummer," however, she applies this intention only to the digression and not even to the rest of the chapter (444). The one positive truth she understands the text to contain – that the colony is a poor man's country – she never demonstrates.

Like the introduction to *Life in the Clearings*, the introduction to *Roughing It* may contain a discomforting truth about the Moodies: the "officers of the army and navy" are not the "instruments" with which "Providence works when it would reclaim the waste places of the earth" (14). J.W.D. Moodie writes that the "long probation in the backwoods of Canada" only brought him back "to the point from whence [he] started" (218). If the Moodies' first seven years in the colony were to be redeemed by a long warning to others of their class not to disobey Providence, then they did indeed toil and suffer in vain.

Mrs Moodie's inability to recognize wider intentions could be due to the unavailability of a genre that would contain these intentions. Her facility with pious and patriotic poetry, didactic children's stories, romance novels, and historical fiction did not serve her attempt to contain Canadian material. Neither could the sketch accommodate the large role she was writing for herself. The genres she brought from England could not be adapted to the amorphous, democratic, vulgar Canadian experience. Her verse production exemplifies this generic collapse. That her poetic output diminished the longer she was in the colony may have to do not only with her desire to be maximally productive but also with the frustration of her lyric impulse by the colony. Few poems were written specifically for *Roughing It*, and many do not relate to the text. The genteel polish of her lyrics never acknowledges the rough life around her. The colony stripped her of the outlines of a unified identity, necessary to the lyric, which she had tried to develop in her pre-emigration poetry. When, offering Bentley her novels, she decides to say nothing of her poetry because "no one reads poetry now," she evinces her sense of the ill fit of traditional poetic genres to colonial life.[14]

Roughing It succeeds when the voices of vulgar characters figure strongly or, often in conjunction with these, undertones in Moodie's voice surface. Her revulsion at the proximity of these people is palpable, but she cannot deny them a prominent place in her "Canadian Life." She attempts to assimilate them into her narrative and subdue them by moralizing or revealing their hypocrisy. She tries to dominate the range of discourse but, finding her voice in response to the voices of others, she begins in compromise. Her attempt to achieve a unitary language is frustrated by the dialogics of communication. She invests this narrative with the hope of restoring a unitary sense of herself. She associates this unified self with England and the lyric, the children's story and the romance. In *Roughing It* the insistence of the words of those she portrays thwarts her. Allowing the voices of the vulgar into her writing, she establishes a zone of contact wherein their discourses subvert hers. Hence she participates in the subversion of her authoritative language. Conjoining monologue and dialogue, Moodie, even if unintentionally, creates polyphony.

Without questioning *Roughing It*'s referentiality, the use of the conventions of fiction in it must also be taken seriously.[15] While reading it as a unified novel is to be avoided, so is reading it as unmediated fact. In dialogue, one of the fictional conventions Moodie most frequently employs, her tacit intentions for using these conventions are particularly transparent. Dialogue is central to each of her eleven chapters in the first volume. Over a third of the prose in this volume is dialogue, and more is quoted monologue. In the volume set on the Douro farm the frequency of verbal exchange decreases as the bush, rather than the neighbourhood, becomes the other; even in this volume her habitual means of depicting relations with the few people she comes in contact with is through represented conversations.

Moodie never claims to have an exceptional memory for recalling others' words, nor does she mention taking notes on them. While she is able to "remember a droll speech or a caracature face for years," this does not imply total recall of long conversations (letter 47). She reconstructs these dialogues, perhaps to construct an imaginary projection of herself. Trying to convey an accurate and truthful impression of the past, she fills in blanks opened up in the intervening years by resorting to a technique she learned writing fiction.

While Moodie occasionally reproduces conversations to relieve the seriousness of the surrounding prose, and sometimes to portray character, her more frequent intention in the dialogues of *Roughing It* is to make characters complicit in the compromise of themselves. Most of the dialogues in volume one are interrogations; they are commonly resolved, however, with a role reversal, as the interrogator inadvertently exposes her or himself. The dialogues are forced to happen by a character given the role of questioner; they end when that character, instead of exacting the desired information, reveals her or his own failings. Dialogue in *Roughing It* becomes an inherently antagonistic tool for communication.[16]

The pattern is established a few lines into the first chapter when two health inspectors interrogate the captain of the Moodies' ship. She introduces this exchange with the notation, "they commenced the following dialogue." The inspectors are made fools of when, to their question concerning births, the captain answers "three at a birth," then has his steward bring in new-born puppies (22). Next, they unknowingly swear the captain in on "Voltaire's *History of Charles XII*" in lieu of a

Bible (23). When the captain denies their request for planking, the inspectors express their pique by ordering him to disembark his passengers. He refuses due to the rough sea, and they leave "in great disdain" (24). Moodie concludes the scene with a comment on the captain's wisdom, as others drown that night attempting to reach shore.

The health inspectors, official interrogators, are mocked, duped, revealed as petty, denied their authority, and finally silenced. She stylizes this dialogue to represent the captain's "peculiar language" (22). The next coerced dialogue, occasioned by the visit of two customs officers and introduced by the same words as the first, is further stylized. Here Moodie uses dramatic conventions, introducing utterances with character tags, colons, and stage directions. This dialogue exposes the officers' greed and abuse of power as each of their questions solicits the expected bribe from the captain (41). Their stylization and prominence in the early pages of *Roughing It* suggest that these passages portray Moodie's primal image of dialogue in the colony.[17]

These initial images of how speech functions in colonial society are refigured in the first dialogue Moodie constructs of her own contact with that society. In "Our First Settlement, and the Borrowing System" her exchanges with Emily Seaton, "Old Satan's" daughter, are interrogatory, if not interrogations, and are further representations of speech as a coercive instrument. Her reluctance even to talk to this "girl of seventeen or eighteen years of age, with sharp, knowing-looking features, a forward, impudent carriage, and a pert, flippant voice" is apparent in every word Emily wrenches from her into the text (93). Equally, and perhaps inadvertently, apparent is Emily's assumption of her own authority as a "*genuine* Yankee[] ... a young lady," and, most importantly, daughter of an early settler, not a "stranger" (94). Moodie, not reliant on quoting Emily's words against her, interposes descriptions and judgments of the girl to ensure her humiliation. Yet Emily's recurring visits always focus on dialogue as she asks for what she wants and simultaneously challenges Moodie's habits and manners. As did the customs officers with the captain, Emily extorts many valuables from Moodie, while Moodie settles for exposing Emily's unscrupulousness.

Emily and other Yankee neighbours further disconcert Moodie by transgressing on her sacred bourgeois privacy, initially by reversing the mastery of seer over seen that she had exercised on the Grosse Isle mob. Upon her entrance Emily "stood, staring at [Moodie] in the most unceremonious manner, her keen black eyes glancing obliquely to every corner of the room" (93). Moodie finds of another borrower that, "once admitted into the house, there was no keeping her away" (102). A third is accustomed to "walking in and out whenever he felt inclined," and "looking at and handling everything" (105). This last is surprised that

Moodie refuses to dress her infant in his sight, and she expels him by assaulting his eyes with a cloud of dust. She ends the chapter with an account of how a candle she had borrowed was stolen, leaving her unable "even to look" at her sick child "to see" if he was recovering (111). This incident, among others, allegorizes her loss of the objectifying mastery of the gaze, even in her own home.

Unhesitating in her condemnation of Emily's affectations, Moodie seems not to recognize the justice of many of her criticisms. "You old country folks are so stiff," Emily tells her, and "You think yourselves smart!" (95, 96) Although Moodie does not acknowledge this identification of the incongruity between her English gentry manners and her reduction to life in the colony, she may grant the next statement she gives Emily more authority: "But old country folks are all fools, and that's the reason they get so easily sucked in, and be so soon wound-up" (96). After silencing Emily's importunities by overpaying her for a plate of butter and requesting that she bring the change next day, Moodie constructs a series of dialogues with others illustrative of the borrowing system. She was exploited by people who not only recognized her vulnerability but also thought she could "well afford to lend" what they wanted (101).

The monetary temptation with which Moodie rids herself of Emily was recommended by "a worthy English farmer" who, knowing "the Canadian Yankees" better than she, offered this solution as an alternative to verbal conquest of her adversary (99). She triumphs verbally over Betty Fye, another borrower, by gradually shifting their roles until she becomes the interrogator. From the beginning of this construction she parries Mrs Fye's requests with her own questions.[18] At last she attains the ideal proportion in dialogue, giving Mrs Fye a long "lecture on honesty." When Mrs Fye responds by quoting Paul, "It is more blessed to give than to receive," Moodie has ready an Old Testament quotation: "The wicked borroweth, and payeth not again" (103). Her satisfaction at routing the enemy is apparent as she sums up the scene: "Never shall I forget the furious passion into which this too apt quotation threw my unprincipled applicant. She lifted up her voice and cursed me ... And so she left me, and I never looked upon her face again" (103–4).

The verse with which Moodie buys her authority by selectively quoting ends, "but the righteous sheweth mercy, and giveth." More importantly, the raising of Betty Fye's voice in curses dramatizes a shattering of dialogue, an end to words. Having established a dialogic context for the representation of the voice of another, Moodie destroys that context and encloses herself in silence. Herself become interrogator, in her smugness at warding off a vulgar American supplicant she has turned the tables once more and become like the anatagonist the scene critizes.

An exchange similar to that which silences Betty Fye shuts the mouth of Joe Harris's mother. Mrs Harris requests a piece of silk to make a hood to keep off the cold. Moodie's comment on the weather provides Mrs Harris the occasion to offer the story of her life. Moodie is "so much interested in the old woman's narrative" that she grants her request. Even when a subsequent request is refused, Mrs Harris is not insulted, for "she commenced the following list of interrogatories" (140). Moodie's replies – to questions intended to elicit no more information than what Mrs Harris has freely given of herself –are terse. This character sympathizes with Moodie over her father's loss of fortune, tells her that her husband had the same experience, and is not critical of Moodie's dislike of the colony. Even in this reconstruction it is apparent that, while Mrs Harris may be prying, she is also trying to establish a friendly relationship of mutual personal exchange. "Provoked by her pertinacity, and seeing no end to her cross-questioning," Moodie abruptly reverses roles and asks, "Mrs. H—, is it the custom in your country to catechise strangers whenever you meet them?" To relieve Mrs Harris's confusion, Moodie explains that she refers to "an evil habit of asking impertinent questions." The denouement once more discloses the self-satisfaction in Moodie's triumph: "The old woman got up, and left the house without speaking another word" (141). In this second creation of a dialogic sphere only to destroy it by silencing the other, she again turns interrogator and exposes herself.

Moodie's work in the first volume of *Roughing It* is concluded by a third conversational conquest tacked on to the chapter on the charivari. Mrs Dean, "an American," pays a call and happens to witness the separation of the Moodies from their servants at mealtime. She asks, "Is not that something like pride?" (213). Moodie agrees with Mrs Dean's scriptural citation that "There is no difference in flesh and blood; but education makes a difference in the mind and manners." During the course of the conversation Mrs Dean reveals her racism in relation to a black ex-servant, and Moodie pounces: "Indeed! Is he not the same flesh and blood as the rest?" (214) Mrs Dean will not grant racial equality, and when Moodie presses the point, "out of the house she sallied in high disdain." The "great disdain" of the inspectors at the opening of the volume is matched at the close. Moodie notes the irony of this being the woman "who had given [her] such a plausible lecture on pride."[19] Concluding with a paragraph on the impending departure for the woods, she misses the irony that, through repeated rebuffs of all interlocutors, she has created a zone of silence in the clearing as deafening as the silence she will find in the bush.

Having suffered through physical proximity with Uncle Joe, Old Satan, and their families, Moodie attempts, almost twenty years later, to restore the authority of her voice by creating temporary spheres of dialogue and then dominating them with biblical citations and verbal aggression. The success of *Roughing It* lies in her failure to attain undisputed priority for her monologue. She left loopholes through which her adversaries in dialogue resist the finalization she would impose. When she allows the speech of Cobourg society contact with her own, the clash escapes her control. In this way some of her characters join her husband and brother, Bentley and Bruce as co-authors of the text in which they appear. The voices of the characters in *Roughing It* enter and speak with their own accents, their own emphases, and persist beyond the authorial attempt to silence them or devalue their words.

The speakers in these represented dialogues stalk each other, eager to take advantage of any opening. But those dialogues in which Moodie vanquishes her opponents do not have to be read univocally. *Roughing It* demonstrates a sinister side to the interpenetration of multiple voices as they jar disconcertingly with hers. She had good reasons to attempt to suppress the cacophonous voices that challenge her own. Peterman, pointing to her ability "in describing or dramatizing extremes and absurdities of human behaviour," argues that "her finest skills as a writer left her uncomfortable" and "seemed to her somewhat frivolous, centrifugal, and lacking in essential seriousness" (1983, 88). The seriousness of her use of these skills is that, through them, she is unsettled by the decentring effect of voices opposed to her own.

Moodie, at home when writing in the lyrical, hortatory, or didactic modes, leaves the doors of this text open to the voices of others. Speaking through her, these voices have a potency she cannot domesticate. They refuse to be reduced to interior decoration and reassert their independence. Her sketches of Uncle Joe and Old Satan only come to rest when she is satisfied that their anarchic tongues have been locked in narratives of their downfall, but she cannot bar all the windows. Her compulsion to engage them in dialogue underscores her anxiety. The section on the borrowing system details her confusion or consternation with the North American pronunciation and use of words like gentlemen, girl, rooster, slack, and sauce. This confusion redoubles her inability to accept a system of commodity exchange she cannot understand. "Uncle Joe and His Family," like the Moodies' house, is occupied by Harris and his mother.[20] Moodie's one-line comments and final challenge to Mrs Harris fail to recuperate the system of narrative, as she fails to grasp the system of land exchange.

In "Trifles from the Burthen of a Life" Moodie depicts the provincial dialect of a Scots landlady and "the most ludicrous enjoyment" Rachel's companion derives from "hearing her talk broad Scotch."[21] That she makes only those characters separate from her in race or class speak dialect points to mockery as part of her intention in using it. The Irishmen, Indians, Yankees, and servants of *Roughing It* speak dialect, but English gentlemen like Tom Wilson, Brian, and Malcolm speak in cadences indistinguishable from hers. She reproduces their speech at length, does not interrupt them or undercut their authority, and their monologues harmonize with hers.

Tom is her proxy in the verbal campaign against the Yankees when he goes to Joe Harris's wife to borrow yeast, since "they are always borrowing from you," he tells Moodie (116). Tom's conflictual conversation with Mrs Harris is stylized in the manner of the captain's with the customs officers and Moodie's with Philander Seaton (105-6). Character tags and stage directions shape a dialogue she admits to inventing: "Would I had been there to hear the colloquy between him and Mrs. Joe; he described it something to this effect:–" (117). Depicting the vulgarity and deceit of Mrs Harris and her mother-in-law, and Tom's outwitting of them (117–19), this dialogue directly follows his routing of Uncle Joe with an impersonation of the devil (114–16). Tom is Moodie's ally in her attempt to quell the Yankees. But the gentlemen, too, harbour a threat, this time a threat from which she cannot distance herself. Unlike others in the text, she internalizes the voices of *Roughing It*'s gentlemen. They do not speak through her; she speaks through them, and their expressions of abandonment and madness resonate with her own.

In the Cobourg setting "Yankee" is a synonym for low-class, and the Indians at Douro are described in terms that are the obverse of those applied to the Yankees. Moodie presents Indians and Yankees, the two recognizable societies she encounters, in paired terms and with similar methods of description. Both are represented as groups. Generalizations on Yankees and Indians abound. "Our First Settlement, and the Borrowing System" is devoted to Yankee customs and her attempt to deal with them; a parallel chapter in the second volume, "The Wilderness, and Our Indian Friends," similarly treats natives. She tries to fix these two alien societies in her writing. The phoneticized dialect spellings and broken sentence structures she puts in the mouths of these characters is matched by her designation of them by their first names and subsumption of individual Indians and Yankees into representative status. They constitute two species distinct from her own. Negations of each other in most ways, they stand in a complementary relationship to the narrator. The Yankee society is vital and thriving, and she rejects it; the Indian society is waning, and so she can eulogize it. Her imperial scorn for the Yankees is equalled by her colonist's condescension to the Indians.

Yankees and Indians are the occasion for numerous moralistic digressions, but the sin at the bottom of Moodie's ethical system is mere foul language. Told by an Indian that they only learned to swear from the English, she laments: "Oh, what a reproof to Christian men! I felt abashed, and degraded in the eyes of this poor savage ... How inferior were thousands of my countrymen to him" (287). What the Yankees are actually guilty of besides vulgarity and lack of respect for their betters comprises an innocuously short list: borrowing, drinking, and swearing. She delivers three lectures on cursing to neighbours (101, 138, 318). Of a man she calls "the most notorious swearer" in the district she writes that "he had converted his mouth into such a sink of iniquity that it corrupted the whole man" and that, with this "foul disease, he contaminated all he touched" (318). What disturbs her about the logging-bee they held is all the "profane songs and blasphemous swearing," all the "bad language" (321, 319).

To understand why this particular sin is so serious for Moodie, her distaste for "bad language" must be connected to the broken dialect she makes her Yankees speak and the ungrammatical speech of her Indians. If these ethno-philological details are then associated with her perception that "the titles of 'sir' or 'madam' were very rarely applied by inferiors" and that "they treated our claims to their respect with marked insult and rudeness," a social explanation for her moral scale becomes possible.[22] In Upper Canada Moodie finds her hierarchy in collapse, and violations of verbal decorum are cathected with the displaced force of this trauma. Each curse she hears is an echo of the shattering of her world.

Indians and Yankees form poles of attraction and repulsion in *Roughing It*. Between these poles are individuals who share Moodie's displacement and nostalgia for genteel standards. This group, curiously, is not represented in the text by her husband, her sister, her brother, or her friend Emilia, all of whom remain ill defined. The real representatives of the colonial gentry are a triumvirate with marked similarities: Tom Wilson, Brian, the still-hunter, and Malcolm, the little stumpy man. There are many differences among these characters, but a concentration on what they share is revealing. R.D. MacDonald and David Stouck have noted the similarities, but their social implications need to be emphasized.

Tom, Brian, and Malcolm, in contrast with the Yankees and Indians, are individualized: a whole chapter is devoted to each; their biographies are fully related; Brian and Malcolm are provided epithets, Tom and

Malcolm given pseudonyms (64, 365). They speak in refined, pointed prose. The epigraph to Tom's chapter reads, "Of all odd fellows, this fellow was the oddest" (63); Moodie writes that "Malcolm was one of the oddest of [nature's] odd species" (384); Brian strikes her as "a strange being" about whom she must find out more (174). As exceptions, they hail her from an ideological position that she recognizes. As subjects of this ideology they address her in a way that ratifies her own subjection to it. She in turn, quoting their words in a voice indistinguishable from her own, speaks to her English readers, hailing them to recognize their shared subjectivity/subjection, their shared oddness before the developing capitalist hegemony.[23]

These three are genteel and educated (65, 179, 370–1). They have all brought relatively large amounts of money to the colony with plans of establishing estates (76, 175, 370). Tom and Malcolm are "indolent," and Brian neglects his farm to spend his time in the woods (65, 371, 180). Inevitably, their settlement schemes have failed, and they have squandered their money (82, 175, 370). Brian and Malcolm relate how they have degraded themselves by keeping vile company, and Tom's only Canadian friend is the bear he buys (180, 372, 82). They all perform acts that strike Moodie as absurd (82, 188, 379). Their narratives seem straightforward illustrations of the proposition that gentlemen should not settle in the bush.

Once more, as in her attempts to secure the voices of the vulgar, Moodie writes her way beyond mere didacticism. She exhibits stronger feelings for these three men than she does for anyone else in the book. Tom loves music, Brian appreciates her painting, and Malcolm writes (69, 181, 379). Tom and Malcolm temporarily live with the Moodies, and Brian is "a frequent guest" (85, 369, 179). Each delivers a moral lesson reflecting sentiments she expresses elsewhere: Tom tells her how her "literary propensities" unsuit her for Canadian society (71); Brian tells a story that ends with the question, "Is God just to his creatures?" (181); Malcolm expostulates, "Oh, the woods! – the cursed woods! – how I wish I were out of them" (380).

These men, unlike the Yankees and the Indians, are capable of, or in Tom's case associated with, serious sin. Brian has attempted suicide, and Malcolm has committed murder (177, 377). Tom, in a lighter tone, uses a false admission of robbery to deflate the seriousness of a fellow passenger on a stage-coach (68). Yet Moodie does not moralize upon these crimes.

The key to the excessiveness of Moodie's treatment of these characters is another of their shared features: they are all mad. Tom, asked if he is going mad, replies, "I never was sane, that I know of" (79). Brian, in another's words, is "as mad as a March hare!" (175) Malcolm asks

Moodie, "Don't you think me mad?" (377) This triumvirate of English gentlemen presents the spectre of madness and sin lurking in the colonial bush beyond the orderly society of the imperial centre and its moral strictures. The stories these characters embody, the words they speak through her, reverberate with her own fears of what she confronts.

Early in her narration of her arrival in the Canadas, Moodie asks, "What heinous crime had I committed, that I ... should be torn from [England's] sacred bosom, to pine out my joyless existence in a foreign clime?" (73) Later she reflects on a period when her "love for Canada was a feeling very nearly allied to that which the condemned criminal entertains for his cell" (135). Plagued by a guilt the source of which she cannot identify, she writes of "the secrets of the prison-house," fearing that madness and death await her (489). Her feelings of guilt derive from an anxiety that, her system of values severely compromised in the colony, the guarantees for moral choice have evaporated. The exercise of "right reason" can no longer establish moral certainty. The triviality of her moral judgments in *Roughing It* is explained from another angle: cursing is execrable but suicide possible.

The mad English gentlemen all die prematurely. Brian makes another, this time successful, attempt on his life (191). Rumours of the murder of Malcolm in Texas reach the Moodies (385). She deletes the end of Tom's story between its *Garland* appearance and the book. He returned to England, married, lost his wife in childbirth, and went to New South Wales, "a melancholy and heart-broken man," to die in his mid-forties (303).

Moodie is trapped between damned Yankees and mad English gentlemen. The rabble are vulgar, vital, exploitative, materialistic, alcoholic, profane, and democratic. The gentry are refined, attenuated, generous, artistic, suicidal, spiritual, and elitist. She is caught between a manifest society and a potential society. One is someone else's reality, for her a nightmare; the other is her dream, a nightmare at its core.

Tom, Brian, Malcolm, and the Moodies are spiritual and poor. The materiality and profanity of the Americans at Cobourg is shown, but their possible suffering is not. The Indians, with no chance of gaining from the wealth of colonial society, have absorbed its profanity. Unable to elevate herself and her kind to the ideal of spirituality synthesized with materiality, Moodie leaves this position in the text vacant. Striving for it, the English gentlemen fall outside of possibility into madness and death. She can find no solution to the contradiction of profanity triumphant other than futilely to ridicule the vulgar between the covers of a book. Providence has indeed deserted her.

T.D. MacLulich, using categories very like Yankees and Englishmen, attributes the presence of these categories in *Roughing It* to the

"European personality structure," but they can be traced to a European social structure (1976, 125). Her positive definitions of self insecure, Moodie seeks identity through negation. She may be unsure of what she is in the colony, but she knows she is not a member of the barbarian Yankee and Indian communities she encounters. They threaten her view of how civilized society should function, but the Englishmen gone wild, in a condition into which she might herself degenerate, threaten her as an individual. Barbarians inhabit the wilderness outside, but wild men come to live in the wilderness within. Her Yankees derive from the gentry attitude towards the newly formed English working class as little better than animals and objects of fear. The connection she makes between "the low-born Yankee" and "the Yankeefied British peasantry and mechanics" reinforces the class antagonism in her rejection of North American society (198).[24]

This antagonism was exacerbated by emigration. Isolated in the genteel rural home, Susanna Strickland had still witnessed the disaffection of the growing class of urban poor. In her letter about the triumphal procession of "Orator" Hunt through London, she needs the reassurance that, six months after July 1830, "thoughts of Revolution ... have died away." She is reluctantly impressed by "the incomparable blacking mass" even as she dismisses "their teeth jarring jargon" of "Radical Reform" (letter 29). The proletarian masses were a murmur from the urban wilderness, to be ridiculed in passing. Sharing the European image of Upper Canada as a natural wilderness, she could not have expected when she left England for the colony that she would land in the midst of the barbarian horde. What were laughable rumblings in the metropolis became impending social chaos in the hinterlands.

As others have noticed, Malcolm especially approximates to the Byronic hero, but so does Brian, and even Tom, if Tom is viewed as a comic inversion of the type. Did Moodie shape her stories of them to suit this type, or were they themselves trying to live a cultural convention? In her conception of the artist and herself as one, the distinction between imagination and reality that this question implies does not hold. The dread her portrait of these English wild men sublimates is also a desire for a possible solution to the uncertainty of British North America.

A link between Tom, Brian, and Malcolm and Moodie's conception of the artist can be forged through her reconstruction of her youthful self as the romantic genius Rachel Wilde. Rejection of and by the world must be the writer's lot. But the artist as outcast and visionary in London, the Lake District, or Geneva had one or two others of similar temperament with whom to share his or her discontent. Youthful daydreams were transformed into a sterner yet far too mundane reality in the colony. The madness and death lurking on the other side of the visionary, anti-materialist stance became realities after that stance may have been discarded. Hence she is called and responds to the characters of Tom, Brian, and Malcolm.

The missing third term, dissolving the binarism of mad Englishmen and damned Yankees, is a class that Moodie does not write about in *Roughing It*. Not until *Life in the Clearings* does she address rising businessmen and professionals, and then to persuade them that "intelligence ... is itself an inexhaustible mine of wealth" (83). They undervalued their writers and intellectuals, and saw a more prosaic meaning in her metaphor. For them artists and workers were only sources of surplus value. When the economy slumped, they were best kept busy in the colonies; otherwise they might become revolutionary workers or radical artists. The "Yankeefied British peasantry and mechanics" and the landless English gentlemen constituted two displaced populations, however disproportionate in numbers, abilities, and expectations.

Moodie was neither radical nor reactionary. All in flux in the colonies, various classes and social orientations jockeying for dominance, she wanted no more than to find a solid basis for a new hierarchy within which she could instal herself at a modest level commensurate with her status in England. She worked with words to affirm the values she knew. While *Roughing It* itself is the emblem of this affirmation, within it she fights a defensive battle. She easily distances herself from the damned Yankees; she knows that she is not like them. The figure of the mad English gentleman is more insidious. The wild man within the gates, he speaks intimately to her of the madhouse and the prison.

Another set of terms in Moodie's socially determined bifurcation can be generated through a consideration of her attempt in *Roughing It* to establish a stable orientation towards colonial customs. The chapter "Our First Settlement, and the Borrowing System" is paralleled in title and content with "The Wilderness, and Our Indian Friends." In the settlement the borrowing system is a custom connected with a society fully developed before the arrival of the Moodies. In the bush their Indian friends are part of an equally developed society. She finds the Yankee customs vulgar and the Indian customs quaint. What she calls the borrowing system may have been, had she learned to manage it, a system of barter pre-dating the circulation of a standard currency and the availability of consumer goods. The Indians also retain barter, but she can control their use of it, as when she refuses to trade "Canoe, venison, duck, fish ... and more by-and-by" for her husband's map, and when she realizes that she could have "demanded a whole fleet of canoes for [her] Japanese sword."[25]

Moodie suffered from ignorance of the customs at Cobourg. Barter was part of an emergent rural economy that failed to survive when industrial capitalism became the dominant social formation. Other customs can be connected with a rural society since peripheralized. Charivaris and bees are among these customs, and she reacts to them as she did to the borrowing system. When she wrote about them, these practices belonged to her past; they did not intrude upon her in Belleville.[26] Ignorant of charivari, when the events of a number of instances of this "queer custom" are related to her she reacts with shock: "Good heavens! are such things permitted in a Christian country?" (208, 211) Her informant assures her that it is "the custom of the country" (210). While "much has been written in ... praise" of bees, to her "they present the most disgusting picture of a bush life" (313–14). "People in the woods have a craze for giving and going to bees," but she has a "hatred to these tumultuous, disorderly meetings," calling their own a "hateful feast" (314, 322). The folk customs of colonials are not to Moodie's taste; she heralds their demise with the advance of civilization.

Moodie is understandably dismayed at the violence to which the charivari sometimes led, but she may have feared it as a carnival folk ritual.[27] According to the woman who explains the custom to her, charivaris are held "when an old man marries a young wife, or an old woman a young husband, or two old people ... enter for the second or third time into the holy estate of wedlock" (208). They respond to carnivalistic mésalliances. So too, they force sacred and profane together, as when the invocation of matrimony as a religious sacrament is followed immediately in the text by a description of riotous behaviour. Carnival annuls the rules of everyday life. Moodie feels "a truly British indignation at such a lawless infringement upon the natural rights of man" as charivari (209). Carnival suspends hierarchy. The charivaris described to Moodie include idlers and gentlemen, booksellers and lawyers. Carnival encourages all to participate, regardless of class. She is told that a charivari "would seldom be attended with bad consequences if people would take it as a joke and join in the spree" (212). Despite this belief that participation would solve the violence associated with charivaris, local legislators used that violence as an excuse for curtailing them. Charivaris threatened the rule of law. Moodie has, after all, a motivation for tacking on to her account of charivari the dialogue with Mrs Dean about the separation of servant and master at mealtime: this defence of her own "custom" confronts the social relativity of "the customs of the country" (213).

The list of the participants in the Moodies' logging-bee establishes it as another occasion for familiar contact across class barriers. The "bad language" against which she rails is integral to the carnival atmosphere. Moodie thinks bees "noisy, riotous, drunken meetings," and theirs ends with the house ringing "with the sound of unhallowed revelry, profane songs and blasphemous swearing."[28] This describes the spontaneous eruption of the carnivalesque. What seems over-reactive in her depiction of the bee is merely commensurate with the degree of threat it represents. She knows how necessary bees are to rural colonial society.

Wholeness of action and unity of tone in the sketches of Tom, Brian, and Malcolm contrast with fragmentation and composition from a wide variety of materials in "The Charivari" and "Our Logging Bee." These chapters contain exhortation, anecdote, social commentary, comedy, autobiography, lyric lament, and dialogue; violating linguistic decorum, they fluctuate wildly between high rhetoric and low slang. Perhaps due to her sense of their literary prototypes, Moodie is able to package her English gentlemen in shapely narratives; but folk customs disorder her text. Tom Wilson, his activities dissociated from social implications, is an innocuous carnival fool. When the carnivalesque presents a distinct intimidation, shrill self-righteousness accompanies a vulnerability to depicting its power. Her contemplation of the "perfect paradise" of Grosse Isle is disrupted by the frolics of "vicious, uneducated barbarians," until the Moodies were "literally stunned by the strife of tongues."[29] Compelled to represent the words of her Yankee interlocutors in her "Canadian Life," so is she compelled to represent charivaris, bees, and, in her next book, camp meetings. Her attempts to monologize "the strife of tongues" at these rituals fail. While these are the darkest scenes of iniquity she conjures up from the colony, they are also scenes of vital communal ritual.

That Moodie absorbs colonial characters and folk customs and attempts to subdue them to her own voice suggests that she really might have heard in that voice the unifying principle of *Roughing It*, so authorizing subsequent attempts to unify the text around her. But her narrative persona, rather than being unified, is dissolved in the tensions between monologism and dialogism, between attraction to wild men and revulsion from barbarians, between narrative system and carnival chaos. Any belief in the author as unifying principle must take into account the collaborative production of the text and recognize that, by welcoming the aid of her husband, Bruce, and Bentley, she dramatizes her dependence upon and limitation by these men in her efforts to attain a unified image of herself. To unify the text would also require showing that the narrator of 1851 really does present a coherent and whole image of herself as protagonist of a story set in the 1830s.

The text as it was initially produced does not achieve formal manifestation of this image. If Mrs Moodie's work alone is considered

– but all of her work, including the introduction and poems – then the two volumes appear to have a parallel structure. Each begins with a voyage into what is the main setting for the volume. The space allotted to the voyages is disproportionate, three chapters on the way to Cobourg and one to Douro, yet they seem to be structural equivalents. Each volume ends with the decision to exit from the setting. Again, the exact parallelism that might establish conscious design is lacking: the departure from the clearing is reserved for the bush volume. In volume one Moodie's main conflict is with a vulgar neighbourhood, in volume two with a hostile environment. The correspondences between "Our First Settlement, and the Borrowing System" and "The Wilderness, and Our Indian Friends" are matched by other correspondences between chapters. The chapters on Old Satan, Uncle Joe, and Phoebe H— in volume one can be paired with the chapters "Burning the Fallow," "The Fire," and "The Whirlwind" in volume two; "Brian, the Still-Hunter" can be paired with "The Little Stumpy Man."

The parallels between the two volumes are, however, incomplete and undeveloped. There are two more chapters in the second volume than the first. Moodie may have wanted a structure flexible enough to be used for each setting and yet contain the varied contents of the two sets of experiences. She may have, but it is more likely that Bruce, Bentley, or his compositors were responsible for deciding that the manuscript should become a two-volume book. On the evidence, she did not divide "Canadian Life" into two discrete units. When she summarizes the book, at the beginning and end, she refers to "the Backwoods of Canada," ignoring altogether the part set in the clearings (15, 589). The first third of the text is but a prelude to the heart of *Roughing It*, in the bush. Early in the second volume she comments on the selectivity governing what follows: "It is not my intention to give a regular history of our residence in the bush, but merely to present to my readers such events as may serve to illustrate a life in the woods" (305). The portion of the text dealing with the seventeen months in the clearing is "a regular history," narrated in detail and containing all the events she felt important. It has the greatest concentration of previously published material, while covering only a fifth of the chronology of the whole. If there is a parallel structure to the two volumes, she does not seem to have grasped it consciously.

Typographical irregularities suggest the manuscript was sent off before Moodie was able to see it as a whole and revise it accordingly. She is inconsistent in her use of dashes to give anonymity to places and people, including herself when she has others address her.[30] A deeper disunity is signalled by the varied internal marks of when the book was written. Five times Moodie measures the distance between the events depicted and the moment of writing, and, apart from his "Canadian Sketches," her husband makes one such reference. These markers, all in portions of the text not previously published, designate a composition period of between late 1848 and early 1850.[31] In her introduction Moodie mentions her "sojourn of nineteen years in the colony," and in "Canadian Sketches" her husband says that he has been "sheriff for the last twelve years."[32] The disjunction between the period of composition and the introduction to the finished text opens up its temporal discontinuities. These inconsistencies suggest a manuscript for the most part in first draft, composed on an elementary chronological structure and never treated as a unit.

Neither was Moodie able consistently to detach herself as narrator from the presentation of her younger self as protagonist. In the first half of "The Charivari," discussing society in the colony, she begins by drawing on her early experiences but gradually modulates to a generalized account, indistinguishable in tone and tense from most of *Life in the Clearings*. Then, having "dwelt long enough upon these serious subjects," she returns to "the close of the summer of 1833" and her first experience of the charivari (206). Likewise, a digression on military half-pay occurs in the narrative present, interrupting a story set in the past (443). While memory is creative throughout *Roughing It*, her description of the St Lawrence shoreline fuses younger and older selves: "I love to recall, after so many years, every object" (36). She then proceeds to recall – or create – her sensations in 1832.

While many passages on homesickness in *Roughing It* arise from specific past events, some bring that emotion into the present, so that it is not always certain whether the "I" in the text is the narrator or the protagonist.[33] Moodie's created dialogues and attempts to place charivaris and bees satisfy desires that persist into the time of writing, and the need to express her yearning for England also persists twenty years after its initial occurrence.[34] One paragraph begins in the protagonist's past with reference to "the few weeks that [she] had sojourned in the country." She then describes homesick dreams of England from which she awoke crying: "I found it but a dream." The paragraph concludes in the narrator's present: "The reader must bear with me in my fits of melancholy, and take me as I am" (89). The reader must ask which Susanna Moodie had fits of melancholy, the one in 1832 or the one in the late 1840s. Similarly, into a meditation tied to her recollections of feelings prior to emigration she obtrudes pleas from the present: "Dear, dear England! why was I forced by a stern necessity to leave you? ... Oh, that I might be permitted to return and die upon your wave-encircled shores, and rest my weary head and heart beneath your daisy-covered sod at last!" That this is the narrator's voice, not her protagonist's, is confirmed by her reference to "melancholy relapses of the spring home-sickness" (73). The text never tells if she ceased to suffer these relapses, so the "home-sickness and despair" she mentions in her introduction belong equally to her experience in 1851 (15).

Moodie likewise mixes past and present in her use of the idea of "home," but home never belongs to the present. In her first meditation on the word she states just this certainty: "Home! the word had ceased to belong to my *present* – it was doomed to live for ever in the *past*; for what emigrant ever regarded the country of his exile as his *home?*" (48) Her last prayer before dreaming of England invokes "Home! Oh, that I could return, if only to die at home!" (89). Considering her unhappiness in the first volume, it is surprising to find her writing "not without regret" of leaving the cleared farm: "in spite of the evil neighbourhood, [she] had learned to love it."[35] The dynamic accounting for this first attachment to a colonial setting is clarified at the end of *Roughing It* when she sheds "regretful tears" at leaving "the dear forest home which [she] had loved in spite of all the hardships" (480). Only when freed from confinement to a place can she forget associated hardships and love it. The one other time she refers to a colonial dwelling as home is when looking back from the deck of the steamboat leaving Belleville (*LC*, 19). For Moodie "home" is always and only the place that is left behind. The ideality expressed by the word can never belong to the reality of her present.

The few glimpses of happiness in the second half of *Roughing It* do not relieve the "many bitter years of toil and sorrow" (270). The "halcyon days of the bush" are confined to the "first spring ... spent in comparative ease and idleness" (278). When a view of the lake is cleared that summer, Susanna's "joy was complete," but the new vista transports her "back to England," and in sitting "for hours" looking at the lake, she neglects "to learn and practice all the menial employments which are necessary in a good settler's wife" (306). "In moments" of oneness with nature she "ceased to regret [her] separation from [her] native land; and ... [her] heart forgot for the time the love of home," but these are only moments amid a more constant homesickness (340). By the mid-1830s hunger, sickness, deprivation, and hard work are also constants. The two occasions that relieve the gloom of the years 1836 to 1838 both involve the gathering in of food:

Oh, how I enjoyed these excursions on the lake; the very idea of our dinner depending upon our success added double zest to our sport! (356)

That harvest [of 1838] was the happiest we ever spent in the bush. We had enough of the common necessaries of life. (425)

But the "winter of 1839 was one of severe trial" (436). She and the children are sick; her husband is in Belleville as paymaster; the Traills have sold their farm and left, and her friend Emilia Shairp is also gone: "I felt more solitary than ever, thus deprived of so many kind, sympathising friends" (437).

Moodie portrays little of what she learned in these years. She retains her fear of cattle and of the woods throughout *Roughing It*.[36] She learns "that manual toil, however distasteful to those unaccustomed to it, was not after all such a dreadful hardship" (352–3). She overcomes her pride and enervation and learns those "menial employments" of "a good settler's wife," working in the garden and kitchen and making the best of the little they have. But if these lessons are part of the independence she gained, it must also be acknowledged that she never gave up the reliance on servants specific to her class in England. And as she states in the introduction to *Mark Hurdlestone*, she quit the jobs taken on in the bush when the family moved to Belleville. She never ceased to distinguish herself from the "hardy labourer" born to manual toil. Even after the experience of poverty allowed her to appreciate the poor, she continued to designate them in the third person.

Moodie implies – through the placing of her claim to have "received more godlike lessons" in the "soul-ennobling school" of "glorious poverty" than she "ever ... acquired in the smooth highways of the world" – that she first entered this school in 1836 (352). If so, she could believe that bush life did teach her something. Once again, however, she blurs her representation of past experience. Of the family events that forced her to emigrate, she writes that "poverty ... became their best teacher" (196), and admits that she enrolled in "this school of self-denial" prior to emigration (197). Groping for the meaning of the years in the backwoods, she looks "back with calm thankfulness on that long period of trial and exertion": "When our situation appeared perfectly desperate, then were we on the threshold of a new state of things, which was born out of that very distress." The succeeding narrative is "to illustrate the necessity of a perfect and child-like reliance upon the mercies of God" (353). The Moodies' release from Douro was not itself born out of distress and required decisive action on their part, which does not accord with a reliance on God. According to her, "Providence was doing great things" for them during these last years in the bush (420). She does not, however, go so far as to characterize John Lovell and Sir George Arthur as emissaries of Providence.

While the Moodies chose to enter the bush, contingency provided the opportunities they needed to exit. Moodie could not shape her life-plot to ratify the providential guidance that presides over her fictional characters. Behind her recognition that gentlefolk are not the "instruments" with which "Providence works when it would reclaim the waste places of the earth" is the menacing possibility that the whole emigration scheme may have been a mistake (14). In "Trifles from the Burthen of a Life" the storm that rages the day the M——s try to leave Suffolk strikes Rachel as "a bad omen." Her husband is angered by her "childish" belief in "an exploded superstition." She insists that "we are all more or less influenced by these mysterious presentiments," but "Rachel's defence of her favorite theory was interrupted."[37] Missing their ship for Scotland a second time, Rachel says, "I should be quite disheartened if I did not believe that Providence directed these untoward events." This time her husband inclines to her opinion despite his "disbelief in signs and omens ... [T]here is something beyond mere accident in this second disappointment" (212). In the expansion of this scene for *Flora Lyndsay*, the heroine asks, "Is it not a solemn warning to us, not to leave England?" Her husband, unwilling to argue, simply states his determination to oppose his will to his wife's message from God (105).

In *Roughing It* Moodie opens her account of the events leading up to emigration by insisting that everyone has "secretly acknowledged" the power of the "mysterious warnings" that "the human heart" receives (193–4). She declares her faith in these warnings and hints that she would have been "saved much after-sorrow" if she had paid "stricter heed" to "the voice of the soul." This digression introduces one such omen: "Well do I remember how sternly and solemnly this inward monitor warned me of approaching ill, the last night I spent at home; how it strove to draw me back as from a fearful abyss, beseeching me not to leave England and emigrate to Canada, and how gladly would I have obeyed the injunction had it still been in my power." Duty to husband and child overrode her premonition: "it seemed both useless and sinful to draw back" (194). She never answers the question of how it "seemed" twenty years later. Whose was right, her husband's interpretation of duty or her own of omens? Her uncertainty must not have been relieved by experience of "much after-sorrow." In her fiction only misguided characters attempt to control their destinies. Was emigration a misguided attempt to circumvent the decrees of Providence?

That *Roughing It* begs for such questions to be asked conditions consideration of the feelings Moodie expresses in it for the colony. The narrator only voices attachment to the colony as a contrast to her protagonist's expressions of dislike for it. Praise for the country never arises spontaneously but only to compensate for the complaints of her younger self. After describing how she sat in her first dwelling "abusing the place, the country, and our own dear selves for our folly in coming to it," she says that "now, when ... loving it," she can "look back and laugh at the feeling with which [she] then regarded this noble country" (91–2). At the end of a year her letters home continue to "abuse[] one of the finest countries in the world as the worst that God ever called out of chaos" (163). Comparing herself to Lot's wife, she writes of the battles "with old prejudices, and many proud swellings of the heart" that she and her husband fought before they "could feel the least interest in the land of [their] adoption, or look upon it as [their] home" (197). She addresses her fullest encomium to the country to "British mothers of Canadian sons!" (38) The phrase implies that first-generation immigrants are never naturalized. She urges these British mothers to raise their sons for the "future greatness" of the colony: "do this, and you will soon cease to lament your separation from the mother country, and ... learn to love Canada as I now love it, who once viewed it with a hatred so intense that I longed to die" (39).

Moodie's persistent homesickness, identification with England, and memories of hatred for the colony combine with her deferral of its greatness into a future only her children would see to create the impression that, in the moment of writing, she is trying as much to convince herself of her love of her present habitat as she is trying to convince her readers. These four sites contain *Roughing It*'s only prose in praise of the colony, and they are overborne by the felt life of the text. Resigned to living out her days in exile, she wished to be buried in England.

Given the lack of typographical uniformity or structural completion, the lack of any view of the experience portrayed as a whole, the lack of any clear moral to be derived from that experience, the lack of any convincing presentation of a positive feeling for the country, to attempt to interpret *Roughing It* as a unified artistic whole would be perverse. What is interesting about the text is not its unity, completion, and wholeness but the expenditure of so much energy and self-examination in a failed attempt to achieve these qualities. When pressure is exerted upon its various cracks and contradictions, it exposes a woman trying to work through words to the terms that could contain the tremendous tensions of her own and her country's histories. Even after she had employed the strategies of fiction at hand, the creation remains unfinalized, and threatens to disprove itself.

Perhaps the most important meaning *Roughing It* had for Moodie was not within its pages but in the book itself: it confirmed her status as author. After 1852 her mature writing no longer languished in defunct colonial periodicals but was available to the whole English-speaking world in a book produced by Richard Bentley of London, "Publisher in Ordinary to Her Majesty." Her attempt to construct an image of self and society uncovered the dangers of dialogue and carnival, the imaginative horrors of damned Yankees and mad Englishmen, and the fractures in her own experience, but once produced, the text was the emblem of her authority. The reality of the book gained for her a status that her various antagonists could not claim.

The frugality of Moodie's publishing practice was manifest once more as she transformed fugitive periodical documents into books. The domestic and creative economy of reselling already-written works to a new audience returned, replete with overtones of a psychological economy. She preserved the continuity between pre-emigration and post-immigration selves by reprinting her British poetry in colonial periodicals, and enacted an imaginative return in her fiction by using British settings. With *Roughing It* she established the other half of the exchange, returning her name to British soil on the covers of a book written in the colony. Her engagement, in D.M.R. Bentley's words, "to explain life on the periphery to those at the centre" was accepted (1990, 119). She threw the second line of an alternating current of psychic energy across the chasm, creating a reciprocal, mutually reinforcing system of literary exchange through which she earned money and a trans-Atlantic identity. Colonial periodicals welcomed the work of the young Englishwoman, and, beginning with *Roughing It*, a British publisher welcomed the work of the middle-aged colonist. This exchange across time and space must have provided a satisfying, if illusory, sense of personal unity. She could disregard the revelations of disunity that her book contains.

"Communication," writes Janet Giltrow, "maintains her attachment ... to the society ... from which she derives her identity." The exchange of language ensured Moodie of her existence. Through it she avoided "vanishing anonymously into a social and cultural void." Giltrow suggests why this textual exchange differs from the verbal exchanges within the text: "the traveller's isolation has a counterpoise in the affinity he feels with the culture he addresses."[38] Dedicated to her sister Agnes, *Roughing It* is metaphorically what Catharine's *The Backwoods of Canada* is literally, a long letter home. Many of its effects result from implicit contrasts of America with England that only those from the latter would understand. Peterman notes her attempt "to fit the imagined needs of a distant and revered audience" (1983, 88); she could risk contact with colonial voices and customs on the assumption that her British readers would respond to these passages in the spirit in which she wrote them. Her application of a line from an Australian poem to the "ruffianly American squatter, who had 'left his country for his country's good,'" is partly an inside joke that only cultured readers could appreciate. Other literary allusions, often biblical, similarly exclude the participation of the vulgar.[39]

On several occasions in *Roughing It* Moodie addresses her reader, sometimes with rhetorical questions. Unlike the interrogations within the text, these queries are meant to establish a communion between author and audience. They invoke shared standards to accentuate the absurdity of particular colonial scenes.[40] The most pointed of these questions, and the most double-edged, concludes the interrogation of Mrs Dean for her double standards on servants and blacks: "Which is more subversive of peace and Christian fellowship – ignorance of our own characters, or of the characters of others?" (215) Moodie exposes the American's self-deception to British readers, and implicates them in her judgment. There is no irony here, no awareness that other readers might find her blind to her own character. She assumes that her readers – British, genteel, educated – will respond sympathetically. As Giltrow phrases it, she dispatches "an appeal to her distant audience. She asks for commiseration" (1981, 142). She has little idea that in this larger dialogue dispute is as possible as consent.

This product of Moodie's domestic, artistic, and psychic economy has won consent, becoming part of the cultural economy of English Canadian literature. That consent has required the silencing of dissonant voices in the text, through editorial censorship or critical deafness. As the English Canadian literary tradition was reaching the point where it could be said to have a canon, *Roughing It* was becoming one of its anchor texts. During this process the text was continually shaped by the hands of others besides its author.

The very title supplied by Bentley is a distortion. The first volume narrates events from the "30th of August, 1832" up to "the close of the summer of 1833" (21, 206). Moodie ends her last chapter in this volume anticipating the "departure for the woods" (215). J.W.D. Moodie's two concluding chapters cover their first year in Canada. He ends by describing the "uncleared land" he has obtained north of Peterborough (253). After the voyage from Grosse Isle to Cobourg this volume deals with life on a previously settled cleared farm less than six miles from Cobourg. In her portion Mrs Moodie tries to come to terms with an established society, while in his chapters J.W.D. Moodie distinguishes between settling on a cleared farm close to markets and developing uncleared land in advance of settlement. In his description of frequent trips into town for "groceries and other necessaries," Cobourg appears as a bustling village (238). Volume one could have been called "life in the clearings." It is as long as volume two, which deals with the bush segment of the Moodie experience.

Bentley and Bruce, producing from a raw manuscript a book directed at a specific market, conditioned all subsequent perceptions of that book and hence its position in English Canadian literature. In the first half a middle-class English woman tries to maintain dignities of caste in the midst of an uncouth, vulgar population. After the bush option is undertaken, she appears against a background of sickness, cold, scarcity, fire, and storm. Class-bound indignation yields to more dramatic and romantic heroism. At this point in the text the creative possibilities of the raw experiences and rawer prejudices of the Moodies unfold. The image of the resourceful gentlewoman, roughing it in the bush of discontent and in a winter of social and mental migration, enlivens and energizes the story. Bentley's "Advertisement," silent on the Cobourg experience, foregrounds the "delineations of fortitude under privation ... contained in her second volume" (x).

That Moodie and her collaborators never achieved consensus on what unifying intention held their fragments together helps to account for the varied composition of each edition. She plays variations on her intention to warn prospective genteel emigrants away from the Canadas, but her husband addresses those coming. Neither of these intentions accords with Bentley's marketing of the text as pioneer romance. A further intention surfaces in 1871 in the first Canadian edition. While this edition cannot be bought by prospective emigrants, the warnings to British gentlemen remain, even in the rewritten and expanded introduction. In "Canada: A Contrast" Moodie remarks only on that part of the narrative set "in the woods, attempting to clear a bush farm" (527). She complains of unjust criticism but traces it to her "account of [their] failure in the bush" (528). She forgets her harsh treatment of the clearings society, and even transfers that criticism to the backwoods by referring to "the first seven years" as if they were all passed there and by writing as if the Moodies had never had a farm "near a village" (527, 528). She asserts that her "love for the country has steadily increased from year to year" (528). She describes how development has erased the conditions they faced in the 1830s. She adds "Forest" to the subtitle "Life in Canada." She changes the epigraph on the title-page from one emphasizing her "Painful experience in a distant land" to a more uplifting one claiming that "poor exiles" are the "first founders of mighty empires" and the civilizers of "barbarous countries."[41] The book becomes a document of a vanished way of life. It provides the basis for a contrast between then and now, between her hatred of the country then and her love for it now.

In contracting for the Canadian edition Moodie was requested to reduce it in size (letters 107, 109). To this end she follows the American pirated edition and cuts most of her verse. By omitting the pieces by her husband and brother, both dead, she becomes the text's sole author keeping one chapter by her husband that accords with her own tone and method but cancelling its attribution to him. His contributions would better suit a "work entirely his own," but plans for such a work were never executed (letter 107). She corrects some factual errors and deletes some mild profanities from dialogue. She changes the word she uses to describe the occupants of Grosse Isle from "harpies" to "women." A general retrospection on "the state of society in Canada," covering a period of "seventeen years" in the 1852 edition (201), covers "forty years" in the 1871, while the statement itself is unchanged. These are her sole attempts to update the text.

Despite refusing to acknowledge the source of criticism of the book, Moodie makes a number of revealing excisions for the Canadian edition. Writing to her daughter a few months before its release, she describes drawing her "pencil through many objectionable passages": "As this edition is for the D.C., we need not arouse their anger by a repetition of them" (letter 109). She deletes a commentary on the disturbing precocity of Canadian children that ends stating that "such perfect self-reliance in beings so new to the world is painful to a thinking mind" and that "it betrays a great want of sensibility and mental culture" (136). She cuts a passage that recounts the Moodies' rejection because "the society of C—" lacked refinement and was resentful of any who had it (201). This omitted passage goes on for ten more paragraphs criticizing local customs. In line with her reconsideration of the Rebellion of 1837 she deletes from the second volume "An Address to the Freemen of Canada," which rails against traitors and "base insurgents." In "Canada: A Contrast" Mackenzie is presented as "a clever and high-spirited man": "the blow struck by that injured man ... gave freedom to Canada" (530). Yet the epigraph to "The Outbreak," drawn from her poetic attack on him and speaking of "a corrupted stream" and "the slave, who lures / His wretched followers," is allowed to stand (407).

All Moodie's changes for the 1871 edition are of this kind. She excises block passages, usually complete paragraphs. She does no rewriting and adds nothing except "Canada: A Contrast," largely taken from the 1852 introduction. Given her chance to oversee an edition, she reduces *Roughing It* from a collaborative production in prose and verse to a story of one woman's trials in the pioneering past. She eliminates the direct social criticism without muting the implicit criticism. She is, at this late date, reclaiming her text, one that attempts, in light of the life she has lived, to speak for her perceptions of self and nation and not for Bentley's perceptions of market and imperial moment. Her reclamation of nation and text is ambiguous and uncreative. It is her post-Confederation re-appropriation of a pre-Confederation imperial blitz on the significance of colonial life. This readdress of intention and text by Moodie in old age salvages authenticities, both fabricated and factual, from the collaborationist text of the two Moodies, Bentley, and Bruce.

Thus she stakes her claim as a canonical figure, for her book as a canonical pioneering text of a new dominion. She also participates in the dismemberment of a text tenuously held together at best.

The 1913 edition, published in Edinburgh by T.N. Foulis and issued in Toronto and New York, is a resetting of the 1871 text. Apart from modernized punctuation, the text is unaltered. In its packaging, however, it extends Moodie's 1871 aim of presenting a document from pioneering forebears. Early photos of the Moodies are included; R.A. Stewart contributes scenic water-colours, and other plates are taken from the British William H. Bartlett's 1842 book *Canadian Scenery Illustrated*. These sketches, executed on his visit to the colony in 1838, thus contemporary with the Moodies' bush experience, reflect a romantic taste for the picturesque that Moodie seldom indulged in the colony. The foreword by the publisher "still further emphasizes the contrast between life in Canada in 1830 and 1913" (xi). The book becomes a piece of a period, the 1830s – in the eyes of 1913, a period piece. In piecing their notions of the 1830s Upper Canada together in an editorial trapping of piety and remembrance, the editors at the Foulis press reveal and reflect their own period.

The 1923 McClelland and Stewart reimpression of the Foulis edition culminates this distancing of the text to a romantic past. Stewart's water-colours and Bartlett's engravings are kept in one issue, but replaced in a second with sketches from various sources. The book is wrapped in an illustrated jacket featuring a log cabin in the foreground, a high silhouette of evergreens in the background. This slip-jacket describes it as a "semi-diary" presenting an "accurate picture of pioneering conditions and life." The blurb steals an afterthought of the 1913 foreword to say that the book has "the additional charm of literary excellence." This edition, available to Canadians through half this century, presents the text as a historical and social document. No longer a warning to emigrants, or a handbook for immigrants, or the grappling of an English gentlewoman with a new world and her place in it, this book is a quaint document from the romance of history, something distant yet engaging, as an exotic tale from a distant land would be engaging for British readers in the middle of the last century.

Klinck's first claim in his introduction to the 1962 New Canadian Library edition rationalizes his completion of the text's dismemberment, as he has made it conform to a specific genre and reduced it to a third of its original length: "Only a successful book requires as much editing as *Roughing It in the Bush* has received" (ix). It is now an "apprenticeship novel" with a central "author-apprentice-heroine" (xiv). His excisions reinforce a reading of it as a novel in which the protagonist resolves her conflicts. Gone is the central "A Journey to the Woods," and with it any indication that Moodie gained limited self-possession only in the bush, after retreat from the clearings. It becomes proof of her 1871 statement that she had grown to feel at home, and, now a unified novel, proof that she has contemporary relevance. An arbitrary critical notion, orthodox within a particular period of academic culture, ratifies the editorial privilege of exclusion.

Roughing It, in play between its various dualities, does not rest in any stable configuration. Its instability exposes it to dismemberment at the call of intentions foreign to itself. It is an instalment in an incomplete serial writing project, not an achieved literary artefact, an open text, not a finished whole. It is one woman's attempt to write through a forest of oppositions and contradictions. While it demands its reader's participation in the effort to negotiate a path, it does not authorize the after-the-fact blazing of this path with critical or editorial sleight-of-hand. While the text as an object – published in England, bound in two volumes, selling for a guinea – may have assured Moodie that she had come through, her journey within it is incomplete.

In the developing English Canadian canon this book has found its place in various forms. Each edition has been constituted by a desire to create a work unified by certain conceptions of what the book should be. Each edition ignores or excludes discordant elements to foreground other elements that accord with the various notions of what the text is. The colony was given it by an English publisher as an exotic narrative of struggle in a distant land. It then became the basis for a contrast showing how far the colony had come on the way to dominion status. Next it was transformed into a quaint document from a distant past. Then it was reduced to the shape of a unified novel. The book has found a home with the Virago Press and the Centre for Editing Early Canadian Texts. The New Canadian Library has published a new edition, re-printing the full text of the first edition. Now that the text has been restored in complete versions, attention to it unbound by the need to unify may be generated.

Margaret Atwood's conception of Moodie as schizophrenic disperses a textual division on to psychological and metaphysical levels. Shields, remarking on Atwood's interpretation, writes that "it is possible that the dichotomy is not rooted in Mrs. Moodie's personality; it may be only a surface splintering, a division which exists for literary purposes, namely the division between person and persona" (1977, 30). Rather, the division exists between literary purposes and the intractability of her linguistic – her ideological – milieu. The split in her personality transposes the split between the institution of *la langue* she carries and *la parole* she finds spoken in the colony. She works at generic and social stability through words but is confuted by the discourse she encounters in her production of self.

Moodie knew that language inscribes social reality. When she quotes the serving-class belief "that no contract signed in the old country is binding in 'Meriky,'" the dialect disavows linguistic contracts as well as legal ones (212). One contradiction she avoids is that of separating language and ideology.[42] She knew that her writing was worth an expenditure of time and effort; even after it was no longer needed to buy children's shoes, it may have bought sanity and sanctity.

This text is central to English Canadian culture precisely because of its problems. In coming to a land that could not be contained by any generic framework, Moodie wrote unabashedly, believing she could capture it all. The inadequacies of language allowed her to catch more of the society around her than she knew. She had little idea of the contradictions riving this text from typography to tone. In her very inability to close the gaps, she delineates the determinate absences upon which she had to build. In its contradictions, its irresolutions, its generic amorphousness, its open-endedness, its disunity, *Roughing It* tells a story of which Moodie had little conscious awareness. She absorbed the contradictions, lived them out, and then reproduced them unresolved. A stronger writer, or one less honest, might have hidden them beneath some aesthetically satisfying resolution. A stronger personality might have imposed a unified presence. As it was, Moodie articulated disturbances molded into the building blocks of Canada. She was the person needed to focus and initiate the textual activity called *Roughing It in the Bush*.

8 Conclusion

"Rachel Wilde," "Trifles from the Burthen of a Life," *Flora Lyndsay,* and many of Moodie's other fictions are concentrated registers of the early nineteenth-century conjunction of economic misfortune and migration. *Roughing It in the Bush* and *Life in the Clearings* are virtual compendia of the concerns of mid-nineteenth-century Upper Canadians. These qualities do not require that Susanna Moodie be read as representative of her class, nation, or sex, or that her works individually or together conform to requirements of artistic unity or overall consistency. As this study has tried to show, there are too many factors contributing to the formation of her work for it to be seen as typical, or unified and consistent. It manifests all the contingency and extemporaneity of a woman using the resources at hand – highly developed resources – to wrest from widely varied circumstances the substance of a self-definition, the subject of her own discourse.[1]

Moodie's struggles to create herself do refer to the position of women writers in her period. Her early children's stories are conventional moral tales with linear plots and clear didactic intent. Their male heroes earn their happy endings by learning self-control. When she began to write serialized novels in the early 1840s, she retained this underlying structure. "Geoffrey Moncton" and "The Miser and His Son" have black and white character systems in which the wicked place their faith in personal will, the good in Providence. She fleshes these stories out not with psychological or narrative complexities but by accreting character studies, sometimes with slim connection to the plot. While the male heroes of many of her stories and novels share her financial anxieties, among the character studies that stretch out the novels are female figures who double for Moodie in less material ways.

Not counting incidental characters, *Geoffrey Moncton* and *Mark Hurdlestone* each have three good women, two of whom die prematurely. The angelic Margaret Moncton marries her cousin Geoffrey just as they discover she is dying of consumption. The poetry-writing enthusiast Juliet Whitmore somehow survives to become one of Anthony Hurdlestone's just deserts. The plots of these novels, however, hinge upon strong female characters, their strength definitive of the evil they embody. In *Mark Hurdlestone* the masculine Mary Mathews leads a vicious life before she loses her mind and saves the hero with her confession. In *Geoffrey Moncton* the demonic Dinah North dominates the plot until Providence turns against her; she confesses and saves both the heroes, but in the madness of damnation kills herself to rob the hangman. Some of the character sketches in the Canadian works also separate strength and insanity from pensiveness and sensibility. In *Roughing It* Mrs Harris plainly contrasts with her granddaughter, Phoebe; in *Life in the Clearings* Grace Marks the mad murderer contrasts with lovelorn Jeanie Burns. Mrs Harris and Grace live into old age; Phoebe and Jeanie die in youth. Through these lunatic Amazons and holy innocents, Moodie examines the imagery of monsters and angels, from Lilith and Eve down, bequeathed to women by male authors.

The insane or captive women of some of Susanna's early poetry are alternative explorations of the condition of women. The title props of "The Broken Mirror" and "The Picture Lost at Sea" frame domestic lives shattered or mislaid, then remade in exile. Moodie's first foray into directly autobiographical fiction, "Rachel Wilde," conjures up a stock romantic visionary to represent her youth. As this figure matures into Rachel M— in "Trifles from the Burthen of a Life," she remains tied to her fictional, angelic prototypes. She is well matched by her foil in *Flora Lyndsay*, the monstrous Wilhelmina Carr, a forceful personality who is extremely eccentric, if not insane. Tom, Brian, and Malcolm mix sensibility and psychosis and may be closest to Moodie's image of the self she fears to become. The self she actually presents in *Roughing It* is both saner and stronger, and indeed is the most fully rounded and convincing character she ever produced. She is neither good nor evil, simply human. In *Life in the Clearings* she engages this character with the public realm, an authority empowered to comment on Upper Canadian society.

Moodie's career developed, however, in the shade cast by men and money. She and Catharine began to write immediately after their father's death. In the stories they both tell of the manuscripts written on blue paper liberated from a trunk, Eliza, their oldest sister, is the instrument of patriarchy's ban on women writing, playing the role of father-figure, which her accounts-keeping and management of the family finances would suggest she actively adopted. The Word of God the Father brought doubts to Susanna about writing, but she only really decided to quit when she married: "My blue stockings, since I became a wife, have turned so pale that I think they will soon be quite white" (letter 31).

While Moodie wrote sporadically and published previously written work in her first years in the colony, the duties of a settler's wife and mother of his children amply filled her time. When her husband was away as militia paymaster, she returned to writing in a concentrated way. With the move to Belleville in 1840 and the birth of her last child in 1843, her second main period of productivity began. J.W.D. Moodie's failure of his husband's duty to provide a secure and stable income was another factor in her increased output. After the publication of six books, all written by 1853, she had no more to say. When her husband was forced to retire in 1863, financial pressure again forced Moodie back to work. She got another children's story and a novel published, but her career could not be revived. Her husband dead, Hunter, Rose and Company approached her in 1869 for a Canadian edition of her books, but only the 1871 edition of *Roughing It* appeared. She spent her last years as a guest in the homes of her sister and children.

Susanna Moodie has had her say and has been listened to. From the children's stories assigned to women writers through the male-dominated novel and her conventional verse and prose, she reached outside the traditional genres to a point from which she could grasp her experience from the perspective of her own gender and class. Her writing was a quest for the forms to represent an identity undictated by social and sexual limitations.

As prophet or moralist Moodie attempted to assimilate the immaterial Word of God throughout her long endeavour to forge an identity in words. But forces of class and gender impelled and imperilled her constructions of self in language: the paternally bequeathed desire for a lost caste; the patriarchal, founders-of-empire ideology of colonization; the anti-genteel, philistine ethos of Upper Canadian society; the democratic threat to hierarchies on both sides of the Atlantic; the unmannered middle-class capture of hegemony. When these forces became too much for her, she withdrew her words from the world, became a receptacle for the Word, and resigned herself to silence. In the mid-1850s she ceased to write for publication and in 1857 became engaged with spiritualism.[2]

Susanna and Catharine studied the zodiac and thrilled at learning that the garret of Reydon Hall was haunted. Of Rachel Wilde, Susanna writes: "Ghosts were her familiars, and with witches and fairies she was well acquainted. She had vague notions of the truth of the second sight" (148). In late 1827 she wrote two poems about spiritual communication with a London friend, and in a letter confirmed that telepathy reconciled her "to the absence of those who are dearer to [her] than life" (letter 4). Three of five "Sketches from the Country" treat Suffolk superstitions or supernatural legends. Later, she wrote two novels about magic for the *Literary Garland*. She recorded her premonitions on the eve of emigration in "Trifles from the Burthen of a Life," *Flora Lyndsay*, and *Roughing It*. In *Geoffrey Moncton* she refers to "the mysteries of mind" as "the links which unite the visible with the invisible" and to dreams as "revelations from the spirit land" (322, 326, 68). In *Roughing It* she tells of communicating spiritually with her husband and argues at length to prove "this mysterious intercourse" of spirits (468).

The apocalypticism of Moodie's early poems reappears in "The Coming Earthquake" in 1848. Natural disaster in this poem is explicitly a synecdoche for the end of the world:

Mortal, behold the toil and boast of years,
In one brief moment to oblivion hurl'd:
So shall it be, when this vain guilty world
Of woe, and sad necessity and tears,
Smiles at the awful mandate of its Lord,
As erst it rose from chaos at his word. (ll. 15–20)

"The Maple Tree," concluding *Roughing It*, foresees the death of "the nation's heart" (l. 78). In *Life in the Clearings* Moodie describes how, after Europeans have reclaimed all the "waste places" of the world and excess population has nowhere else to go, "the world ... will be struck out of being by the fiat of Him who called it into existence" (282). Her apocalypticism becomes millennarian in other writing in the 1840s. In "Canada," the prolegomenon to both the *Victoria Magazine* and *Roughing It*, she has a "prophetic glance" of "Visions of thy future glory" (ll. 2, 3). The weight of "Nations old, and empires vast" is upon the colony, "the last – not least" to be born (ll. 47, 50). Canada's future as a Christian nation assured, the poem ends predicting the second coming: "Joy! to the earth – when this shall be / Time verges on eternity!" (ll. 115-16) She is reconciled to her present by interpreting it as preparation for the millennium. After discussing telepathy in *Roughing It*, she foretells that humanity will know its "mysterious nature" when Christianity has "transformed the deformed into the beauteous child of God. Oh, for that glorious day! It is coming" (469). Millennarianists claimed spiritualism to be a new religion; she asserts that it is "a new revelation from God to man" (letter 68). Many of her poems strike a visionary stance, and the "pleasing madness" of the poet returns as the "glorious madness" of the spiritualist ("The Poet," l. 17, letter 68). As a spiritualist visionary, however, she no longer communicated her visions to the world.

Between 1853 and 1855 Moodie became engrossed in the new literature of spiritualism, reading at least four books on the subject (letters 51, 56, 61). In the fall of 1855 she had "several visits from Miss Kate Fox the celebrated Spirit Rapper." Margaret and Kate Fox had devised table-rapping as the favoured means of spiritualist communication. She depicts Kate as "a witch" with a "pure spiritual face" incapable of deceiving and explains her demonstration as due to an ability "to read unwritten thoughts" (letter 59). In May 1858 she recounts her spiritualist progess over the preceding year. Despite witnessing further demonstrations, she "persisted in [her] vain unbelief." She "had several sharp mental conflicts on the subject" with her husband, who had "become an enthusiastic spiritualist." In the spring of 1857, after he went to visit "another spiritual friend," she "wept very bitterly." Alone, she had her final proof as Thomas Harral and Thomas Pringle communicated to her from among the dead (letter 68). This event initiated her activity as a spiritualist medium.

The Moodies' spiritualism coincided with the intensification of their economic and social insecurity. Her first year as a medium was "a year of great anxiety," during which they were "in continual jeopardy of losing all that [they] possessed in the world." Spiritualism was an alternative to direct action as a response to their conditions. The spirits repeatedly told J.W.D. Moodie that he had the power to heal by laying on of hands, and he tried to exercise this power. In communication with the dead, Susanna wrote out "whole pages of connected and often abstruse matter, without ... knowing one word about it" (letter 68) – this, rather than writing out whole pages on more mundane matters for which she might have been paid. A "Spiritualist Album" contains messages from the dead received by the Moodies from 1857 to 1863. She did not, after all, stop writing. She just stopped writing about the living and for the living. In the "Spiritualist Album" as in *Roughing It*, she accepted the aid of collaborators and ventriloquized the voices of others in a dangerous dialogue with her own. In the "Spiritualist Album," however, her collaborators and conversationalists are dead.

Moodie turned from words to the Word. While her spiritualist activities did not continue after 1863, neither did she return, except briefly, to writing. The bulk of her surviving correspondence is from the last years of her life and makes for painful reading. These letters put to rest any idea that *Roughing It* is the success story of a displaced English gentlewoman coming to terms with a colonial environment. She laments how hard it is "to be called upon to endure greater privations at the close of life, than ... in the Bush" (letter 77). Any claim that she came to love her adopted country must face the persistence of her thoughts of leaving it. For thirty-five years after their arrival in the colony the Moodies discussed plans to emigrate again; their discussions only ceased when his health forbid the prospect. The idealized, romantic figure of a founding pioneer, so often put forward in the commentary on *Roughing It*, did not exist.

Susanna Strickland began to write with a faith in the power of words to work for personal needs and desires. She soon felt doubts about this power. Being lionized, then criticized, in London taught her that language could not be trusted. Being accused of lying and playing ape for the aristocracy in the colony forced her to see that language does not mean in any unequivocal way. She had her own words subverted by the alien tongue of damned Yankees and infected by the nightmare speech of mad Englishmen. The work of words failed her, and only the Word remained.

Susanna Moodie remains integral to English Canadian literary and popular culture because her life and writing are bound up with the history and ideology of nineteenth-century Upper Canada. Her life and writing were produced by and in turn produce that period. Still, our continuing response to the disunity in her voice may be due to the unresolved disunity in our own.

Notes

INTRODUCTION

1 The verse is from a handwritten book of poems, mostly unpublished (PHEC, ser. II, Manuscripts, box 6, p. 3). It was written after the spring of 1852, when the arrival of the British edition of *Roughing It* in the colony first brought Moodie widespread fame, and before 1854, the date of the poem following it. It is also the first poem in a manuscript book of verse, now in the Thomas Fisher Rare Book Library, University of Toronto, which Moodie wrote for and dedicated to her daughter in 1866. The prose passage is from a letter to her British publisher, Richard Bentley, dated 8 October 1853 (letter 49).

2 Letter 72; for a survey of reviews of Moodie's work (listed in Secondary Sources in the Bibliography, mainly under Anonymous) and a more complete discussion of the criticism, see Thurston 1989, 31–124.

3 Douglas 1875, 106; O'Hagan 1899, 170; for the connection of nationalism, mimesis, and Canadian literary criticism, see Davey 1988, 12; Lecker 1990, 662–3; McCarthy 1991, 32–3; Surette 1982 and 1991, 17.

4 She is referred to as a "pioneer of Canadian literature" by the *Anglo-American Magazine*, Anon. 1852, 173; Canniff 1869, 360; MacMurchy 1906, 23; see also Weaver 1917.

5 Skelton 1924, 241; Rhodeniser 1930, 61.

6 Lorne Pierce and Albert Watson (1922) create "On First Seeing Quebec"; Edmund and Eleanor Broadus (1923) "The Bear"; John Robins (1946) "A Settler's Wife Alone at Night"; and Malcolm Ross (1954) "Lot's Wife," all from short passages of *Roughing It*.

7 The essays include McCourt 1945, Needler 1946, Partridge 1956, Scott 1959, Thomas 1966, and von Guttenberg 1969. The group biographies include Needler 1953, and Morris 1968.

8 MacLulich 1984–85, 19; Lecker 1990, 656–67.

9 As Ross's *Our Sense of Identity* (1954) is a title indicative of the preoccupations of its time, so is David Staines' *The Canadian Imagination* (1977) typical of its. Donna Bennett has analysed the "affirmation of prose fiction as the central form of contemporary literature" in Canadian criticism during the same period as that covered by these two dates (1991, 136). The version of *Roughing It* canonized by the late 1970s accords with the canonical fiction of that time as described by Lawrence Mathews: "The central character struggles to find meaning, purpose, authenticity, identity ... The significance of the protagonist's experience is *personal*; ... Social and political reality may hardly exist at all" (1991, 159).

10 Moss 1974, 86; Moss detaches the historical Susanna Moodie from the distasteful social attitudes of "the created being who has her author's name" (85).

11 While *Roughing It* is in Moss's *A Reader's Guide to the Canadian Novel*, none of Traill's texts is. Elizabeth Thompson's *The Pioneer Woman* is the one extended attempt to elevate Traill over Moodie as the founder of "a female character type, one which is arguably unique to Canada," and to give her a chief place on "any list of Canadian heroines" (1991, 3, 8). Leon Surette coined the neologism "topocentric" in 1982.

12 Among these critical texts are Murray 1990, Dean 1989, and Freiwald 1989. Susan Glickman, in the only essay devoted to *Enthusiasm; and Other Poems*, uses it to demonstrate that Moodie resisted "oversimplification" and was willing to be self-contradictory, qualities that "enabled her to be the most complete chronicler of the settlement experience in English Canada" (1991, 23). Glickman's stress on Moodie's "spiritual autobiography" (22) is the foundation of Susan Greenfield's dissertation (1990) on Moodie. In a thesis on the *Victoria Magazine* Klay Dyer (1992) argues for reintegrating Moodie's work in its historical context. D.M.R. Bentley places *Roughing It* among a group of texts on emigration in his search for the social and cultural significance of the experience. While some of these texts risk returning to the earlier orthodoxy that saw Moodie as a simple chronicler of Canadian experience, lacking responsibility for producing the meaning of that experience, all argue against the construction of Moodie as archetypal mother of the Canadian imagination. Lucas 1989, however, reverts to the view of *Roughing It* as unified, and Buss 1990 accepts the once conventional linkage of women and the land that Murray 1986 dismantles. Peterman 1988 and Ballstadt 1990 continue to produce new empirical material. Their collection, with Elizabeth Hopkins, of *Letters of Love and Duty* (Toronto: University of

Toronto Press 1993) appeared too late for the present book, which uses the manuscript versions of the letters it prints.

13 Lecker refers to many discussions of the English Canadian canon (1991, 9, 198–9 n 17). The essays in Lecker's collection that are most pertinent to Moodie's place in the canon are those by Surette, McCarthy, Bennett, and Mathews.

14 The methodological assumptions here summarized derive from study of a number of theorists, including Louis Althusser, Mikhail Bakhtin, Antonio Gramsci, Stephen Greenblatt, Fredric Jameson, Pierre Macherey, Franco Moretti, Edward Said, and Raymond Williams. For a full discussion of these assumptions and their indebtedness to these theorists, see Thurston 1989, 1–30.

CHAPTER ONE

1 Sources for the British historical context are listed in the Bibliography but, since I have worked from a consensual view of the period, will remain in the background.

2 Catharine Parr Traill's manuscripts in the Traill Family Collection are a substantial source of information for Susanna's childhood. Mary Agnes FitzGibbon, Moodie's granddaughter, used these papers to write her "Biographical Sketch" for Traill's *Pearls and Pebbles* (1894). Biographies of her sister Agnes by Jane Strickland (1887) and Una Pope-Hennessy (1940) are also sources of information for Susanna's British years but must be read with caution. Moodie's "Rachel Wilde," "Trifles from the Burthen of a Life," and *Flora Lyndsay* carry information on her youth, while *Roughing It in the Bush* and *Life in the Clearings* cover her later years. Her letters provide details from the whole of her life from late 1826 to late 1882. Ballstadt's dissertation on "The Literary History of the Strickland Family" contains a scholarly treatment of the early years of the family. Other sources of biographical information are Audrey Morris (1968), Michael Peterman (1983), Ballstadt, Peterman, and Elizabeth Hopkins (1985), and Ballstadt (1988 and his annotations to the CEECT edition of *Roughing It*).

3 On "the salaried," a growing segment of the middle class in the late eighteenth century, see Davidoff and Hall 1987, 265–70.

4 This paragraph and the following examination of Susanna's youth are informed by Althusser's analysis of the ideological function of such institutions as family, education, and religion (1970).

5 FitzGibbon 1894, iv; for the grandfather's disinheritance, see TFC, 8188–91, 8265. Traill writes that their grandfather "obtained a clerkship in the Wells and Hallets Dockyard" (8191) and that their father later "had the management" of the same (8188). Leonore Davidoff and Catherine

Hall mention the importance of "kin, friends or patrons ... to gaining a salaried post" (1987, 266). The Greenland Dock is in the inner London borough of Southwark.

6 TFC, 8196; Strickland may have continued working for his former employers while in East Anglia (Pope-Hennessy 1940, 7).

7 In "Trifles" the narrator describes her heroine's home: "R– Hall, was an old fashioned house, large, rambling, picturesque and cold." It had "been built in the first year of the reign of good queen Bess. The back part of the mansion appeared to have belonged to a period still more remote" (186). Traill claims that Reydon Hall bore "on one of its gables, in iron figures the date 1517" (TFC, 8335). The editors of the *Letters*, however, give 1682 as the year in which it was built (2).

8 Strickland 1884, 1; an unpublished autobiographical sketch by Moodie (PHEC, ser. II, Manuscripts, box 5, f. 31). Ballstadt, Peterman, and Hopkins call Reydon Hall "the summit of Thomas Strickland's ambitions" (*Letters*, 2; see also Pope-Hennessy 1940, 15; Peterman 1983, 63). In 1808 the Strickland children were aged as follows: Eliza 14, Agnes 12, Sarah 10, Jane 8, Catharine 6, Susanna 5, Samuel 3, Thomas 1.

9 All sources agree that Strickland was forced to be in Norwich more than he had planned, although there is no consensus on the reason; see TFC, 8345; Strickland 1887, 7–8; FitzGibbon 1894, viii; Pope-Hennessy 1940, 15; Ballstadt 1965, 10, 10 n 4; Peterman 1983, 64; *Letters*, 2). From the beginning of the move to Suffolk, Strickland was likely making trips to Norwich to superintend both his partner and his town house. These trips may have increased as his business difficulties began and more formal arrangements may have developed later.

10 TFC, 8434; Catharine describes the alternation of her sister and mother; see also Strickland 1887, 7–11; FitzGibbon 1894, xii–xiii; Pope-Hennessy 1940, 15–17; Ballstadt 1965, 10.

11 FitzGibbon 1894, xii (see also TFC, 8486); *RI*, 196 (see also *FL*, 6); Strickland 1887, 14; the will is quoted in Ballstadt 1965, 10, 13). It is unlikely that Strickland could have saved enough money from his manager's wages to buy both a house in Norwich and a country estate. Davidoff and Hall, after describing the "relatively low status and ... youthfulness" of the salaried, suggest that "men in such positions might, in middle age, move into partnership or become independent entrepreneurs" (1987, 267, 268). Strickland's frequent business trips to Norwich point to his active management of the coach manufactory and, since limited-liability was not instituted until 1844, he may have suffered full liability for the bankruptcy. Coach manufacturing, one of East Anglia's few industries, flourished prior to the post-Napoleonic War depression (Davidoff and Hall 1987, 403). It is possible, then, that Strickland made much of his money in the coach manufactory during the

prosperous years of 1803–15, saw this company start to fail with the onset of the post-war depression, protected his property by willing it to his wife in early April 1818, but lost his liquid capital in the collapse of his business before his death.

12 Hobsbawm 1968, 84; mention of John Sedley, William Dorritt, and Arthur Clenham substantiates Hobsbawm's remark about novels. Davidoff and Hall also refer to real-life instances of "the twists of fortune which became the stuff of Victorian novels" (1987, 207). On the economic fortunes during the depression of East Anglia in general, see Davidoff and Hall, 44, and of Norwich specifically, see Hobsbawm, 25, 48, 56, 68.

13 Quoted in Pope-Hennessy 1940, 5; on the education of the elder girls, see TFC, 8196; Strickland 1887, 3–4; FitzGibbon 1894, viii, letter 117. The younger girls are never mentioned in relation to their father's educational regime, and Catharine remarks that their education "devolved on the two elder sisters" (TFC, 8288; see also Pope-Hennessy 1940, 6).

14 See Strickland 1887, 3; FitzGibbon 1894, vi; Pope-Hennessy 1940, 5; the library also contained a history of the Turks that had been popular in the eighteenth century (TFC, 8413; Pope-Hennessy 1940, 5).

15 Strickland 1897, 3; letter 77; see also Pope-Hennessy 1940, 5; Ballstadt 1965, 11. A confusion, originating with Jane, about the Harrison text, indicates that the Stricklands might have possessed an edition of Holinshed's *Chronicles*, a possibility also suggested by Catharine's mention of being told "stories from the old chronicles" (FitzGibbon 1894, vi). Catharine probably refers to the same text as Susanna when she describes "a fine Atlas in two quarto volumes" with "Geographical histories of the European countries" (TFC, 8422).

16 Letter 117; see also TFC, 8200.

17 Strickland 1887, 4–5; see also TFC, 8200-01.

18 Perkin 1969, 295; Pope-Hennessy says Strickland had the older girls produce abstracts of their prescribed reading for discussion (1940, 5–6); Jane and Catharine mention that the girls began writing creatively in their youth (Strickland 1887, 4; TFC, 8418, 8484). Catharine recounts how their father tried to teach them mathematics but only succeeded with Eliza (8194), perhaps because of the aid she gave him with accounts. Davidoff and Hall note that a Birmingham Unitarian "urged teaching girls arithmetic ... to enable them to understand income and expenses" (1987, 384). In general, "the relatively progressive view of female education ... was a characteristic of Unitarian thinking" (145).

19 Catharine later laments that she had not paid attention to her correspondent's teaching because, studying North American flowers, she cannot "understand as you would do their botanical arrangement" (1836, 190). The editors of the *Letters* mention "Eliza's attempt to instruct her in botany and the natural sciences" (4–5).

20 Letter 117; Catharine, recounting how Agnes and her father "were often in opposition" about contemporary politics, continues: "Agnes was a true Jacobite and our father upheld the Hanoverian dynasty. William of Orange was his hero. While Agnes' interest lay with the fallen house of Stuart of whose rights she considered him a usurper–" (TFC, 8311–12). Jane also mentions her father's admiration for William III and, referring to an anti-republican poem by Agnes, expresses her own hatred of Cromwell (1887, 5, 12). Agnes's insistence on connecting the family with the Stricklands of Sizergh Castle, who were Roman Catholic, an "elder branch" of the family according to Catharine, who doubts the connection and states that their "father sprung from the Protestant or Reformed Church branch" (TFC, 8224), was part of her royalist allegiances.

21 Strickland 1887, viii, 39, 85; Pope-Hennessy 1940, 181–2, 237; criticisms of Agnes as a closet Catholic were especially frequent during the Tractarian 1840s. Agnes herself complained of being accused by reviewers of "tory and high church principles" (PHEC, ser. I, Correspondence, no. 120). After Agnes's death Catharine defended her: "It has been frequently said that my sister was at heart a Romanist. This was not the case for she was a consistent liberal protestant woman brought up in the tenets of the Church of England" (TFC, 8208). Elsewhere, however, she implicates her oldest sister: "I believe that my sister Agnes held sound gospel doctrines ... With respect to Elizabeth I am not so confident" (8495).

22 Quoted in Pope-Hennessy 1940, 181.

23 Pope-Hennessy 1940, 20, 45; Letters, 14–15; DNB; the Childses specialized in cheap editions of good literature. That they gained from the popularization of reading is one point of contact they, as dissenters, had with secular utilitarianism.

24 Perkin 1969, 349–50; on nonconformist resistance to church rates and its connection with "a widespread demand for the disestablishment of the church," see also Davidoff and Hall 1987, 98.

25 Pope-Hennessy 1940, 45; see also Letters, 71; Susanna displeased a sister of her mother's, with whom she visited when she was sixteen, by falling in love with a nonconformist (TFC, 9885).

26 Letters, 14, 16; Glickman also sees Susanna's marriage "in an Anglican ceremony" as proof she abandoned dissent (1991, 10).

27 "It was against the wishes of my Mother and my sisters that I cast my lot, as a colonial emigrant's wife," Catharine writes (TFC, 10034). James Hammerton substantiates the "acknowledgement of loss of caste" that emigration represented (1979, 12): "emigration ... was a response to the fearful experience of downward social mobility" and had a "disreputable image" (13, 17). About the conclusion to Gaskell's Mary Barton, Williams writes: "all the objects of her real sympathy ... are going to Canada; there could be no more devasting conclusion" (1958, 91).

28 TFC, 8349, 8487–8; Jane Strickland and Pope-Hennessy both dwell extensively on the literary and social activities of Agnes and Eliza. On the social isolation of the Stricklands at Reydon Hall, see also *Letters*, 3–4, and the quotation given there from a contemporary who knew the family in Suffolk.

29 TFC, 8494; given her youth when he died and critical comments on "fashionable ritualistic forms" she makes in another context (8208), that Catharine fully understood the social and political implications of ascribing High Church beliefs to her father can be doubted. In an unpublished autobiographical sketch, Susanna writes that up to the age of seven her "education ... had been more moral than religious" (PHEC, ser. II, Manuscripts, box 5, f. 31).

30 The editors of the *Letters* suggest that the connection with the Childses "likely went back to the years the Stricklands had spent at Stowe House" (14). They also provide information on "Allen Ransome (1806–75), a Quaker from Ipswich," who was a friend of the family (14, 49 n 2, 199), and print Susanna's letters to him.

31 Perkin 1969, 204; Perkin describes "the familiar progress from Anglicanism to Dissent and back to Anglicanism again, which usually accompanied social mobility from the labouring poor through the middle ranks to a landed estate" (35). Davidoff and Hall note that "it was a not uncommon pattern for nonconformists who became very wealthy and wanted to mix with the upper middle classes for social or political reasons, to abandon their chapel and join the church" (1987, 104). In nineteenth-century England "religious belief had become 'a character and function of class' rather than a basis for a wider social unity. Religious belonging gave distinctive identity to particular communities and classes in a society which was increasingly aware of its divisions and in which the established church was gradually losing its claim for national rather than sectarian status" (77).

32 Hobsbawm 1968, 203; Clark 1985, 371; Davidoff and Hall 1987, 80–1, all confirm the strength of dissent in East Anglia. On the political orientation of Anglicans and non-Anglicans, see Perkin 1969, 207; Clark 1985, 90.

CHAPTER TWO

1 TFC, 8418, *Letters*, 4; these literary efforts by Catharine and Susanna were aborted by the intervention of Eliza, who scorned her younger sisters' waste of time (TFC, 8425–6). Agnes may have been writing poetry from age nine (letter 117; Strickland 1887, 4; Pope-Hennessy, 15).

2 Letter 78; Susanna says she wrote *Spartacus* when thirteen, and it is likely one of the productions the sisters worked on in the winter of 1816. At Eliza's response to their literary endeavours, Catharine tore up most of

her manuscript but saved a story from it for later publication. Susanna, who "flung [her manuscript] into the fire" (TFC, 8426), may have saved some part of it for publication as *Spartacus* six years later.

3 They wrote "over 60 books for children" (Ballstadt 1965, 41).

4 On children's books as a genre that, because children were part of the "proper sphere" of women, was their particular reserve, see Gilbert and Gubar 1979, 72; Davidoff and Hall 1987, 304–5. On anonymous publication as one of the ways women dealt with the barriers to claiming a professional identity, see Showalter 1977, 17; Poovey 1984, 36.

5 TFC, 8418, 9742; Mary Poovey describes anonymous publication or writing for a small circle of friends as widespread practices that "allowed women an indirect, disguised entrance into the competitive arena of literary creation" (1984, 36). The early lives of Catharine and Susanna were actually more like the lives of Ann and Jane Taylor, who came from an impoverished middle-class family, collaborated in writing, and, like the Brontës and the Stricklands, tried to start a school. Darnton and Harvey, the publisher of the Taylors' children's books, was also Catharine's, and, like Susanna, they dedicated their first book of poetry for adults to James Montgomery (Davidoff and Hall 1987, 64–7, 479 n 76).

6 TFC, 8428; letter 78; Susanna's letters and Catharine's memoirs seldom mention payment for their early publications, other than in these two locations. "The practice of having a father, brother, or husband negotiate with a publisher was common for a young woman writer": not only were financial affairs not a proper preoccupation for women; publishing for profit was particularly unfeminine (Poovey 1984, 36–7; see also Showalter 1977, 17). Davidoff and Hall use Elizabeth, Agnes, and Jane Strickland's occasional refusal to accept payment for their work as an example of how "status considerations encouraged women to play down selling themselves or their products" (1987, 286).

7 Jane is quoted in Pope-Hennessy 1940, 18; Agnes founded the Sunday School at St Margaret's Church, Southwold, and in the 1850s hoped to build a schoolhouse (*Letters*, 26 n 2; letter 117; TFC, 8332). Susanna taught at Agnes's Sunday school and later at the Congregationalist school (letters 9, 22). She considered becoming "a lady's companion" (Thomas Pringle to Susanna Strickland, 26 May 1829, Susanna Moodie Collection, 2. Correspondence and Clippings, folder 4, Moodie, Susanna Strickland 1828–29). Davidoff and Hall note that "teaching became the only occupation in which middle-class women could preserve something of their status" (1987, 293). "The shift towards acceptability of middle-class women's need to earn money came very slowly," Showalter writes, and then shows how writers earned twice what governesses did (1977, 48). "Employment for impecunious ladies was no easy matter throughout the nineteenth century" (Hammerton 1979, 28).

8 Most of Susanna's children's books are undated, and it is difficult to date them precisely. Her corpus of separately published juvenile stories will thus be restricted to those she lists in a later letter: *Spartacus, Profession and Principle, Hugh Latimer, Rowland Massingham, The Little Prisoner,* and *The Little Quaker.* Her implication that these tests preceded her major periodical work is accepted (letter 78). *Hugh Latimer* (issued three time in its original form and once in two parts) and *The Little Prisoner* are the only stories known to have gone beyond a first edition, and so may say something about the market they supplied.

9 Gilmour 1981, 8–11; *Hugh Latimer* anticipates by thirty years the assertion by Smiles, the popular doxographer, that "riches and rank have no necessary connexion with genuine gentlemanly qualities. The poor man may be a true gentleman ... The poor man with a rich spirit is in all ways superior to a rich man with a poor spirit" (1859, 328). Davidoff and Hall conclude that in the middle-class appropriation of the concept, "real gentility ... was a matter of the inner state, not the outer casing" (1987, 113).

10 In Moretti's terms, "literary formalization ... has a double function: it *expresses* the unconscious content and at the same time *hides* it" (1983, 103). In this story Susanna does what Poovey argues many women writers did: "Through the use of thinly disguised characters, these writers explore, expand, and sometimes revise their own situations in such a way as to express or repress their own deeply felt desires" (1984, 45). This transformation of autobiography became one of her common techniques.

11 That Hugh's schoolmates scorn his mother's occupation suggests that Susanna was unsure whether her father's business success – momentary though it was – was a legitimate source of status.

12 Peter Hulme's discussion of Providence applies to its function in Susanna's fiction: "Nothing defines Providence more clearly than its reliance on plot: Providence is history with a plot, authored by God" (1986, 177). The compatibility of Providence with romance but not realism partly determines Susanna's choice of narrative mode.

13 1799, 1:44; on the Victorian belief in the innate depravity of children, see David Grylls (1978, 24–8).

14 Poovey describes how "the very act of a woman writing during a period in which self-assertion was considered 'unladylike' exposes the contradictions inherent in propriety: just as the inhibitions visible in her writing constitute a record of her historical oppression, so the work itself proclaims her momentary, possibly unconscious, but effective, defiance" (1984, xv). This analysis underscores the contradictions in Susanna writing children's stories that counsel resignation and humility.

15 On the changing relations of literary production during this period, see Perkin 1969, 255–6; Feltes 1986, 5–6. Davidoff and Hall say that "writing … was a favoured occupation for large numbers of men and women … the vast majority of whom wrote for their own pleasure and edification and that of their relatives and friends" (1987, 162). Poovey quotes an early nineteenth-century woman writer who describes writing as "an ornament, or an amusement, not a duty or profession," for women (1984, 40).

16 On Cheesman, see *LC*, 169; TFC, 8229; Strickland 1887, 15; Pope-Hennessy 1940, 21; *Letters*, 6; *DNB*; he was an artist and engraver who lived on Newman Street, 500 metres from the British Museum. In 1829 Susanna published a poem "On Being Asked by T. C—, Esq. to Turn His Italian Sonnets Into English Verse." Thackeray situates Rebecca Sharp's "lazy, dissolute, clever, jovial" artist father in the Newman Street area, called in *Vanity Fair* "the artist's quarter" (1848, 11). On Leverton, see *LC*, 170; Strickland 1887, 17; Pope-Hennessy 1940, 23; *Letters*, 5; she was the widow of architect Thomas Leverton, who in 1795 built Bedford Square, the most elegant of the squares of Bloomsbury, where Mrs Leverton continued to live after his death in 1824. In *Vanity Fair* Amelia Osborne's pompous father-in-law has as two frequent guests "old Sir Thomas Coffin and Lady Coffin from Bedford Square," the former "celebrated as a hanging judge" (1848, 442). The Stricklands abandoned Cheesman in Bohemia for solid Bedford Square when the death of Mr Leverton opened that address to them.

17 On Eliza as editor of a fashionable periodical, most likely the *Lady's Magazine*, see letter 39; Strickland 1887, 18; Pope-Hennessy 1940, 33–4; Ballstadt 1965, 16–17; *Letters* 14, 96 n 4.

18 Pope-Hennessy 1940, 24–9; Strickland 1887, 34, 39, 48, 164, 183; Lady Morgan was a popular novelist; Letitia Elizabeth Landon was the fashionable poet L.E.L.; Anna Jameson wrote a range of non-fiction prose (on her 1836 trip to Upper Canada, Jameson was not asked by Agnes to look up the Stricklands who were there); Jane Porter was a popular novelist, and her sister, Anna, a poet and novelist.

19 Mary Russell Mitford's sketches had been appearing in periodicals since 1819, the five-volume collection of them as *Our Village* beginning in 1824 (–1832). Ballstadt (1972) traces her influence on Susanna's writing. A letter from Pringle dated 26 May 1829 mentions a letter from Mitford that he is passing on to Susanna because it concerns her (Susanna Moodie Collection, 2. Correspondence and Clippings, folder 4, Moodie, Susanna Strickland 1828–29). At the beginning of June, Susanna wrote a poem to Mitford that Pringle delivered (letter 15; see also *Letters*, 12).

20 "The Pope's Promise," 6; all quotations are from the reprint in *Voyages*.

21 "The Earthquake" was first published in August 1827 and has nine stanzas of six lines each (*ababcc*) and slightly irregular metre. Copies in her commonplace book indicate that those poems to be discussed, "The Earthquake," "On the Ruins ...," and "The Old Ash Tree," were all written in 1827 (PHEC, ser. II, Manuscripts, box 8, pp. 30–2, 49–51, 25–6). The commonplace book seems to have been compiled in the late 1820s, but two other manuscripts, also dating some poems, were written later, one in the mid-1850s (PHEC, ser. II, Manuscripts, box 6) and the other in the mid-1860s (Thomas Fisher Rare Book Library). The dating in the earliest manuscript, when present, will be accepted.

22 Published in *La Belle Assemblée* seven months after "The Earthquake," "On the Ruins ..." is eight stanzas of eight lines. In *Enthusiasm* the title becomes "Lines Written Amidst the Ruins of a Church on the Coast of Suffolk," suggesting this elegy on how "the paths of glory lead but to the grave" had a precursor known to have been in the family library. The eight-line stanzas are really linked quatrains, rhyming *ababcdcd*, the stanza of Gray's Elegy.

23 "Stanzas," ll. 7–8, 14–15; "Autumn" was published two months after "The Old Ash Tree," while "Stanzas" appeared in the August 1827 issue with "The Earthquake." The manuscript copy of "Stanzas" indicates that it was written in 1823 (PHEC, ser. II, Manuscripts, box 8, pp. 91–2).

24 Susanna herself gives this explanation in 1854 when she describes for Bentley the poems of *Enthusiasm*, in which all of those discussed appear: "the sorrows of a very unhappy home ... will account for the deep tone of melancholy that pervades most of them, for I wrote exactly as the spirit prompted me – as I felt" (letter 54). Glickman suggests that "this experience lies behind the preoccupation in *Enthusiasm* with grief, loss, disaster, graves, ruins, and the exemplary deaths of Christians" (1991, 11).

25 *Letters*, 8, 9; five months after Susanna began submitting work to Harral, "To —" appeared, and the next month, "To A.L.H.–l." In August 1830 she writes that her "stay in London was greatly saddened by the loss of a very dear young friend" (letter 24), probably Anna Laura Harral, who died in London in 1830 (*Letters*, 9, 51 n 2).

26 Discussion of the annuals has been informed by Norman Feltes's analysis of the "commodity-text" (1986, 9). The annuals provide an example of how "the organization of the market for books was only an extension of the organization of the production of books" (5). Information on them has been drawn from Altick 1957, 362–3; Bain 1973; Boyle 1967; Faxon 1912; Jamieson 1973.

27 "Stanzas on War," l. 1; this poem was written and published in 1827 (PHEC, ser. II, Manuscripts, box 8, pp. 62–4).

28 At one hundred and thirty-six lines "The Overthrow of Zebah and Zalmunna" is one of her longest early poems. The lines of four stresses, end-stopped and in couplets, give the poem a bouncy rhythm at odds with its martial subject. A copy of this poem in Susanna's commonplace book is undated, but it was probably written the same year it was published. Specifically religious poems, most undated, are clustered near the end of this commonplace book. In January 1829 she describes "a couple of sacred pieces" as the only poems she is working on (letter 12). It is among these "Hymns" and "Sacred Songs" that "The Overthrow of Zebah and Zalmunna" appears (PHEC, ser. II, Manuscripts, box 8, pp. 107–12).

29 That Dale may have commissioned Susanna to write "The Deluge" for an already existing "Series of Scripture Illustrations" does not undermine its connection with her other writing. In *Enthusiasm* a note is appended to "The Child's First Grief" saying that it was written to illustrate a plate (110), and it is likely that "The Boudoir" was written for an engraving, yet both of these poems are characteristic of her.

30 Doleful captives do not appear in Susanna's poetry until the end of 1830. *The Little Prisoner* was written before 1828, but imprisonment in this story is a positive event, leading to moral reformation, not the source of anguish it becomes in the lyrics of captivity. So, too, "Francis I. In Captivity," written in early 1828 (PHEC, ser. II, Manuscripts, box 8, pp. 10–13), uses captivity as a source of insight, not despair. "The Captive" was written by the fall of 1830, "The Release of the Caged Lark" by the fall of 1831. "The Captive Squirrel's Petition," a poem very like the latter, was published in the fall of 1830. That none of these poems appears in her commonplace book suggests that they were written in 1829, when she ceased compiling it, or later.

The classic discussion of the relation of "spatial imagery of enclosure and escape" to the historical situation of women remains that of Gilbert and Gubar: "Dramatizations of imprisonment and escape are so all-pervasive in nineteenth-century literature by women that ... they represent a uniquely female tradition in this period" (1979, 83, 85). Susanna joins this tradition in 1830 and remains in touch with it for much of her writing career.

31 "There's Joy when the Rosy Morning" was published in 1828, the same year it was written; "O Come to the Meadows" was published in 1829. One stanza of "The Spirit of Spring" is in *The Amulet*, about which she writes in November 1829: "It is a splendid book and I am glad that I am one of its contributors even at the expense of the mutilation of one of my best pieces" (letter 20). "The Wood Lane," written in 1824, and "Awake!" were published in 1830 (PHEC, ser. II, Manuscripts, box 8, pp. 7–9, and box 6, pp. 69–72).

32 For her contributions to the *Ecclesiastic*, see letter to her from Thomas Pringle, 6 Mar. 1829, Moodie-Strickland-Vickers Family Fonds, 2nd acc., letter 14. Besides *The Iris*, she was also in *The Amulet; or Christian and Literary Remembrancer* and *The Spirit and Manners of the Age: A Christian and Literary Miscellany* late in 1829. She probably had other publications in annuals in this and other years. "The Heir of Jeroboam" was likely in *The Iris* for 1830 under her own name. She had two poems signed Z.Z. in *Emmanuel: A Christian Tribute of Affection and Duty* for 1830 (*Letters*, 42 n 5, 47 n 6). Under Moodie, Boyle lists the following titles, and the editors of the letters confirm that she published in these annuals: "The Young Tyrolese," *Juvenile Keepsake* for 1829; "The Mock Coral Necklace; or, The Young Spanish Emigrants," *Juvenile Keepsake* for 1830; "Lady Lucy's Petition," *New Year's Gift* for 1830; "Visit of the Sea Fish to the River Fishes," *Ackermann's Juvenile Forget Me Not* for 1831 (Boyle 1967, 203; letters 20, 22; *Letters*, 14, 42 n 5, 48 n 6).

33 Letter 13; she had already written two poems on this figure, "Arminius" (published in 1835) and "Flavius and Arminius" (unpublished: PHEC, ser. II, Manuscripts, box 6, pp. 69–82; box 8, pp. 80–90). After subtitling previous short prose "sketches," she called "The Son of Arminius" a "tale," perhaps to acknowledge the genre she was really working in. She inserts twenty years into the chronology of known events to open up a space within which to tell her wholly fictional tale. Arminius had already been taken up by German nationalists as the "heroic leader who fought for the liberty of Germany" (78), an anachronistic judgment made by Tacitus and repeated in the story.

34 "The Son of Arminius" (*Victoria Magazine* version), 78; the story's first paragraph emulates the stately rhythms of the English translation of Tacitus's *Annals*, 2.41. The next four paragraphs derive from various sections of the *Annals*. The rest of the story is Susanna's invention. She cites Tacitus in a footnote to "Nero: An Historical Sketch," a poem in *La Belle Assemblée* in 1828, which also has little to do with Tacitus, relying on the apocryphal additions to his text that created the anti-Christian Nero.

35 "The Son of Arminius," 80; the uncle admits that he himself has been a slave to "Envy! avarice! ambition!" (80)

36 "My Aunt Dorothy's Legacy," "The Disappointed Politician," "Black Jenny: A Tale Founded on Facts," "The Picture Lost at Sea," and "The Vanquished Lion" all appear in annuals for 1832. The last is in the same volume of *Ackermann's Juvenile Forget Me Not* as "The Boudoir" and, like it, was commissioned to illustrate a plate.

37 For the legacy from an aunt that may have figured in the writing of "My Aunt Dorothy's Legacy," see TFC, 8265, 9886; "Trifles," 162; FitzGibbon 1894, xv; Griffiths 1949, 84, 87.

38 Poovey describes this same urge for imaginative compensation: "far from encouraging women to come to conscious terms with their social position, sentimental fiction often provided them with compensatory gratifications, ideal rewards, and ideal revenges ... One of the most persistent dilemmas of the woman writer during this period proved to be the problem of controlling her own attraction to ideal compensations" (1984, 38).

39 "The Vanquished Lion," 31; all quotations are from the reprint in *Voyages*. Compare this description of the plight of the family to Moodie's laconic statement about her own family: "The world sneered, and summer friends forsook them" (*RI*, 196).

40 In "The Picture Lost at Sea" the character even takes up his author's medium momentarily: the rich jeweller "wished to see his son distinguished for his wealth rather than for his literary talents" (153).

CHAPTER THREE

1 In Gramsci's terms, she was rejecting a place among the "traditional intellectuals," who "put themselves forward as autonomous and independent of the dominant social group," precisely during a period when the middle class was "struggl[ing] to assimilate and conquer 'ideologically' the traditional intellectuals" (1971, 7, 10). By choosing to orient herself with Evangelicism, she was joining "organic intellectuals" tied openly to a segment of the middle class bent on defining intellectual activity in their own moral and social terms (10–12). Said, working from Gramsci's concept of hegemony, distinguishes between filiation as the system of cultural relationships inherited through birth and affiliation as a consciously chosen alternative system based on shared beliefs and values (1983, 16–25).

2 Susanna's fortunes with *La Belle Assemblée* can be measured by her signatures. Her first story in it appears anonymously in September 1825. In May 1827 her first poem in it carries her initials, as do the rest of her verse and prose for 1827. She gets a byline in early 1828, but not again until the end of that year. Her first prose with a byline is her last "Sketch from the Country," in January 1829, and she keeps her byline for the rest of that year. She has three short poems in *La Belle Assemblée* in the first three months of 1830 but is again reduced to "S.S." Her last piece in it is a reprint of an 1828 poem. While she gets her byline back, Harral may have resurrected this poem as filler.

3 "The Besieged City" was written in 1827; "Francis I. In Captivity" in 1828 (PHEC, ser. II, Manuscripts, box 8, pp. 33–6, 10–13). "The Besieged City" (identified as Marseilles in a later version) is based on the battles of the Duke of Bourbon with Francis I in 1524–25. Francis, after freeing

Marseilles, attacked Italy, where he was captured by the army of Emperor
Charles V (later Holy Roman emperor), who is referred to in "Francis I."
as "Invidious Charles!" (l. 71)

4 *The Romance of History* secured Ritchie's literary career. Susanna's poems
on the romance of French history would have shown Pringle her
suitability as a reviewer of his friend Ritchie's book. Through him she
had by early 1831 "become intimately acquainted ... with Mr. and Mrs.
Leitch Ritchie both of whom I love much" (letter 29).

5 Letter 29; since most reviews were anonymous, Susanna's are known
only through the correspondence. The three reviews discussed are the
only ones mentioned in the surviving letters, apart from her husband's
reference in 1838 to her "review of poor Pringle's book" (PHEC, ser. I,
Correspondence, no. 65). This review has not been located but would be
of Ritchie's posthumous edition of the *Poetical Works of Thomas Pringle,
with a Sketch of his Life* (1838).

6 Letter 26; in the same issue as her review of Ritchie, "God Preserve the
King!" is announced, under "New Musical Publications," as separately
published with music.

7 She provides an account of the event in *Life in the Clearings:* "I must
remark ... the powerful effect produced upon my mind by having 'God
save the King' sung by the thousands of London on the proclamation of
William IV ... It seemed to me the united voice of a whole nation" (144–5).

8 Letter 117; no copy of *Patriotic Songs* has survived. The reviewer in *La
Belle Assemblée* notes that it contains "seven or eight poems." Ballstadt
cites a later publication by Agnes listing six poems in *Patriotic Songs.* Two
of these, "The Banner of England" and "Britannia's Wreath," are
Susanna's (Ballstadt 1986, 91, 96 n 14).

9 All the poems in this paragraph were published in 1831 except "The Fall
of Warsaw," published in 1832. Manuscript material provides a date of
composition, 1828, only for "The Spirit of Motion" (PHEC, ser. II,
Manuscripts, box 8, pp. 37–8).

10 "The Miser" and "The Doctor Distressed" were published in 1833 and
1836. Susanna may have sent "Music's Memories" (North American title,
"The Strains We Hear in Foreign Lands"; see letter 35) from Canada, but
Eliza did retain some of her work for publication after she had left. At the
beginning of 1831 Susanna comments on "The Miser" to an editor: "The
story is dreadful but partly founded upon facts. I should be greatly
obliged by your opinion as to its merits" (letter 28). In 1842 she
introduces "The Miser and His Son" to the editor of the *Literary Garland:*
> An abridgement of this story, bearing the same title, was published in
> the *Lady's Magazine,* in ... 1833. I should not attempt to send you a
> story which had been published before, were it not for the following
> circumstances: My eldest sister was one of the principal conductors of

that Magazine ... I left with her many of my papers, and ... an imperfect sketch of this story, which I intended filling up at my leisure ... This I had nearly accomplished, when, to my great mortification, my sister sent me a copy of the Magazine, with the rough draft of the story, forming one of the contributions. (letter 39)

"The Doctor Distressed" and three poems in the *Lady's Magazine and Museum* may also have been left with Eliza. "The Emigrant's Bride" (1837), a ballad dramatizing love's conquest of a father's strictures and fear of emigration, is related to her attempts to deal with the prospect of parting from England seen in "The Vanquished Lion." "What Is Death?" (1833) and "The Lover's Dream" (1837) also do not reveal that they were written in Canada. "The Doctor Distressed" can thus be treated as part of Susanna's work for the *Lady's Magazine*. All quotations are from the reprint in *Voyages*.

11 When Susanna knew the Birds, James (1788–1839) owned a stationery shop. He was a farmer's son who gained some popularity in the 1820s and 1830s for his poetry. His reputation may be likened to that of two other Suffolk poets in this period, Bernard Barton and Robert Bloomfield.

12 In the *DNB* Harral is said to have been Bird's "most intimate friend" and to have produced a posthumous selection of Bird's verse with memoir. There is a macabre allusion in the title of Bird's poem. At Peterloo, "Orator" Hunt wore a white hat, which, crushed by a sword in the massacre, became a symbol for radical reformers.

13 Throughout the later eighteenth century Unitarians provoked and were attacked by both church and state. A well-known confrontation was occasioned by Richard Price's sermon on the birthday of William III, which connected the Glorious Revolution and the French Revolution and urged the English to follow the example of the latter. This sermon drew forth Edmund Burke's *Reflections on the Revolution in France* (1790), which equated heterodox dissent and jacobinism. Thomas Strickland's dispute with Agnes over William III and the Stuarts may shadow this dispute. Unitarianism owed its influence to the large proportion of educated men and wealthy manufacturers it drew. Clark writes that those "who fell away from Trinitarian orthodoxy ... provided by far the greater part both of the radical intelligentsia and its rank and file" (1985, 282).

14 "In the 1820's it was a short step from Unitarianism to sceptical Utilitarianism" (Perkin 1969, 205). J.S. Mill was a regular in W.J. Fox's *Monthly Repository*, the Unitarian organ, while Fox was in the first number of the utilitarian *Westminster Review*. Unitarians and utilitarians collaborated in founding the *London Review* and in supporting Mechanics Institutes. Thomas Strickland's possible sympathies with utilitarianism should be recalled.

15 Letter 31; Agnes writes that "some malignant person, Mrs. Harral I suspect, put a hoaxing announcement ... into the 'Globe' ... [of] poor Kitty's marriage" (quoted in *Letters*, 62 n 3). The Moodies throughout the second half of the 1850s were practising spiritualists and compiled a "Spiritualist Album" of communications from the dead. Mrs Moodie received messages from Harral, who told her that he was not happy in his marriage and that his dead wife "is a miserable Spirit." Mrs Harral communicated with Mrs Traill to tell her that she hated Catharine and her own son and daughter (PHEC, ser. II, Manuscripts, box 5, pp. 103, 58, 69).

16 Letter 12; "the sacred pieces" she refers to are those at the end of her commonplace book, where the poem she includes in this letter is also to be found (PHEC, ser. II, Manuscripts, box 8, pp. 99–106; p. 100).

17 TFC, 9883, 9884–5; while the clergyman to whom Catharine refers has not been identified, that he was an itinerant who, when he left the area, commended Susanna "to the care of a worthy earnest Nonconformist Pastor" (9884) increases his resemblance to a man described by Davidoff and Hall: "the Rev. John Charlesworth, an enthusiastic Anglican Evangelical, travelled all over east Suffolk, often with a nonconformist 'brother minister'" (1987, 93). George Burmeister, a temporary minister at Southwold who greeted Susanna in London in early 1831 as "my little Neophyte" is another candidate (letter 29; *Letters*, 58 n 10).

18 "The old Dissenting congregations ... were as suspicious of enthusiasm as members of the Church of England" (Briggs 1959, 66). Evangelicism "appeal[ed] to men and women who were dissatisfied with the 'rational Christianity' of both church and chapel" (67). The Evangelicals condemned "the characteristic vices of the aristocracy" and assumed "middle-class moral superiority" (Perkin 1969, 286, 283–4). Their "zeal could imply a condemnation of squire and parson" (Clark 1981, 378).

19 Letter 19; the last quotation echoes Hannah More's recommendation that a woman "should be carefully instructed that her talents are only a means to a higher attainment ... that merely to exercise them as instruments for the acquisition of fame and the promoting of pleasure, is subversive of her delicacy as a woman" (1799, 2:12). The comments on Agnes in this letter may obliquely criticize her, as may Susanna's description in "Fame" of "Ambition's laurel" as "stained with kindred blood" (ll. 57, 58).

20 "The Hymn of the Convalescent," ll. 5–6; her experience during this period corresponds to options taken by other women, her contemporaries, who chafed against limitation and dependency: "Daughters ... practised a form of passive resistance by falling ill or becoming so intensely religious as to effectively withdraw from family affairs" (Davidoff and Hall 1987, 334).

21 Letter 22; in fact Susanna produces twenty-eight biblical texts to prove to Bird that she does not believe "in a cunningly devised fable." As a Unitarian he would believe neither in the atonement nor in any proof of it based on scripture.

22 Letter 22; TFC, 9884; as part of her conversion she had to produce "reasons for dissent from the establishment" (letter 22). While everyone automatically belonged to the local Anglican church, "becoming a member of a nonconformist congregation required individual choice ... The congregation provided a community" (Davidoff and Hall 1987, 85–6).

23 In 1854 she claims that *Enthusiasm's* forty-nine poems are "most of the poems" she wrote "between the ages of 14 and 20" (letter 54). The poems with the earliest composition date that can be established were written in 1822 and 1823 (PHEC, ser. II, Manuscripts, box 8, pp. 49–51, 91–2), while the majority were written in 1827–29. By the time she dedicated the collection she had published over fifty poems, half of which are in *Enthusiasm*. The main reason for the exclusion of any given poem seems to have been unsuitability for the religious theme: "Of its moral tendency, there can be no doubt," she writes (letter 78).

24 Letter 54; see also letter 78; she mentions the copies in a letter to her husband (PHEC, ser. I, Correspondence, no. 81).

25 "Enthusiasm," ll. 63–8; given the traditional gender of the Muse, it is significant that she invokes a neuter "bright spirit."

26 "Enthusiasm," ll. 159–60; she includes a prose paraphrase of these lines in *Mark Hurdlestone* (154–5). For an alternative interpretation of Susanna's enthusiasm, see Peterman 1983, 69–70.

27 "Enthusiasm," ll. 386, 393, 409–11; Susanna's "stream of time" comprises "twice three thousand years" (l. 388), alluding to Bishop Ussher's calculation that the Creation occurred 26 October 4004 BC.

28 By the early seventeenth century enthusiasm was associated with bacchanalians and Baptists. *OED*, "Enthusiasm," 2: "Fancied inspiration ... Ill-regulated or misdirected religious emotion, extravagance of religious speculation." (Definition 1 was obsolete by the end of the seventeenth century.) "Enthusiasm," 3: "The current sense: Rapturous intensity of feeling in favour of a person, principle, cause, etc." Glickman surveys the history of the word and its relations to poetry (1991, 15–17). She concludes her analysis of the poem by stating that it is "framed by rhetorical, and filled with lyrical and dramatic, self-contradiction" (19).

29 "Fame" is two hundred and ten lines in heroic couplets. Once again, when exercising her ambition in a long poem, she turns to her father's library, Pope being a likely model.

30 The poem flattens a subtle biblical legal code under a one-dimensional moral. That the manslayer in this poem is "the victim of passion" (l. 37)

recalls all her stress on restraint of emotion and leads back to the impulsive brother of "The Two Fishermen" and to *The Little Prisoner*.

31 "To the Memory of R.R. Jun," ll. 18–21; a manuscript version provides the full name, "Robert Ransom," likely the son of her friend Allan Ransome (PHEC, ser. II, Manuscripts, box 8, p. 112).

32 "Lines on a New-born Infant," ll. 3, 6, 16; a note says that this poem was for James Bird's son, now dead.

33 Letter 25; Catharine corroborates this information (TFC, 9885).

34 The poems of disappointed love in *Enthusiasm* are "The Dream" (written 1824, published 1827), "Stanzas: Thou Wilt Think of Me Love" (published 1830), "The Warning," "Mary Hume," and "The Ruin" (written 1827). Other poems on this theme include "The Rover's Farewell to His Mistress" (published 1828) and "The Maniac" (written 1821, published 1829). The latter poem is based on the same situation as "The Ruin" (PHEC, ser. II, Manuscripts, box 8, pp. 70–1, 17–27, 44–6).

35 J.W.D. Moodie met Pringle (1789–1834) in Edinburgh as early as 1813. Susanna first mentions him in a letter in 1828 (letter 6). In October of that year he sent Susanna a business letter with a copy of *Friendship's Offering*, which he was editing, and payment for her first piece in it. By May 1829 he was addressing her as "My Dear Child" and signing himself "Your loving papa T.P.," helping her negotiate with the *Ecclesiastic* and getting "Zebah and Zalmunna" published in *The Iris*. He demurred from her views on her "darling pet Croly" because Croly is "a most intolerant and intolerable ultra" and Pringle "a sour and bitter Whig." The Reverend George Croly, a minor poet, had been profiled by Harral (*La Belle Assemblée*, 3rd ser., 8 [1828]: 2–10), so Pringle's divergence from him may have influenced Susanna (Thomas Pringle to Susanna Strickland, 20 Oct. 1828, Susanna Moodie Collection, 2. Correspondence and Clippings, folder 4, Moodie, Susanna Strickland 1828–29; Moodie-Strickland-Vickers Family Fonds, 2nd, letter 14; PHEC, ser. 2, Correspondence, no. 101; Thomas Pringle to Susanna Strickland, 26 May 1829, Susanna Moodie Collection).

36 "An Appeal to the Free," ll. 33–4; the poem is historically specific in noting that, with trade in slaves outlawed, abolition is in reach. It was reprinted in *Literary Garland* in 1850, directed then at slavery in the United States. In 1854 Susanna explicitly addressed a new poem, "Freedom for the Slave," at the United States (PHEC, ser. II, Manuscripts, box 6, pp. 9–11). *Hugh Latimer* includes an episode about a "black youth," tormented by the same group that plagues Hugh, who is rescued by Hugh and his friend in sympathy for his "suffering[,] ... exile from his country," and control by "a tyrannical master" (37, 41–2).

37 Mary had been, according to Pringle, "for fourteen months ... a domestic servant in [his] own family" (1831b, 105). She had come to London from

Antigua with her owner, John Wood. In England she was technically free, but she was entirely dependent upon Wood. She came to the attention of Pringle and the Anti-Slavery Society, who worked to attain her manumission, meanwhile employing her as a servant and using her story to press their case.

38 Letter 29; Henry "Orator" Hunt, was a demagogic radical leader whom sixty thousand gathered to hear at Peterloo. The procession Susanna witnessed was to mark Hunt's assumption of his parliamentary seat on 3 February 1831. Whatever his motives, Hunt expressed the aspirations of a broad segment of the working class.

39 The characterization of the working class as slaves was common during this period. Susanna herself later connects slavery and wage slavery. Praising the colony in "Trifles," she points to the improved situation of "the trampled and abused child of man": he can now be "a free inheritor of the soil, who so long labored ... as an ignorant and degraded slave" (187–8).

40 An editorial comment on Mary Prince's story of being sold from her family projects the slave as spectacle. A long footnote describes a slave market "at the Cape of Good Hope." The "unhappy group" of a mother and children is characterized as "a fine[] subject for an able painter" (1831, 53). The tableau illustrates a moral point, but this reification of slavery shows how deeply ingrained were the attitudes upon which it was based. "Anti-slavery was recognized," Davidoff and Hall point out, "as a peculiarly feminine concern, dealing as it did with such questions as dependence, children, marriage and family life" (1987, 433).

41 Prince 1831, 120; Susanna mentions the latter name once, to Bird: "I send you twenty copies of Mary's *History*, and 2 of *Ashton Warner*. If you can in the way of trade dispose of them, I should feel obliged" (letter 31). These two statements are the only evidence that she also transcribed Ashton Warner's narrative.

CHAPTER FOUR

1 Emigration is a common motif in novels set in this period. When a character in *Vanity Fair* is faced with disinheritance, one of his alternatives is to "go and dig in Canada" (Thackeray 1848, 194). In *Shirley* an industrialist, anticipating the failure of his mill, begins "packing ... for ... Canada" (Brontë 1849, 593). Other novels show working-class characters actually leaving for North America. In *Mary Barton* the male hero, his reputation ruined, marries Mary and leaves with her for a job in "the Agricultural College they are establishing at Toronto in Canada" (Gaskell 1848, 446). Alton Locke dies en route to America. Middle-class heroes are saved from emigration while working-class figures embark,

reflecting in fiction the loss of caste that emigration represented (Hammerton 1979, 12–13). In *Bogle Corbet* John Galt clearly states the social distinctions involved in the decision to emigrate:

> Money, the want of it, or to get it, is the actuating spring ... of intending emigrants of the middle ranks ... The lower classes are governed by motives sufficiently manifest; ... swarms of operatives ... have no other resources; as their vocation is labour, a shifting of the scene is comparatively of little consequence to them. But it is only amidst the better class of emigrants that the mingled and combined feelings of necessity, interest, and sorrow are found. (1831, 11)

This dismissal of the attachments of members of the "redundant population" who made up the mass of emigrants none the less reveals the contradictory emotions of middle-class economic refugees like the Moodies. Bird and Pringle also wrote on emigration, Bird publishing *The Emigrant's Tale and Miscellaneous Poems* in 1833 and Pringle publishing "The Emigrant's Farewell" in 1828.

2 J.W.D. Moodie 1866, viii, xiii; on the Moodies in South Africa, see xiii–xiv; Gerson 1985, 36–7.

3 *RI*, 219, 220; John Lyndsay says: "My *own* inclinations would lead me back to a country where I have dear friends, a large tract of land, and where some of the happiest years of my life were spent" (*FL*, 7).

4 *FL*, 8; this novel is an expansion of "Trifles from the Burthen of a Life" (1851), for which additions but no deletions were made. The statements about South Africa and the Pringles were added. Rachel M— of the story becomes Flora Lyndsay. In her Canada trilogy Moodie provides an almost continuous narrative of her life from marriage into the years in Belleville. *Flora Lyndsay* "contains [their] voyage to Canada" (letter 107); "it is Canadian, and the real commencement of *Roughing It*" (letter 112). *Roughing It* carries their story from the arrival at Quebec in the fall of 1832 to the departure from Douro Township for Belleville in 1840. From *Life in the Clearings* can be gathered details of their life in Belleville.

5 Traill 1826, iii; the family mentioned was likely the Blacks. Ruth Marks's comment in the preface to the reprint that Catharine "relied heavily on two typical travelogues of the day for scenic and historic landmarks" (1969, ix) suggests that the Stricklands had access to information on Canada. Catharine's later reference to Howison's 1821 text provides one possibility (1836, 50). This story also begins with a fall in the family fortunes that requires choosing between a lower social status in England or emigration: "Give up Roselands, papa!" exclaims one of the heroines; "Where shall we go if we leave this place, so dear to us all?" (2–3)

6 On the meeting of Susanna and Dunbar at the Pringle's home, see *RI* 220; J.W.D. Moodie 1866, ix; TFC, 9888. Mrs Strickland wrote Moodie in July, telling him that she would not interfere with her daughter's desire to

marry him, even though his "income is at present too confined to support a wife." When Moodie left for the Orkneys at the beginning of August, their engagement was settled (PHEC, ser. I, Correspondence, nos. 135, 56). Susanna first mentions it on 3 August (letter 23).

7 Letter 24; in a long letter written in the Orkneys, Moodie concedes the possibility of their following her plan of living in "a cheap house" in Suffolk. He goes on to his thoughts of living in the Orkneys and his attempts to find a house there (PHEC, ser. I, Correspondence, no. 57).

8 Letter 26; in "Trifles" the narrator says that "poor Rachel would have followed him to the deserts of Arabia" (162).

9 When she announces her marriage to Bird, she is "perfectly satisfied" with being "settled in very pleasant lodgings" and does not mention the prospect of emigration. She also notes that "Mr. Pringle 'gave me' away," performing once more his role as surrogate father (letter 31). Catharine mentions this detail and that she was bridesmade (TFC, 9888). She remained in London after the Moodies returned to Suffolk, and only when she rejoined them "many months" later did she learn that her "brother-in-law had determined upon emigrating to Canada" (9889).

10 Moodie quotes her husband's thoughts: "You are happy and contented now, but this cannot always last; the birth of that child ... is to you the beginning of care. Your family may increase in proportion; out of what fund can you satisfy their demands?" (RI, 195) In "Trifles" M—, noting that his unborn child and potential siblings "must all be clothed and fed, and educated" (160), insists the family has "no alternative but to emigrate" (161).

11 "Trifles," 161; RI 195; while their decision to emigrate is often seen as one in which both Moodies shared, its necessity was clear only to him. If J.W.D. Moodie was the one to insist on emigration, leaving his wife little choice but to comply, he was merely acting the prescribed and respected role of a poor gentleman. When Bina Freiwald argues that "the decision to emigrate ... is presented as a specifically maternal moment" because of its connection with the birth of a child (1989, 157), she ignores the paternalistic pressure brought to bear on Mrs Moodie in this moment.

12 RI, 220; FL, 8; before his African experience Moodie had "entertained similar notions" (FL 220), based on books he had read. In his own book he emulated the practice of collecting "high-flavoured dishes" (221).

13 Letters 32, 34; see also FL, 8. While living with the Blacks, Strickland married their daughter. She died bearing his son. His neighbour, Robert Reid, who had immigrated in 1820, invited Samuel to live with his family while he got over his loss. He married Reid's daughter in 1827. Reid was in England in 1831–32.

14 The map provided by Ballstadt (CEECT, 276) shows the distribution of the group's holdings. While Thomas Wales, the Tom Wilson of *Roughing*

It (see CEECT, 559, note to 55.8), is mentioned in "Trifles" (169), the plan for him to meet them in the colony is not. James Bird, Jr, is mentioned in both texts ("Trifles," 169, where he appears as James Hawke; *RI*, 393; CEECT, 594, note to 416.11), as is the ex-servant of Reydon Hall ("Trifles," 192–3; *RI*, 199). If Pope-Hennessy's account of Catharine's and Susanna's departure from Suffolk is accurate, then it is with this event that Moodie most consciously distorts her own experience for fictional purposes: "on the 20th of May, 1832, Mr. and Mrs. Moodie, nurse and baby, and Mr. and Mrs. Traill, together with Agnes and Jane Strickland, got into a rowing-boat at Southwold and were conveyed to the vessel lying at anchor off the shore" (1940, 42). In "Trifles" and *Flora Lyndsay* the Traills and the Strickland sisters are not represented. The fictionally significant three attempts to rendezvous with the steamer for Scotland and the omens adduced from their difficulty in departing smack of fictional shaping.

15 "Trifles," 181, 193; these contrasts between the heroine's early innocence and later experience collapse the distinction between author and character. Other narrative interjections added to *Flora Lyndsay* that insist the story is truth, as witnessed by the narrator, not fiction, have the same result (see 16, 32, note to 79). "Flora, as my readers must long ago have discovered, was no heroine of romance," we are told, "but a veritable human creature" (67). Moodie ends the novel by leaving "our emigrants ... preparing to go on shore, having described the voyage from thence to Quebec, and up the St Lawrence elsewhere" (342).

16 Mary Barton, asked if she knows where Canada is, replies, "Not rightly" (Gaskell 1848, 430). Howison aims to relieve "the ignorance and misconception that have prevailed with respect to [Upper Canada's] real condition" (1821, v). In 1831 Cattermole published his lectures "with a view of correcting the erroneous idea" in England about Upper Canada (v). Strickland, as late as 1853, comments on the English misconception of Canada West: "Many persons, on leaving England for Canada, fancy they shall see nothing but interminable woods and lakes" (1853, 2.150).

17 Letter 34; PHEC, ser. I, Correspondence, nos. 58, 59, 59a. In *Flora Lyndsay* the husband returns from London in May, having "satisfactorily arranged all his pecuniary matters" and "engaged a passage in a fine vessel that was to sail from Leith" (86).

18 On Edinburgh, the ship, and its departure and arrival times, see "Trifles," 229–39; *FL*, 140–1, 166; *RI*, 21–3. D.M.R. Bentley discusses *Roughing It* in his examination of "a variety of significant responses ... to the three stages of the trans-Atlantic crossing – the departure, the voyage itself, and the arrival – in the hope of revealing at each stage some of the personal, social, and cultural ramifications of the emigrant experience" (1990, 94).

19 Letter 34; in 1833–34 Moodie's Douro land was increased by purchase to three hundred and sixty acres (*RI*, 253). Moodie was entitled to a "military grant of four hundred acres," only some of which Strickland got for him in Douro. He refers to three hundred and sixty acres concentrated in one location, sixty of them granted lands, but he had land spread over three townships (*RI*, 253; Ballstadt 1988, liv n 12). Mrs Moodie also refers to a concentrated holding of sixty-six acres grant and three hundred purchased on Katchawanook Lake (*RI*, 275).

20 On their arrival and stay at Cobourg, see *RI*, 76–7, 83–5; *LC*, 212–13. In the latter source she quotes her words to an acquaintance: "Did I only consult my own feelings, I would be off by the next steam-boat to England" (213).

21 *RI*, 228; witnessing the "clearing up a thick cedar-swamp," Moodie's "heart almost sickened at the prospect of clearing such land, and [he] was greatly confirmed in [his] resolution of buying a farm cleared to [his] hand" (*RI*, 225). Cattermole says of free grants in inaccessible areas, "they are not worth accepting" (88).

22 1831, 84; a month prior to emigrating, J.W.D. Moodie heard Cattermole lecture in Yoxford, fifteen kilometres from Southwold (*RI*, 63). Moodie may also have seen William Dunlop's *Statistical Sketches of Upper Canada*, available in Edinburgh in mid-1832, in which emigrants are instructed to choose ships sailing early in the season in order to plant food for the winter: "the difference of a fortnight or three weeks in arriving at your destination may make the difference of nearly a year's subsistence to the emigrant" (1832, 74). This common-sense advice is also given in Howison's book (1821, 247) and may have been standard in such texts.

23 For settlement patterns, see Spelt 1955, 58–63; Harris and Warkentin 1974, 116–19; map in Craig 1963, 127.

24 On the cult of loyalism, see Craig 1963, 75; Errington 1987, 97. On criticism of the government as disloyal and pro-American, see Craig, 91–8, 115–17; Errington, 107–11, 166–75; Russell 1981, 16–37; Wise 1967a. On Upper Canadian political instability, see Buckner 1985, 72; Errington, 118. On the interrelatedness of all three issues, see Mills 1988, passim.

25 Strickland, finding Whitby in 1825 "partially settled, and chiefly by Americans," bought land in Douro Township (1853, 2.17), where Robert Reid and Thomas Stewart, both firm Tories, had amassed large holdings since settling in the early 1820s. Thomas Need took "3000 acres as a first investment" in Verulam Township in 1832 (1838, 37). In 1833 John Langton describes the Newcastle District, specifically Fenelon Township, as "the most English of all the districts" (1950, viii). Traill went straight to his grant in Douro. On the location of Moodie's land, see Ballstadt 1988, liv n 12.

26 Anti-Americanism, directed at both Canadians and Yankees, is a constant in books written about Upper Canada. Mrs Moodie refers to "Canadian Yankees" and J.W.D. Moodie to "Americans, Canadians as well as Yankees" (*RI*, 99, 240). The United States had yet to appropriate the adjective "American" exclusively to itself.

27 St Thomas *Liberal*, 19 Sept. 1833, quoted in Craig 1963, 229; having been in the colony less than a month, Traill, too, had "heard ... much of the odious manners of the Yankees in this country" (1836, 73). Moodie tells how "the American settlers from the United States ... generally mistook the reserve which is common with the British towards strangers for pride and superciliousness," and quotes one who told him, "'You Britishers are too *superstitious*' ... It was some time before I found out what he meant by the term '*superstitious*,' and that it was generally used by them for 'supercilious'" (*RI*, 251).

28 *RI*, 236; see also 232, 249; *FL*, 86. The difficulties of taking possession of this farm are detailed by Mrs Moodie (*RI*, 88–9, 126–34, 162–3). Ballstadt identifies many of the people involved and illuminates what actually happened at Cobourg (CEECT, 563, notes to 81.25–6 and 81.28–9; 564, note to 89.2–3; 570, note to 139.33).

29 *RI*, 248; emigration guides recommend that half-pay officers and gentlemen buy cleared farms (Cattermole 1831, 89; Dunlop 1832, 81; Strickland 1853, 2.135–6), but also contrast the poor agricultural practices of Canadians and the "scientific agriculture" of recent British immigrants (Howison 1821, 146, 234; Dunlop 1832, 81). Moodie claims that "a considerable portion of the cleared land was light and sandy" because of earlier farming practices (236). Harris and Warkentin note that "a few gentlemen farmers ... many of them officers retired on half pay ... were able to pursue a European agricultural ideal" based on "the writings of the English agricultural improvers" (1974, 136–7). For evidence that Moodie probably would have done well if he had stayed in Cobourg and produced wheat for export, see McCalla 1978; Russell 1981, 68–81; Johnson 1989, 16–17.

30 *RI*, 255; see also CEECT, 577, notes to 269.34–5 and 270.5–6; J.W.D. Moodie 1866, viii–ix; Morris 1968, 49–50.

31 *RI*, 248; Moodie mentions that "a small legacy of about £700 fell into [his] hands" (248). Ballstadt, Peterman, and Hopkins identify this as what Susanna "received from the estate of Rebecca Leverton" (*Letters*, 71), who died in 1834.

32 Anon. 1833, 117; Johnson notes "the distinction accorded to some few regionally prominent men of being appointed to the Legislative Council" (1989, 40). Strickland, after three years with the Canada Company, had come back to the area north of Peterborough in 1831. He resumed his friendships with Stewart and Reid and became a partner with the latter

in several developments. By 1839 both Traill and Strickland were also magistrates (Morris 1968, 139, 175). Gaining a magistracy was a mark of recognition and a step towards more lucrative and prestigious public appointments. A high proportion of magistrates were conservative (Johnson 1989, 61–7).

33 Magrath 1833, 13; among the disadvantages of the bush, Magrath cites "difficulty of access" and "the absolute want of roads" (13). For Cattermole, the disadvantages outweigh the advantages: "No people make more fatal mistakes than the English in this one particular, often times simply because some old acquaintance is settled in a distant township" (1831, 89). Harris and Warkentin conclude "that settlers took up land as close to neighbors, kin, or their own national groups as was possible" (1974, 123). On influence and grants, see Johnson 1989, 52–4; Morris 1968, 73.

34 Wise 1967b, 28; on the power of local officials, see Craig 1963, 30; Johnson 1989, 61–4. Johnson shows the importance of loyalty, respectability, and religious belief in gaining the patronage appointments necessary to membership in a local elite. Ability, talent, and intelligence were seldom factors (87–96). Strickland's personal relations with Reid and Stewart, plus his later offices of magistrate, president of the Court of Requests, county councillor, and his captaincy in the militia, establish his membership in the local elite.

35 Morris 1968, 107; Sara Jeanette Duncan sketches a process very like what occurred in Douro: "Such persons would bring their lines of demarcation with them, and in their new *milieu* of backwoods settlers and small traders would find no difficulty in drawing them again ... The little knot of gentry-folk soon found the limitations of their new conditions; years went by in decades, aggrandizing none of them ... The original dignified group broke, dissolved, scattered ... It was a sorry tale of disintegration" (1904, 48–9).

36 *RI*, 275; see also Traill 1836, 61. J.W.D. Moodie, contrary to his wife, says he bought land in 1833 and 1834 at prices "considered cheap at the time" (*RI*, 253). While she claims they lost money when they sold this land in the late 1840s, Ballstadt shows that they made a profit (CEECT, 579, note to 293). Moodie's land speculations occurred early enough in the development of the Douro area that, had the improvement of the waterways been achieved, he would have gained substantially. As it was, he lost his time and effort but not his money.

37 Craig 1963, 159; Harris and Warkentin note the "positive correlation between land values and improvements in transportation" (1974, 139; see also Morris 1968, 71). Fraser discusses the politics and economics of canals during this period (1979, 149–99). In 1837 Traill mentions "large sums voted" for "opening the navigation of the Otonabee from Peterboro

to the Bay of Quinte" (TFC, 9687). Moodie in "The Otonabee" writes: "A hand is on thy mane / That will bind thee in a chain" (ll. 31–2), but later annotates these lines: "Alluding to the projected improvements on the Trent, of which the Otonabee is a continuation. Fifteen years have passed away since this little poem was written; but the Otonabee still rushes on in its own wild strength" (RI, 272).

38 RI, 424; most of the letters between the Moodies from 1838–39 contain some mention of their attempts to deal with debts (PHEC, ser. I, Correspondence, nos. 60–70, 80–8).

39 RI, 409; "The people in the Backwoods," she later states, "were profoundly ignorant of how the colony was governed; ... and when the rebellion actually broke out it fell upon them like a thunder-clap" (LC, 36). According to Traill, they had been "slumbering in fancied security on a fearful volcano" (TFC, 9635).

40 Need mentions the "attempt on the part of a few low radicals to get up a 'grievance' meeting, as seditious assemblies are here denominated," in Peterborough in January 1833 (1838, 45). He participated in the Peterborough Tory campaign in the election of 1836, hoping to return the "constitutional candidate" (119). Another recent immigrant writes of the same contest: "in common with all good & loyal subjects I have been as busy as possible – The revolutionists have been defeated" (Read and Stagg 1985, 19). Strickland's summary of local male perception of events indicates a broader awareness than that of the women: "For several years preceding the rebellion of 1837–8, the country had been agitated by the inflammatory speeches and writings of William Lyon Mackenzie and his political coadjutors ... however, ... the loyal inhabitants of the counties of Northumberland and Peterborough ... were completely taken by surprise on hearing that a body of rebels, headed by William Lyon Mackenzie, were actually in arms and on their march to invest Toronto" (1853, 2.259–60). The men knew of Mackenzie, but were surprised by the rebellion. So was everyone in Toronto except Colonel James FitzGibbon.

41 RI, 411; she reports reading the proclamation on the evening of 4 December, long before any news of the events in Toronto that day could have reached Douro. The dispatch of Head's to which the loyal volunteers in the area responded arrived on 6 December (Read and Stagg 1985, 293). Traill's journal covering the rebellion begins on 7 December 1837 (TFC, 9635). A more precise account of the involvement of Moodie, Traill, and Strickland with the rebellion is in Morris (1968, 144–8).

42 RI, 413; see also letter 38. "Canadians! Will You Join the Band?" best supports her claim. It appeared in the Palladium of British America on 20 December, was reprinted in following weeks in the Montreal Transcript, the Kingston Chronicle and Gazette, and the St Catharines Journal. "On Reading the Proclamation Delivered by William Lyon Mackenzie" (1838),

"The Burning of the Caroline" (1838), and "The Oath of the Canadian Volunteers" (1839) were printed once, twice, and three times, respectively.

43 *RI*, 416; the period referred to might be any time in the first half of 1838. The first issue of the *Garland* was published in December 1838. When she later writes that the magazine started "in the fall of 1837" and Lovell wrote to her "in the December of that year" (286), she must mean the fall of 1838 (Intro to *MH*, 286). Clearly, she associated the beginning of her work for the *Garland* with the absence of her husband. She first mentions Lovell in her correspondence to Moodie in February 1839: "I have never received any answer from Mr Lovel, about contributing to the Garland" (PHEC, ser. I, Correspondence, no. 81). Her first piece in it appeared in May 1839.

44 *RI*, 424; Moodie was in Toronto in early 1838. His company was moved to the Niagara frontier in March and disbanded at the end of July. He is preoccupied by two themes in his letters from this period: money and war (PHEC, ser. I, Correspondence, nos. 60–4). He began sending home money in February. From the beginning of his militia duty he felt that war with the United States was imminent.

45 Buckner 1985, 254; Craig 1963, 254; on Arthur as assistant to Thomson, see Buckner 260; Craig 269–72; Mills 1988, 113–17.

46 Moodie states that her husband's appointment as paymaster "was Sir George Arthur's doing" (*RI*, 436). She wrote to Arthur thanking him for giving her husband the paymaster job (CEECT, 599, note to 448.9–10). Arthur's later regret that "it was not earlier in [his] power to confirm some appointment on" Moodie (quoted in *Letters*, 72, and Morris 1968, 178) suggests he had little to do with it. Moodie left Douro to take up his appointment on 14 December (PHEC, ser. I, Correspondence, no. 65; CEECT, 601, note to 460.12). The paymaster's job went with the reduction of the militia in 1839, and Moodie was back in Douro in late summer (see *RI*, 475; PHEC, ser. I, Correspondence, nos. 69, 70, 87, 88).

47 *Letters* 72; Lieutenant Colonel George, Baron de Rottenburg, "the provincial government's chief representative and militia commander" in the Quinte region from late 1838 to mid 1840 (Gerald Boyce 1967, 81), helped Moodie to get the sheriff's job. They became friends, and Moodie mentions "the Baron" in most of his letters to his wife in 1839. "I really think he will yet be of great service to us as he has much influence with Sir George Arthur having formerly acted as his Private Secretary," he writes in January, and then continues: "He ... promised to use all his influence with Sir George in our favor" (PHEC, ser. I, Correspondence, no. 70; for de Rottenburg, see also Betsy Boyce 1992, 127, 131, 143–4, 162–3, 215 n 30). The Victoria District, created out of the Midland District in 1839, became Hastings County after Moodie's appointment. Johnson writes of the increase in district governments in the late 1830s and

competition for the new offices, among which, as one of "the main positions," he lists sheriff (1989, 21).

48 PHEC, ser. I, Correspondence, nos. 65, 66; in the spring he writes that "the population is disaffected" (no. 67). He believes that "this is the most desirable situation in Upper Canada ... excepting the population which is very much disaffected but the *worst* are clearing out" (no. 68). Read and Stagg discuss the reputation of Belleville in the post-rebellion years (1985, lxxi–lxxii). Betsy Boyce's book details the political disturbances in Hastings County surrounding the rebellion; for the years 1838 and 1839, see 1992, 63–153. "The Bay of Quinte district was the oldest settled area and the one most accessible" in south-central Ontario (Spelt 1955, 45).

49 In December 1838 Moodie writes of the chance of another job in the "New District of Hastings" in the spring; he would sell his farm if he "should get a permanent appointment" (PHEC, ser. I, Correspondence, no. 65). She writes in January about her disappointment that his job is temporary: "I had wished that I could get out of the discomforts and miseries of Douro" (no. 80). In light of this letter and the others that follow, her claim in *Roughing It* that the "winter of 1839 was one of severe trial to me" (436) is an understatement. He raises the possibility of making an "exchange of wild land for a cleared farm near to the mouth of the Trent" (no. 66; see also no. 67) and of exchanges on the front west of Port Hope (no. 83) and on the Bay of Quinte (no. 68). She raises the possibility of Texas or the Cape (nos. 87, 88). By 1 June 1839 she concludes "that this must be the *last winter* of exile and widowhood" (no. 87) and in July pleads, "Oh Heaven keep me from being left in these miserable circumstances another year" (no. 88). The main preoccupation of the letters from this period is getting off their Douro farm (see also nos. 68, 84, 85).

50 Moodie had trouble posting his sheriff's bond before taking up his new post. His difficulty seems to have been bureaucratic, but he took it more seriously (Morris 1968, 174–6).

51 Belleville became district town of the Victoria District in 1840 and by 1846 had a population of 2,040 (Smith 1846, 14). After Toronto and Kingston, it was the third largest urban centre in south-central Ontario throughout the second quarter of the century, by 1851 reaching a population of 4,569 (Spelt 1955, 91). Population figures recorded by the Moodies confirm these statistics (*RI*, 510; *LC* 49). "The shores of the Bay of Quinte were originally occupied principally by U.E. Loyalists and retired officers," according to J.W.D. Moodie, "but the emigration from Europe has chiefly consisted of the poorer class of Irish Catholics, and of Protestants from the North of Ireland" (*RI*, 509). Texts for prospective emigrants habitually specify the origins of the population of various regions.

52 Mills discusses "two distinctive definitions" of loyalty current during this period: "The Tory definition ... stressed the exclusive nature of loyalty and ... the commitment to the British connection. In addition, the Tories totally rejected the legitimacy of opposition." The definition of loyalty articulated by the reform movement "was assimilative rather than exclusive; loyalty could be earned ... Moreover, there was an acceptance of the legitimacy of dissent; loyalty did not require acquiescence in abuses" (1988, 32–3). These two definitions parallel perceptions of loyalty in Douro and in Belleville, respectively.

53 Intro to *MH*, 288; elsewhere she contradicts this statement: "The native-born Canadian regarded with a jealous feeling men of talent and respectability who emigrated from the mother country, as most offices of consequence and emolument were given to such persons" (*LC*, 56). After recounting the scramble for the sheriff's position, Morris claims that Moodie was consistently treated as "an outsider [and] a Britisher" (1968, 173) by the local establishment. Johnson, discussing the rivalry between native-born and immigrants, concludes that by 1841 there was "an unmistakable decline" in the acquisition of "appointed positions" by "the native-born" (1989, 104). J.W.D. Moodie's assessment of the situation in 1839 differs from his assessment in 1850. Shocked at the *Kingston Whig's* attack on him as "an out and out advocate of *responsible Govt*," he is pleased that the *Toronto Patriot* defends him as "a loyal and trusty man." He believes he can avoid partisanship "by steadily pursuing a conciliatory course to all" (PHEC, ser. I, Correspondence, no. 70).

54 Local elites expected sheriffs and magistrates to be appointed from among their ranks (Craig 1963, 107; Read and Stagg 1985, xxii). For two out of three bonds Moodie posted before having one accepted, he appealed to his Douro connections, signing up Traill, Strickland, Stewart, and a Rev. Armour as sureties. For his third bond he had two Belleville area men (Morris 1968, 175–6; PHEC, ser. I, Correspondence, no. 70). These difficulties highlight the purely local nature of the local elites, as well as Moodie's lack of direct connection with the central elite. His lack of influence in Toronto was likely crucial to his career in Belleville and only partially remedied by his friendship with Baldwin. Describing another case, Johnson writes "that it was central, not local, influence that mattered most" (1989, 86).

55 Moodie's memorial of 23 November 1840 to the governor's secretary, quoted in Morris 1968, 179; Ponton, a Scots immigrant of 1834 aligned with the Belleville reformers, was still looking for an appointment in 1842, when Moodie told Baldwin that, due to the meddling of Dougall, "our friend Ponton has been disappointed in obtaining the office of Clerk of the Council" (Moodie to Baldwin, 25 Feb. 1842, Baldwin Papers, Correspondence, vol. A58, letter 52). Ponton went on to become

Belleville's registrar and mayor (Sheldon and Judith Godfrey 1991, 77, 79, 85 nn 2, 7; *Letters*, 83; Smith 1846, 201). On Parker and Dougall, see Morris, 171–3, 184–5, 187–92, 201–3; *Letters*, 85; Betsy Boyce 1992, 72, 86, 172.

56 In his recommendations to Baldwin for reform of the shrievalty, Moodie suggested a guaranteed income of three hundred pounds. By 1848 he was willing to take a replacement position worth as little as two hundred if it was free of "the risk of [his] present office" (Moodie to Baldwin, 15 Feb. 1845, 8 Oct. 1848, Baldwin Papers, Correspondence, vol. A58, letters 56, 60). For his difficulty collecting fees, see *Letters*, 85, 87; Morris 1968, 184, 202. Peter Russell presents abundant information on incomes during this period. Moodie's income put him in the top category of Russell's hierarchy, the "Respectable," who earned from two to three hundred pounds a year (1981, 25–9).

57 Moodie's petition to the governor, quoted in Morris 1968, 185; according to Johnson, it was standard for prominent individuals to have several occupations and "also fairly common for one government employee to hold more than one government office" (1989, 18).

58 1866, ix; he makes the same statement in a letter to Bentley in 1865 (PHEC, ser. I, Correspondence, no. 78). Gerson discusses the defensiveness of this introduction (1985, 42–3).

59 Letter 89; this letter from 1868 summarizes the difficulties experienced by her husband when in office: "They kept us from the larger emoluments of the office by never paying their accounts and by bringing constantly vexatious suits against my husband in the name of parties who were unable to pay their costs, which though he always *won*, yet in the end was out of pocket by having to pay for the defence." In "Perhaps, or Honesty the best policy," an unpublished autobiographical sketch written in the 1860s, Moodie writes about the poor morals of "a new country": "In politics – in trade – even in the grave professions, the want of honor ... seldom stands in the way of preferment" (PHEC, ser. II, Manuscripts, box 4, f. 31, unnumbered p. 1).

60 Quoted in Morris 1968, 195; Morris characterizes the petition as "routine" and quotes the Assembly's view of it as "frivolous and vexatious." The Godfreys, however, conclude that Moodie's "independence of action was questionable" (1991, 48). Moodie himself later admits that he has "not always acted up to the principle" that "a sheriff should ... keep clear of *party politics*" (Moodie to Baldwin, 15 Feb. 1845, Baldwin Papers, Correspondence, vol. A58, letter 56). Most of the petition's charges dealt with Baldwin and his election committee, not Moodie. On the provincial election of 1841, see Buckner 1985, 263; Careless 1967, 41–7. On the Belleville campaign, see Gerald Boyce 1967, 95–7; Morris 1968, 192–5; *Letters*, 86–7. On Murney, see Morris, 184, 192–201; *Letters*, 87, 114; Johnson 1989, 217; Sheldon and Judith Godfrey 1991, 48–51, 82–3.

61 Careless 1967, 75; Mrs Moodie claimed there was a "large body of Reformers" in Belleville at this time (*LC* 56). The earliest dated evidence for their first meeting is a letter from Moodie to Baldwin from 3 February 1842, which refers to two letters from Baldwin (Baldwin Papers, Correspondence, vol. A58, letter 49). In subsequent letters the same month, Moodie refers to "our party" and advises Baldwin how "we" can triumph over the Tories (letter 51). By 1845 Moodie had distanced himself from the reformers, although he still saw the virtues of responsible government. The Moodies responded to Baldwin's qualities as a man, and he provided a connection with the central elite necessary to a civil servant.

62 Upset that anyone should contest the election of his attorney general, Bagot dismissed Murney from his job as clerk of the peace. Morris provides an account of the second election (1968, 196–9; see also Gerald Boyce 1967, 97; Careless 1967, 71; Read and Stagg 1985, 377; Sheldon and Judith Godfrey 1991, 49–50). Baldwin was offered and took a safe reform seat in Rimouski after the Hastings election. Murney did not take his seat until his win in 1844.

63 Moodie to Baldwin, 4 May 1848, Baldwin Papers, Correspondence, vol. A58, letter 57.

64 On Doctors Hope and Lister, see *Letters*, 83, 114, and letter 53 on the latter only. On William FitzGibbon, son of Colonel James FitzGibbon, important in the defeat of the rebellion, see *Letters*, 114; Morris 1968, 200; Smith 1846, 201.

65 Moodie's deposition to the governor on 18 April 1842, quoted in Morris 1968, 187, who provides an account of his conflict with Judge Dougall based on this source (189–91). The surety involved was Major Adam Henry Meyers, the very Loyalist with whom Moodie was "pretty *thick*" in January 1839 and with whom he hoped to exchange his Douro holding (PHEC, ser. I, Correspondence, nos. 66, 70).

66 The minute-book of the Congregational Church of Belleville is explored at greater length in Thurston 1994, where the statements made here are substantiated. Rufus Holden, drugstore owner, magistrate, and later reeve of Belleville, is the one founding member who attained some local prominence.

67 The historical details of this paragraph come from Buckner 1985, 167–71; Careless 1967, 58–131; Mills 1988, 121–9.

68 Moodie to Baldwin, 6 Feb. 1845, Baldwin Papers, Correspondence, vol. A58, letter 55.

69 Moodie to Baldwin, 8 Oct. 1848, Baldwin Papers, Correspondence, vol. A58, letter 60.

70 *LC*, 66; in *Roughing It* Moodie believes "that they expected to find an author one of a distinct species from themselves" (202).

71 A clear expression of this argument about the decline of both ultra-Tory conservativism and agrarian radicalism and their replacement by capitalist hegemony is in Fraser, who believes that they shared more with each other than they did with what succeeded them (1979, 107, 240–1, 249–50, 329, 343–4). Mills also discusses how loyalty to England remained unimpaired by responsible government, which in turn was necessary for capitalism to develop in the Canadas (1988, 99–100, 135).

CHAPTER FIVE

1 Strickland may have received some of Moodie's work through correspondence or British periodicals shipped to him. The poems in the *Star* in the fall of 1831 are "The Vision of Dry Bones" (20 Sept.), "Morning Hymn" (4 Oct.) and "Elijah in the Wilderness" (18 Oct.). The first two are in *Enthusiasm*.

2 *Letters*, 74; the poems in the *Star* in 1832 are "On the Ruins of Walberswick Church in Suffolk" (19 Sept.), "Autumn" (17 Oct.), "Uncertainty" (31 Oct.), "O Come to the Meadows" (23 Nov.), and "Youth and Age" (19 Dec.).

3 "Song. The Strains We Hear in Foreign Lands," ll. 1–2, 11; the passage in *Roughing It* that this poem concludes expands on her inability to respond to colonial culture. She tells of musicians playing through the night on board the ship at anchor in the St Lawrence, then writes: "Nothing tends so much to increase our melancholy as merry music when the heart is sad; and I left the scene with eyes brimful of tears, and my mind painfully agitated by sorrowful recollections and vain regrets" (48).

4 *Letters*, 74; Ballstadt 1988, xxi; her first two Canadian poems, "The Strains We Hear in Foreign Lands" and "The Sleigh-Bells," were published with her letter to Bartlett in the *Albion*, but the author was identified as Agnes Strickland. Bartlett corrected his error several months later when he published "There's Rest," written in August 1832, when she was on the St Lawrence.

5 In her initial letter to Bartlett, Moodie compliments him on the reception of the *Albion* "into the study of every respectable family on this side of the Atlantic" (letter 35), and she later notes that it has "a wide circulation in Canada" (Intro to *MH*, 293). Anna Jameson describes it as "compiled for the use of the British settlers in the United States, and also in Canada, where it is widely circulated" (1838, 251).

6 Intro to *MH*, 289; Moodie does not mention her contributions to the *Canadian Literary Magazine*, although she does write that its "list of contributors embraced some of the cleverest men in the Colony." Klinck notes that the "contributors were all promising *litterateurs* such as Mrs. Susanna Moodie, Dr. 'Tiger' Dunlop, and Robert Douglas Hamilton, all

British-trained authors who had published before arriving in Canada" (1965, 154–5).

7 Quoted in Gundy 1965, 193; Moodie's poems "The Convict's Wife" and "Oh Can You Leave Your Native Land" are in the first issue of the *Canadian Literary Magazine*, with her story "Achbor." The second issue has her "I Loved You Long and Tenderly."

8 Before discussing Fairfield, Moodie admits she "had never been able to turn my thoughts towards literature during my sojourn in the bush" (*RI*, 416–17). At least one of the poems he published was written in 1824 (PHEC, ser. II, Manuscripts, box 6, pp. 69–98).

9 "Oh Canada! Thy Gloomy Woods" (ll. 1–2) and "Home Thoughts of an Emigrant" (ll. 19–22), both published in 1836; the absence of bird-song in these lines recalls Alexander McLachlan's *The Emigrant*: "Lovely birds of gorgeous dye ... songless, ev'ry one." Moodie anticipates McLachlan more fully in a letter: "We have few birds, and I miss the rich tones of the nightingales, blackbird, lark and thrush, the sweet piping of the robin, linnet and woodlark, whose united chorus from ... Reydon wood ... filled the whole air" (letter 91).

10 On newspaper coverage of the activities of the fall of 1837, see Read and Scagg 1985, extracts A67, A68, A71–4, A81; Mackenzie's constitution is extract A78. Head's challenge, "Let them come if they dare!" is echoed in "The Oath of the Canadian Volunteers": "Let the foe come ... if they dare" (ll. 12–13).

11 J.W.D. Moodie met Fothergill in Toronto (PHEC, ser. I, Correspondence, no. 60). On Fothergill and the *Palladium*, see Craig 1963, 192; Errington 1987, 100, 158, 175; Johnson 1989, 17, 52–3, 191; *Letters*, 76–7; Read and Scagg 1985, 74 n 151.

12 "The Banner of England," a battle hymn to "the standard of the free, / That dared the might of France" (ll. 35–6), is in *Patriotic Songs* (1831) and was in the *Palladium* on 24 January (Ballstadt 1986, 91, 96 n 14, 88). "Stanzas on War" and "The Avenger of Blood" appeared in the *Palladium* on 21 February and 11 April 1838, respectively.

13 Letter 38; in late 1837 the British sinking of the *Caroline*, a supply ship for Navy Island, brought the threat of war with the republic very close. Moodie's poem on the *Caroline* was published the next fall. Letter 38 is taken from a reprint in the *Montreal Transcript*, 11 Oct. 1838, of a letter that accompanied the poem in the *Palladium* (*Letters*, 95 n 1). A complete run of the *Palladium* has not survived, so the original publication date is not known.

14 The *Palladium* died with Fothergill in 1840. The *York Correspondent and Advocate*, before Mackenzie incorporated it into the *Constitution*, had been the first paper to pick up "The Sleigh-Bells" from the *Albion*. Another reform paper, the *Kingston Spectator*, had taken "There's Rest" from the *Albion*.

15 PHEC, ser. I, Correspondence, no. 65; this letter also encloses a copy of the *Palladium* "to file with the rest."

16 PHEC, ser. I, Correspondence, nos. 80, 66; Moodie travelled to Kingston regularly to pick up pay for the troops. Nothing came of his offer to arrange for a book of her poems. In her next letter she returns to the attempt to sell *Enthusiasm*: "Could you make any engagement for the hundred copies that are unbound I would sell them cheap for cash" (PHEC, ser. I, Correspondence, no. 81).

17 PHEC, ser. I, Correspondence, no. 83; she makes the standard division of literary labour: "I could take all the light reading. Tales, poetry &c. and you the political and statistical details."

18 David Arnason, describing the *Literary Garland* as the "longest single publishing enterprise before Confederation," notes that "the average life expectancy of literary magazines ... was about two years" (1973, 127, 128). Lovell's attachment to England and active service in suppressing the Lower Canadian rebellion supports this presentation of the *Garland* as an apparatus of the colonial elite. He had government printing contracts and an office in Toronto (Gundy 1965, 195). Douglas Fetherling details how, after the rebellion and into the next decade, "the Tories virtually eliminated the Reform press" (1990, 24).

19 PHEC, ser. I, Correspondence, nos. 81, 87; Lovell "offered to pay the postage on all manuscripts to his office, and left [her] to name my own terms of renumeration" (*RI*, 417).

20 "London: A National Song" was first published in 1832. The other two poems in the *Garland* in 1839 are short lyrics on frustrated love like those Moodie wrote in the late 1820s. According to an editorial note to one of the stories, it "was written as far back as the year 1824." The other two stories deal with European subjects; one of them, about two British boys, would have suited a juvenile annual. The second is her one piece in the first volume that the editor does not designate as original.

21 On the pre-emigration composition of "The Royal Quixote," see the editorial comment appended to it in the *Garland*; on "The Miner" and "The Miser and His Son," see letters 13 and 28, respectively; a version of "Jane Redgrave" is in *La Belle Assemblée* in 1829.

22 Not counting poems by J.W.D. Moodie and verse emblems, *Roughing It* has twenty-four poems. Only "The Forgotten Dream" has not been identified as previously published. *Life in the Clearings* has twenty-three poems, four of which are not known to have been previously published: "Indian Summer," "The Song of Faith," "Song" ["There's hope for those who sleep ..."], and "A Freak of Fancy."

23 Gerson 1989, 138; in Gerson's view, the colonial novel "suffered more than any other literary form from the absence of a solid foundation of acknowledged social and historical experience" (42). She suggests that

the long story "Noah Cotton" was inserted in *Flora Lyndsay* because it "includes enough murder, illegitimacy, theft, and romance to compensate for Flora's more mundane activities, thus bridging the gap between the conventions of popular fiction and the material offered by the New World" (43). MacLulich also notes that "Richardson and Moodie ... started their literary careers with the assumption that the only proper setting for genteel fiction was a European one" (1988, 26). Thompson believes that "in the orientation towards the Old World that is demonstrated in her fiction, Moodie is more representative of her era than is Traill" (1991, 28).

24 Moodie asked Bentley to discard only the American subtitle of *Geoffrey Moncton*, "The Faithless Guardian" (letter 60). She disagreed with his intention to call it "The Monctons," fearing a confusion with "The Monktons of Wincot Abbey, a story in the *Albion*," but left the decision up to him (letter 61, *Letters*, 165 n 4).

25 Fredric Jameson writes that in fiction "real social contradictions, insurmountable in their own terms, find a purely formal resolution in the aesthetic realm" (1981, 79), an insight he derives from "Levi-Strauss's seminal characterization of mythic narrative, the imaginary resolution of ... real contradictions" (256). This discussion of Moodie's novels is indebted to Jameson. He believes that "the literary 'character' ... is to be seen rather as an 'effect of system' than as a fully representational identity in its own right" (243). Behind this analysis of characters in Moodie's fiction is an alignment of her system of values with the "semiotic rectangle" Jameson borrows from Greimas (47–8, 166–8, 254–6).

26 "Matrimonial Speculations," 362; Rachel Beauchamp's mother hopes that Rachel might be a means of conciliating the maternal grandfather and recouping some of the fortune that had been estranged by her father's contempt for his in-laws. Rachel's narrative satirizes the vulgar, materialistic London relatives, from whom she retreats back to the country after one day. Susanna's first trip to London was for a visit to her mother's sister, who "had not seen any of [them] for a number of years," but "after a few weeks [she] did not find her sojourn a pleasant one" and left (TFC, 9885–6).

27 Letter 52; see also the opening of the story: "The principal events in my tale, though whimsical enough, are, I believe, founded upon facts; the circumstances having been related to me by an intelligent West Indian merchant" (413).

28 When the European features of the voluntary slave, being signs not only of cleverness but also a spirit of liberty, are the prime point of contention among potential buyers, the suspicion arises that Moodie had little understanding of slavery. This suspicion is confirmed when Richard's "slavery" leads directly to marriage with his master's daughter. "Richard

Redpath" is her one attempt in fiction to enter the territory charted by Hulme: "Sentimental sympathy began to flow out along the arteries of European commerce in search of its victims" (1986, 229; on anti-slavery and sentimentality, see also Pratt 1992, 87). The caricaturing of blacks combined with a condemnation of slavery is also found in *Flora Lyndsay*.

29 *Belleville Intelligencer*, 26 Dec. 1862, quoted in *Letters*, 89; in their biography of Benjamin, Sheldon and Judith Godfrey use "Richard Redpath" for many descriptions of him and his business. For his conflict with the Moodies, see especially 45–53, but also see *Letters*, 88; Read and Stagg 1985, 286 n 86; Morris 1963, 193; Ballstadt 1988, 608, note to 538.3; Betsy Boyce 1992, 51, 73, 89–90. According to Boyce, "a fire in January 1863 destroyed almost all the files" of the *Intelligencer* (1992, 10).

30 *Letters*, 89; the Godfreys write that Benjamin "had helped incite tory and Orange feelings ... against [J.W.D.] Moodie" (1991, 50), and Moodie complained to Baldwin of Benjamin's attacks (Moodie to Baldwin, 25 Feb. 1842, Baldwin Papers, Correspondence, vol. A58, letter 52). Benjamin concealed his religion and Levi "passes ... for a Christian," but is "a Jew by birth, and one at heart and in practice, and belongs to the very worst tribe of them" (442). One vignette concerning Levi has no point other than to introduce the lines, "I took a piece of pork, / And stuck it on a fork, / For the old Jew's dinner" (558). These lines echo a mock-elegy on the hanging in effigy of Benjamin, printed in the Kingston *Whig* in 1836: "For Pork's the meat Jews must not eat, / No doubt it killed the Jew" (quoted in Palmer 1978, 30, and Sheldon and Judith Godfrey, 25). Robert Redpath, after reading a paragraph on himself in Levi's newspaper, seeks his revenge. He finds Levi "reading his paper aloud to a knot of idlers," his dangling legs having "a strange resemblance to the cloven feet with which painters have invested his Majesty of Evil." The "submissive Jew" is no match for the bluff Anglo-Saxon, and he is made literally to eat his words on Robert (561). These scenes bear little relation to the rest of the story. On anti-semitism in Upper Canada during this period, see Russell 1981, 297, 304.

31 Errington 1987, 116; see also Craig 1963, 200. "Political asperities," Cattermole claimed in 1831, are "chiefly confined to the editors of newspapers, whose disputes have been alike annoying to their own immediate friends, the public at large, and injurious to the best interests of the colony" (110). In 1838 Anna Jameson remarked that through Upper Canadian newspapers "a great deal of base, vulgar, inflammatory party feeling is ... circulated" (153).

32 The introductory quotation is from a passage in the January 1848 "Editor's Table" of the *Victoria Magazine*, which begins: "A man of an enlightened and elegant mind is not at all likely to stain his pages by low and vulgar abuse, a practice too commonly resorted to by the editors of

papers." It concludes with the hope that "as the Colony advances in literature and refinement," the abuse will disappear (120). The three block quotations are from "Richard Redpath," 283, *RI*, 83, and Intro to *MH*, 292–93.

33 "Old Woodruff and His Three Wives," 174; all quotations are from the reprint in Edwards, ed. 1973.

34 Ballstadt identifies the characters in *Roughing It* in his notes to the CEECT edition.

35 *RI*, 488; five-eights of "Old Woodruff" go into two-thirds of the chapter "Adieu to the Woods" in *Roughing It*. The main additions are "a laughable extempore ditty" by her husband (479); her retrieval of their daughter from a friend's and the picking up of a parcel left by a friend (483–4); and the narration of their second night's lodging at the house of a friend (484–5). The revisions thus shift the focus from Woodruff to people closer to her.

36 Jenny appears throughout the later chapters of *Roughing It* (see especially 440–2, and PHEC, ser. I, Correspondence, nos. 80, 81, 84, 88). Emilia Shairp is Moodie's good friend in the bush (see *RI*, 437, 448–9, and PHEC, ser. I, Correspondence, nos. 80, 83, 88). The "Captain N—" of "The Walk to Dummer" (442) seems to be the "wicked Captain L— of Dummer" mentioned earlier (*RI*, 318; see CEECT 586, note to 338.2–3, 605, note to 488.5–7; PHEC, ser. I, Correspondence, nos. 61, 63).

37 While the evils of alcohol appear throughout Moodie's work, she went through an especially concentrated period of ruminating on them in late 1846, early 1847. A dramatic poem, "The Drunkard's Return. A Tale for the Teetotallers," dated December 1846, appears in the February 1847 issue of the *Literary Garland*; "The Walk to Dummer" is published the next month. The anecdote "A Tale for Teetotallers" is in the *Victoria Magazine* the following September. Poem, sketch, and anecdote feature a poor wife and children starving due to a drunken husband and father. The poem and anecdote are fictions. Comparing the poem with the sketch shows how permeable was the barrier between fact and fiction for Moodie and how readily people she knew stimulated her imagination to fictionalize on them.

38 On its title page the *Victoria Magazine* was identified as "A Cheap Periodical, for the Canadian People," and Moodie later refers to it as "a periodical for the people" (Intro to *MH*, 291). New believes the Moodies "were mistaken in their audience" (1989, 34). Referring to her comment that Canadians appreciate a "good political article" over "romantic tales and poetry" and their decision to "banish from the pages of the *Victoria*, all subjects ... that might lead to angry discussion" (*VM*, 287), he argues that the works that would appeal to Canadians "were exactly the sort of thing ... that she chose to omit from *The Victoria Magazine*" (35). According

to Mary Lu MacDonald, however, "it was customary for the prospectus of a new literary periodical to emphasize that it would be politically neutral" (1990, 37).

39 "Rachel Wilde," 100, 101; all quotations are from the reprint in *Voyages*.

40 The one major part of "Rachel Wilde" not attested to in other sources is the year Rachel spends with friends of her father when she is six. Traill's account of her and Susanna's first attempts as authors is particularly close to Moodie's in "Rachel Wilde" (compare TFC, 8418–26, and "Rachel Wilde," 145–9).

41 Letter 47; in *Flora Lyndsay* itself there is an acknowledgment that it is incomplete: "And here we shall leave our emigrants, in the bustle, confusion and excitement of preparing to go on shore, having described the voyage from thence to Quebec, and up the St Lawrence elsewhere" (342). Moodie's original title for the book was "Rachel Macgregor's Emigration" (letter 48). She later asks for the removal of "the Emigrants" from the title and the addition of its original title as subtitle (letter 52). Her correspondence with Bentley between this letter and the publication of *Flora Lyndsay* does not mention its new title, so it likely came from Bentley.

42 "The Well in the Wilderness," 95, quoted from the reprint in *Voyages*. Besides the discussions in *Roughing It* and *Flora Lyndsay* of her terror of wild animals, Moodie has the mother in "The Broken Mirror" cite "the wild beasts" as a reason not to emigrate to South Africa (*Voyages*, 68). In *Roughing It* she mentions a "dread of encountering wild beasts in the woods," which she "never could wholly shake off" (276), and describes her "cowardice" during a walk with her husband at night when a bear followed them (404).

43 The quotation on *Wilson's Canada Casket* is from an advertisement for it in the July 1848 *Victoria Magazine* (264). *Wilson's Experiment* is favourably noticed in the previous December's issue (96). Canniff notes that the *Victoria Magazine* was succeeded by the *Eclectic Magazine* and the other two journals, none of which lasted beyond 1852 (1869, 362). According to New, Wilson's "interests were moving in another direction" (1968, x). Klay Dyer adduces a combination of competition from American periodicals, local politics, and the interfering enterprises of Wilson as reasons for the failure of the *Victoria Magazine* (1992, 10–18). A hint of political disagreements between Wilson and the Moodies is provided by a notice in Benjamin's *Intelligencer* wishing *Wilson's Experiment* "every success" (quoted in Dyer, 16). The Moodie's first contact with Wilson may have been through the Congregationalist church, which he joined in January 1845. Among the many reviews and notices of the *Victoria Magazine* is one suggesting that the Moodies did proceed some way with their plan to become proprietors of their own periodical: "The Prospectus

of '*Moodie's Magazine*' to take the place of this monthly, will probably appear next week" (*Huron Signal*, 15 Dec. 1848, quoted in Dyer, 18).

CHAPTER SIX

1 *RI*, 511; on Benjamin's career, see Sheldon and Judith Godfrey 1991. He must have left Moodie alone after he gave up the *Intelligencer*. Ten years further still, Moodie probably wanted to retract his praise. As MP for North Hastings, Benjamin intervened directly with John A. Macdonald in the campaign to get Moodie fired from his sheriff's job (Sheldon and Judith Godfrey, 128–9).

2 *VM*, 89; the epigraph to "Education the True Wealth of the World" has thirteen lines. When she revises this essay to make it the chapter "Free Schools – Thoughts on Education" in *Life in the Clearings*, the first seven lines are deleted and the line quoted becomes the first line, the three qualities now capitalized (77).

3 The epigraph first used for "Rachel Wilde" is retained when she transforms "A Word for the Novel Writers" with a few introductory pages into the chapter "Toronto" in *Life in the Clearings* (249).

4 Letter 44; she says the same elsewhere (Intro to *MH*, 286).

5 Geoffrey Moncton, despairing at being a bastard outcast in England, is told that "there are other countries, where the conventional rules that govern society in this, are regarded with indifference – *America*, for instance" (91). The unconventional Wilhemina Carr in *Flora Lyndsay* congratulates the heroine on going to Canada: "In that wild country you will enjoy the glorious privilege of living as you please" (59). Elsewhere Moodie cautions "those persons who have been brought up in the old country, and accustomed ... to the conventional rules of society": "the mixed society must for a long time, prove very distasteful" (*LC*, 59). "The distinctions, unavoidable among persons of wealth and education, are hardly felt or recognised here," she later says (148).

6 Moodie readily reconciles equality before Christ with social inequality (*LC*, 331). In *Flora Lyndsay*, Wilhelmina Carr voices the same view: "as to pure democracy ... that's all humbug. No well-educated, wealthy persons, ever consider themselves upon an equality with their servants" (59).

7 Chapter 3, "Free Schools – Thoughts on Education," and chapters 5 and 6, "Trials of a Travelling Musician" and "The Singing Master," had been published in the *Victoria Magazine* in 1847; chapter 8, "Wearing Mourning for the Dead," and chapter 11, "Michael Macbride," had been in the *Literary Garland* in 1851; chapter 12, "Jeanie Burns," and chapter 13, "Lost Children," sent for *Roughing It*, had been in *Bentley's Miscellany* in 1852; most of chapter 14, "Toronto," had appeared in the *Garland* in 1851. Parts

of the *Victoria Magazine*'s "Editor's Table" were transferred to *Life in the Clearings* (*VM*, 71 and 240 become 81 and 331–3). At least 18 of its 23 poems were previously published. Bentley, holding copyright on a bunch of post-*Roughing It* sketches, may himself have fleshed out a scanty manuscript with them. It may have been his decision to include "Michael Macbride," "Jeanie Burns," and "Lost Children."

8   A visit to the Moodies by "The Hon. R. B–" is mentioned in *Life in the Clearings*, and he is quoted (94). More surprisingly, "our beloved and excellent chief-justice Robinson" is quoted (150). While Ryerson is not named, Moodie would be aware that he was largely responsible for "the present liberal provision made for the education of the rising generation," which she praises (77). The various aspects of Upper Canadian society that she comments on are all of the ideological state apparatuses listed by Althusser (1970, 143).

9   *LC*, 330, 9, 10; in the introduction she writes that *Roughing It* "was prompted by the hope of deterring well-educated people, about to settle in this colony, from entering upon a life for which they were totally unfitted by their previous pursuits and habits" (9). Her recommendations that gentlemen immigrants become speculators or take cleared land are also in both places (10, 330).

10   *LC*, 297, 296; Traill thought the settlements along Lake Ontario looked pleasing (1836, 47) but knew that bush settlers were "dispirited by the unpromising appearance of things about them" (87). She also realized that for "the mere passing traveller ... there is certainly a monotony in the long unbroken line of woods." But Traill sought out "the minute beauties of scenery" and found much "to charm and delight the close observer of nature" (63). She comments throughout her book on the flora, finding, indeed, "an Arcadia of fruits and flowers in the Backwoods of Canada." This contrast between what they were each able to see provides a telling focus for the common differentiation of the sisters (see, for example, Gairdner 1972; Jackel 1977; Fowler 1982, 93–8; Thompson 1991, 45–6, 160 n 1). Moodie's implied support for primogeniture aligns her with colonial conservatives (see Craig 1963, 207–8).

11   *LC*, 88; Cattermole says that "society in York is equal to any provincial town in Britain" (1831, 18).

12   *LC*, 253; "The piracies of the Americans" that stock the Toronto bookstores, Moodie recognizes, "must always make the Canadas a bad market for English publications," but the benefits of having cheap reprints available outweigh the loss to authors published in Britain, herself included, presumably (253).

13   *LC*, 89; the Moodies acquired their own piano in 1842, bought and shipped to them by Lovell, with money he owed her (letter 40). J.W.D. Moodie also mentions the proliferation of pianos in Belleville as evidence of cultural and economic progress (*RI*, 514).

14 *LC*, 327; her comments to Bentley on the New Year's Day custom make her awareness of the class dimension even clearer: "You must keep open house that day, and be dressed up to receive *all* who choose to come ... The gentlemen go round in their sleighs to wish the females in every house, (in their own class) the returns of the season" (letter 54).

15 *LC*, 328; when Moodie mentions children's parties at her own house, then ties them to the disrespect of children for their parents, she hints at a personal source for her hostility.

16 1853, 1.219–20; the dominance of American Methodist clergy in this period is a common theme (see Magrath 1833, 112, 115; Howison 1821, 142; Traill 1836, 247). William Westfall shows that between 1842 and 1881, while the population of Ontario "almost quadrupled," the Methodists "increased their combined membership more than sevenfold." The Anglicans almost kept pace with population growth (1989, 10; see also Craig 55–6). For the Anglican preference for parishes in settled areas and the Methodist missions to the backwoods, see Errington 1987, 52; Wise 1965, 82.

17 Westfall's discussion of the antagonism between Anglican order and Methodist enthusiasm in Upper Canada in the nineteenth century supports this argument about Moodie's attitude towards Methodism (1989, 19–49; see also Craig 1963, 165–7). "By mid-century the animosity and bitterness that had divided the Anglicans and the Methodists had begun to disappear" (11), he writes, but Moodie, at least when writing *Life in the Clearings*, seems still to have shared Thomas Radcliff's opinion of colonial religion as he expressed it twenty years earlier: "In the democratic principle, ... in the instigation to discontent, and in disaffection to the laws, may always be traced the absence of the Church of England principles" (Magrath 1833, 116). Moodie's daughter was given a copy of Magrath's book in 1844 (PHEC, ser. V, Printed Materials).

18 *LC*, 35; on the dates at which Methodist preachers from the United States and England came to Upper Canada, see Craig 1963, 166–7; Grant 1988, 45, 70. There were three Methodist churches in Belleville (Smith 1846, 14); Moodie does not refer to the third.

19 *LC*, 34–5; Moodie's attraction to the Free Church is also indicated by her description of its Toronto church: "I was greatly struck with the elegant spire of Knox's church, which is perhaps the most graceful in the city" (253).

20 On St Thomas's, see Betsy Boyce 1992, 23, 26, 121–2. On Benjamin's association with it, see Sheldon and Judith Godfrey 1991, 67, 71, 136, 139. Murney was Anglican (Johnson 1989, 217).

21 Bentley's active role in the production of *Roughing It* opens the possibility that it was his decision to include "Michael Macbride" in *Life in the Clearings* and so risk offending Irish Catholics. Westfall writes that "anti-

Catholicism forms a persistent theme in the religious history of the nineteenth century in Canada" (1989, 22). Among the first things to unite all the Protestant denominations was their antipathy to Catholics (123; see also Russell 1981, 276-8). Moodie's toleration towards them in *Life in the Clearings* is thus notable, even if due to defensive motives.

22 *LC*, 30; Moodie's comment on the chastity of Suffolk "female peasantry" may derive from the indiscretion of the unwed servant girl she brought with her to Canada (*RI*, 199; "Trifles," 192). Irish Catholic wit is illustrated by several anecdotes, which lead to Scottish Catholic anecdotes told to Moodie by "the late Bishop Macdonald, a man whose memory is held in great veneration in the province" (*LC*, 29). Alexander Macdonell, a Highland Scot who came to Glengarry County in 1804, became Catholic bishop of Kingston in 1826. Moodie likely had these anecdotes through her husband, who may have met Macdonell in Kingston in 1838–39. On Father Brennan, see Gerald Boyce 1967, 209.

23 PHEC, ser. I, Correspondence, no. 70.

24 PHEC, ser. I, Correspondence, no. 69.

25 J.W.D. Moodie in "Religion and Loyalty" argues "that almost any religion is better than no religion, and the sooner the ideas of moral restraint are impressed on the mind the better" (1848, 105). He insists that "mutual forbearance and charitable feelings towards our opponents in religion" are necessary because of "the difficulties religious prejudices create in the civil government of the country." He wants religious "harmony" to arise through "a voluntary sacrifice of illiberal prejudices by all sects" (106, 107).

26 PHEC, ser. I, Correspondence, nos. 69, 70; *RI*, 500, 501; on the fear that party politics meant instability and Baldwin's perception that this need not be so, see Buckner 1985, 144, 160–1, 233, 259, 268, 270, 280.

27 *LC*, 13, 56, 59; "The Garland" (1843) voices support for union:
> Union is strength – whilst round the boughs
>> Of thine own lofty maple tree,
> The threefold wreath of Britain flows,
>> Twined with the graceful fleur-de-lis. (ll. 41–4)

She reprints part of this poem in 1853 (*LC*, 17), but by 1856 she is complaining that "the free industrious, British population of Upper Canada are kept in a minority by the Catholic votes of Lower Canada, which is most injurious to the general interest and prosperity of the Colony." Her fears of political instability and resentment of the French are palpable: "The Feud between the protestants and their Catholic fellow subjects grows stronger every hour. I fear, that we shall have a fearful struggle for power between these hostile parties before long" (letter 64).

28 *LC*, 24; while there were early supporters for various types of Protestant establishment in all the Protestant denominations, supporters of

voluntarism were at first mainly in the dissenting congregations. Although Strachan maintained his opposition, by mid-century "Anglicans, Presbyterians, and Methodists had in effect reached the same position" (Westfall 1989, 118; see also 100–1, 116–18; Grant 1988, 93–4, 137–40; Russell 1981, 269–72). In her remarks on "the voluntary principle," then, Moodie is promoting the consensual position.

29 In 1835 Charles Duncombe went to the United States to report "on schools ... but also lunatic asylums, and on prisons and penitentiaries" (Houston 1972, 33; see also Craig 1963, 187). Duncombe was a radical reformer, and a reform Assembly commissioned him; discipline and education were linked in this period, regardless of political orientation. Palmer writes that in the "contest for hegemony, schools became a counterpart of the prisons, and by mid-century one chief superintendent's report described the educational system of Upper Canada as 'a branch of the national police,' aiming 'to occupy a large part of the population' and 'support and restrain many of the grown-up populations'" (1983, 57; see Prentice 1977, 132, for the source of this quotation).

30 Instead of the steamboat entering Lake Ontario through the passage between Prince Edward County and Amherst Island, Moodie has it travel along the North Channel to Kingston, thirty kilometres in a direction opposite to that of its destination.

31 Moodie's visit to the Kingston jail pre-dated the Penitentiary Act of 1851, which was intended to correct abuses uncovered by the Royal Commission on Penitentiaries and was "the small but vital beginning of a long and extensive development of state social action" (Careless 1967, 221). The only other state-maintained social-welfare institutions extant at the time were "a marine hospital and quarantine hospital at Quebec" and the "provincial asylum in Toronto" (220). Moodie clearly understood the significance of the prison and asylum as first among the repressive state apparatuses and saw their relationship to the developing educational institution. A common thread in "the argument of the school promoters," showing their view of education as an ideological state apparatus, "was their expanding conception of the role of the state in education. Thus they pushed the constant extension of government control over schooling" (Prentice 1977, 170).

32 LC, 77; Baldwin and the reformers actually opposed the 1846 bill, drafted by Ryerson, for a common school system. Reform opposition was based on middle-class resistance to paying for schools that the poor would attend while their children went to grammar schools. By 1850 reform had been won over to a school system supported by all. On the School Acts of 1846 and 1850 and the political bickering over them, see Houston 1972, 48–9; Prentice 1977, 125. This discussion of education is indebted to the work of Susan Houston and Alison Prentice.

33 On educational reform as a reaction to social unrest, and the attempt to convince the middle class to pay for the education of the poor, see Houston 1972, 33, 35, 40–1; 1975 85–6, 89–90; Prentice 1977, 46, 50–1, 56, 67, 119–27, 131–3, 171. In 1851 the *Globe* pointedly expressed the issue: "Educate the people and your gaols will be abandoned and your police may be disbanded; all the offenses which man commits against his neighbour and against his own peace will be comparatively unknown ... If we make our people intelligent, they cannot fail to be prosperous; intelligence makes morality, morality industry, industry prosperity" (quoted in Houston 1975, 89).

34 *LC*, 82; Moodie explicitly connects ignorance and drunkenness only once (85). Her chapter on education follows immediately upon her discussion of drunkenness, however, and her references to "every idle ragged child" and "these neglected children" (77, 78) show her agreement with one reformer's advocacy of schools as guardians for the "pitiable victims of neglect and wretchedness": "Accustomed ... to witness at home nothing ... but what is degrading; early taught to observe intemperance, and to hear obscene and profane language without disgust; obliged to beg, and even encouraged to acts of dishonesty to satisfy the wants induced by the indolence of their parents – what can be expected, but that such children will ... become responsible to the laws for crimes?" (quoted in Houston 1972, 35) Prentice observes that "school promoters attacked the family as educationally inadequate" (1977, 61) and shows how the development of public education depended on the derogation of family education: "The public itself was a 'family' and the education of future citizens therefore required the parental interference of the state" (171; see also Prentice 1972). Moodie's emphasis on the failing of poor families to care for their children keeps her in touch with this theme in educational reform.

35 Quoted in Houston 1972, 44; Prentice attributes the opposition of Ryerson and the Methodists to Strachan's scheme for an educational system run by the Church of England "in part to the belief ... that the church had retarded the progress of education in Upper Canada by its attempted monopoly" (1977, 60; see also 172). She describes the centrality of non-sectarian (but Protestant) Christianity in the development of public education (71–5, 128–9).

36 Quoted in Houston 1972, 45; Prentice's conclusion is that the school promoters, among whom Moodie must be numbered, had "an essentially inegalitarian view of society and an equally inegalitarian approach to schooling" (1977, 184). She shows how an ostensibly democratic system had built into it from the start hierarchies of gender, class, and race (108–13, 138–44, 162–4). One of the contradictions school promoters attempted to deal with was that between their belief that education could improve the lives of workers and restore harmony between the classes,

and their commitment to a class society (96, 106–7): "Class conflict and 'arbitrary' ... class distinctions were to be eliminated, but not the classes themselves" (123). She discusses "how education was often virtually equated with restraint" (33), how it was "intended to produce discipline in its lower class graduates," and how one of the goals was to develop "the practical habits and values that were held to be necessary to all working men in an urban, industrial economy" (131; see also Palmer 1983, 56–7; Westfall 1989, 6–7).

37 Intro to *MH*, 287–8; when dealing in *Roughing It* with the period when she had to work the farm with Jenny, Moodie makes a similar statement: "You must become poor yourself before you can fully appreciate the good qualities of the poor – before you can sympathise with them, and fully recognize them as your brethren in the flesh" (423). She is tapping into what Hammerton calls "familiar sermons stressing the 'dignity of labour'" (1979, 34).

38 *LC*, 13; emigrant manuals commonly recommend the colony especially to the poor and working class (Howison 1821, 238; Cattermole 1831, 99; Dunlop 1832, 69–70; Strickland 1853, 1.134–6). Russell has a chapter critically examining "The Popular Image of Upper Canada: 'The Poor Man's Country'" (1981; see especially 373–83), and social historians have questioned whether Canada lived up to this image (see Fingard 1974, 266).

39 *LC*, 36. She later describes Canada as "exempt from pauperism" (86); the same assertion appears in *Roughing It*: "To the benevolent philanthropist, whose heart has bled over the misery and pauperism of the lower classes in Great Britain, the almost entire absence of mendicity from Canada would be highly gratifying" (205; see also "Trifles," 187). Moodie's brother and sister were also pleased at the apparent lack of poverty (Traill 1836, 47; Strickland 1853, 1.120). According to David Gagan, "most authors agreed that what really distinguished rural society in Upper Canada was not the absence of a class structure, but rather the absence of a wholly impoverished class of rural agriculturalists or artisans" (1975, 315). Russell provides further evidence for the "conviction ... that there was no poverty in Upper Canada" (1981, 431).

40 Moodie's assumption of pioneering or service as fit work for working-class immigrants underlies her books on Canada. On one occasion she distinguishes the proper roles for the various classes in developing the transportation network: "The many plank-roads and railways in the course of construction in the province, while they afford high and remunerative wages to the working classes, will amply repay the speculator who embarks a portion of his means in purchasing shares in them" (*LC*, 10).

41 Moodie quotes the Toronto reviewer in letters 50 and 51. The pertinent passages on servants are in *RI*, 40, 197–201, and *FL*, 67–9 (see also "Trifles," 190–2).

42 Strickland 1853, 1.137; on trouble with servants, see Need 1838, 17; Traill 1855, 5–6; Langton, ed. 1950, 71–2, 104–5. "The evidence from English gentlewomen's letters and journals," writes Marjorie Cohen, indicates "that the turnover rate for servants was high in Canada, and the likelihood of keeping one for a long period remote" (1988, 86). According to R.G. Moyles and Doug Owram, "the scarcity of domestic servants" became "a cliché" (1988, 218).

43 On the developments of labour relations outlined in this paragraph and in the section in general, see Fingard 1974; Langdon 1973; Palmer 1983, 10–12, 60–2; Russell 1981, 32–59.

44 *FL* 31, 177–8; a conversation in "Trifles" also associates Mrs Grundy with the society Rachel M— is leaving (180–1), and in her 1871 introduction to *Roughing It* "the Mrs. Grundys of society" are left in "the mother country" (*RI*, 531; see also Magrath 1833, 67). Given the clash between their economic status and their own social pretensions, the Stricklands would have suffered acutely from Grundyism before they emigrated.

45 Strickland 1853, 1.xi–xii; he repeats this assertion twice more (1.81, 1.140). Education enhanced "one's social status, being a necessary component of gentility" (Russell 1981, 255; see also 255–64). Prentice discusses the linkage of education and respectability in this period (1977, 67–9) and concludes that "respectable religion, education and status all went together" (75). Thompson discusses Traill's "meritocracy based on education and manners" (1991, 44). None the less, money came first: it could buy education, but education could not replace it.

46 The opposition between formulated theology and individual experience is close to Westfall's opposition between a rational Anglican religion of order and an emotional Methodist religion of experience (1989, 19–49). While Moodie's social orientation may have swung back towards the former during her life in the colony, she did not regain the religious certainty it offered, as her spiritualism in the 1850s testifies.

47 *LC*, 331, 332, 81; both these passages were first published in the *Victoria Magazine*. The first was part of the "Editor's Table" (240) and became two pages of the conclusion of *Life in the Clearings*. The second was part of an otherwise favourable review (71); Moodie's criticism of the author for republicanism becomes her own defence against the same charge.

48 Letter 116; for other protestations that *Roughing It* is a true story that has been distorted, see letters 78, 105, 109, 112.

CHAPTER SEVEN

1 The critical approach outlined in this paragraph takes one of its cues from Macherey's program of bringing "out a *difference* within the work by demonstrating that it is *other than it is*" (1966, 17). *Roughing It* readily reveals what Macherey believes of every literary work: it is characterized by a "*diversity of the letter* – the text is saying several things at once" (22).

2 PHEC, ser. I, Correspondence, no. 59a. *Ten Years in South Africa* was passed between Colburn and Smith, Elder before Bentley accepted it in 1834, although in "Trifles" M— has placed his South African book with Bentley by the spring of 1832 (179).

3 J.W.D. Moodie's letter to Bentley in 1834 is quoted by Peterman (1983, 82); Bentley's response is quoted by Ballstadt (1988, xxvii). By the late 1830s Moodie was more concerned about *Ten Years in South Africa* than about any new colonial narrative. De Rottenburg thought he should have got four hundred pounds for it, and Agnes Strickland advised him to have someone in London pressure Bentley for payment (PHEC, ser. I, Correspondence, nos. 65, 80). Moodie had material ready for inclusion in *Roughing It*, and after his death Susanna found "a large portion of a work on Canada" that he had written before the rebellion (letter 105).

4 J.W.D. Moodie's chapters are "The Village Hotel," "The Land-Jobber," "The 'Ould Dhragoon,'" and "Canadian Sketches." His poems are "To the Woods! – To the Woods!" (215), "Stanzas" ("Where is religion found?" 229–30), the thirty-one-line poem opening "The Land-Jobber" (231–2), "Oh, Let Me Sleep!" (257), the thirty-one-line poem opening "The 'Ould Dhragoon'" (342–3) and the thirty-six-line poem closing it (349–50), "Oh, the Days When I Was Young!" (385–7), "The Bears of Canada" (406), "A Song of Praise to the Creator" (437–8), "The Magic Spell" (477), and "God Save the Queen" (522–4). To reap the benefits accruing to them from his involvement, Mrs Moodie notes at the end of her introduction that she has been assisted by her "husband, J.W. Dunbar Moodie, author of 'Ten Years in South Africa'" (15). Strickland's "Description of a Whirlwind" (*RI* 433–5) first appeared in the *Victoria Magazine*, signed PIONEER (100–2) and later became part of *Twenty-Seven Years in Canada West* (1853, 1.241–6). All the surviving correspondence with Bentley about *Roughing It* was written by Mrs Moodie.

5 *RI*, 219; at both the beginning and the end of his linking chapters J.W.D. Moodie explains that he has provided details necessary to making their "situation" intelligible (219, 255).

6 Peterman 1983, 83; Heather Murray finds the "ever-hopeful spirit and entrepreneurial zeal" of J.W.D. Moodie's chapters "dissonant with Moodie's own chapters" (1990, 94).

7 See Parker 1979, 145–6, 156 n 8, for details of the prior publication of Mrs
   Moodie's portions of *Roughing It*. The passage on dandelion coffee (*RI*,
   353–6) had also appeared in the *Victoria Magazine* (22). Fothergill had
   published J.W.D. Moodie's "The Bears of Canada" and "Oh, Let Me
   Sleep" in the *Palladium* in 1838 (PHEC, ser. 1, Correspondence, no. 60)
   and may have published other poems by him. "The 'Ould Dhragoon'"
   was in the *Literary Garland* (ns 2 [1844]: 360–2), as were his poems
   "Stanzas" (as "Religion"; 2 [1839–40]: 164), "A Song of Praise to the
   Creator" (ns 2 [1844]: 548), and "The Magic Spell" (ns 5 [1847]: 39). "To
   the Woods!" and "Oh, the Days When I Was Young!" had been in the
   Victoria Magazine (117, 145–6). "Canadian Sketches" may expand on an
   1836 essay.
8 The first phrase is Ballstadt's (1988, xxvi–xxvii), the second Peterman's
   (1983, 84). These critical texts contain the only treatment of revisions
   made to the sketches for *Roughing It*.
9 *The List of the Publications of Richard Bentley and Son 1829–1898* contains
   entries on the first three issues of the first edition of *Roughing It* and the
   second edition of 1857. The first issue is represented most fully. Towards
   the end of the entry the following description is given: "The First Edition
   consisted of 2,250 copies. A New Edition, with additional matter, was
   issued November 29, 1852. Cheaper Editions appeared July, 1854 ... and
   1857 ... the latter with slight modifications" (folio 616). The entry on the
   second issue carries a note only: "*November* 29, 21s. A NEW EDITION
   WITH SOME ADDITIONAL MATTER. For particulars see the FIRST
   EDITION, published January 28, 1852" (folio 650). The entry on the third
   issue again refers to "the First Edition" and also ahead to "A Popular
   Edition," that of 1857 (folio 751). The entry on the 1857 edition, a wholly
   new printing, once more describes the book in full (folio 846).
10 The *OED* lists several meanings for the gerund "roughing" current in the
   first half of the nineteenth century. Besides "the fact of undergoing
   hardships, or living under hard conditions," it could also mean the
   "operation of preparing roughly or treating in a preliminary manner."
   Thackeray activates both senses when he writes that a bankrupt in *Vanity
   Fair* may have to "go and dig in Canada, or rough it in a cottage in the
   country" (1848, 194).
11 The Centre for Editing Early Canadian Texts has weeded out errors
   attributable to the printing process but includes the chapter "Jeanie
   Burns," which Moodie at one time wanted in *Roughing It*. The theory of
   textual bibliography that the Centre endorses rests on the concepts of
   authorial autonomy and intention. Jerome McGann has worked out an
   alternative to these principles that stresses authorial collaboration and
   shared intentions. For a fuller discussion of McGann's theories as they
   apply to *Roughing It*, see Thurston 1987, 198. Since the text is being

viewed as a collaboration between its authors and its editors, the first full version they produced will be the one analysed. This is the second issue of the 1852 edition (without "Jeanie Burns"), the copy-text for the 1989 NCL edition. For the in-press revisions, corrections and additions to the copy-text, see CEECT 637–48.

12 This description is derived from Bakhtin's analysis of one of the roots of the novel as "multi-styled and hetero-voiced ... mixing high and low, serious and comic ... prosaic and poetic speech, living dialects and jargons ... Alongside the representing word there appears the *represented* word" (1963, 108). Susan Johnston emphasizes Moodie's representation of "alien sociolects," especially "sociolects of landscape appreciation" (1992, 29).

13 *RI*, 489. That Strickland saw his book not only as a promotion of the colony but a refutation of his sister's book is clear in his preface, the last paragraph of which echoes and alludes to her last paragraph: "If the facts and suggestions contained in the following pages should prove useful and beneficial to the emigrant, by smoothing his rough path to comfort and independence, my object will be attained, and my first literary effort will not have been made in vain" (1853, 1.xix).

14 Letter 44. Bakhtin characterizes poetry as based on "the idea of a unitary and singular language and a unitary, monologically sealed-off utterance." He opposes the poet to the prose writer, who "welcomes the heteroglossia and language diversity of the literary and extraliterary language into his own work." While "poetic forms reflect lengthier social processes ... requiring centuries to unfold," prose forms "register[] with extreme subtlety the tiniest shifts and oscillations of the social atmosphere" (1934–35, 296, 298, 300). These distinctions are useful in understanding Moodie's different talents for prose and verse.

15 Mary Louise Pratt's comments on the development of travel writing, once it became "a profitable business," help to explain the production of *Roughing It*: "travel-writers and their publishers relied more and more on professional writers and editors to ensure a competitive product, often transforming manuscripts completely, usually in the direction of the novel" (1992, 88).

16 Jameson writes "that the normal form of the dialogical is essentially an *antagonistic* one" and that "class discourse ... is essentially *dialogical* in its structure" (1981, 84).

17 Pratt stresses the importance of "arrival scenes" as "a convention of almost every variety of travel writing"; they "serve as particularly potent sites for framing relations of contact and setting the terms of representation" (1992, 78, 80).

18 Moodie's first questions arise from her confusion (99). She progresses to personal queries (101). She has learned the effectiveness of being blunt,

bringing Betty to the point with questions that are in effect challenges: "Oh, you want to borrow some?"; "Well, Mrs. Fye, what do you want *to-day*?" (100, 102). The analysis of these scenes of dialogue applies one of Bakhtin's insights: "In dialogue the destruction of the opponent also destroys that very dialogic sphere where the word lives ... This sphere is very fragile and easily destroyed (the slightest violence is sufficient, references to authority, and so forth)" (1970–71, 150).

19 *RI*, 215. She next writes: "Alas, for our fallen nature! Which is more subversive of peace and Christian fellowship – ignorance of our own characters, or of the characters of other?" Upon these words Johnston speculates that "the Moodie character is able to respond to Mrs. D. as a subject whose language can penetrate her own" (1990, 40). The whole scene has led up to Moodie's irony about Mrs Dean's lecture on pride, however, and has been structured in the same way and with the same conclusions as the scenes with Mrs Fye and Mrs Harris. Johnston credits Moodie with a self-reflexive irony inconsistent with the rest of her writing. "The Moodie character" was first used by Moss (1974) to absolve Moodie of responsibility for now-distasteful social attitudes.

20 Moodie's prolonged animosity towards Joe Harris would be further explained if he was the same Joseph Harris who in early 1846 became minister of the Belleville Congregationalist church that had expelled the Moodies in April 1845. The evidence for this possibility is in the minutes for 3 June 1846; Smith 1846, 281; "Uncle Joe and His Family" (1847), 429 (see also *RI*, 170); Traill 1852, 86n; Martin, McGillis, and Milne 1986, 44, 97, 234. This evidence is presented in detail in Thurston 1994.

21 "Trifles," 234; Moodie also represents the dialect of blacks in this text and in *Hugh Latimer* and "Richard Redpath."

22 *RI*, 197, 198. Bentley analyses Moodie's reaction to language in the colony in terms similar to those developed here: "The very speech of the men whom Moodie describes on arrival in Canada thus reflects her fearful sense of a social and personal disintegration ... during the transition from the hierarchical civilization that she cherishes to the independent or republican culture that she knows to exist in North America" (1990, 116–17). Howison reports that when lower-class immigrants "hear themselves addressed by the titles, *sir, master,* or *gentleman,* a variety of new ideas begin to illuminate their minds" (1821, 174). Moodie tells how her "bare-legged, ragged Irish servants were always spoken to, as 'sir' or '*mem*'" (197–8). There are also similarities in their analyses of natives (Howison, 148, 149; *RI*, 287, 295). These parallels and others suggest the influence of Howison on Moodie.

23 Althusser's theory of ideology underlies these statements about the relationship of Moodie and Tom, Brian and Malcolm. Gubar and Gilbert write of "the extent to which a female artist ... is keenly aware that she

must inevitably project herself into a number of uncongenial characters and situations" and of "the degree of anxiety a literary woman may feel about such a splitting or distribution of her identity, as well as the self-dislike she may experience in feeling that she is 'really closest to' those characters she 'appears to detest'" (1979, 69).

24 These remarks are informed by Hayden White's discussion of wildness and civilization (1979, 151–2). White also distinguishes between wild men and barbarians (165–7) and connects notions of them with the difficulties the upper and middle classes were having with the concept of nobility and with the working class (192–3). Yankee levellers and British peasants can be reconnected with North American natives through Greenblatt's observation that the European "response to the savages ... strikingly resembles the response of the European elite to the unreformed carnivalesque customs of the lower orders" (1990, 67).

25 *RI*, 281, 282. "All mercantile business," writes Howison in 1821, "is carried on by means of barter; circulating medium being so scarce, that it cannot be obtained in exchange for almost any thing" (112). While Traill shares some of her sister's reservations, she sees "legimate reasons for borrowing, and all kindly, well-disposed neighbours will lend with hearty good-will" (1855, 25). The Yankee customs are, in Williams's terms, emergent, among those "new meanings and values, new practices, new relationships and kinds of relationships [that] are continually being created" (1977, 123). The native customs are residual, having "been effectively formed in the past" and "at some distance from the effective dominant culture" (122, 123). The offers the natives make to Moodie hint at a social system based on reciprocity and foreign to the European predilection for unequal exchange (see Hulme 1986, 147–48; Pratt 1992, 80–1, 84–5).

26 Bees, organized around activities like quilting, were still being held in parts of rural Ontario thirty-five years ago, although the practice seems to have since disappeared. Likewise, charivaris or shivarees, apparently restricted to rural districts, seem to be held with less and less frequency.

27 Moodie's unfamiliarity with charivaris is an index of her insulation from popular culture, since Palmer traces its roots to medieval Europe (1978, 9). "But despite its rather mundane purpose," he writes, "the charivari often posed acutely the problem of social order and disorder" (24). While early Upper Canadian charivaris had both "patrician" and "plebian" participation, by 1850 they were "exclusively an affair of the lower orders, ... associated with the barbarism and savagery of the masses" and "harshly condemned" (52). This "proletarianization" occurred unevenly: "where bourgeois consciousness matured earliest, the charivari was first attacked" (54). Palmer's description of it in Williams' terms helps to place Moodie's motives in criticizing the charivari as a custom of the working

class : "an autonomous culture reared its head, an implicit challenge to the hegemony of the bourgeoisie. Built on the residual, it could move towards an emergent purpose" (60). Elsewhere, Palmer describes the charivari as "a world turned upside down, a carnival atmosphere of disguise, producing the possibility of overthrowing the social relations of a paternalistic order" (1983, 44). For the charivari's carnivalesque features, see Bakhtin 1963, 122–3.

28 *RI*, 314, 321; Moodie lists the participants in their bee on 314–15, 338. Profanation, or "playing with the symbols of higher authority," is central to Bakhtin's category of carnival (1963, 125). In Moodie's description of their bee may be perceived "*the life of the carnival square*, free and unrestricted, full of ambivalent laughter, blasphemy, the profanation of everything sacred, full of debasing and obscenities, familiar contact with everyone and everything" (129–30). For approving accounts of what Traill calls "friendly meetings of neighbours," see Howison 1821, 253; Cattermole 1831, 87; Traill 1836, 102–3. Strickland, after a favourable report of a bee, concludes "the general practice is bad" (1853, 1.37; see Harris and Warkentin 1974, 127–8).

29 *RI* 28, 29; on Grosse Isle as carnival, see Kroetsch 1983.

30 The variant treatments of proper names occur as follows:
   Peterborough, usually spelled out, but P— 154, 399, 450, 461, 463 (also for Port Hope, 97)
   Cobourg 59, 61, 305; but — 76, 85, 89, 95, 97, 114; and C— 133, 157, 201, 208, 260, 380, 484 (twice), 485 (twice)
   Rice Lake 266; but — lake 176 (twice)
   Douro 215, 258, 260, 330, 456; but D— 79, 207, 450
   Dummer 318, 355, 407, 439ff; but D— 146, 155
   Mr Young 301, 315; but the Y—s 327 (twice), 330 (twice), 331, 333, 334 (twice), 387, 409
   Mr Wood and Mr W— 297
   Moodie, usually spelled out, but M— 80
   Mrs Moodie, usually spelled out, but Mrs M— 84, 213 (changed to Mrs Moodie in the NCL edition)
   Susanna 399; but S— 277, 468

31 Moodie mentions that "sixteen years have slowly passed away" since the first letters she received from England late in 1832 (122). After recalling the birth of her daughter on 9 June 1833, she writes that "sixteen years have passed away since" she heard anything of the Harris family (170). Referring to Cobourg in 1833, she writes that "seventeen years has made ... a great ... difference in the state of society" (201). To a poem likely written February 1834 she adds a note stating that "fifteen years have passed away since this little poem was written" (272n). To the description of land bought in late 1833, early 1834, she adds the note: "After a lapse

of fifteen years, we have been glad to sell these lots." Ballstadt dates sales of portions of this land to May 1848 and November 1849 (274n; CEECT, 579, note to 293). J.W.D. Moodie refers to "a residence of sixteen years in Canada" (218).

32 *RI*, 15, 507; J.W.D. Moodie is more cagey at the beginning of the "Canadian Sketches" when he refers to the previous text as containing "truthful pictures ... observed fifteen or twenty years ago" (518).

33 Those passages on homesickness that begin and end in the narrative past are at 121–2, 134, 163, and 337. The collapse of narrator and protagonist further discredits attempts to separate Moodie the writer from "the Moodie character."

34 Indeed, Moodie never seems to have lost her homesickness entirely. In 1869 she again refers to her "own heartsickness, to return and die upon my native soil" (letter 91). Nevertheless, two years later she writes in the introduction to the Canadian edition of *Roughing It* that she "cannot imagine any inducement ... which could induce me to leave the colony" (528).

35 *RI*, 258. When she writes that "it was much against [her] wish" that the Cobourg farm be sold, she may be suggesting that she already intuited that the bush was no place for gentlefolk. When she writes of her dislike of "emigrant roving and unsettled habits," she shows her awareness of the tendency of early nineteenth-century settlers to become nomadic, the adventurous or insolvent retreating from the advance of civilization to the frontier (Gagan 1975, 316–17; Harris and Warkentin 1974, 127).

36 Moodie first confesses to being "terribly afraid of cattle" when her request for help in milking is mocked by Mrs Harris. She perseveres and does the milking herself: "I had learned a useful lesson of independence, to which, in after-years I had often again to refer" (183). But on the next occasion she is confronted with the task she writes that she "never could overcome [her] fear of cattle." Malcolm mocks her at this point, and again she does the job (375). That Mrs Harris's words to her ("A farmer's wife, and afraid of cows!") and Malcolm's ("A farmer's wife, and afraid of a cow!") are the same is another indication of invented rather than remembered dialogue. The first time she experiences fear of the woods she writes that she "never could wholly shake [it] off," and she experiences the same fear later (276, 403–4).

37 "Trifles," 197, 198. In the expansion of this scene for *Flora Lyndsay* the presentiments of doom are more pointed: "If we may judge of the future by the present – it looks dark enough" (90).

38 Giltrow 1981, 134, 143, 132; other critics have made observations similar to Giltrow's. Hallvard Dahlie, for instance, sees transatlantic correspondence as the exiles' way of maintaining a "tangible link ... with their homeland" (1986, 13). "Traill throws into relief the gender-

dimensions of the long letter home to mother," writes Bentley, "a type of writing that affirms a female connectedness of the blood and heart across enormous geographical barriers" (1990, 104). For "pioneer women autobiographers," Helen Buss places writing among those activities "motivated and enlarged by ... the desire to remain connected" (1990, 129).

39 *RI*, 104; see also CEECT, 566, note to 97.8–9; Briggs 1959, 389. Samuel Strickland also quotes this line (1853, 1.113). Moodie makes literary or biblical allusions on the following pages: 21, 25, 32, 64, 76, 135, 196, 201, 213, 214, 276, 299, 385, 407, 422, 441, 453, 455, 462, 487.

40 For addresses to the reader, see 524 and 589; for rhetorical queries of the reader meant to highlight a colonial absurdity, see 108 and 170.

41 For changes to the title-page of the 1871 edition, see CEECT, 618. For the changes made for the 1871 edition, see CEECT, 657–68.

42 Moodie pragmatically unites writing and living. She compares writing to bread-baking (121) and milking (183). She compares contemplating a field of potatoes to contemplating a painting (353). Her fungus paintings are on a par with her writing as a means to supplement the family income (420).

CHAPTER EIGHT

1 This section is indebted for its orientation and some of its terms to Gilbert and Gubar 1979, 67–8, and Poovey 1984, 35–47. The expansion on the following statement by Gilbert and Gubar will be especially apparent: "a woman writer must examine, assimilate, and transcend the extreme images of 'angel' and 'monster' which male authors have generated for her" (17).

2 This section is indebted to Ballstadt (1981) and Ballstadt, Peterman, and Hopkins (1982–83; *Letters* 118–21). The treatment of Moodie's spiritualism here is very different from that produced in these places. Much of the following information comes from the "Spiritualist Album" in PHEC, ser. II, Manuscripts, box 5. For a more extensive treatment of this material, see Thurston 1994.

Bibliography

PUBLISHED WORKS

By Susanna Moodie

This list of Susanna Moodie's published works is provisional. It will be added to and corrected, but given its cautious policy regarding unconfirmed, anonymous, and pseudonymous titles, it will not likely need to be subtracted from. It records an impressive career, but Moodie probably published even more widely than this checklist shows.

Besides primary research, a number of sources have aided in the identification of Moodie's works. Mary Markham Brown's *Index to the Literary Garland* and Carl Ballstadt's "The Literary History of the Strickland Family" have been invaluable. Moodie herself provides a list of her publications (letter 78). The editorial apparatus to *Letters of a Lifetime* and to the CEECT edition of *Roughing It*, both representing the work of Carl Ballstadt, Elizabeth Hopkins, and Michael Peterman, have also been very useful.

The list is arranged chronologically, according to first appearance in whatever form. When appropriate, items are grouped under the title of the periodical. Titles first appearing in annuals are also grouped separately, for which the year prior to the date of the annual is given as year of publication. Items are entered under first known publication; subsequent publication will be indicated either with the title of the book or periodical or with abbreviations. Year(s) of publication will be given when appropriate. Poems that were published before *Enthusiasm* and included in it are listed under their first known appearance. Under *Enthusiasm* are listed the poems first published in it, many of which were subsequently reprinted. Verse items will be identified by a *v* following the entry.

1822

Spartacus; A Roman Story. London: Newman.

[1825–28]

Hugh Latimer; or, The School-Boys' Friendship. London: A.K. Newman and Dean and Munday.

The Little Prisoner; or Passion and Patience; with *Amendment; or Charles Grant and his Sister*. London: Dean and Munday.

The Little Quaker; or, The Triumph of Virtue. A Tale for the Instruction of Youth. London: Cole.

Profession and Principle; or, The Vicar's Tales. London: Dean and Munday.

Rowland Massingham; or, I Will Be My Own Master. London: Dean.

1825
La Belle Assemblée

"The Native Village." 3rd ser. 2: 109–12. *VM* 1848.

1827
La Belle Assemblée

"To Mary, Leaving England." 3rd ser. 5: 221. As "Song" ("When kindred hearts are parting ..."), *LG* 1847. *v.*

"The Witch of the East Cliff. Sketches from the Country. No. I." 3rd ser. 6: 15–19.

"Serenade Song" ("Lady awake! – it is the hour –"). 3rd ser. 6: 26. *v.*

"Song" ("Tell me where the God of love ..."). 3rd ser. 6: 27. *v.*

"Serenade Song" ("Oh lady! dost thou fear to fly ..."). 3rd ser. 6: 71. *v.*

"The Two Fishermen. Sketches from the Country. No. II." 3rd ser. 6: 109–14. *VM.*

"The Earthquake." 3rd ser. 6: 121. *EO, LG* 1841–42, *LC. v.*

"Stanzas" ("There is a pause in nature, ere the storm ..."). 3rd ser. 6: 121. As "The Pause," *EO, LG* 1841–42. *v.*

"The Dream." 3rd ser. 6: 165. *EO, LG* 1843. *v.*

"To —." 3rd ser. 6: 215. As "Sympathy," *LG* 1843. *v.*

"Song" ("Sleep ye in peace? – in danger's hour ..."). 3rd ser. 6: 215. *v.*

"Naomi. Sketches from the Country. No. III." 3rd ser. 6: 247–51.

"Lines Written in Sickness." 3rd ser. 6: 256. *v.*

"To A.L.H.–l." 3rd ser. 6: 256–7. *v.*

"Stanzas to a Young Friend." 3rd ser. 6: 257. *v.*

Annuals

"Stanzas on War." *Pledge of Friendship; A Christmas Present, and New Year's Gift* for 1828: 356–9. As "War," *EO, Palladium of British America.* 21 Feb. 1838. *v.*

1828
La Belle Assemblée

"Helena, of Saxe Altenburg." 3rd ser. 7: 9–12, 143–8, 254–7.
"Count Ravenstein." 3rd ser. 7: 22–4, 60–3.
"Winter." 3rd ser. 7: 27. *EO. v.*
"The Dead Man's Grave. Sketches from the Country. No. IV." 3rd ser. 7: 51–5. *Family Herald* (Montreal), 25 Jan. 1860.
"On the Ruins of Walberswick Church in Suffolk." 3rd ser. 7: 119. As "Lines Written Amidst the Ruins of a Church on the Coast of Suffolk," *EO, Star* (Cobourg), 19 Sept. 1832, *North American Quarterly Magazine* 1834, LG 1843. *v.*
"Nero: An Historical Sketch." 3rd ser. 7: 211. *Canadian, British American, and West Indian Magazine,* Mar. 1839, LG 1844. *v.*
"To the Son of a Bard (By a Lady who had been requested to answer for him at the Font)." 3rd ser. 7: 257. *v.*
"The Old Ash Tree." 3rd ser. 8: 23. *EO,* LG 1840–41, LG 1849. *v.*
"The Trial by Fire." 3rd ser. 8: 56–60, 106–9.
"A Dream." 3rd ser. 8: 69–70.
"Boat Song." 3rd ser. 8: 72. *v.*
"The Sleep of Death." 3rd ser. 8: 73. As "Stanzas" ("Oh! restless as the ceaseless troubled flow ..."), *La Belle Assemblée* 1830. *v.*
"Autumn." 3rd ser. 8: 119. *EO, Star* (Cobourg) 17 Oct. 1832, LG 1839–40, *Chronicle and Gazette* (Kingston) 10 Oct. 1840, *Bytown Gazette and Ottawa and Rideau Advertiser* 29 Oct. 1840, LG 1846. *v.*
"The Cistus." 3rd ser. 8: 164–5. *v.*
"The Pope's Promise." 3rd ser. 8: 245–50. *VM.*
"The Nameless Grave." 3rd ser. 8: 264. As "The Stoneless Grave," *Athenaeum* 3 Apr. 1830, *EO. v.*

Annuals

"There's Joy when the Rosy Morning." *Friendship's Offering: A Literary Album, and Christmas and New Year's Present* for 1829: 148–9. *EO. v.*
"The Rover's Farewell to His Mistress." *Forget Me Not: A Christmas and New Year's Present* for 1829: 369. *v.*

1829
La Belle Assemblée

"Old Hannah; or, The Charm. Sketches from the Country. No. V." 3rd ser. 9: 21–4.

"The Rover's Serenade." 3rd ser. 9: 32. *v.*

"The Maniac." 3rd ser. 9: 74. From "The Native Village," *La Belle Assemblée* 1825, LC. *v.*

"The Reaper's Song." 3rd ser. 9: 75. *EO. v.*

"The Harper's Song." 3rd ser. 9: 163. *v.*

"The Lover's Promise." 3rd ser. 9: 265. As "The Promise," *LG* 1843. *v.*

"Jane Redgrave: A Village Tale." 3rd ser. 10: 53–8, 107–13. *LG* 1848.

"Sylla at Orchomenus." 3rd ser. 10: 70. *LG* 1844. *v.*

"On Being Asked by T. C——, Esq. to Turn His Italian Sonnets Into English Verse." 3rd ser. 10: 119. *v.*

"The Song of the Hours." 3rd ser. 10: 165, 268–9. *EO. v.*

Annuals

Z. Z. "The Child's First Grief." *Friendship's Offering: A Literary Album, and Christmas and New Year's Present* for 1830: 217. *EO. v.*

Z. Z. "O Come to the Meadows." *Juvenile Keepsake* for 1830: 93. *EO, Star* (Cobourg), 23 Nov. 1832, included in "Rosamond Hartford," *LG* 1845. *v.*

Z. Z. "The Overthrow of Zebah and Zalmunna." *The Iris: A Literary and Religious Offering* for 1830: 153–7. *EO. v.*

"The Son of Arminius." *Ackermann's Juvenile Forget Me Not: A Christmas, New Year's, and Birth–Day Present* for 1830: 241–61. *VM*, as "The Song of Arminius," in *The Hyacanth: Or, Affection's Gift* for 1850.

Z. Z. "The Spirit of Spring." *The Amulet; or Christian and Literary Remembrancer* for 1830: 367. *The Spirit and Manners of the Age: A Christian and Literary Miscellany*, Dec. 1829, *EO, Chronicle and Gazette* (Kingston), 9 Dec. 1840, *LG* 1840–41, *VM, The Odd–Fellow's Offering* for 1852. *v.*

1830
La Belle Assemblée

"Adieu." 3rd ser. 11: 75. *v.*

"The Blind." 3rd ser. 11: 113–14. *v.*

"The Rain." 3rd ser. 11: 114. *v.*

Athenaeum

Z. Z. "Love and Ambition." 16 Jan.: 29. *Forget Me Not* for 1831. *v.*
Sophia Sandys. "Stanzas: Thou Wilt Think of Me Love." 23 Jan.: 42. *EO, LG*
    1848, *Mark Hurdlestone. v.*
Sophia Sandys. "To Water Lilies." 6 Mar.: 136. *EO. v.*
"The Besieged City." 22 May: 314. *LG* 1848. *v.*
"Francis I. In Captivity." 17 July: 442. As "Francis the First in Captivity," *LG*
    1841–42. *v.*
"God Preserve the King!" 4 Sept.: 555–6. *v.*
"An Appeal to the Free!" 20 Nov.: 728. *EO, LG* 1850. *v.*
Review of "*The Romance of History – France*. By Leitch Ritchie. 3 vols." 11 Dec.:
    769–71.

Lady's Magazine, or Mirror of the Belles Lettres

"The Captive Squirrel's Petition." Improved ser. 2: 238–40. *Ackermann's Juvenile
    Forget Me Not* for 1831. *v.*
"Hymn of the Convalescent." Improved ser. 2: 295–6. *EO, LG* 1846, *LG* 1850.
    v.

Annuals

"Awake." *The Juvenile Forget Me Not: A Christmas and New Year's Gift, or Birthday
    Present* for 1831: 104. *v.*
"The Captive." *Friendship's Offering: A Literary Album, and Christmas and New
    Year's Present* for 1831: 184–6. *VM. v.*
"The Deluge." *The Iris: A Literary and Religious Offering* for 1831: 170–4. *EO. v.*
"Winter Calling up His Legions." *The Forget Me Not: A Christmas, New Year's,
    and Birth-day Present* for 1831: 321–4. *EO. v.*
"The Wood Lane." *The Juvenile Forget Me Not: A Christmas and New Year's Gift,
    or Birthday Present* for 1831: 145–6. *LG* 1843, *Family Herald* (Montreal), 21
    Mar. 1860. *v.*

1831
Athenaeum

Review of "*An Only Son; a Narrative*. By the Author of 'My Early Days.'" 1
    Jan.: 7–8.
Review of "*Beauties of the Mind, a Poetical Sketch; with Lays, Historical and
    Romantic*. By Charles Swain." 22 Jan.: 57–8.
"Random Thoughts." ("When is youth's gay heart the lightest?"). 15 Oct.:
    664. *LG* 1842, *LC. v.*

Star (Cobourg)

"The Vision of Dry Bones." 20 Sept. *EO. v.*
"Morning Hymn." 4 Oct. *EO. v.*
"Elijah in the Wilderness." 18 Oct. *v.*

Lady's Magazine, or Mirror of the Belles Lettres

"England's Glory: A Loyal Song." Improved ser. 3: [1]. *v.*
"The Royal Election: A Historical Sketch from Polish History." Improved ser.
    3: 62–6. *LG* 1840–41.
"Song." ("'I'll never love!' young Cora cries"). Improved ser. 3: 71. *v.*
"The Spirit of Motion." Improved ser. 3: 80. *EO. v.*
"Sunlight." Improved ser. 3: 120. Extract from "Enthusiasm," *EO. v.*
"The Forest Rill." Improved ser. 3: 191–2. *EO, LG* 1840–41. *v.*
"Home." Improved ser. 4: 26–7. *Canadian, British American, and West Indian Magazine* 1839. *v.*
"Britannia's Wreath." Improved ser. 4: 90. *v.*

Annuals

"Black Jenny: A Tale Founded on Facts." *Marshall's Christmas Box, a Juvenile Annual* for 1832: 3–22. As title story in a collection of stories by various authors, *The Little Black Pony and Other Stories* (Philadelphia: Collins 1850).
"The Boudoir." *Ackermann's Juvenile Forget Me Not: A Christmas, New Year's, and Birth-Day Present* for 1832: 31. *v.*
"The Disappointed Politician." *The Gem, a Literary Annual* for 1832: 34–48.
"My Aunt Dorothy's Legacy." *Comic Offering; or Ladies' Melange of Literary Mirth* for 1832: 118–28. As "Tom Singleton; or, How My Aunt Dorothy Left Her Money," *Family Herald* (Montreal), 28 Dec. 1859.
"The Picture Lost at Sea." *Marshall's Christmas Box, a Juvenile Annual* for 1832: 152–68. As "The Picture," *The Violet: A Christmas and New Year's Gift* for 1842.
"The Release of the Caged Lark." *Marshall's Christmas Box, a Juvenile Annual* for 1832: 91–3. *The Violet: A Christmas and New Year's Gift* for 1842. *v.*
"The Vanquished Lion." *Ackermann's Juvenile Forget Me Not: A Christmas, New Year's, and Birth-Day Present* for 1832: 97–115.

Enthusiasm; and Other Poems. London: Smith, Elder.

"Enthusiasm." *v.*
"Fame." *v.*
"The Avenger of Blood." *Palladium of British America*, 11 Apr. 1838. *v.*
"Paraphrase, (Psalm XLIV)." *v.*
"Paraphrase, (Isaiah XL)." *LG* 1843. *v.*

"The Destruction of Babylon." *LG* 1841–42. *v.*

"To the Memory of Mrs. Ewing." *v.*

"To the Memory of R. R. Jun." *v.*

"Uncertainty." *Star* (Cobourg), 31 Oct. 1832. *v.*

"The Warning." *v.*

"Lines on a New-Born Infant." *v.*

"The Christian Mother's Lament." As "The Mother's Lament," *Maple Leaf* 1852, *LC. v.*

"The Lament of the Disappointed." *LG* 1839–40. *v.*

"Youth and Age." *Star* (Cobourg), 19 Dec. 1832. *v.*

"Mary Hume." *LG* 1843, *Bytown Gazette and Ottawa and Rideau Advertiser*, 19 Jan. 1844. *v.*

"Lines Written During a Gale of Wind." *v.*

"Fancy and the Poet." *LG* 1839–40. *v.*

"Night's Phantasies." *v.*

"The Luminous Bow." *v.*

"The Sugar Bird." *LG* 1841–42. *v.*

"The Ruin." *LG* 1843. *v.*

"Love." *LG* 1848. *v.*

"Evening Hymn." *v.*

1832

"London: A National Song." *Fraser's Town and Country* (Feb.–Mar.): 154. *LG* 1838–39, as "For London. A National Song," *LC. v.*

Lady's Magazine, or Mirror of the Belles Lettres

"The Brigand's Song." Improved ser. 5: 187–8. *v.*

"On the Fall of Warsaw." Improved ser. 5: 245–6, *LG* 1840–41, *Bytown Gazette and Ottawa and Rideau Advertiser*, 11 Feb. 1841. *v.*

1833
Albion (New York)

"The Sleigh-Bells. A Canadian Song." 2 Mar.: 72. *Correspondent and Advocate* (Toronto), 16 Mar. 1833, *Star* (Cobourg), 20 Mar. 1833, *Canadian Magazine* 1833, *The Patriot* (Toronto), 12 Apr. 1833, *Friendship's Offering* for 1834, *Bytown Gazette and Ottawa and Rideau Advertiser*, 12 Jan. 1837, *RI*, *The Remember Me: A Token of Love* for 1853. *v.*

"Song. The Strains We Hear in Foreign Lands." 2 Mar.: 72. As "Song," *Star* (Cobourg), 20 Mar. 1833, "Music's Memories," *Lady's Magazine and Museum* 1834, "The Strains We Hear," *LG* 1844, *RI. v.*

"There's Rest." 25 May: 161. *Kingston Spectator*, 24 July 1834, *Lady's Magazine and Museum* 1834, *North American Quarterly Magazine* 1834, RI. *v.*

"The Mountain Air." 15 June. LG 1843, RI. *v.*

Canadian Literary Magazine

"The Convict's Wife: – A Sketch." 1: 44. LG 1840–41, RI. *v.*

"Achbor: An Oriental Tale." 1: 45–9. *North American Quarterly Magazine* 1834, VM.

"Oh Can You Leave Your Native Land. A Canadian Song." 1: 56. *North American Quarterly Magazine* 1834, included in "Trifles from the Burthen of a Life," RI, *Selections from Canadian Poets. v.*

"I Loved You Long and Tenderly. A Song." 1: 82. Included in *Geoffrey Moncton*. *v.*

Lady's Magazine and Museum

"What is Death?" Improved ser. and enlarged 2: 76. LC. *v.*

"The Miser." Improved ser. and enlarged 2: 247–57. Expanded to become "The Miser and His Son," LC 1842.

1834

"The Canadian Herd-Boy." *Albion* (New York), 28 June. *Ladies' Musical Library*, Aug. 1843, *Chronicle and Gazette* (Kingston), 16 Sept. 1843, LG 1847, *Bentley's Miscellany* 1852, LC, *Selections from Canadian Poets. v.*

"The Canadian Woodsman." *Kingston Spectator*, 10 July: 1. *Montreal Herald for the Country*, 14 July 1834, *Chronicle and Gazette* (Kingston), 19 July 1834, *Montreal Herald for the Country*, 18 Sept. 1834, as "The Backwoodsman," LG 1841–42, *Bytown Gazette and Ottawa and Rideau Advertiser*, 9 Feb. 1843, *Brockville Recorder*, 19 Mar. 1846, *St. Catharines Journal*, 7 May 1846, RI. *v.*

1835
Albion (New York)

"Human Changes." 17 Jan. *v.*

"My Native Land." 24 Jan. Included in "The Fugitive," LG 1838–39, LC. *v.*

North American Quarterly Magazine

"Arminius." 5: 403–6. LG 1844. *v.*

"Lines: On a Bunch of Withered Flowers." 6: 22. *v.*

"A Scene in Harvest." 6: 108–10. *v.*

"The Poet." 6: 262. *LC. v.*
"Solitary Thoughts." 6: 283. *v.*

1836

"The Doctor Distressed. A Sketch from Life." *Lady's Magazine and Museum* improved ser. and enlarged 9: 241–3. As Chapter II, "The Worst Fool is an Old Fool," in "Rosamond Hartford," *LG* 1845, under original title in *Flowers of Loveliness* for 1852.

North American Quarterly Magazine

"A Funeral Hymn." 7: 187. *v.*
"Oh! Canada, Thy Gloomy Woods!" 8: 198. *RI. v.*
"Home Thoughts of an Emigrant." 8: 366. *LG* 1841–42, as "The Lament of a Canadian Emigrant," *RI. v.*
"The Bride of Every Day." 8: 366. *LG* 1839–40. *v.*

1837

"Canadians Will You Join the Band. A Loyal Song." *Palladium of British America, and Upper Canadian Mercantile Advertiser* (Toronto), 20 Dec.: 4. *Transcript* (Montreal), 28 Dec. 1837, *Chronicle and Gazette* (Kingston), 3 Jan. 1838, *St. Catharines Journal*, 11 Jan. 1838, as "An Address to the Freemen of Canada," *RI. v.*

Lady's Magazine and Museum

"The Emigrant's Bride. A Canadian Song." Improved ser. and enlarged 10: 53–4. As "The Waves That Girt My Native Isle," *LG* 1840, under original title, *RI. v.*
"The Lover's Dream." Improved ser. and enlarged 10: 79. As "Once in the Prime of Rosy Youth," *LG* 1844. *v.*

1838

"On Reading the Proclamation Delivered by William Lyon Mackenzie, on Navy Island." *Palladium of British America, and Upper Canadian Mercantile Advertiser* (Toronto), 17 Jan. *v.*
"The Wind That Sweeps Our Native Sea." *Novascotian* (Halifax), 5 July. *v.*
"There is Not a Spot in This Wide Peopled Earth." *Chronicle and Gazette* (Kingston), 24 Oct.: 1. *St. Catharines Journal*, 13 Dec. 1838, as "The Land of Our Birth," *LC. v.*

Transcript (Montreal)

"The Banner of England." 1 Feb. *LG* 1840–41, *LC. v.*
"The Burning of the Caroline." 11 Oct. *LG* 1840–41, *RI. v.*

1839

"The Waters." *Bytown Gazette and Ottawa and Rideau Advertiser*, 11 Sept.: 1. *LG* 1839–40, as "A Canadian Song," *RI. v.*

Literary Garland

"The Otonabee." 1: 275. *RI. v.*
"The Oath of the Canadian Volunteers – A Loyal Song for Canada." 1: 281. *Transcript* (Montreal), 11 June 1839, *Bytown Gazette and Ottawa and Rideau Advertiser*, 26 June 1839, *RI. v.*
"The Royal Quixote." 1: 321–30, 351–63.
"The Gold Medal." 1: 385–8.
"The Disappointed Lover." 1: 480. *v.*
"The Fugitive." 1: 566–70.
"A Song." ("Sinks the broad sun o'er the wide heaving ocean ..."). 1: 577. *v.*

1840
Literary Garland

"Geoffrey Moncton." 2: 3–12, 75–82, 125-32, 165–72, 193–203, 256–67, 327–30, 352–60, 385–400. Published in book-form as *Geoffrey Moncton; or, The Faithless Guardian* (New York: De Witt and Davenport 1855), *The Moncktons* (London: Bentley 1856).
"On a Wreath of Wild Flowers." 2: 164. *Bytown Gazette and Ottawa and Rideau Advertiser*, 12 Mar. 1840. *v.*
"Rise, Mary! Meet Me on the Shore." 2: 164. As "The Emigrant's Farewell," *RI. v.*
"The Reproof." 2: 204. *v.*
"The Faithful Heart that Loves Thee Still." 2: 307. *RI. v.*

1841
Literary Garland

"The First Debt. A Tale of Every Day." 3: 217–24, 241–9, 289–301, 355–64, 399-408, 433–45, 481–97, 529–50.
"A May-Day Carol." *v.*

"Welcome, Welcome, Little Bark." 3: 522–3. *v.*
"To Violets." 3: 562. *v.*
"The Wish." 3: 562. *v.*
"The Sailor's Return: Reminiscences of our Parish." 4: 13–18.

1842
Literary Garland

"The Apostate." 4: 55–7, 113–16, 157–60, 210–14. *v.*
"The Miser and His Son." 4: 319–27, 348–56, 389–403, 447–66, 485–505, 533–59. Published in book-form as *Mark Hurdlestone, The Gold Worshipper* (London: Bentley 1853).

1843
Literary Garland

"The Garland." ns 1: 15. *v.*
"Ernest von Weber." ns 1: 23–35.
"The Fisherman's Light." ns 1: 63. *Selections from Canadian Poets*, as "The Indian Fisherman's Light," *RI. v.*
"The Canadian Hunter's Song." ns 1: 63. *RI. v.*
"The Broken Mirror. A True Tale." ns 1: 145–54.
"A Song." ("'Twas night – and not a single gleam ..."). ns 1: 327. *v.*
"To Adelaide." ns 1: 357. *LC. v.*
"Richard Redpath." ns 1: 413–18, 441–9. 481–90, 549–64. *Star* (Toronto), 1843, included in *Matrimonial Speculations* (London: Bentley 1854).
"The Dying Hunter to His Dog." ns 1: 548. *RI. v.*

1844
Literary Garland

"The Miner. A Tale." ns 2: 28–32.
"Random Thoughts." ("The soul has a language the lips cannot learn ..."). ns 2: 45. *v.*
"Mildred Rosier. A Tale of the Ruined City." ns 2: 63–8, 111–19, 155–63, 215–23, 241–6, 299–305, 401–5, 433–45, 481–90, 529–48.
"Sympathy." ns 2: 452. *v.*

1845
Literary Garland

"The Messenger of Death." ns 3: 65–6. *v.*
"The Wind." ns 3: 137. As "To the Wind," *LC. v.*

"Rosamond Hartford, or Waiting for Dead Men's Shoes. Matrimonial Speculations. No. I." ns 3: 289–96, 357–64, 396–404. Included, as "Waiting for Dead Men's Shoes," in *Matrimonial Speculations* (London: Bentley 1854).
"May Morning Song." ns 3: 335. As "Morning Song," *LC. v.*
"A Song of Disappointment." ns 3: 350. Included in "Chess. From the Persian," *VM. v.*

1846
Literary Garland

"Monica; or Witchcraft." ns 4: 1–12, 59–69, 97–106, 145–52, 206–11, 241–7.
"Sonnet. To the Memory of Dr. James Haskins." ns 4: 76. *LC. v.*
"Lines Written Upon the Prospect of War with the American States." ns 4: 297. *v.*
"The Miss Greens. Matrimonial Speculations. No. II." ns 4: 298–307, 337–42. Included in *Matrimonial Speculations* (London: Bentley 1854).

1847
Literary Garland

"Old Woodruff and His Three Wives. A Canadian Sketch." ns 5: 13–18. As, in part, "Adieu to the Woods," *RI.*
"To the Early Lost." ns 5: 76. As "The Early Lost," *LC.*
"The Drunkard's Return – A Tale for Teetotallers." ns 5: 87–8. *LC. v.*
"The Walk to Dummer. Canadian Sketches. No. II." ns 5: 101–9. *RI.*
"Our Borrowing. Canadian Sketches. No. III." ns 5: 197–205. As part of "Our First Settlement, and the Borrowing System," *RI.*
"Song. Imitation of the Moorish." ns 5: 262. *v.*
"Tom Wilson's Emigration. Canadian Sketches. No. IV." ns 5: 283–6, 293–303. Divided between "Tom Wilson's Emigration" and "Old Satan and Tom Wilson's Nose," *RI.*
"Uncle Joe and His Family. Canadian Sketches. No. V." ns 5: 363–8, 423–9. *RI.*
"Brian, the Still Hunter. Canadian Sketches. No. VI." ns 5: 460–6. *RI.*

Victoria Magazine

"Canada." 1: 3. *Metropolitan Magazine* 1848, *RI. v.*
"Wolsey Bridge." 1: 12–13.
"Scenes in Canada. A Visit to Grosse Isle." 1: 14–17. *RI.*
"A Tale for Teetotallers." 1: 20.
"Editors' Table. The Dandelion and the Uses to Which it is Applied." 1: 22. *RI.*
"The Well in the Wilderness; A Tale of the Prairie. – Founded Upon Facts." 1: 54–8. *The Odd-Fellow's Offering* for 1852, *Bentley's Miscellany* 1853.

"Scenes in Canada. No. II. First Impressions. Quebec." 1: 65–8. *RI.*
"The Nautical Philosophers. A Sketch from Life." 1: 88–9. *v.*
"Education the True Wealth of the World." 1: 89–92. As "Free Schools – Thoughts on Education," *LC.*
"A Close Cut." 1: 93.
"A Detected Cheat." 1: 93.

1848

"Jane Redgrave – A Village Story." *Literary Garland* ns 6: 1–10, 49–58, 97–103, 145–54, 210–21, 251–60, 309–20, 347–58, 395–404, 443–52, 491–500, 539–59.

Victoria Magazine

Item *re* hurricane in Douro, 19 August 1837. 1: 102–3. *RI.*
"The Coming Earthquake." 1: 112. *LG* 1848, as "The Earthquake," *LC. v.*
"Rachel Wilde, or, Trifles from the Burthen of a Life." 1: 113–15, 126–8, 156–9, 183–7, 212–14, 234–7, 250–2.
"Papers on Practical Jokes. No. I." 1: 139–41. As "Practical Jokes: Lambeth Church," *Bentley's Miscellany* 1853.
"Papers on Practical Jokes. No. II." 1: 151–4. As "Practical Jokes: Ben Backstay," *Bentley's Miscellany* 1853, "Practical Jokes," *The Odd-Fellow's Offering* for 1852.
"Papers on Practical Jokes. No. III." 1: 177–81. As "Practical Jokes: Wat Robinson," *Bentley's Miscellany* 1854.
"The Light of His Soul Has Departed." 1: 181. *v.*
"Chess. From the Persian." 1: 181–2. As "Chess," *Belford's Monthly Magazine* 1877.
"The Quiet Horse; A Domestic Sketch." 1: 265–8.

1849

"The Maple Tree. A Song for Canada." *Literary Garland* ns 7: 214. *RI. v.*

1850

"The Calling of Gideon." *Literary Garland* ns 8: 201–2. *v.*

1851
Literary Garland

"Michael Macbride." ns 9: 49–55. *LC.*
"Trifles from the Burthen of a Life." ns 9: 97–104, 170–7, 228–35, 258–62, 308–14. Expanded and published in book-form as *Flora Lindsay, or Passages in an Eventful*

Life (London: Bentley 1854).

"A Word for the Novel Writers." ns 9: 348–51. As part of "Toronto," LC.

"Noah Cotton: A Tale of Conscience." ns 9: 396–406, 444–9, 481–93, 529–36.
Included in *Flora Lyndsay*.

"Wearing Mourning for the Dead." ns 9: 540–6. LC.

1852

"The Foundling of the Storm." *Maple Leaf* 1: 13–14. v.

"Jeanie Burns." *Bentley's Miscellany* 32: 143–52. *Graham's Magazine* 1852, *Home
Circle* 1853, LC.

Roughing It in the Bush; or, Life in Canada. London: Bentley.

1853

Life in the Clearings versus the Bush. London: Bentley.

1854

"Grace Marks." *Anglo-American Magazine* 5: 598–604. LC.

1860
Family Herald (Montreal)

"Our Lady's Well." 15 Feb.: 109–10.

"The Wraith." 22 Feb.: 117–18; 21 Mar.: 149–50.

1862

"To Elizabeth in Heaven." *Hastings Chronicle* (Belleville), 25 June: 1. v.

1863

"My Cousin Tom. A Sketch from Life." *British American Magazine* 1: 12–20.

1864
British American Magazine

"The Accuser and the Accused." 2: 285–96, 350–5. Published in book-form as
George Leitrim; or, The Mother's Test (Edinburgh: Hamilton 1875).

"Dorothy Chance." 2: 569–77. *Daily News* (Montreal), 18 May 1867, published
in book-form as *The World Before Them. A Novel* (London: Bentley 1867).

1865

"To Mrs. Murney on the Sudden Death of an Only and Beloved Son."
Intelligencer, (Belleville) 1 June: 1. *v.*

1871

"Washing the Black-a-Moor White." *Canadian Literary Magazine* 1: 163–5.

1872
Canadian Monthly and National Review

"The Orphan." 1: 527. *v.*
"Genius." 1: 353. *v.*

MANUSCRIPT SOURCES

Baldwin Papers, Robert Baldwin Room, Toronto Public Library.
Manuscript book of poems, dedicated to Agnes Dunbar FitzGibbon, 1866, Thomas
    Fisher Rare Book Library, University of Toronto.
Minute Book of the Congregationalist Church of Belleville, Hastings County
    Museum, Belleville, Ontario.
Patrick Hamilton Ewing Collection of Moodie-Strickland-Vickers-Ewing
    Family Papers, Rare Book Room, National Library of Canada.
Susanna Moodie Collection, MG29, D100, National Archives of Canada.
Traill Family Collection, MG29, D81, National Archives of Canada.

SECONDARY SOURCES

Althusser, Louis. 1970. "Ideology and Ideological State Apparatuses." *Lenin and
    Philosophy and Other Essays.* Trans. Ben Brewster. New York and London:
    Monthly Review Press, 1971. 127–86.
Altick, Richard D. 1957. *The English Common Reader. A Social History of the Mass
    Reading Public 1800–1900.* Chicago: University of Chicago Press.
Anon. 1828. Rev. of annuals. *Athenaeum,* 22 Oct.: 819.
– 1828. [Harral, Thomas]. Rev. of *Friendship's Offering. La Belle Assemblée,* 3rd
    ser., 8: 214–16.
– 1829. [Harral, Thomas]. Rev. of annuals. *La Belle Assemblée,* 3rd ser., 10: 215.
– 1829. Rev. of *Ackermann's Juvenile Forget Me Not. Literary Gazette,* 24 Oct.: 697.
– 1830. Notice of *Enthusiasm. Athenaeum,* 3 Apr.: 207.
– 1830. [Jerdan, William]. Rev. of annuals. *Literary Gazette,* 9 Oct.: 655.
– 1830. Notice for "God Preserve the King." *Athenaeum,* 11 Dec.: 780.

– 1831. [Harral, Thomas]. Rev. of *Patriotic Songs*. *La Belle Assemblée*, 3rd ser., 14: 82.

– 1831. [Strickland, Elizabeth]. Rev. of *Patriotic Songs*. *Lady's Magazine, or Mirror of the Belles Lettres*, improved ser., 4: 155.

– 1831. [Jerdan, William]. Rev. of *Enthusiasm*. *Literary Gazette*, 21 May: 328.

– 1831. [Strickland, Elizabeth]. Rev. of *Enthusiasm*. *Lady's Magazine, or Mirror of the Belles Lettres*, improved ser., 3: 375–7.

– 1831. Rev of *Enthusiasm*. *Ladies Museum*, improved ser., 2: 182–4.

– 1833. Rev. of *Enthusiasm*. *Canadian Literary Magazine* 1: 107–10.

– 1833. "The Emigration of 1832." *Canadian Literary Magazine* 1: 110–21.

– 1847. Adv. for *Victoria Magazine*. *Pilot* (Montreal), 31 Aug.: 2.

– 1847. Rev. of *Victoria Magazine*. *Pilot* (Montreal), 19 Oct.: 2.

– 1848. Rev. of *Literary Garland*. *Prince Edward Gazette* (Picton), 16 June 1848: 2.

– 1851. "A Hint to Whom it May Concern." *True Witness and Catholic Chronicle* (Montreal), 21 Feb.: 4.

– 1852. "Mrs. Moodie's Life in Canada." *Spectator*, 7 Feb.: 133–4.

– 1852. Rev. of *Roughing It*. *Observer*, 15 Feb.; rpr in *Pilot* (Montreal), 27 Mar.: 2.

– 1852. Rev. of *Roughing It*. *Literary Gazette*, 21 Feb.: 178–81.

– 1852. Rev. of *Roughing It*. *Athenaeum*, 28 Feb.: 247–8.

– 1852. "Forest Life in Canada West." *Blackwood's Edinburgh Magazine* 71: 355–65.

– 1852. Rev. of *Roughing It*. *Pilot* (Montreal), 27 Mar.: 2; rpr from *Observer*, 15 Feb.

– 1852. Adv. for *Blackwood's*. *Examiner* (Toronto), 31 Mar.: 3.

– 1852. Adv. for *Roughing It*. *Pilot* (Montreal), 1 July: 3.

– 1852. Rev. of *Roughing It*. *Daily Evening Transcript* (Boston), 6 July: 2.

– 1852. Adv. for *Roughing It*. *Daily Colonist* (Toronto), 9 July: 2.

– 1852. Rev. of *Roughing It*. *British Colonist* (Toronto), 9 July: 2.

– 1852. Rev. of *Roughing It*. *Mercury* (New Bedford, Mass.), 9 July 1852: 2.

– 1852. Rev of *Roughing It*. *Albion* (New York), 10 July: 333.

– 1852. Rev. of *Roughing It*. *Norton's Literary Gazette and Publisher's Circular*, 16 July: 131.

– 1852. Rev. of *Roughing It*. *Literary World* (New York), 17 July: 39.

– 1852. Rev. of *Roughing It*. *Spirit of the Times* (New York), 17 July: 264.

– 1852. "The Editor's Shanty." *Anglo-American Magazine* 1: 168–77.

– 1852. Rev. of *Roughing It*. *Godey's Magazine and Lady's Book* 45: 296.

– 1852. Rev. of *Roughing It*. *Graham's Magazine* 41: 336.

– 1852. Rev. of *Roughing It*. *Globe* (Toronto), 7 Aug.: 378.

– 1852. Rev. of *Roughing It*. *Weekly Tribune* (New York), 25 Sept.: 6–7.

– 1852. Rev. of *Roughing It*. *Provincial: or, Halifax Monthly Magazine*, Oct.: 383–9.

– 1853. Rev. of *Mark Hurdlestone*. *Spectator*, 8 Jan.: 37.

– 1853. Rev. of *Mark Hurdlestone*. *Athenaeum*, 15 Jan.: 73–4.

– 1853. Adv. for *Mark Hurdlestone*. *Putnam's Monthly Magazine*, Feb.: 233.

– 1853. Rev. of *Life in the Clearings*. *Spectator*, 13 Aug.: 783–4.

– 1853. Rev. of *Life in the Clearings*. *Athenaeum*, 27 Aug.: 1012–13.

– 1854. Rev. of *Flora Lyndsay*. *Athenaeum*, 6 May: 554–5.

– 1854. Rev. of *Flora Lyndsay*. *Spectator*, 13 May: 519.

– 1854. Rev. of *Matrimonial Speculations*. *Athenaeum*, 2 Dec.: 1462.

– 1855. Rev. of *Geoffrey Moncton*. *Hastings Chronicle* (Belleville), 29 Nov.: 2.

– 1856. Rev. of *Geoffrey Moncton*. *Spectator*, 9 Feb.: 170.

– 1856. Rev. of *Geoffrey Moncton*. *Athenaeum*, 23 Feb.: 231.

– 1859. Adv. for "Tom Singleton; or, How My Aunt Dorothy Left Her Money." *Family Herald* (Montreal), 21 Dec.: 44.

– 1866. Rev. of *Scenes and Adventures of a Soldier and Settler*. *Daily Witness* (Montreal), 15 Oct.: 2.

– 1868. Rev. of *The World Before Them*. *Athenaeum*, 4 Jan.: 16.

– 1872. Rev. of *Roughing It*. *Canadian Monthly and National Review* 1: 182–3.

– 1884. "Susanna Moodie. An Interview with a Celebrated Canadian Authoress. Early Life in the Bush. Reminiscences of Napoleon, Carlyle, Cruikshank, O'Connell, and Others." *Globe* (Toronto), 8 Mar.: 5.

– 1885. "The Late Susanna Moodie. A Biographical Sketch of a Well-Known Canadian Author." *Globe* (Toronto), 10 Apr.: 5.

– 1913. Notice for *Roughing It in the Bush*. *Daily Mail and Empire* (Toronto), 29 Nov.: 27.

– 1913. Rev. of *Roughing It in the Bush*. *Daily Mail and Empire* (Toronto), 13 Dec.: 24.

– 1966. "Susanna Moodie's Life a Conflict Between Writing, Harsh Necessity." *Peterborough Examiner*, 21 Oct.: 11.

– 1966. "Historians in Writer's Debt." *Peterborough Examiner*, 21 Oct.: 11.

– 1977. "Moodie, Susanna (Strickland)." *Encyclopedia Canadiana*.

– 1987. "Unique Find of Moodie Collection Reported." *Intelligencer* (Belleville), 7 Aug.: 3.

– 1987. "Moodie Collection Finds New Home." *Feliciter* 33.9: 1.

– 1988. "Spiritualism Pervades Documents of Belleville's Pioneer Author." *Intelligencer*, 7 Mar.: 9.

– 1988. "When the Spirits Came Knocking, Susanna Was at the Door." *Intelligencer*, 26 Nov.: 9.

Arnason, David. 1973. "Canadian Literary Periodicals of the Nineteenth Century." *Journal of Canadian Fiction* 2.3: 12–28.

Atwood, Margaret. 1970. Afterword to *The Journals of Susanna Moodie*, by Margaret Atwood. Toronto: Oxford University Press. 62–4.

– 1986. Introduction to *Roughing It in the Bush*. London: Virago Press. vii–xiv.

Bain, Iain. 1973. "Gift Book and Annual Illustrations." *Literary Annuals and Gifts Books: A Bibliography 1823–1903*. Rpr with supplementary essays by Eleanore

Jamieson and Iain Bain. Pinner, Middx: Private Libraries Association. [19–25].

Baker, Ray Palmer. 1920. *A History of English-Canadian Literature to the Confederation*. Rpr New York: Russell and Russell 1968.

Bakhtin, Mikhail. 1934–35. "Discourse in the Novel." *The Dialogic Imagination*. Ed. Michael Holquist. Trans. Caryl Emerson and Michael Holquist. Austin: University of Texas Press 1981. 259–422.

– 1963. *Problems of Dostoevsky's Poetics*. Ed. and trans. Caryl Emerson. Minneapolis: University of Minnesota 1984.

– 1970–71. "From Notes Made in 1970–71." *Speech Genres and Other Late Essays*. Ed. Caryl Emerson and Michael Holquist. Trans. Vern McGee. Austin: University of Texas Press 1986. 132–58.

Ballstadt, Carl. 1965. "The Literary History of the Strickland Family: Elizabeth, 1794–1875; Agnes, 1796–1874; Jane Margaret, 1800–1888; Catharine Parr, 1802–1899; Susanna, 1803–1885; Samuel, 1809–1867." PhD, University of London.

– 1972. "Susanna Moodie and the English Sketch." *Canadian Literature* 51: 32–8.

– 1974. "Proficient in the Gentle Craft." *Copperfield* 5: 101–9.

–, ed. 1975. *The Search for English-Canadian Literature: An Anthology of Critical Articles from the Nineteenth and Early Twentieth Centuries*. Toronto: University of Toronto Press. xi–l.

– 1981. "Lives in Parallel Grooves." *Kawartha Heritage*. Peterborough: Peterborough and Atlas Foundation. 107–18.

– 1982. "Strickland, Susanna (Moodie)." *Dictionary of Canadian Biography*. Vol. XI. Toronto: University of Toronto Press.

– 1986. "Secure in Conscious Worth: Susanna Moodie and the Rebellion of 1837." *Canadian Poetry* 18: 88–98.

–, ed. 1988. *Roughing It in the Bush*. Ottawa: Carleton University Press. xvii–lx.

– 1990. "'The Embryo Blossom': Susanna Moodie's Letters to Her Husband in Relation to *Roughing It in the Bush*." *Re(dis)covering Our Foremothers: Nineteenth-Century Women Writers*. Ed. Lorraine McMullen. Ottawa: University of Ottawa Press. 137–45.

Ballstadt, Carl, Michael Peterman, and Elizabeth Hopkins. 1982–83. "'A Glorious Madness': Susanna Moodie and the Spiritualist Movement." *Journal of Canadian Studies* 17.4: 88–100.

– ed. 1985. *Letters of a Lifetime*. Toronto: University of Toronto Press.

[Bartlett, John Sherren]. 1833. Notice preceding poems and letter. *Albion* (New York), 2 Mar.: 72.

[–]. 1833. Correction. *Albion* (New York), 25 May: 161.

Bennett, Donna. 1991. "Conflicted Vision: A Consideration of Canon and Genre in English-Canadian Literature." *Canadian Canons: Essays in Literary Value*. Ed. Robert Lecker. Toronto: University of Toronto Press. 131–49.

Bentley, D.M.R. 1990. "Breaking the 'Cake of Custom': The Atlantic Crossing as a

Rubicon for Female Emigrants to Canada?" *Re(dis)covering Our Foremothers: Nineteenth-Century Women Writers*. Ed. Lorraine McMullen. Ottawa: University of Ottawa Press. 91–122.

Boyce, Betsy. 1992. *The Rebels of Hastings*. Toronto: University of Toronto Press.

Boyce, Gerald. 1967. *Historic Hastings*. Belleville: Ontario Intelligencer.

Boyle, Andrew. 1967. *An Index to the Annuals*. Vol. 1. *The Authors (1820–1850)*. Worcester: Andrew Boyle Ltd.

Briggs, Asa. 1959. *The Age of Improvement 1783–1867*. Rpr London: Longman 1979.

[Briggs, Charles Frederick]. 1852. "Preface to the American Edition." *Roughing It in the Bush; Or, Life In Canada*. New York: Putnam. [iii].

Broadus, Edmund Kemper and Eleanor, ed. 1923. *A Book of Canadian Prose and Poetry*. Toronto: Macmillan.

Brontë, Charlotte. 1849. *Shirley*. Rpr Harmondsworth, Middx: Penguin 1974.

Brown, Mary M. 1962. *An Index to the Literary Garland (Montreal 1838–1851)*. Toronto: Bibliographical Society of Canada.

Buckner, Phillip A. 1985. *The Transition to Responsible Government: British Colonial Policy in British North America*. Westport, Conn.: Greenwood Press.

Buss, Helen. 1990. "Women and the Garrison Mentality: Pioneer Women Autobiographers and Their Relation to the Land." *Re(dis)covering Our Foremothers: Nineteenth-Century Women Writers*. Ed. Lorraine McMullen. Ottawa: University of Ottawa Press. 123–36.

Canniff, William. 1869. *History of the Settlement of Upper Canada (Ontario) with Special Reference to the Bay Quinte*. Rpr Belleville: Mika 1971.

Careless, J.M.S. 1967. *The Union of the Canadas: The Growth of Canadian Institutions, 1841–1857*. Toronto: McClelland and Stewart.

Cattermole, William. 1831. *Emigration: The Advantages of Emigration to Canada*. London: Simpkin and Marshall.

Clark, J.C.D. 1985. *English Society 1688–1832: Ideology, Social Structure and Political Practice during the Ancien Regime*. Cambridge: Cambridge University Press.

Cohen, Marjorie Griffin. 1988. *Women's Work, Markets, and Economic Development in Nineteenth-Century Ontario*. Toronto: University of Toronto Press.

Craig, Gerald M. 1963. *Upper Canada: The Formative Years 1784–1841*. Toronto: McClelland and Stewart.

Dahlie, Hallvard. 1986. *Varieties of Exile: The Canadian Experience*. Vancouver: University of British Columbia Press.

Davey, Frank. 1988. *Reading Canadian Reading*. Winnipeg: Turnstone.

Davidoff, Leonore, and Catherine Hall. 1987. *Family Fortunes: Men and Women of the English Middle Class, 1780–1850*. Chicago: University of Chicago.

Dean, Misao. 1989. "Concealing Her Blue Stockings: Femininity and Self-Representation in Susanna Moodie." Paper delivered at "New Visions of the Quebec and Canadian Literary Corpus," conference of the Association of Canadian and Quebec Literatures, Learned Societies, Laval University, 28–30 May.

Dewart, Edward Hartley, ed. 1864. *Selections from Canadian Poets; With Occasional Critical and Biographical Notes, and an Introductory Essay on Canadian Poetry.* Rpr Toronto: University of Toronto Press 1973.

Douglas, James. 1875. "The Present State of Literature in Canada." *Canadian Monthly and National Review.* Rpr in *Towards a Canadian Literature.* Ed. Douglas Daymond and Leslie Monkman. Ottawa: Tecumseh 1984. 99–107.

Duncan, Sara Jeannette. 1904. *The Imperialist.* Rpr Toronto: McClelland and Stewart 1990.

[Dunlop, William]. 1832. *Statistical Sketches of Upper Canada for the Benefit of Emigrants: by a Backwoodsman.* Rpr in *Tiger Dunlop's Upper Canada.* Ed. Carl Klinck. Toronto: McClelland and Stewart 1967.

Dyer, Klay. 1992. "A Periodical for the People: Mrs. Moodie and *The Victoria Magazine.*" MA, University of Ottawa.

Edwards, Mary Jane, ed. 1973. *The Evolution of Canadian Literature in English: Beginnings to 1867.* Toronto: Holt, Rinehart and Winston.

Errington, Jane. 1987. *The Lion, the Eagle, and Upper Canada: A Developing Colonial Ideology.* Kingston: McGill-Queen's University Press.

Evans, Jack. 1989. "Students Rough It in the Bush to Find Author's Rural Home." *Intelligencer* (Belleville), 5 Aug.: 9.

[Fairfield, Sumner Lincoln.] 1834. "Mrs. Moodie's Poems." *North American Magazine* 5: 126–8. Rpr in *Chronicle and Gazette* (Kingston), 21 Mar. 1835: 2.

Faxon, Frederick Winthrop. 1912. *Literary Annuals and Gift-Books: A Bibliography with a descriptive introduction.* Rpr with supplementary essays by Eleanore Jamieson and Iain Bain. Pinner, Middx: Private Libraries Association 1973.

Feltes, N.N. 1986. *Modes of Production of Victorian Novels.* Chicago: University of Chicago Press.

Ferguson, Moira, ed. 1987. *The History of Mary Prince.* London: Pandora. 1–41.

Fetherling, Douglas. 1990. *The Rise of the Canadian Newpaper.* Toronto: Oxford University Press.

Fingard, Judith. 1974. "The Winter's Tale: The Seasonal Contours of Pre-Industrial Poverty in British North America, 1815–1860. Rpr in *Interpreting Canada's Past.* Vol. 1. *Before Confederation.* Ed. J.M. Bumsted. Toronto: Oxford University Press 1986. 248–72.

FitzGibbon, Mary Agnes. 1894. Biographical Sketch for *Pearls and Pebbles; or, Notes of an Old Naturalist,* by Catharine Parr Traill. Toronto: William Briggs. [iii]–xxxiv.

[Fothergill, Charles.] 1837. Notice preceding poem. *Palladium of British North America* (Toronto), 20 Dec.: 4.

Fowler, Marian. 1980. "*Roughing It in the Bush*: A Sentimental Novel." *The Canadian Novel: Beginnings.* Ed. John Moss. Toronto: New Canada Publications. 80–96.

– 1982. *The Embroidered Tent: Five Gentlewomen in Early Canada.* Toronto: Anansi.

Fraser, Matthew. 1987. "National Library Acquires 'a Real Treasure Trove.'" *Globe and Mail* (Toronto), 7 Oct.: A23.

Fraser, R.L. 1979. "Like Eden in Her Summer Dress: Gentry, Economy and Society: Upper Canada, 1812–1840." PhD, University of Toronto.

Freiwald, Bina. 1989. "'the tongue of woman': The Language of the Self in Moodie's *Roughing It in the Bush.*" *Re(dis)covering Our Foremothers: Nineteenth-Century Women Writers.* Ed. Lorraine McMullen. Ottawa: University of Ottawa Press. 155–72.

French, William. 1986. "Atwood is Reunited with Susanna Moodie." *Globe and Mail* (Toronto), 2 Sept.: A13.

Frye, Northrop. 1965. Conclusion to *Literary History of Canada. Canadian Literature in English.* Gen. ed. Carl Klinck. 2nd ed. Toronto: University of Toronto Press. 1976. 2:333–61.

Gagan, David. 1975. "'The Prose of Life': Literary Reflections of the Family, Individual Experience, and Social Structure in Nineteenth Century Canada." Rpr in *Interpreting Canada's Past.* Vol. 1. *Before Confederation.* Ed. J.M. Bumsted. Toronto: Oxford University Press 1986. 308–20.

Gairdner, William. 1972. "Traill and Moodie: Two Realities." *Journal of Canadian Fiction* 1.2: 35–42.

Galt, John. 1831. *Bogle Corbet.* Ed. Elizabeth Waterston. Toronto: McClelland and Stewart 1977.

Garebian, Keith. 1986. "Historic Paths to Our National Psyche." *Quill and Quire* 52: 22.

Gaskell, Elizabeth. 1848. *Mary Barton.* Rpr Harmondsworth, Middx: Penguin 1970.

George, Marge. 1990. "Lakefield Spawned Writers." *Toronto Star,* 18 Aug.: E14.

Gerson, Carole. 1980. "*The Snow Drop* and *The Maple Leaf:* Canada's First Periodicals for Children." *Canadian Children's Literature* 18/19: 10–23.

– 1985. "Mrs. Moodie's Beloved Partner." *Canadian Literature* 10: 34–45.

– 1989. *A Purer Taste: The Writing and Reading of Fiction in English in Nineteenth-Century Canada.* Toronto: University of Toronto Press.

Gerson, Carole, and Kathy Mezei, ed. 1981. Introduction to *The Prose of Life.* Downsview: ECW Press. 1–15.

Gilbert, Sandra M., and Susan Gubar. 1979. *The Madwoman in the Attic: The Woman Writer and the Nineteenth-Century Literary Imagination.* New Haven: Yale University Press.

Gilmour, Robin. 1981. *The Idea of the Gentleman in the Victorian Novel.* London: George Allen and Unwin.

Giltrow, Janet. 1981. "'Painful Experience in a Distant Land': Mrs. Moodie in Canada and Mrs. Trollope in America." *Mosaic* 14.2: 131–44.

– 1986. Rev. of *Letters of a Lifetime. University of Toronto Quarterly* 56: 164–5.

Glickman, Susan. 1989. Afterword to *Roughing It in the Bush.* Toronto: McClelland and Stewart. 535–43.

– 1991. "The Waxing and Waning of Susanna Moodie's 'Enthusiasm.'" *Canadian Literature* 130: 7–26.

Godfrey, Sheldon and Judith. 1991. *Burn This Gossip: The True Story of George Benjamin of Belleville, Canada's First Jewish Member of Parliament 1857–1863.* Toronto: The Duke and George Press.

Grace, Sherrill. 1980. "Moodie and Atwood: Notes on a Literary Reincarnation." *The Canadian Novel: Beginnings.* Ed. John Moss. Toronto: New Canada Publications. 73–9.

Grady, Wayne, ed. 1980. *The Penguin Book of Canadian Short Stories.* Harmondsworth, Middx: Penguin.

Gramsci, Antonio. 1971. *Selections from the Prison Notebooks.* Ed. and trans. Quintin Hoare and Geoffrey Nowell Smith. New York: International Publishers.

Grant, John Webster. 1988. *A Profusion of Spires: Religion in Nineteenth-Century Ontario.* Toronto: University of Toronto Press.

Greenblatt, Stephen. 1990. *Learning To Curse: Essays in Early Modern Culture.* London: Routledge.

Greenfield, Susan. 1990. "The Follies Incident to Human Nature: Susanna Moodie's Life Story as Spiritual Autobiography in 'Rachel Wilde,' *Flora Lyndsay, Roughing It in the Bush,* and *Life in the Clearings.*" PhD, University of Western Ontario.

Griffith, Alice Louise. 1949. "Susanna Strickland Moodie: A Biography." MA, University of Toronto.

Groening, Laura. 1983. "*The Journals of Susanna Moodie*: A Twentieth-Century Look at a Nineteenth-Century Life." *Studies in Canadian Literature* 8: 166–80.

Grylls, David. 1978. *Guardians and Angels: Parents and Children in Nineteenth-Century Literature.* London: Faber and Faber.

Gundy, H. Pearson. 1965. "Literary Publishing." *Literary History of Canada. Canadian Literature in English.* Gen. ed. Carl Klinck. 2nd ed. Toronto: University of Toronto Press, second ed. 1976. 1:188–202.

Hammerton, A. James. 1979. *Emigrant Gentlewomen: Genteel Poverty and Female Emigration, 1830–1914.* London: Croom Helm.

Harris, R. Cole, and John Warkentin. 1974. *Canada before Confederation: A Study in Historical Geography.* New York: Oxford University Press.

Heward, Burt. 1988. "New Look at Sisters of Moodie." *Citizen* (Ottawa), 23 Apr.: C3.

Hill, Heather. 1987. "Library Gets 19th-Century Windfall Featuring Canadian Literary Legend." *Gazette* (Montreal), 7 Aug.: A1.

Hobsbawm, E.J. 1968. *Industry and Empire.* Harmondsworth, Middx: Pelican, 1969.

Hopkins, Elizabeth. 1982. "Susanna Moodie." *Profiles in Canadian Literature: 3.* Ed. Jeffrey Heath. Toronto: Dundurn. 33–40.

– 1986. "British Gentlewoman Immigrant: Susanna Moodie." *Polyphony* 8.1–2: 5–8.

Houston, Susan E. 1972. "Politics, Schools, and Social Change in Upper

Canada." Rpr in *Education and Social Change: Themes from Ontario's Past.* Ed. Michael B. Katz and Paul H. Mattingly. New York: New York University Press 1975. 28–56.

– 1975. "Victorian Origins of Juvenile Delinquency: A Canadian Experience." *Education and Social Change: Themes from Ontario's Past.* Ed. Michael B. Katz and Paul H. Mattingly. New York: New York University Press. 83–109.

Howison, John. 1821. *Sketches of Upper Canada, Domestic, Local, and Characteristic.* Edinburgh: Oliver and Boyd.

Hulme, Peter. 1986. *Colonial Encounters: Europe and the Native Caribbean, 1492–1797.* London: Methuen.

Hume, Blanche. 1928a. *The Strickland Sisters: Catharine Parr Traill and Susanna Moodie.* Toronto: Ryerson.

– 1928b. "Grandmothers of Canadian Literature." *Willison's Monthly* 3: 474–7.

Jackel, David. 1979. "Mrs. Moodie and Mrs. Traill, and the Fabrication of the Canadian Tradition." *Compass* 6: 1–22.

Jameson, Anna. 1838. *Winter Studies and Summer Rambles in Canada.* Rpr Toronto: McClelland and Stewart 1990.

Jameson, Fredric. 1981. *The Political Unconscious: Narrative as a Socially Symbolic Act.* Ithaca: Cornell University Press.

Jamieson, Eleanore. 1973. "The Binding Styles of the Gift Books and Annuals." *Literary Annuals and Gift Books: A Bibliography 1823–1903.* Rpr with supplementary essays by Eleanore Jamieson and Iain Bain. Pinner, Middx: Private Libraries Association. [7–17].

Johnson, J.K. 1989. *Becoming Prominent: Regional Leadership in Upper Canada, 1791-1841.* Kingston: McGill-Queen's University Press.

Johnston, Susan. 1992. "Reconstructing the Wilderness: Margaret Atwood's Reading of Susanna Moodie." *Canadian Poetry* 31: 28–54.

Jones. D.G. 1970. *Butterfly on Rock: A Study of Themes and Images in Canadian Literature.* Toronto: University of Toronto Press.

Keith, W.J. 1985. *Canadian Literature in English.* Harlow, Essex: Longman.

Kennedy, Roderick, and Jean Anderson. 1939. "Susanna Moodie: Brilliant Realist of the Bush." *Standard* (Montreal), 4 Mar.: 21.

Klinck, Carl. 1959. "A Gentlewoman of Upper Canada." *Canada Literature* 1: 75–7.

–, ed. 1962. *Roughing It in the Bush.* Toronto: McClelland and Stewart. ix–xiv.

–, gen. ed. 1965. "Literary Activity in the Canadas (1812–1841)." *Literary History of Canada. Canadian Literature in English.* 2nd ed. Toronto: University of Toronto Press 1976. 1:139–58.

Kline, Marcia. 1970. *Beyond the Land Itself: Views of Nature in Canada and the United States.* Cambridge, Mass.: Harvard University Press.

Kroetsch, Robert. 1983. "Carnival and Violence: A Meditation." *Open Letter,* 5th ser., 4: 111–22.

Kröller, Eva-Marie. 1981. "Resurrections: Susanna Moodie, Catharine Parr

Traill and Emily Carr in Contemporary Canadian Literature." *Journal of Popular Culture* 15.3: 39–46.

Langdon, Steven. 1973. "The Emergence of the Canadian Working-Class Movement, 1845–1867." Rpr in *Interpreting Canada's Past*. Vol. 1. *Before Confederation*. Ed. J.M. Bumsted. Toronto: Oxford University Press 1986. 345–58.

Langton, H.H., ed. 1950. *A Gentlewoman in Upper Canada: The Journals of Anne Langton*. Toronto: Irwin.

Lecker, Robert. 1990. "The Canonization of Canadian Literature: An Inquiry into Value." *Critical Inquiry* 16: 656–71.

– 1991. *Canadian Canons: Essays in Literary Value*. Toronto: University of Toronto Press. 3–16.

Lighthall, William Douw, ed. 1889. *Songs of the Great Dominion: Voices from the Forests and Waters, the Settlements and Cities of Canada*. Rpr Toronto: University of Toronto 1971.

The List of the Publications of Richard Bentley and Son 1829–1898. 1899. Microfich rpr Cambridge: Chadwyck-Healey 1975.

Lucas, Alec. 1989. "Mrs. Moodie Re-Visited." *Re(dis)covering Our Foremothers: Nineteenth-Century Women Writers*. Ed. Lorraine McMullen. Ottawa: University of Ottawa Press. 146–54.

McCalla, Douglas. 1978. "The Wheat Staple and Upper Canadian Development." Rpr in *Interpreting Canada's Past*. Vol. 1. *Before Confederation*. Ed. J.M. Bumsted. Toronto: Oxford University Press 1986. 184–95.

McCarthy, Dermot. 1979. "Ego in a Green Prison: Confession and Repression in *Roughing It in the Bush*." *Wascana Review* 14.2: 3–16.

– 1991. "Early Canadian Literary Histories and the Function of the Canon." *Canadian Canons: Essays in Literary Value*. Ed. Robert Lecker. Toronto: University of Toronto Press. 30–45.

McCourt, Edward. 1945. "Roughing It with the Moodies." *Queen's Quarterly* 51. Rpr in *Masks of Fiction*. Ed. A.J.M. Smith. Toronto: McClelland and Stewart 1961. 81–92.

MacDonald, Mary Lu. 1987. "Susanna Moodie: The Patrick Hamilton Ewing Collection of Moodie-Strickland-Vickers-Ewing Family Papers." *National Library News* 19.12: 1–5.

– 1990. "Reading Between the Lines: An Analysis of Canadian Literary Prefaces and Prospectuses in the First Half of the Nineteenth Century." *Prefaces and Manifestoes*. Ed. E.D. Blodgett and A.G. Purdy. Edmonton: University of Alberta. 29–42.

MacDonald, R.D. 1972. "Design and Purpose." *Canadian Literature* 51: 20–31.

MacDougall, Heather. 1987. Rev. of *Letters of a Lifetime*. *Canadian Historical Review* 68: 126–7.

McDougall, Robert L., ed. 1959. *Life in the Clearings*. Toronto: Macmillan. vii–xxiii.

McGann, Jerome. 1983. *A Critique of Modern Textual Criticism*. Chicago: University of Chicago Press.

McGregor, Gaile. 1985. *The Wacousta Syndrome: Explorations in the Canadian Langscape*. Toronto: University of Toronto Press.

Macherey, Pierre. 1966. *A Theory of Literary Production*. Trans. Geoffrey Wall. London: Routledge and Kegan Paul 1978.

Mackenzie, William Lyon. 1837. "The Navy Island Proclamation." *The Colonial Century: English-Canadian Writing before Confederation*. Ed. A.J.M. Smith. Toronto: Gage 1973. 152–8.

MacLulich, T.D. 1976. "Crusoe in the Backwoods: A Canadian Fable?" *Mosaic* 9.2: 115–26.

– 1984–85. "What Was Canadian Literature? Taking Stock of the Canlit Industry." *Essays in Canadian Writing* 30: 17–34.

– 1988. *Between Europe and America: The Canadian Tradition in Fiction*. Toronto: ECW Press.

MacMurchy, Archibald. 1906. *Handbook of Canadian Literature*. Toronto: Briggs.

Magrath, Thomas. 1833. *Authentic Letters from Upper Canada*. Ed. Thomas Radcliff. Rpr Toronto: Macmillan 1953.

Marks, Ruth. 1969. Preface to *The Young Emigrants; or, Pictures of Canada*, by Catharine Parr Traill. New York: Johnson Reprint Corporation. vii–xii.

Marquis, T.G. 1914. "English-Canadian Literature." *Canada and Its Provinces: A History of the Canadian People and Their Institutions*. Ed. Adam Shortt and Arthur G. Doughty. Vol. 12. Toronto: Glasgow, Brook. 493–589. Rpr Toronto: University of Toronto 1973.

Martin, Norma, Donna S. McGillis, and Catherine Milne. 1986. *Gore's Landing and the Rice Lake Plains*. Gore's Landing: Heritage Gore's Landing.

Mathews, Lawrence. 1991. "Calgary, Canonization, and Class: Deciphering List B." *Canadian Canons: Essays in Literary Value*. Ed. Robert Lecker. Toronto: University of Toronto Press. 150–66.

Mathews, Robin. 1975. "Susanna Moodie, Pink Toryism, and Nineteenth Century Ideas of Canadian Identity." *Journal of Canadian Studies* 10.3: 3–15. Rpr in *Canadian Literature: Surrender or Revolution*. Ed. Gail Dexter. Toronto: Steel Rail Educational Publishing 1978. 27–44.

– 1985. "Moodie, Susanna." *The Canadian Encyclopedia*. Rev. ed. Edmonton: Hurtig 1988. 1385.

Mills, David. 1988. *The Idea of Loyalty in Upper Canada, 1784–1850*. Kingston: McGill-Queen's University Press.

Moir, John S. 1965. "Four Poems on the Rebellion of 1837 by Susan Moodie." *Ontario History* 57: 47–52.

Moodie, J.W. Dunbar. 1835. *Ten Years in South Africa*. London: Richard Bentley.

– 1848. "Religion and Loyalty." *Victoria Magazine* 1: 104–7, 137–9.

– 1866. *Scenes and Adventures as a Soldier and Settler, During Half a Century.*

Montreal: Lovell.

More, Hannah. 1799. *Strictures on the Modern System of Female Education*. 2nd ed. London: Cadell and Davies.

Moretti, Franco. 1983. *Signs Taken For Wonders: Essays in the Sociology of Literary Forms*. Trans. Susan Fischer, David Forgacs, and David Miller. Rev. ed. London: Verso 1988.

Morgan, Henry J. 1862. "Mrs. Moodie." *Sketches of Celebrated Canadians, and Persons Connected with Canada*. Quebec: Hunter, Rose. 742–4.

– 1867. "Moodie, Mrs. Susanna." *Bibliotheca Canadensis*. Ottawa: Desbarats. 281–2.

Morris, Audrey. 1968. *The Gentle Pioneers. Five Nineteenth-Century Canadians*. Toronto/London: Hodder, Stoughton.

Moss, John. 1974. *Patterns of Isolation in English Canadian Fiction*. Toronto: McClelland and Stewart.

– 1981. *A Reader's Guide to the Canadian Novel*. Toronto: McClelland and Stewart.

Moyles, R.G., and Doug Owram. 1988. *Imperial Dreams and Colonial Realities: British Views of Canada, 1880–1914*. Toronto: University of Toronto Press.

Murray, Heather. 1986. "Women in the Wilderness." *A Mazing Space: Writing Canadian Women Writing*. Ed. Shirley Neuman and Smaro Kamboureli. Edmonton: Longspoon Press/NeWest Press. 74–83.

– 1990. "The Woman in the Preface: Atwood's Introduction to the Virago Edition of Moodie's *Roughing It in the Bush*." *Prefaces and Manifestoes*. Ed. E.D. Blodgett and A.G. Purdy. Edmonton: University of Alberta. 90–7.

[Need, Thomas]. 1838. *Six Years in the Bush; or, Extracts from the Journal of a Settler in Upper Canada. 1832–1838*. London: Simpkin, Marshall, & Co.

Needler, G.H. 1946. "The Otonabee Trio of Women Naturalists – Mrs. Stewart – Mrs. Traill – Mrs. Moodie." *Canadian Field Naturalist* 60: 97–101.

– 1953. *Otonabee Pioneers: The Story of the Stewarts, the Stricklands, the Traills and the Moodies*. Toronto: Burns and MacEachern.

New, William. 1968. Introduction. *Victorian Magazine 1847–1848*. Vancouver: University of British Columbia Library. vii–x.

– 1987. *Dreams of Speech and Violence: The Short Story in Canada and New Zealand*. Toronto: University of Toronto Press.

– 1989. *A History of Canadian Literature*. London: Macmillan.

Nickels, Nick. 1948. "Suggest Making Old Church Memorial to Traill, Moodie." *Examiner* (Peterborough), 29 Oct.: 15.

Noonan, G. 1980. "Susanna and Her Critics: A Strategy of Fiction for *Roughing It in the Bush*." *Studies in Canadian Literature* 5: 280–9.

Northey, Margot. 1984. "Completing the Self-Portrait: Moodie's 'Rachel Wilde.'" *Essays on Canadian Writing* 29: 117–27.

O'Hagan, Thomas. 1899. "Canadian Women Writers." *Canada: An Encyclopaedia of the Country*. Vol. 5. Ed. J. Castell Hopkins. Toronto: Linscott. 170–6.

Palmer, Bryan D. 1978. "Discordant Music: Charivaris and Whitecapping in

Nineteenth-Century North America." *Labour/Le Travailleur* 3: 5–62.

– 1983. *Working-Class Experience: The Rise and Reconstitution of Canadian Labour, 1800–1980.* Toronto: Butterworth.

Parker, George. 1979. "Haliburton and Moodie: The Early Publishing History of *The Clockmaker*, 1st Series, and *Roughing It in the Bush.*" *Papers of the Bibliographical Society of Canada* 3: 139–60.

– 1985. *The Beginnings of the Book Trade in Canada.* Toronto: University of Toronto Press.

Parks, Malcolm. 1960. Rev. of *Life in the Clearings. Dalhousie Review* 39: 577–8, 581.

Partridge, Florence G. 1956. "The Stewarts and the Stricklands, the Moodies and the Traills." *Ontario Library Review* 40: 179–81.

Perkin, Harold. 1969. *The Origins of Modern English Society 1780–1880.* London: Routledge and Kegan Paul.

Peterman, Michael A. 1981. "A Tale of Two Worlds – From There to Here." *Kawartha Heritage.* Peterborough: Peterborough Historical and Atlas Foundation. 93–106.

– 1983. "Susanna Moodie (1803–1885)." *Canadian Writers and Their Works: Fiction Series 1.* Ed. R. Lecker, J. David, E. Quigley. Downsview: ECW. 63–104.

– 1988. "*Roughing It in the Bush* as Autobiography." *Autobiography and Canadian Literature.* Ed. K.P. Stich. Ottawa: University of Ottawa Press. 35–44.

Pierce, Lorne. 1927. *An Outline of Canadian Literature (French and English).* Toronto: Ryerson.

Pierce, Lorne, and Albert Durrant Watson, ed. 1922. *Our Canadian Literature: Representative Prose and Verse.* Toronto: Ryerson.

Poovey, Mary. 1984. *The Proper Lady and the Woman Writer.* Chicago: University of Chicago Press.

Pope-Hennessy, Una. 1940. *Agnes Strickland. Biographer of the Queens of England 1796–1874.* London: Chatto and Windus.

Pratt, Mary Louise. 1992. *Imperial Eyes: Travel Writing and Transculturation.* London: Routledge.

Prentice, Alison. 1972. "Education and the Metaphor of the Family: The Upper Canadian Example." Rpr in *Education and Social Change: Themes from Ontario's Past.* Ed. Michael B. Katz and Paul H. Mattingly. New York: New York University Press 1975. 110–32.

– 1977. *The School Promoters: Education and Social Class in Mid-Nineteenth Century Upper Canada.* Toronto: McClelland and Stewart.

Prince, Mary. 1831. *The History of Mary Prince, a West Indian Slave. Related by Herself.* [Transcriber Susanna Strickland, ed. Thomas Pringle]. Rpr ed. Moira Ferguson, preface Ziggy Alexander. London: Pandora 1987.

[Pringle, Thomas.] 1831a. Preface to *The History of Mary Prince.* Ed. Moira Ferguson. London: Pandora 1987. 45–6.

– 1831b. "Supplement to the History of Mary Prince by the Editor." In *The*

History of Mary Prince. Ed. Moira Ferguson. London: Pandora 1987. 85–115.

Purdy, A.W. 1971. "Atwood's Moodie." *Canadian Literature*. 47: 80–4.

Rashley, R.E. 1958. *Poetry in Canada; The First Three Steps*. Toronto: Ryerson.

Read, Colin, and Ronald J. Stagg, ed. 1985. *The Rebellion of 1837 in Upper Canada*. Ottawa: Carleton University Press 1985.

Rhodenizer, V.B. 1930. *A Handbook of Canadian Literature*. Ottawa: Graphic.

Robins, John D., ed. 1946. *A Pocketful of Canada*. Toronto: Collins.

Ross, Malcolm, ed. 1954. *Our Sense of Identity*. Toronto: Ryerson.

Russell, Peter A. 1981. "Attitudes to Social Structure and Social Mobility in Upper Canada (1815–1840)." PhD, Carleton University.

Said, Edward. 1983. "Introduction: Secular Criticism." *The World, the Text, and the Critic*. Cambridge, Mass.: Harvard University Press. 1–30.

Scott, Lloyd. 1959. "The English Gentlefolk in the Backwoods of Canada." *Dalhousie Review* 39: 56–69.

Shields, Carol. 1977. *Susanna Moodie: Voice and Vision*. Ottawa: Borealis.

– 1989. Afterword to *Life in the Clearings versus the Bush*. Toronto: McClelland and Stewart. 335–40.

Showalter, Elaine. 1977. *A Literature of Their Own: British Women Novelists from Brontë to Lessing*. Princeton: Princeton University Press.

Skelton, Isabel. 1924. *The Backwoodswoman: A Chronicle of Pioneer Home Life in Upper and Lower Canada*. Toronto: Ryerson Press.

Smiles, Samuel. 1859. *Self-Help*. London: John Murray.

Smith, W.H. 1846. *Smith's Canadian Gazetteer*. Toronto: H. & W. Rosell.

Spalding, Lincoln. 1959. "Diary in a Young Country." *Saturday Night*, 1 Aug.: 26.

Spelt, Jacob. 1955. *Urban Development in South-Central Ontario*. Rpr Toronto: McClelland and Stewart 1972.

Staines, David, ed. 1977. *The Canadian Imagination: Dimensions of a Literary Culture*. Cambridge, Mass.: Harvard University Press.

Stephen, S. 1972. "*The Journals of Susanna Moodie*: A Self-Portrait of Margaret Atwood." *White Pelican* 2: 32–6.

Stevenson, Lionel. 1926. *Appraisals of Canadian Literature*. Toronto: Macmillan.

Stouck, David. 1974. "'Secrets of the Prison-House': Mrs. Moodie and the Canadian Imagination." *Dalhousie Review* 54: 463–72.

– 1984. "Susanna Moodie." *Major Canadian Authors*. Lincoln: University of Nebraska. 15–28.

Strickland, Jane Margaret. 1887. *Life of Agnes Strickland*. Edinburgh and London: William Blackwood and Sons.

Strickland, Samuel. 1853. *Twenty-Seven Years in Canada West; or, The Experience of an Early Settler*. Ed. Agnes Strickland. London: Bentley.

Stuewe, Paul. 1990. "New Editions Bring Susanna in from the Bush." *Toronto Star*, 13 Jan.: M9.

Surette, Leon. 1982. "Here Is Us: The Topocentrism of Canadian Literary Criticism." *Canadian Poetry: Studies, Documents, Reviews* 10: 44–57.

– 1991. "Creating the Canadian Canon." *Canadian Canons: Essays in Literary Value*. Ed. Robert Lecker. Toronto: University of Toronto Press. 17–29.

Sutherland, Ronald. 1968. "The Body-Odour of Race." *Canadian Literature* 37: 46–67. Rpr in *Second Image: Comparative Studies in Quebec/Canadian Literature*. Don Mills: newpress 1971. 28–59.

Thackeray, William Makepeace. 1848. *Vanity Fair*. Rpr New York: Random House 1950.

Thomas, Clara. 1966. "The Strickland Sisters." *The Clear Spirit: Twenty Canadian Women and Their Times*. Ed. Mary Quayle Innis. Toronto: University of Toronto Press. 42–73.

– 1972. "Journeys to Freedom." *Canadian Literature* 51: 11–19.

– 1986. Rev. of *Letters of a Lifetime*. *Queen's Quarterly* 93: 659–61.

Thompson, Elizabeth. 1991. *The Pioneer Woman: A Canadian Character Type*. Kingston: McGill-Queen's University Press.

Thurston, John. 1987. "Rewriting *Roughing It*." *Future Indicative: Literary Theory and Canadian Literature*. Ed. John Moss. Ottawa: University of Ottawa Press. 195–204.

– 1989. "Susanna Moodie (1803–85): The Canonization of a Colonial Writer." PhD, Queen's University.

–, ed. 1991. Introduction to *Voyages: Short Narratives of Susanna Moodie*. Ottawa: University of Ottawa Press. vii–xxix.

– 1994. "'The Casket of Truth': The Social Significance of Susanna Moodie's Spiritual Dilemmas." *Canadian Poetry* 35: 31–62.

Tinkler, John. 1982. "Canadian Cultural Norms and Australian Social Rules: Susanna Moodie's *Roughing It in the Bush* and Marcus Clarke's *His Natural Life*." *Canadian Literature* 94: 10–22.

[Traill, Catharine Parr]. 1826. *The Young Emigrants; or, Pictures of Canada*. Rpr New York: Johnson Reprint Corporation 1969.

[–] 1836. *The Backwoods of Canada: Being Letters from the Wife of an Emigrant Officer, Illustrative of the Domestic Economy of British America*. Rpr Toronto: McClelland and Stewart 1989.

– 1852. *Canadian Crusoes: A Tale of the Rice Lake Plains*. Rpr Ottawa: Carleton University Press 1986.

– 1855. *The Canadian Settler's Guide*. Rpr Toronto: McClelland and Stewart, 1969.

von Guttenberg, Antoine Charles. 1969. "Susanna Moodie." *Early Canadian Art and Literature*. Vaduz, Liechtenstein: Europe Printing Establishment. 99–119.

Wachtel, Eleanor. 1989. "Telling It Slant." *Books in Canada* 18.4: 9–14.

Weaver, Emily P. 1917. "Pioneer Canadian Women. III. Mrs. Traill and Mrs. Moodie: Pioneers in Literature." *Canadian Magazine* 48: 473–6.

Westfall, William. 1989. *Two Worlds: The Protestant Culture of Nineteenth-Century*

Ontario. Montreal and Kingston: McGill-Queen's University Press.

White, Hayden. 1978. *Tropics of Discourse: Essays in Cultural Criticism*. Baltimore: Johns Hopkins University Press.

Whitlock, Gillian. 1985. "The Bush, the Barrack-Yard and the Clearing: 'Colonial Realism' in the Sketches and Stories of Susanna Moodie, C.L.R. James and Henry Lawson." *Journal of Commonwealth Literature* 20.1: 36–48.

Wilberforce, William. 1797. *A Practical View of the Prevailing Religious System of Professed Christians, in the Higher and Middle Classes, Contrasted with Real Christianity*. Rpr New York: American Tract Society, n.d.

Williams, Raymond. 1958. *Culture and Society 1780–1950*. Rpr London: Hogarth 1990.

– 1977. *Marxism and Literature*. Oxford: Oxford University Press.

Wise, S.F. 1965. "Sermon Literature and Canadian Intellectual History." Rpr in *Pre-Industrial Canada, 1760–1849*. Vol. 2. *Readings in Canadian Social History*. Ed. Michael S. Cross and Gregory S. Kealey. Toronto: McClelland and Stewart 1982. 79–97.

– 1967a. "Colonial Attitudes from the Era of the War of 1812 to the Rebellions of 1837." *Canada Views the United States: Nineteenth-Century Political Attitudes*. Ed. S.F. Wise and R.C. Brown. Toronto: Macmillan 1972. 16–43.

– 1967b. "Upper Canada and the Conservative Tradition." *Profiles of a Province: Studies in the History of Ontario*. Ed. Edith Firth. Toronto: Ontario Historical Society. 20–33.

Woodcock, George. 1986. "O, Susanna!" *Canadian Literature* 109: 101–3.

W.P.C. 1848. "Our Literature Present and Prospective." *Literary Garland*, ns 6: 245–6.

Young, Aileen. 1967. "The Strickland Family." *Through the Years in Douro: 1822–1967*. Ed. J. Alex Edmison. Peterborough: Newson. 20–9.

Young, Kathryn. 1988. "Ouiga-Board, Seances Played Big Role in Life of Roughing It In Bush Author." *Citizen* (Ottawa), 5 Mar.: C3.

Index